CHINA'S MILITARY POWER

Once termed the world's largest military museum, the Chinese military has made enormous progress over the past twenty years. With skyrocketing military budgets and new technology, China's tanks, aircraft, warships, and missile capabilities are becoming comparable to those of the United States. If these trends continue, how powerful will the Chinese military be in the future? Will its capabilities soon rival or surpass those of the United States?

The most comprehensive study to date, this book provides a detailed assessment of China's military capabilities in 2000 and 2010 with projections for 2020. It is the first to outline a rigorous, theoretically, and empirically grounded framework for assessing military capability based on not just weaponry but also doctrine, training, equipment, and organizational structure. This framework provides not only the most accurate assessment of China's military to date but an important new tool in the study of military affairs.

Roger Cliff is a Senior Fellow at the Atlantic Council. He has previously worked for the Office of the Secretary of Defense and conducted research for the RAND Corporation on China's foreign policy, military modernization efforts, and defense industry. He received his PhD from Princeton University.

China's Military Power

ASSESSING CURRENT AND FUTURE CAPABILITIES

ROGER CLIFF

Atlantic Council

CAMBRIDGE
UNIVERSITY PRESS

32 Avenue of the Americas, New York NY 10013-2473, USA

Cambridge University Press is part of the University of Cambridge.

It furthers the University's mission by disseminating knowledge in the pursuit of education, learning and research at the highest international levels of excellence.

www.cambridge.org
Information on this title: www.cambridge.org/9781107502956

First published 2015

A catalogue record for this publication is available from the British Library

Library of Congress Cataloguing in Publication data
Cliff, Roger.
China's military power : assessing current and future capabilities / Roger Cliff, Atlantic Council.
    pages   cm
Includes bibliographical references and index.
ISBN 978-1-107-10354-2 (hardback : alk. paper) – ISBN 978-1-107-50295-6 (pbk. : alk. paper)
1. China–Armed Forces.   2. China–Military policy.   3. National security–China.
4. China–Strategic aspects.   I. Title.
UA835.C568 2015
355'.033251–dc23   2015005489

ISBN 978-1-107-50295-6 Paperback

Contents

Figures

Tables

Acknowledgments

I could not have written this book without the help of many people. I should begin with Allan Song of the Smith Richardson Foundation. When I first approached him to request support for a book on the Chinese military, I was thinking that I would simply write a distillation of everything I had learned about China's military over the decade and a half I had spent doing research on it. Allan, however, insisted that I do more than that, that I have a rigorous analytic framework for the book. Over the next few months, with his prodding, I developed such a framework and am extremely glad that I did. The result is not just a far more rigorous assessment of the capabilities of the Chinese military than I would have written otherwise, but also what I believe is a significant contribution to the field of security studies more broadly. The creation of this framework also contributed to my proposal to the Smith Richardson Foundation being approved, and I received a substantial grant from the Foundation that alleviated the need for me to find other sources of income while writing the book. Without Allan Song and the Smith Richardson Foundation, therefore, this book would not have been written.

Several people provided direct assistance as I researched and wrote the book. Ken Allen and Dennis Blasko supplied me with important insights into the organization of the Chinese military (as well as many other aspects of the Chinese military), and Dave Johnson, John Gordon, and John Stillion supplied me with important insights into the organization of the U.S. military. Beth Asch provided me with valuable guidance regarding resources for assessing the quality of U.S. military personnel. As detailed in Chapter Eight, several current and retired U.S. military officers who had served as attachés in China filled out a survey instrument on the organizational culture of the Chinese military. I promised them confidentiality so I cannot name them here, but without their contributions I would not have been able to write what may be the most interesting chapter of the book. Norman Cliff provided me with guidance in interpreting ordinal statistics so that I could properly assess the results of the survey. When the manuscript was complete, Dave Shlapak read it in its entirety and provided numerous comments and suggestions that have vastly improved the book. Robert Button read the scenario analysis chapter (Chapter Nine) and similarly provided numerous comments and suggestions that made that chapter much better, including recommending that I talk to John Yurchak, who gave me an invaluable tutorial in submarine warfare.

Randy Shriver and the Project 2049 Institute provided me with the institutional home under which I was able to receive the Smith Richardson Foundation grant. The RAND Corporation, aside from giving me a venue for conducting research on East Asian security issues for 14 years, also provided me with access to several important reference databases that greatly facilitated my research for this book. Carolyn Pumphrey and the Triangle Institute of Security Studies gave me an opportunity to share my findings during the early stages of the project, and Dave Ochmanek and the Office of the Secretary of Defense provided me with an opportunity to share my findings at a later stage in the project.

My ability to write this book, of course, was not simply the result of the direct support and assistance I received while I was writing it, but also of all the training and mentoring I received in Chinese studies, social science, and military analysis prior to (and during) the writing. I would particularly like to thank Paul Pickowicz, Richard Madsen, and Barry Naughton of UC San Diego; Richard Falk, the late Richard Ullman, Samuel Kim, Michael Doyle, Aaron Friedberg, and Lynn White of Princeton University; my former RAND colleagues, too numerous to list here; and my colleagues in the field of Chinese military studies, also too numerous to enumerate.

I am very happy that Cambridge University Press has chosen to publish this book. Thanks, therefore, to John Berger for first expressing interest in the manuscript and then getting it approved for publication. Thanks also to Stephen Acerra, Ezhil Sugu Maran, and David Anderson for all their help in turning the manuscript into an actual book.

Finally, I want to thank my family: my father and late mother for supporting and believing in me regardless of what direction I took my life; my brothers, Larry and Paul, for being unconditional friends; my children, Michelle and Conrad, for simply being themselves; most of all, my wife, Renee. In particular, it was she who suggested that I find grant support for the writing of the book, which caused me to contact Allan Song, who, in turn, as noted above, caused me to write a better book. Then, throughout the writing of the book, she supported and encouraged me, even as the process stretched out far longer than initially planned. To her I owe the greatest debt.

Abbreviations

AWACS	Airborne Warning and Control System
CEP	circular error probable
CMC	Central Military Commission
CPC	Communist Party of China
DOTMLPF	doctrine, organization, training, material, leadership, personnel, and facilities
EEZ	exclusive economic zone
GAD	General Armaments Department
GDP	gross domestic product
GED	General Educational Development
GLCM	ground-launched cruise missile
GLD	General Logistics Department
GPD	General Political Department
GPS	Global Positioning System
GSD	General Staff Department
HBCT	Heavy Brigade Combat Team
IBCT	Infantry Brigade Combat Team
ICBM	intercontinental ballistic missile
JASDF	Japanese Air Self-Defense Force
JASSM	Joint Air-to-Surface Stand-off Missile
JASSM-ER	Joint Air-to-Surface Stand-off Missile – Extended Range
JSOW	Joint Standoff Weapon
LPD	landing platform dock
LRASM	Long-Range Anti-Ship Missile
MRAF	military region air force
NCO	noncommissioned officer
NTC	National Training Center

PACOM	U.S. Pacific Command
PAI	Primary Aircraft Inventory
PLA	People's Liberation Army
ROTC	Reserve Officer Training Corps
SRBM	short-range ballistic missile
TAI	Total Aircraft Inventory
THAAD	Terminal High-Altitude Air Defense System
UN	United Nations
WEI	Weapon Effectiveness Index
WUV	Weighted Unit Value

1

Introduction

As recently as the late 1990s, China's military, known as the People's Liberation Army (PLA), was being described as a "junkyard army" or "the world's largest military museum."[1] Aside from being equipped primarily with weapon systems based on 1950s Soviet designs, the PLA's combat doctrine was also outmoded, its training was lackadaisical, and its personnel were poorly educated and led. Indeed, the primary focus of the PLA was not on conducting military operations but on making money from a wide range of commercial operations.

Changes since that time have been rapid. Today China's defense industries are now producing weapon systems comparable to the M1 Abrams tanks, Aegis destroyers, and F-15 and F-16 fighter aircraft that are the mainstays of the U.S. military. In 2007, China tested a ground-launched missile that intercepted one of China's own weather satellites, making it only the third nation (after the United States and Soviet Union) to demonstrate the capability to destroy a satellite in orbit. In 2011, while U.S. defense secretary Robert Gates was in Beijing for meetings with China's leadership, China conducted a test flight of an advanced stealth fighter that looks remarkably like those recently developed by the United States.

In addition to modernizing its weaponry since the late 1990s, moreover, the PLA has revised its combat doctrine, upgraded its training, personnel, and leadership, and divested itself of its business interests. All of this progress has been accompanied by a massive increase in defense spending. In 1998, China's official defense budget was $11.3 billion. Beijing's announced defense budget for 2014 was $132 billion.[2] If these trends continue, how powerful will the PLA be in the future? Will its military capabilities soon rival or surpass those of the United States? Or is the U.S. military edge over China so great that it will take decades for the PLA to catch up?

The answers to these questions are of more than just abstract interest. Although China's economy is increasingly intertwined with that of the rest of the world, China has territorial disputes with many countries in Asia and is becoming increasingly assertive regarding its claims. Most significantly, China claims that Taiwan, which has been politically independent from the main-land since 1949, is part of Chinese territory, and Beijing asserts that it has a right to use force to incorporate the island under its governance.[3] The United States, on the other hand, in the 1979 Taiwan Relations Act (passed by the U.S. Congress after Washington established diplomatic relations with the People's Republic of China in Beijing and severed them with the Republic of China in Taipei), has declared that any effort to determine Taiwan's political future "by other than peaceful means" would be "a threat to the peace and security of the Western Pacific area and of grave concern to the United States."[4] This phrase has generally been interpreted as implying an intention by the United States to defend Taiwan against military pressure or attack by the People's Republic. In addition, the United States has defense treaties with Japan and the Philippines, both of which have territorial disputes with China (albeit over sparsely inhabited islands). Thus, there is a real possibility of a war between the United States and China. In the words of one senior China expert, "For at least the next decade ... the gravest danger in Sino-American relations is the possibility the two countries will find them-selves in a crisis that could escalate to open military conflict."[5]

A war between the United States and China, regardless of its outcome, would likely have a transformative effect on the international system. As the United States and China are the world's two largest economies, the immediate impact on international trade and finance would be enormous. More last-ingly, a war, even if it ended quickly, would likely result in a subsequent relationship of mutual suspicion and hostility for a long period. Much as during the Cold War, both sides would significantly increase their military spending, increase the numbers and combat readiness of their military forces in the region, and vie for political influence with other countries in the region and throughout the world.

China's military capabilities affect not only the potential outcomes of such a war, moreover, but also its likelihood. Empirical research has shown that movements toward approximate military parity between great powers are correlated with an increase in the likelihood of war between them.[6] If China's military capabilities begin to approach those of the United States, therefore, the risk of war between the two countries is likely to increase.

Even if war never comes, China's military capabilities will affect its relations with the rest of the world. In disputes between China and other countries, knowledge of the likely outcome of a military conflict will implicitly shape the positions of both Beijing and its interlocutors. Although China's leaders have been at pains to reassure Asia and the world that China's rise will be peaceful, therefore, China's influence in regional and global affairs will be in part a function of its military power. Thus, understanding China's current and future military capabilities is essential to an understanding of how China affects the international system, including an understanding of the likelihood of a great power war that would fundamentally transform the international system.

Although substantial work has been published describing the history and current conditions of the PLA, no significant attempts have been made to assess its overall capabilities as a fighting force and what these capabilities are likely to be in the future. The work published to date on developments in the PLA since the 1990s has generally been descriptive in nature or focused on the *processes* involved in the PLA's modernization effort. Neither of these approaches provides an understanding of the actual military capabilities of the PLA, because the former merely describe the constituent elements of military capability without providing a framework for evaluating their relative quality, and the latter are focused on explaining the causes for activities rather than on assessing the results of those activities. As a result, no comprehensive assessment has been published of the ability of the PLA to effectively conduct military operations.

The major books and reports on China's military that have been published over the past decade or so may be divided into four categories. The first consists of comprehensive examinations of the entire PLA.[7] These studies, however, have several limitations. First, some of them focus primarily on the weapon systems China is acquiring, without considering the other dimensions of military capability such as organization, doctrine, training, and personnel. Second, even those that do consider such dimensions do not locate them within a generalized framework that would enable China's capabilities in these dimensions to be evaluated and compared to those of other countries. Finally, although some of these works describe the PLA's *aspirations* for different types of military capability, they do not provide a methodology for estimating when those aspirations might be achieved.

The second category of books and reports on China's military that have been published over the past decade consists of in-depth analyses of selected elements of the PLA. Topics include the PLA Army, PLA Navy, and PLA Air Force; China's defense industries; the history of the PLA; civil-military relations in China; and the PLA's combat doctrine.[8] Studies such as these provide a wealth of valuable information about different aspects of China's military. In many cases, however, they are also primarily descriptive and lack a comparative perspective or analytic framework that could be used to make judgments about China's military capabilities in these different dimensions. In addition, by their nature these are examinations of a single aspect of China's military power and cannot provide a comprehensive assessment of China's overall military capabilities.

A third category of books and reports on China's military consists of assessments of the possible outcomes of a China-Taiwan conflict.[9] These studies have been extremely valuable in providing in-depth analysis of the scenario that is by far the most likely to result in direct military conflict between the United States and China – a war over Taiwan. However, they generally focus on the material capabilities of the militaries involved without attempting to assess the impact of intangible qualities such as organizational structure, personnel quality, training, and organizational culture.

A final category consists of books warning of China's aggressive intentions and efforts to increase its military capabilities. The number of books of this type that have been published is large. These books generally present arguments for why conflict between the United States and China is likely in coming years and identify potential conflict scenarios between the United States and China. Some provide overviews of China's military or describe weapon systems that the PLA is reportedly attempting to acquire, but none attempts to systematically assess China's current or future military capabilities.[10]

ASSESSING MILITARY CAPABILITY

To assess China's current and future military capabilities, a rigorous, theoretically and empirically grounded methodology is needed. To date, however, none has been developed. Many estimates of the military power of nations, including those used by international relations scholars, simply count the number of military personnel or major weapon systems such as tanks, warships, and combat aircraft that a country possesses.[11] During the Cold War, academic analyses of the military balance between the United States and the Soviet Union similarly centered on comparisons of the weapon systems that the two sides possessed. Much of this literature was focused on the nuclear balance, but during the 1980s a number of studies of the conventional military balance in Europe were published as well. These analyses, too, were weapon system-centric, with the unit of comparison being the "armored division equivalent," a measure computed based on the total number of each type of weapon possessed by the combat forces of the two sides multiplied by numerical estimates of the quality of those weapons.[12] Just as the Cold War was ending, however, the inadequacy of this way assessing of military capability was dramatically demonstrated in the 1991 Gulf War between a U.S.-led coalition and Iraq. Before the war, estimates, based primarily on comparisons of the weapon systems and numbers of soldiers each side had, were that the U.S. coalition would suffer as many as sixteen thousand casualties in expelling the "battle hardened" Iraqi army from Kuwait.[13] As it turned out, however, these estimates were more than an order of magnitude too high.[14]

After the Gulf War ended, most accounts attributed the unexpectedly easy coalition victory to the technological superiority of a new generation of weapons such as M1 tanks, stealth fighters, and laser-guided bombs.[15] Careful analysis of the Gulf War, however, decisively refutes this view. Coalition forces not equipped with advanced weapon systems performed no more poorly than forces equipped with the most advanced technology, and forces equipped with advanced technology performed far better than can be explained by superior technology alone. The one-sided coalition victory in the Gulf War was not primarily the result of the coalition's technological superiority but rather of its superior tactics, training, personnel quality, and other nonmaterial factors.[16]

Indeed, many instances can be identified in which materially inferior forces have decisively defeated materially superior adversaries. The most prominent example is the 1940 Battle of France, in which the German army in ten days decisively defeated the combined British and French armies, which had numerical superiority and comparable technology (British and French tanks were better, the Germans had better aircraft). A more extreme example from World War II is Operation Compass in Egypt and Libya from December 1940 to February 1941. In this campaign, thirty-six thousand British Commonwealth soldiers armed with 120 artillery pieces, 275 tanks, and 140 aircraft took on 150,000 Italian soldiers armed with 1600 artillery pieces, 215 tanks (not including 339 "tankettes" equipped only with light machine guns), and 330 aircraft. Although the British artillery, tanks, and aircraft were unquestionably superior to their Italian counterparts, it is difficult to imagine that the material superiority of what were, in any case, relatively small numbers of these weapons was alone sufficient to make up for the Italian's overwhelming numerical superiority in soldiers and weapons. And yet the British Commonwealth forces decisively defeated the Italians, driving the Italians out of Egypt and deep into Libya, taking most of the Italian force prisoner.[17]

More recent examples include 5 Commando's defeat of the more-numerous and better-armed rebels of the Simba Rebellion in the Congo between 1964 and 1965 and Executive Outcomes' defeats of União Nacional para a Independência Total de Angola (UNITA) in Angola from 1993 to 1995 and the Revolutionary United Front in Sierra Leone between 1995 and 1996.[18] Perhaps the most dramatic example, however, is the Battle of 73 Easting during the 1991 Gulf War. In this battle, nine M1 tanks and twelve M3 Bradley infantry fighting vehicles engaged thirty-seven T-72 tanks and more than seventy other armored vehicles, destroying all thirty-seven T-72 and seventy-six other armored vehicles, with the loss of only one M3. According to Lanchester's Law, a commonly used formula for predicting the results of such engagements based on material factors, such a lopsided outcome would have been possible only if each M1 was the equivalent of thirty-six T-72s, which is highly implausible.[19]

More generally, a comprehensive analysis of a wide range of modern conflicts indicated that nonmaterial factors were far more important than material factors in explaining combat outcomes.[20] Thus, any assessment of military capability that is based primarily on material measures is fundamentally flawed. As Biddle (2004) has noted, given the centrality of military power to many theories of international relations, this is a critical deficiency.[21]

Although some academic studies have recognized the inadequacy of purely material factors in assessing military power, they have not systemically specified or analyzed the nonmaterial contributors to military capability. Biddle (1996) and Biddle, Hinkle, and Fisherkeller (1999), for example, refer to "skill" without explicitly defining what that term encompasses. Biddle (2004) identifies "force employment," defined as "the doctrine and tactics by which armies use their materiel in the field" as "one key nonmaterial variable," but does not state what other key nonmaterial variables might be.[22] Others have written about the importance of other nonmaterial features of military organizations, but none has attempted to comprehensively characterize the totality of nonmaterial dimensions of military capability.[23]

The U.S. military, however, has long recognized that military capability is a function of more than just weapons and numbers of soldiers. U.S. military discourses often refer to military capability as comprising "doctrine, organization, training, materiel, leadership and education, personnel, and facilities," acronymized as DOTMLPF.[24] That is, the U.S. military believes that the effectiveness of military forces depends on the combat doctrine they employ, how the forces are organized, how they are trained, the weapons and supplies that they are provided with, how well they are led, how well they are educated, the quality of the people who make them up, and the capacities of the facilities that support them.

Although members of the U.S. military frequently use the term "DOTMLPF," however, they do not appear to have a detailed conception of what each component entails, and publications of the U.S. military do not provide further explication. For example, the official U.S. Department of Defense dictionary does not have definitions for the terms "organization," "training," "leadership," or "education," and even for those terms that have definitions (doctrine, materiel, personnel, and facilities), what specific characteristics of those dimensions are important is not specified.[25]

This book, therefore, employs the overall perspective represented by the DOTMLPF concept, but builds on it and converts it into an analytically applicable methodology by postulating that military capability is a function of seven distinct dimensions (which differ slightly from the DOTMLPF construct): doctrine, organizational structure, weaponry, personnel, training, logistics, and organizational culture. Each of these dimensions is defined in terms of key characteristics that can be used to assess a military's relative strength in that particular dimension and to compare its strength in that dimension to that of other militaries.

In some cases the key characteristics for a dimension were identified by drawing on previous research on that particular aspect of military capability (e.g., personnel quality) or on the more general social science literature related to that dimension (e.g., organization theory). For some dimensions, however, there was no preexisting theoretical literature or research on which to draw. In these cases, a theory of what the key characteristics of that dimension of military capability are was first developed based on analysis of publications of the U.S. military and other organizations. The specific theory and methodology used for assessing each particular dimension are described in the chapters in this book on each of the seven dimensions of the PLA (Chapters Two through Eight).

A key and unexpected discovery of this study was about the interrelationships between the different dimensions of military capability. The operational doctrines of militaries can be arrayed along a spectrum, from, at one end, doctrines based on direct engagement with an adversary, to, at the other end, doctrines based on indirection and maneuver. The type of doctrine a military employs affects its requirements in the other dimensions. A military that employs a doctrine that focuses on direct engagement can have an organizational structure that is more centralized and standardized and has low levels of horizontal integration. Its personnel do not need to be highly qualified, its training can be less sophisticated, its logistics support can be less robust and its organizational culture does not need to emphasize initiative, innovation, or risk taking. It does, however, need large quantities of capable weapons.

A military that employs a doctrine that emphasizes indirection and maneuver, on the other hand, needs an organizational structure that is decentralized and has low levels of standardization, but has high levels of horizontal integration. It needs highly qualified personnel, high levels of training, highly robust logistics, and an organizational culture that emphasizes initiative, innovation, and risk taking. The quality and, especially, the quantity of its weaponry are less important.

As described in the next chapter, since 1999 the PLA has had a doctrine that emphasizes indirection and maneuver. The key question, therefore, is whether the PLA has, or will have, the organizational structure, personnel, training, logistics, and organizational culture needed to effectively employ this doctrine.

As implied by this last sentence, the goal of this project was not just to assess China's military capabilities at a particular point in time, but to measure its rate of progress in recent years and, based on this rate of progress, estimate its likely capabilities in the future. To this end, the PLA's capabilities in each of the seven dimensions were assessed at two different points in time: around 2000, when China's military modernization program was just beginning, and around 2010, the most recent year for which data were available at the time this study commenced in 2011. Based on the observed progress between 2000 and 2010, estimates of the PLA's capabilities in 2020 were then made for each of the seven dimensions. Given that many of the measures of military capability used in this study are not amenable to precise quantification, and that progress in any case cannot be expected to proceed at a uniform rate over a period of two decades, these estimates are necessarily approximate. Nonetheless they are useful for identifying which areas of military capability are likely to be relative strengths of the PLA in the future and which areas are likely to persist as weaknesses.

When this study commenced, the expectation was that information about the characteristics of the Chinese military in each of the seven dimensions would be found in the extensive body of (largely descriptive) secondary literature on the Chinese military and that the present project would essentially be a "meta-analysis" that simply applied an overarching framework to an existing body of information. It turned out, however, that because the various books, articles, and reports that constitute the secondary literature on the PLA were generally written without reference to any theoretical or conceptual framework, in many cases the needed data were not found in the extant literature or were insufficient. As a result, a substantial amount of primary source research was required to supplement the existing secondary literature. In most cases this consisted of analysis of publications (in Chinese) of the PLA and related organizations, but in one case (organizational culture) it entailed developing and administering a survey instrument.

Military capabilities, of course, are relevant only in particular contexts: That is, what is most important is not the abstract capability of a military but its ability to conduct specific types of operations at specific places in the world. The final analytic task for this project, therefore, was to examine two hypothetical conflict scenarios involving China and the United States in 2020. Analyzing these scenarios provided a concrete way of assessing whether the Chinese military will have the capability to challenge U.S. military dominance in the region given China's projected improvements (or lack thereof) in each of the seven dimensions of military capability. The scenarios were analyzed based on the estimates that were developed of China's future military capabilities in each of the seven dimensions, estimates of the overall military capabilities of the United States and any other participants in the conflict (given that it was not practical to conduct in-depth analyses of the future military capabilities of the participants other than China, this was done using publicly available information and a few general assumptions), and basic military-operational analysis techniques for estimating movements and combat effects of forces. The performance characteristics of the forces involved were estimated using publicly available information about the capabilities of specific weapon systems as well as the historical performance records of different types of weapons, along with estimates of the effects of differences in doctrine, organizational structure, personnel quality, training, logistics capabilities, and organizational culture. The quantitative aspects of the scenario analysis were simple enough that all calculations could be done using a pocket calculator. Although such an approach cannot capture the effects of multiple interacting parameters in the way that a detailed computer simulation can, it has the advantage of being intelligible to any reader with a knowledge of high school mathematics and, given the uncertainties about how weapon systems that have never been tested in combat would actually perform, its results are not necessarily any less accurate.

A BRIEF HISTORY OF THE PEOPLE'S LIBERATION ARMY

The PLA was founded in 1927 as the military arm of the Communist Party of China (CPC). Initially an insurgent guerilla army, the PLA took advantage of the protection provided by the Soviet occupation of northern China at the end of World War II to develop into a more conventional military equipped with weaponry provided by the Soviets or captured from the forces of the Chinese government, which was then controlled by the rival Nationalist Party, and over the next four years the PLA was able to defeat the government's military in a series of increasingly large-scale conventional battles.[26]

After the government military had been defeated and the CPC-controlled People's Republic of China had replaced the Nationalist Party–controlled

Republic of China as the government of the Chinese mainland in 1949, the PLA benefited from increased assistance from the Soviet Union, especially after China's entry into the Korean War in 1950. This assistance included training, provision of Soviet weapons to China, and the construction of factories in China capable of producing Soviet-designed aircraft, ships, tanks, and other weapon systems.[27]

Soviet assistance to the Chinese military continued after the Korean War until 1960, at which point political friction between Beijing and Moscow resulted in the Soviets withdrawing most of their military and industrial assistance to China. In the years that followed, China struggled to master autonomous production of the Soviet weapons it had acquired. The task was made more difficult by the political and economic upheavals of the 1960s and 1970s including the "Great Third Line" (大三线) program, which relocated China's defense and other industries from cities near the coast and the Soviet border to China's interior, where poverty and transportation bottlenecks hampered their development.[28]

The PLA of this time was poorly equipped and largely filled by minimally educated conscripts drawn from the countryside. PLA strategy and tactics until the 1970s were based on the concept of "People's War," which envisioned a guerrilla-like campaign in response to a large-scale invasion of China. Under this concept, the PLA would initially avoid direct engagement with the invader (at first assumed to be the United States, but from the late 1960s on assumed to be the Soviet Union) and instead allow the invader to penetrate deep into China before initiating counterattacks that would begin as small-scale, low-intensity operations but gradually increase in scale and intensity until the invader was expelled again.[29]

When China's economic reform program began in 1978, the PLA, although huge (more than four million active-duty personnel) and relatively well funded (the official defense budget, which represented only a portion of total defense spending, was nearly 5 percent of China's gross domestic product [GDP] in 1978), was a backward and unwieldy fighting force. It was equipped mainly with 1950s-era Soviet weaponry, manned primarily by poorly educated conscripts; training was rudimentary and unsystematic; and its strategy and tactics were designed for territorial defense against a large-scale invasion. These flaws were exposed in China's 1979 punitive invasion of Vietnam, when the PLA took an estimated twenty thousand casualties in a month-long campaign.[30]

The economic reform program China's leadership initiated in 1978, moreover, did not immediately result in a revitalization of the PLA. Instead it resulted in further stagnation and neglect. By 1996, official defense expenditures had grown by only 25 percent compared to 1978, even as the economy had grown by more than 400 percent in that time.[31] During this period, the PLA had been encouraged to supplement its budgetary allocations by generating revenue through other means. In response, it had become heavily involved in a variety of business activities, from operating ice cream shops to using its military airlift aircraft to provide commercial air transportation.[32]

A turning point occurred in 1996, however. In July and August 1995 and again in March 1996, in response to what appeared to be a possible upgrading of relations between the United States and Taiwan, the Chinese leadership instructed the PLA to test-fire short-range ballistic missiles (SRBMs) into the ocean near Taiwan. In response to the March 1996 tests, which occurred on the eve of elections in Taiwan, the United States dispatched two aircraft carrier task forces to the region. The deployment of these carriers and their associated warships was intended to signal American resolve to come to Taiwan's defense if China used force against Taiwan. It also had the effect of demonstrating the PLA's complete inability to successfully use force against Taiwan if the United States intervened, because China had no answer for U.S. carrier power.

In the aftermath of these events, the Chinese leadership chose to launch a sustained program of modernization and reform of the PLA. China's official 1997 defense budget was more than 11 percent higher than the 1996 budget, and between 1996 and 2014 defense budgets grew on average by that same rate.[33] During this time the overall size of China's armed forces was reduced by nearly a quarter, with much of the reductions coming from China's oversized ground forces (which made up an estimated 75 percent of the PLA's personnel in 1996). In addition, entire layers of command were eliminated, with corresponding reductions in the number of generals and admirals.

Much of the PLA's weaponry was modernized as well. In 1996 the most advanced main battle tank in the PLA's inventory was the Type 85, a descendent of the Soviet 1950s-era T-54; the most advanced submarine in service, other than two Kilo-class vessels recently purchased from Russia, was the Ming class, an improved version of the Soviet 1950s-era Romeo class; and the most advanced fighter aircraft in operation, other than two squadrons of Su-27s recently imported from Russia, was the J-8, based on the Soviet 1950s-era MiG-21. Today the most advanced main battle tank in the PLA's inventory is the Type 98A, roughly equivalent to the U.S. M1A1; the most advanced submarine in service, the Shang class, is comparable to early versions of the U.S. Los Angeles class; and the most advanced fighter aircraft in service, the J-10 and J-11B, are roughly equal in capability to the U.S. F-16 and F-15.

All of these systems, moreover, as well as many other advanced weapon systems in China's inventory, are domestically produced.

In addition to the modernization of its traditional weaponry, the PLA has also acquired a range of new types of weapons that provide "asymmetric" capabilities that could present particular challenges for adversaries. Most notable among these are its conventional ballistic missiles. The PLA now possesses more than eleven hundred conventional ballistic missiles with ranges between two hundred and eleven hundred miles. Because ballistic missiles are so difficult to intercept, these missiles give China a virtually assured conventional strike capability against targets within one thousand miles of China that could be used for a variety of purposes, including neutralizing other countries' land-based airpower and, with the development of an antiship ballistic missile, America's sea-based airpower. China is also developing a variety of other weapons and tactics that could be used to counter the U.S. military's dominance in conventional military operations.[34]

Along with acquiring more advanced weapon systems, the PLA has promulgated two new generations of operational doctrine since 1996 and has been improving the quality of its personnel and training as well. Improving personnel quality has involved several lines of effort. One is increasing the educational requirements for new officers and enlisted personnel. Today, to be inducted into the PLA as an enlisted person, recruits from rural areas must have at least graduated from middle school, and those from urban areas must have graduated from a vocational high school or three-year technical college, or else be enrolled in a four-year college. Similarly, all officers are required to possess college degrees, and approximately half of the PLA's new officers are now recruited from civilian universities.

Another aspect of the PLA's efforts to improve the quality of its personnel has been the creation of a professional noncommissioned officer (NCO) corps in 2000. As of 2008, moreover, all NCOs must have at least a high-school education and a "certificate of professional qualification," such as a diploma from a vocational high school, and senior NCOs are required to have a degree from a three-year technical college.

The PLA is attempting to improve the quality of its training by increasing the realism, complexity, and integration of the operations of different services in its training activities. Training is now routinely conducted on unfamiliar terrain, at night or in bad weather, and against opposing forces whose actions are not predetermined. The frequency of "combined-arms" (different branches within a single service) and "joint" (different services training together) training has also increased, as has the scale of the exercises. Some training areas now have dedicated opposition forces that simulate the weapons and tactics of potential adversaries and are allowed to defeat the visiting units during exercises. In addition, rigorous evaluation and critique have become an integral part of PLA training, with units required to meet standardized performance benchmarks or else undergo remedial training.

The PLA's modernization process is not complete. Although the most modern systems in the PLA inventory are comparable to those that make up the bulk of the U.S. inventory, many PLA weapon systems are still based on 1950s Soviet designs. Personnel and training quality, although improved, are still regarded by most outside observers as falling short of Western standards. China's military capabilities are continuing to improve, however. Only recently have China's defense industries demonstrated the ability to produce fully modern weapon systems, but those systems are now entering China's forces in increasing numbers. In addition, even more advanced systems are in development and are likely to enter service in the next few years. Perhaps most importantly, China's military leadership is keenly aware of the PLA's shortcomings in the intangible dimensions of military power – personnel, training, leadership, and so on – and is engaged in a concerted effort to eliminate those shortcomings. The question is how long it will take the PLA to catch up to world standards in these and other dimensions of military capability.

THE ORGANIZATIONAL STRUCTURE OF THE PEOPLE'S LIBERATION ARMY

The PLA is nominally under the dual command of the CPC and the Chinese government, but the CPC's authority takes priority, a fact the CPC frequently reiterates because of the Chinese leadership's concern that, in the event of an uprising or split in the leadership, the PLA might choose to side with opposition forces or a populist leader, not the CPC. This dual command is exercised by two nominally separate organizations, both called the Central Military Commission (CMC). One CMC belongs to the CPC (and officially is appointed by the CPC's Central Committee); the other belongs to the Chinese government (and is appointed by China's National People's Congress, officially the government's highest decision-making authority). The membership of the two organizations, however, is identical. In practice, therefore, the two CMCs are effectively a single organization.[35]

The membership of the CMC is not fixed but has been relatively stable in recent years. It is usually chaired by China's most senior civilian leader, currently Chinese president and secretary-general of the CPC, Xi Jinping. Presently it has two vice chairmen, both active duty generals, but occasionally has a civilian vice chairman, usually the current chairman's designated successor. From 2010 to 2012, for example, when Hu Jintao was president and CPC secretary-general, Xi Jinping was a vice-chairman of the CMC. The other members of the CMC include the current minister of defense, the directors of the four "general departments" (see below) and the commanders of the Navy, Air Force, and long-range surface-to-surface missile force, known as the Second Artillery Force. All of these, including the minister of defense, are uniformed, active duty military officers.

Below the CMC, the chain of command divides into several threads. First, there are four "general departments": the General Staff Department (GSD), the General Political Department (GPD, the General Logistics Department (GLD), and the General Armaments Department (GAD). These general departments do not have direct authority over any combat units, but they are important for setting overall policy, strategy, and regulations for China's military. They also simultaneously function as the headquarters of the PLA Army, which, unlike the other services in the PLA, does not have a separate headquarters organization. Also directly under the CMC are the headquarters organizations of each of China's three other services–the PLA Navy, PLA Air Force, and the Second Artillery Force, which is officially an "independent branch" (兵种)," not a full-fledged "service" (军种).[36]

In addition, also directly under the CMC are seven military region (大军区) commands that represent the seven geographic regions of China shown in Figure 1.1. All PLA Army forces are directly under the control of one of these military region commands. In addition, each military region also has a military region air force (MRAF), and three of the seven military regions have one of the PLA Navy's three fleets headquartered in them. The commanders of the MRAFs and fleets are deputy commanders of the military regions in which they are located (the military region commander is always a PLA Army officer), but are respectively under the command of the PLA Air Force headquarters or PLA Navy headquarters, not the commanders of the military regions in which they are located. Second Artillery Force units are divided among six missile "bases" that do not correspond to the seven military regions and the missile base commanders are not deputy commanders of the military regions in which they are located. The Second Artillery controls China's land-based nuclear missiles, and these are likely to remain under centralized control during wartime. The Second Artillery also controls conventionally armed surface-to-surface (ballistic and cruise) missiles, however, and it is likely that, in a war, some of these conventional missiles would be assigned to joint military region commanders or to the commander who was in overall charge of the war. The PLA's organizational structure is shown in Figure 1.2.[37]

FIGURE 1.1 China's Military Regions
Source: Office of the Secretary of Defense, 2006

Although this cross-cutting system of regional and service organizations may seem overly complicated and ambiguous, it is not unlike that of the U.S. military, which also employs a system that includes both military services and geographic commands. Thus, for example, the U.S. Pacific Command (PACOM), which is responsible for U.S. military forces operating anywhere between the West Coast of the United States and Pakistan, also contains within it separate "component commands" for the Army, Navy, Air Force, and Marine Corps. The commanders of each of these components report both to the overall PACOM commander and to the commanders of their respective services. In the U.S. system, the responsibilities of these different lines of command are distinguished by specifying that the geographic commander is responsible for joint operations and overall military policy and strategy in the region, while the service commanders are responsible for ensuring their forces in the region are trained, equipped, and supplied.

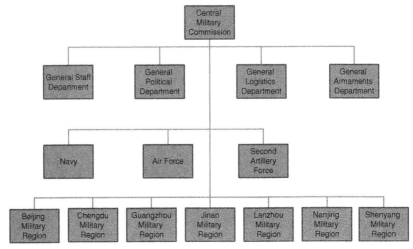

FIGURE 1.2 The Chinese Military's Organizational Structure

OVERVIEW OF THE REST OF THE BOOK

The seven chapters that follow examine and assess the Chinese military's doctrine, organizational structure, weaponry, personnel quality, training, logistics, and organizational culture at each of three times: 2000, 2010, and 2020. The ninth chapter examines how China's capabilities would measure up against those of the United States in two hypothetical conflicts – a full-scale invasion of Taiwan and a clash in the South China Sea.[38] Finally, the book concludes by describing the implications of the findings of the preceding chapters for the policies of the United States and China, as well as for the study of military power more generally.

2

Doctrine

Strategy and tactics play a key role in determining victory and defeat. In 1940, when the German military decisively defeated the combined forces of Britain and France even though the material capabilities of the British and French armies were arguably equal or superior to those of the Germans, this was in large part because of the strategy and tactics employed by the German military as compared to the French and British militaries. More recently the ability of U.S.-led forces to defeat the Iraqi insurgency beginning in 2006, after three years of futile efforts, was due not to improvements in the weaponry of the coalition forces but to a change in strategy and tactics.

A strategy is an overall plan for winning a war as a whole or a campaign within the war. Tactics are the methods used to win individual battles and engagements. The optimal strategy and tactics for any given war, campaign, or battle always depend on the specific circumstances – the objectives of the operation, the capabilities of the two sides, the geography, what the other side is doing, and so on. However, most militaries have a set of principles that they use to guide the selection of strategy and tactics. These principles are based on understandings about what methods were most effective in past wars as well as beliefs about what is most likely to be effective in contemporary conflicts, given changes in technology and other aspects of warfare. The term for these principles is *doctrine*. Sometimes militaries codify their doctrine in publications that they make available to their personnel, but in other cases doctrine is purely an oral tradition passed on from senior personnel to their juniors.[1] In the U.S. and Chinese militaries doctrine is codified in official publications, although in each military there are undoubtedly also unofficial doctrinal principles that exist as purely oral traditions. Even when there is standardized official doctrine, moreover, different militaries treat it differently. In the U.S. military, doctrine is regarded as flexible, and the commander's personal military judgment is said to take precedence over official doctrine.[2] Other militaries are more rigid about following doctrine than the U.S. military is.[3]

ASSESSING THE QUALITY OF DOCTRINE

Although successes and failures of strategy, tactics, and doctrine are favorite subjects of books and studies on military affairs, these successes and failures are generally explained in terms of the particular circumstances in which the strategy, tactics, and doctrine were employed. These circumstances include factors such as terrain, weather, the technology available, enemy capabilities, enemy intentions, and so on. No studies have identified or even proposed a set of objective measures for assessing the quality of military doctrine that are independent of the specific circumstances in which it is employed. Reflection on the desirable general characteristics of doctrine that are independent of specific circumstances, however, suggests the following three criteria.

First is whether the doctrine is designed for the types of contingency the country is likely to encounter. For example, a doctrine for long-range amphibious operations would not be useful for a country that had no overseas interests that it might be called upon to defend. Conversely, if the country had an ongoing land border dispute with a neighboring nation, its doctrine would be deficient if it did not include warfighting principles appropriate for border conflicts.

A second criterion is whether the doctrine is consistent with the capabilities of the country's military and the capabilities of its likely adversaries. A doctrine optimal for the employment of industrial-age armor and artillery against a similar adversary, for example, might be inappropriate for employment of the same type of forces against an adversary employing information-age precision weapon systems or, alternatively, against an adversary employing the weapons and tactics of an insurgency. A country's military doctrine can, of course, simultaneously account for the possibility of conflict against different types of adversaries. The U.S. military, for example, currently has doctrine both for fighting adversaries who use modern weapon systems and conventional tactics and for fighting adversaries who employ low-technology weapon systems and irregular tactics.

A third important characteristic of a country's doctrine is the extent to which it integrates the capabilities of different services and branches. In some doctrines, the operations of different branches or services are conducted without regard for the operations of other branches and services. During World War II, for example, even though the Army Air Corps was part of the U.S. Army, its doctrine emphasized operations that were unrelated to the operations of the Army ground forces.[4] Another possible doctrinal flaw is for the operations of all but a single dominant combat element to be focused solely on supporting that dominant element. Again during World War II, within the U.S. Army ground forces, infantry was the dominant branch. U.S. Army ground force doctrine was, consequently, based on armored forces being used primarily to support infantry operations, rather than armor providing a unique capability that could be used independently or in combination with infantry operations.[5]

CHINESE MILITARY DOCTRINE

There are many misconceptions about Chinese military doctrine. The most common mistake is to regard anything published by the Chinese government or military as representing official doctrine. One example of this was a book entitled *Unrestricted Warfare* (超限战) that was published in China in the late 1990s.[6] This book advocated the use of a variety of unconventional methods, including terrorist attacks, in the event China found itself at war with a powerful opponent such as the United States. Both authors were active duty officers in China's military, and the book was published by a Chinese military publishing house. China's military controls many publishing houses, however, and the one that published this book, the PLA Literature and Arts Press, mostly publishes works of fiction, poetry, and so on that are for sale to the general public in China, not books that are used for training military officers. Although *Unrestricted Warfare* obviously represented the thinking of at least two Chinese military officers in the late 1990s, it was not, and is not, official doctrine.

A similar mistake is to treat articles in popular Chinese military magazines on as representing official doctrine. These magazines, with titles like *Aerospace Knowledge*, *Naval and Merchant Ships*, and *Modern Weaponry*, are published by China's defense industries and trade associations. Articles in them are frequently translated and disseminated within the U.S. government and defense contractor community by the U.S. government's Open Source Center. China's defense industries, however, are controlled by the civilian part of China's government and are not owned or controlled by the Chinese military. The purpose of these magazines is primarily to serve the huge popular appetite in China for information on military affairs and weaponry and secondarily to tout the accomplishments of China's defense industries. The articles are written by journalists, writers of popular fiction, and even students at civilian universities.[7]

Even articles in official Chinese military journals cannot be regarded as describing official doctrine. These journals, just like their counterparts in the United States, such as U.S. Army's *Parameters* or the U.S. Navy's *Proceedings*, exist to facilitate debate and discussion. Many of the articles in Chinese military journals are written by junior officers who are studying for master's degrees at China's military universities and academies and are probably based on term papers or master's theses. That these articles do not represent official doctrine is demonstrated by the fact that many of them contradict each other.

That none of these articles and books constitute official doctrine, however, does not mean that the PLA does not have doctrine. The PLA's doctrine, moreover, is not just an oral tradition; it is codified in publications issued by the PLA. These publications are called "campaign guidance" (战役纲要) and "combat regulations" (战斗条令).[8] These publications are not available outside of China and are probably regarded as military secrets (unlike in the U.S. military, which makes much of its doctrine publicly available). Nonetheless, it is possible to learn quite a bit about them from other publications of the Chinese military, particularly textbooks that are used in China's military academies and universities. Thus, although we cannot directly examine the Chinese military's doctrinal publications, it is still possible to assess the quality of its doctrine.

THE CHINESE MILITARY'S DOCTRINE IN 2000

The type of doctrine employed from the time of the PRC's founding until the mid-1970s is usually referred to as "People's War" and was essentially a doctrine of guerilla warfare that advocated initially avoiding direct engagement with an invader's[9] main forces and instead employing small-scale hit-and-run attacks in the enemy's rear areas. Only after the invader had been worn down and weakened would the PLA begin a counteroffensive to push the invader out.[10]

In the mid-1970s the "People's War" doctrine was replaced by one that is sometimes called "People's War under Modern Conditions." The new doctrine emphasized engaging an adversary closer to China's borders, put more emphasis on the importance of early battles, allowed for positional warfare, and deterred nuclear attacks through the threat of retaliatory nuclear counterstrikes, which China had by then acquired the capability to carry out.[11]

In the mid-1980s, the PLA's warfighting doctrine was revised again, with the new doctrine sometimes called "Local Wars under Modern Conditions." Unlike the previous two generations of doctrine, the new version did not assume that future wars would be total wars for national survival. This was because China's senior leadership had pronounced that large-scale, global war was unlikely for the foreseeable future.[12] Instead, future wars were assumed to more likely be fought for limited objectives, such as enhancing diplomatic strength, intimidating an adversary, or acquiring economic resources. As a result, they would be fought within a limited space and time with limited levels of force.

This assumption implied new warfighting principles, including the importance of seizing the initiative by going on the offensive early on in a war, concentrating the most capable forces in the battlespace (instead of conducting dispersed operations with large numbers of modestly trained and equipped forces), and seeking large-scale, decisive battles from the beginning of the conflict.[13]

The overwhelming success of U.S. forces against Iraq in Operation Desert Storm in 1991 prompted a third revision of the PLA's warfighting doctrine. At a meeting of the CMC in early 1993, the then-president of China and chairman of the CMC, Jiang Zemin, directed the PLA to prepare for "local wars under conditions of modern technology, especially high technology" (现代技术特别是高技术条件下局部战争, later referred to as "local wars under conditions of high technology" 高技术条件下局部战争 or simply "high-technology local wars" 高技术局部战争).[14] Shortly thereafter, the PLA began drafting a new set of doctrinal publications. In January 1999, the CMC issued a set of six campaign guidance documents – one each for the PLA Army, Navy, Air Force, and Second Artillery, one for joint operations, and one for logistics. Based on these campaign guidance documents, the CMC and GSD issued a set of eighty combat regulations publications. These publications included one on combined arms operations for the PLA as a whole, one on Army division-level operations, one on Army regiment-level operations, one on Navy operations, one on Air Force operations, a set of combat logistics support regulations, and specific combat regulations for each of the individual branches and specialized forces and other major force elements of each service as well as the logistics forces (twenty-five for the Army, twenty-two for the Navy, fourteen for the Air Force, four for the Second Artillery, and nine for logistics forces).[15]

Although these campaign guidance and combat regulation documents are not publicly available, according to other publications of the Chinese military, the joint campaign guidance described the following:

- The types and characteristics of joint campaigns
- Basic "guiding thought" (指导思想) for joint campaigns
- General principles for conducting joint campaigns
- How forces are to be organized, what tasks they are to perform, and how they are to be employed
- How command and control and information warfare are to be conducted
- How planning and organization for joint campaigns is to be conducted
- How combat support, logistics support, and equipment support are to be provided
- What political work is to be conducted as part of a joint campaign.[16]

The joint campaign guidance is said to have been developed for operations to maintain China's unity, protect the sovereignty of its territorial waters and its oceanic interests, protect the territorial sovereignty of its border areas, protect critical coastal areas, and ensure the security of China's airspace over critical strategic areas. The joint campaign guidance provided direction for five specific types of joint campaigns: island blockade, island offensive, border region counterattack, joint air defense, and counterlanding. The first two of these appear to be types that would have been employed against Taiwan, the third appears to be a type that would have been employed against India or other country with which China might have a border conflict, and the last two appear to be designed for defense of the Chinese homeland against a coercive air campaign or amphibious invasion (presumably by the United States, the only nation with the capabilities to even contemplate a coercive air campaign or amphibious invasion against China in this time period). Little official information is available about the campaign guidances for the PLA Army, PLA Navy, or logistics forces, but the PLA Air Force campaign guidance provided direction for three types of air force campaigns – air offensive campaigns, air defense campaigns, and air blockade campaigns – and the Second Artillery Force campaign guidance apparently provided direction for two types of campaign – nuclear counterattack campaigns and conventional missile strike campaigns.[17]

Although descriptions of the specific contents of the campaign guidance documents and combat regulations are not publicly available, the Chinese military publishes numerous textbooks and reference books that describe military strategy, operations, and tactics. These books cannot be construed as being identical to official doctrine, but those that were published in the years after 1999 are presumably broadly consistent with the 1999 campaign guidance and combat regulation publications and thus the general principles, at least, of the 1999 doctrinal publications can be inferred from them.[18]

One fundamental principle consistently emphasized in Chinese military publications, including those issued in the years after 1999, is that military goals are subordinate to political goals. Thus, the goal of a "local war under conditions of high technology" was not the destruction of the adversary's military but the achievement of the political goals of the war, which, because of the nature of twenty-first century wars – including the fact that they might be fought with an adversary who possessed chemical, biological, or nuclear weapons – were necessarily limited. By the same token, all instruments of national power, including diplomacy, economics, and international public opinion, would be brought to bear in a conflict and could constrain the actions of both China and its adversaries.[19]

Related to this was the principle of seeking a quick decision in a conflict. Because the political and economic factors constraining a conflict could change, China had to seek to achieve its political goals quickly, before those factors changed in a way that prevented the achievement of its goals. The principle of seeking a quick decision was also based on the recognition that, in some conflicts, China's adversary could be a country, such as the United States, whose overall military capabilities significantly exceeded those of China. In such cases, China had to seek to achieve a temporary, localized military advantage and bring the conflict to a conclusion before the adversary could marshal all of its capabilities. At the same time, however, China also had to be prepared to fight a protracted conflict if it was unable to bring it to a conclusion in a short amount of time.[20]

A corollary of the principle of seeking a quick decision was the importance of seizing the initiative early on in the conflict. If China sought the rapid resolution of a war on terms favorable to it, then it could not allow the adversary to hold the initiative, even if the adversary was the aggressor. This implied an emphasis on offensive operations, even in an essentially defensive war. It also implied a further principle described in Chinese military publications, namely, the principle of preemption. The best way to seize the initiative in a conflict would be to initiate combat operations before the adversary had completed its preparations for combat or launched an attack. Again, preemption was seen as desirable even if the adversary was the actual instigator of the conflict.[21]

Another principle implied by the importance of seizing the initiative early in a conflict was the principle of surprise. One of the best ways of seizing the initiative was said be to conduct a significant surprise operation that the adversary would have to react to and thereby cede the initiative. And, of course, a *preemptive* surprise operation would be particularly effective for seizing the initiative.[22]

Another principle emphasized by Chinese military publications in the years after the 1999 doctrine was issued was avoiding direct engagement with an adversary's combat forces and instead focusing attacks on "key points" – vulnerable but critical elements of its overall combat system. These were said to include command-and-control centers, information systems, bases (particularly air bases and aircraft carriers), logistics systems, and the linkages between systems. Such attacks were to have entailed precision strikes conducted by multiple services from multiple directions throughout the combat theater, rather than attacks on the adversary's frontline forces.[23]

Related to the principle of key point attacks was the principle of concentration of force. Particularly in a conflict with a militarily superior adversary,

China could not afford to disperse its forces but would instead need to focus them on attacking the most critical elements of the adversary's combat system.[24]

Chinese military publications of the early 2000s put particular emphasis on the importance of having an advantage in the quality and amount of information available to one's side. This implied efforts both to attack enemy sensors, computers, and communication systems, and to defend friendly sensors, computers, and communication systems from enemy attack. Attacks could come in the form of physical destruction, electronic warfare, or attempts to disrupt the enemy's information systems via computer software attacks.

Finally, Chinese military publications emphasized the importance of unified leadership and centralized command. For China to defeat a militarily superior adversary, its attacks not only needed to be focused on certain critical weak points, they needed to be carefully synchronized and coordinated. This was seen as possible only under a unified and tightly centralized command system.[25]

Assessment

In 2000 China had military doctrine that appeared to largely, but not completely, correlate with most of the contingencies that could plausibly have occurred in that timeframe. China's military doctrine in 2000 also appears to have been well designed with respect to the military capabilities of likely adversaries, but appears to have been based on capabilities that were more advanced than the PLA actually possessed at the time. Finally, PLA doctrine seems to have integrated fairly well the capabilities of the different specialties and branches within each service, but not between services.

Correspondence with Likely Contingencies

The most important, and perhaps the most likely, type of military contingency in which China could plausibly have become involved in the years around 2000 was a conflict over Taiwan. Bringing about the unification of Taiwan with the rest of China was a major policy goal of the Chinese government, and its efforts to achieve this goal were an important basis for the government's legitimacy. The Chinese government explicitly asserted that it had the right to use military force to achieve this goal and, if Taiwan had taken actions that were seen in the mainland as amounting to an attempt to make its independence a permanent condition, the Chinese government could well have felt compelled to use force against the island in response. Conceivable uses of force included an outright invasion, a blockade, a seizure of one or more of the small islands close to China's coast that were controlled by Taiwan, or perhaps a coercive air and missile bombardment designed to force Taiwan to capitulate.[26] Any use of force against Taiwan would have been complicated by the possibility of intervention by the United States.

Other military contingencies in which China could plausibly have become involved in the years around 2000 included the following:

- Conflict over territorial claims in the South China Sea, where China's claims overlapped with those of Vietnam, the Philippines, Malaysia, and Brunei
- Conflict over territorial claims in the East China Sea, where China's claims overlapped with those of Japan
- A war between North and South Korea (since Pyongyang was Beijing's only formal treaty ally)
- Conflict along China's land borders, either due to China's territorial disputes with India or due to the actions of separatist or terrorist groups conducting operations within China but enjoying sanctuary across the border in a neighboring country
- A collapse of governance in a country on China's periphery, such as North Korea.

In addition, it was also possible that China's military could have been called upon to suppress a purely internal uprising. The People's Armed Police, a paramilitary force that is separate from the PLA, has primary responsibility for suppressing internal conflicts but, if an uprising had exceeded the capability of the People's Armed Police to control, there is little doubt that the PLA would have been called upon, just as it has been in the past. Indeed, when riots occurred in Tibet in 2008, there were reports that Chinese government security forces included PLA vehicles (with their insignia covered up).[27]

Comparing these possible contingencies with what we know about the PLA's doctrine in the early 2000s suggests that the types of campaign addressed by the doctrine were well matched to the type of contingency the country was likely to encounter in this period. That is, with the exception of a purely internal uprising in China, all of the plausible contingencies that China might have become involved in during the years around 2000 would have been localized, conventional international conflicts fought for limited aims, not total wars for national survival on the one hand, nor protracted, low-intensity guerrilla wars on the other. Moreover, since many of them, particularly a conflict over Taiwan, would have involved the United States, Japan, or South Korea, all countries with sophisticated modern militaries, they would have been wars in which advanced military technology played a key role.[28]

As noted above, the 1999 joint campaign guidance provided direction for five specific types of joint campaign: island blockades, island offensives, border region counterattacks, joint air defense, and counterlanding. Thus, it appears that, of the specific military contingencies China could have become involved in, the PLA's doctrine would have supported an outright invasion or blockade of Taiwan, a seizure of one or more of the small islands close to China's coast that were controlled by Taiwan, seizure of islands in the South China Sea or East China Sea, and conflicts along China's land borders.[29] It is not clear, however, that China's military doctrine was designed for a coercive air and missile bombardment of Taiwan, for securing China's claims to the *waters* of (as opposed to islands in) the South China Sea and East China Sea, a land conflict on the Korean peninsula of a scale larger than a border conflict, or counterinsurgency and stability operations in a country on China's periphery or within China itself. A coercive air and missile bombardment of Taiwan, involving as it would have both the PLA Air Force and the Second Artillery, would by definition have been a joint campaign, and the 1999 campaign guidance did not include such a joint campaign.[30] This omission could be seen as a shortcoming of China's military doctrine in 2000, but it could also represent a judgment by China's military leadership that a purely coercive air and missile bombardment of Taiwan (or any other adversary) was not a plausible contingency. They may have judged that the only effective uses of force against Taiwan would require either an outright invasion or at least a blockade of the island.

As for securing China's claims to the waters of the South China Sea or East China Sea, it is possible that this was regarded as purely a PLA Navy mission, and therefore that the PLA Navy campaign guidance, but not the joint campaign guidance, included a campaign appropriate for this contingency. A textbook about military campaigns used by the Chinese military in the early 2000s called *Campaign Studies* 《战役学》, for example, lists possible navy campaigns as including sea blockades, interdiction of sea lines of communication, destruction of enemy surface forces, and protection of sea lines of communication, all of which could have been used as templates for defending China's claims to the waters of the South China Sea or East China Sea, although none of them appears to be a perfect match for such a scenario.[31]

There is no evidence to suggest that Chinese military doctrine in 2000 was designed for intervention in a conflict between North and South Korea. Intervention in a conflict between North and South Korea would have been a joint campaign involving, at a minimum, the PLA Army, Air Force, and Second Artillery. None of the types of campaign said to be included in the 1999 joint campaign guidance, however, appear to correspond to the likely characteristics of a major conventional conflict on the Korean peninsula.[32] China would certainly have had the option of not intervening in a conflict between North and South Korea, however, and the lack of doctrinal guidance for a joint large-scale conventional ground conflict may have reflected a judgment by China's military or civilian leadership that China's involvement in such a conflict was undesirable or implausible. Obviously such a conflict did not occur in the 2000s, so this judgment may have been accurate, but if it had occurred and the Chinese leadership had decided that it in fact needed to intervene, the lack of doctrinal guidance, and the thinking and analysis that the development of such guidance represents, would likely have made China's operations in the conflict more costly and less effective than they would otherwise have been.

Chinese military doctrine in 2000 did not include principles for counterinsurgency and stability operations, as a 2009 article notes that regulations on counterterror actions were not added to the PLA's doctrinal system until the next generation of doctrine was issued in the late 2000s.[33] It should be noted, of course, that the PLA was not the only military in this timeframe whose doctrinal guidance for conducting counterinsurgency operations was lacking, as the U.S. military discovered in Iraq beginning in 2003, so the lack of a current doctrine for counterinsurgency campaigns was not unique to China.

The 1999 joint campaign guidance also included at least two campaign types – a joint air defense campaign and a joint counterlanding campaign – that do not obviously correspond to any of the plausible contingencies identified above. A war over Taiwan, however, could well have required a joint air defense campaign. Although China's efforts against Taiwan in such a conflict would likely have been covered by the "island offensive" campaign type, Chinese military leaders probably assumed that, if the United States intervened, the offensive orientation of U.S. air force doctrine would cause it to conduct offensive air strikes against China. Thus, an invasion of Taiwan would have entailed both an "island offensive campaign" and a "joint air defense campaign."

The contingency in which a joint counterlanding campaign might have been conducted, however, is less clear. It is possible that this doctrine was designed for defending Chinese-held islands in the South China Sea. It is also conceivable that the joint counterlanding campaign was intended to apply to a contingency such as a U.S.-led reinvasion of Taiwan after the island had been conquered and occupied by China, but the likelihood of such a campaign seems too remote for doctrine to have been developed solely for it. Thus, the counterlanding campaign does not clearly correspond to any plausible contingency that China might have faced in the years around 2000.

Match between Doctrine and Capabilities

Although China's military doctrine in 2000 appears to have corresponded fairly well to the types of contingencies in which China was most likely to have become involved during that timeframe, the doctrine does not appear to have been consistent with the capabilities of the PLA at the time. Western analysts at the time noted that China lacked the "surveillance, warning, intelligence, and target acquisition capabilities" and command, control, communications, and intelligence systems "capable of effectively coordinating multi-service operations" that would have been needed to implement the principles of the doctrine. They also noted that the Chinese armed forces were limited in "rapid response, mobility, and the lethality of their weapons systems," and that the PLA's logistics system was not "capable of supporting the levels of consumption created by high-intensity joint warfare."[34]

More generally, if military doctrines are arrayed along a spectrum, with doctrines based on defeating an enemy by closing with and destroying his main combat forces at one end, and doctrines based on maneuver and indirection at the other, then the PLA's doctrine in 2000 clearly fell closer to the latter end of the spectrum.[35] Successfully implementing this type of doctrine, however, requires specific kinds of organizational structure, weaponry, personnel, and organizational culture. As is detailed in subsequent chapters of this book, the PLA was deficient in all of these areas in 2000.

China's military doctrine in 2000 appears to have been better designed with regard to the military capabilities of likely adversaries. The campaign guidance publications issued in 1999 are said to have been specifically designed for a conflict with an adversary that possessed an advantage in high-technology weapons. In 2000, this would have been the case in a conflict with any of China's most likely adversaries including the United States, Japan, Taiwan, and South Korea. Indeed, as described above, many of the key principles of China's military doctrine in 2000 were chosen precisely because of the possibility of a conflict with a technologically superior adversary. At the same time, however, China's 1999 campaign guidance documents were said to recognize that potential future adversaries were diverse, and that not all of them would have an advantage in high-technology weapons.[36]

Integration of the Capabilities of Different Services and Branches

Other than for the PLA Air Force, Chinese military doctrine at the operational and tactical levels in the years around 2000 has not been well studied.[37] Thus, it is difficult to directly assess the degree to which China's military doctrine in 2000 integrated capabilities within services other than the PLA Air Force, but within the PLA Air Force, at least, doctrine appeared to reasonably well integrate the capabilities of its different specialties and branches. The PLA Air Force consists of four combat arms: aviation, surface-to-air missiles, anti-aircraft artillery, and paratroopers. An analysis of Chinese military publications on air force employment principles from the early 2000s found that, although aviation was clearly the organizationally dominant branch, the capabilities and functions of the other three arms were well represented within the doctrine.[38] Indeed, the integration between aviation and ground-based air defenses was arguably better in the PLA than in the U.S. military, where the U.S. Air Force controls land-based fixed-wing combat aircraft but the U.S. Army controls ground-based surface-to-air missiles and anti-aircraft artillery. Assuming that the PLA Air Force was not an anomaly within the PLA, therefore, it seems likely that the doctrine for the PLA Army, Navy, and Second Artillery also did a good job of integrating the capabilities of their different specialties and branches.

Chinese military doctrine in 2000 does not appear to have integrated capabilities well *between* services, however. The analysis of Chinese military publications on air force employment principles, for example, found no information on how PLA Air Force and PLA Navy aviation would coordinate their actions in providing air defense over water or conducting strike operations against enemy naval vessels.[39] The PLA leadership seems to have concluded that PLA force employment principles were not sufficiently integrated across the services as well, as a major emphasis of the next set of doctrinal guidelines to be issued was on improving joint operations.

THE CHINESE MILITARY'S DOCTRINE IN 2010

By 2003 Chinese military publications had stopped referring to the type of conflict China was preparing for as "Local Wars under High-Technology Conditions" and begun referring to them as "informationized local wars" (信息化局部战争) or "local wars under informationization conditions" (信息化条件下局部战争).[40] Then, in December 2004, Chinese president and new chairman of the CMC Hu Jintao (having replaced his predecessor, Jiang Zemin, in the latter position in September 2004), gave a speech in which he declared a new set of "historical missions for the new stage of the new century" (新世纪新阶段历史使命) for the PLA. These were the following:

- Providing an important source of strength for consolidating the ruling position of the CPC
- Providing a solid security guarantee for sustaining the important period of strategic opportunity for national development
- Providing a strong strategic support for safeguarding national interests
- Playing a major role in maintaining world peace and promoting common development.[41]

The implication of these "New Historical Missions" appears to be that the PLA must be prepared for a range of operations other than just high-intensity warfare, including international peacekeeping operations. China's 2006 national defense white paper, for example, describes the PLA's responsibility as "winning local wars under conditions of informationization" and "enhancing national sovereignty, security, and *interests of development*" (emphasis added), and Chinese military publications after 2004 began referring to "diversified military missions" (多样化军事任务) and "nonwar military actions" (非战争军事行动).[42]

A third new development after 2000 was an effort to strengthen joint operations. In 2004, the PLA began using a new term, "integrated joint operations," to refer to military actions in which the services actually interacted with each other during the operation. Previously, an operation was described as "joint" simply if more than one service participated in it, even if their actions did not directly affect each other. For example, an exercise in which PLA Army forces attacked a simulated enemy army while PLA Air Force aircraft attacked a simulated enemy air base was described as having been a "joint" operation even though the two battles were not directly connected to each other. As a result, the PLA needed to coin a new term to refer to operations in which different services actually interacted with each other in the course of an operation.[43]

As a result of these developments, in 2004 the PLA began drafting new doctrinal publications. In contrast to past practice, however, instead of writing an entirely new set of doctrinal publications that would be issued together as a group, the CMC stipulated the adoption of a "rolling development" approach in which new regulations would be issued on an ongoing basis as needed in response to changing requirements or new theoretical insights.[44] Thus, there is no single time at which we can say that this "fifth generation" of doctrinal regulations was issued, and there does not appear to have been an official announcement of when the new doctrinal publications were issued. However, articles published in 2008 and through early September 2009 imply that the writing of the regulations had been completed and that they would soon be approved, and an article published in December 2009 implies that they had been issued.[45]

The new generation of doctrinal regulations are said to differ from the previous generation in several ways. First is a greater emphasis on joint operations. Accordingly, more than ten new campaign guidance publications based on the requirements, actions, and functions of integrated joint operations were issued, in addition to the six types of campaign guidance documents issued in 1999. A second difference is an increase in the number of combat regulation publications, including the addition of combat regulations for new forms of warfare that "open up new domains of struggle with an enemy in wartime." It is not clear what all of these "new domains" are but, based on other publications of the Chinese military they probably include things such as computer network warfare or psychological warfare. A third characteristic of the new doctrinal documents is said to be an expansion of the scope of operations that they cover, in response to the "New Historical Missions" assigned to the PLA by President Hu. In particular, doctrine for counterterrorist operations has been added.[46]

The revisions to PLA doctrine that began in 2004 are probably reflected in teaching materials issued after that date.[47] The 2006 edition of *Campaign Studies*, for example, describes several new types of campaigns. Two new types of army campaigns have been added – "mountain offensives" and "counterterrorist and stability operations" – as has a new type of navy campaign – "offensive campaigns against coral islands and reefs." The 2006 edition also eliminates several campaign types described in the 2000 edition. The "border region counterattack" and "counterlanding" joint campaigns have been eliminated, as have the "urban offensive" and "urban defense" army campaigns, the "sea blockade" and "coastal raid" navy campaigns, the "air blockade" air force campaign, and the "nuclear counterattack" Second Artillery campaign.[48]

The logic for these deletions is not clear in all cases. The PLA leadership may have concluded that a purely sea or air blockade campaign was unlikely and therefore eliminated both types in favor of the already-existing joint blockade campaign. In the case of the counterlanding, urban offensive, urban defense, and coastal raid campaigns, the PLA leadership may have determined that these campaigns were either improbable or else that they would simply be part of broader campaign types, and therefore were not deserving of identification and discussion as distinct campaigns. A border conflict (e.g., with India or one of China's Central Asian neighbors), however, appeared to still be a plausible contingency in 2006, so it is unclear why this campaign type was eliminated.

The elimination of the nuclear counterattack campaign is most puzzling. It is possible that this campaign type was considered too sensitive for discussion in an openly published volume (distribution of the 2000 edition of *Campaign Studies* was officially restricted to military personnel, although it was widely available within and outside of China, whereas the 2006 edition has no distribution restrictions), or perhaps the 2006 edition was intended to only discuss campaigns involving conventional military capabilities.

The changes in PLA doctrine that began in 2004 are seen not just in textbooks but also in training. After the issuing of the 1999 doctrinal publications, in 2001 and 2002 the official training guidelines of the Chinese armed forces were revised to reflect the new doctrine. Similarly, in early 2009 the GSD and the headquarters of the services issued a new set of training guidelines that, among other things, increased the emphasis on joint training as well as training in a "complex electromagnetic environment," a reference to battlefields characterized by extensive jamming of radars and communications equipment, computer hacking, and other forms of electronic or information warfare.[49]

Assessment

The correspondence between the different types of campaigns described by the PLA's military doctrine and the plausible military contingencies involving China that might have occurred in 2010 appears to be strong and further improved over 2000. The match between China's doctrine and the capabilities of the PLA likely improved as well, and the match between its doctrine and the capabilities of China's most-capable potential adversaries (e.g., the United States) was probably still good. The degree to which China's doctrine integrated the capabilities of different services and branches also appears to have significantly improved over 2000, especially with regard to integrating the capabilities of different services.

Correspondence with Likely Contingencies
The set of plausible major contingencies in which China's military might have become involved in 2010 is largely the same as those that were plausible in 2000:

- War with Taiwan, probably involving the United States
- Conflict over territorial claims in the South China Sea
- Conflict over territorial claims in the East China Sea
- A war between North and South Korea
- Conflict along China's land borders, either due to territorial disputes or due to the actions of cross-border separatist or terrorist groups
- Regime collapse in a country on China's periphery, such as North Korea
- A purely internal uprising.

Although information on the specific campaigns for which guidance documents have been issued since 2004 is not available, based on the 2006 campaigns textbook it appears that some of the less-likely campaign types have been deleted and some plausible new types have been added. In particular, the "counterterrorist and stability operations" army campaign that appears in the 2006 edition of *Campaign Studies* seems to be relevant to countering the actions of cross-border separatist or terrorist groups, regime collapse in a country on China's periphery, a purely internal uprising, and even the occupation of Taiwan after a successful conquest of the island (a possibility that the Chinese military leadership may have become more aware of after the U.S. experience in Iraq). The addition of the "mountain offensive" army campaign provides specific focus on the type of terrain in which a border conflict with India or one of China's Central Asian neighbors would be conducted. Similarly, the naval "offensive campaign against coral islands and reefs" appears to be highly relevant to a conflict over territorial claims in the South China Sea, more so than the generic "island offensive campaign" included in the 1999 joint campaign guidance, as that campaign type was probably designed primarily for an invasion of Taiwan, an island many times larger than those of the South China Sea.[50]

Of the campaign types that appear to have been eliminated, given that none of the plausible contingencies in which China's military might have become involved in 2010 was likely to entail an amphibious invasion of China, the apparent elimination of the "counterlanding" campaign type seems appropriate. The rationale for eliminating the joint "border region counterattack" campaign is less clear. A border conflict would most likely occur in the mountains and thus might be covered by the newly added "mountain offensive" army campaign type, but that is not the only possibility and it seems likely that the PLA would wish to employ substantial air forces, not just army forces, in the event of a conflict with a country along China's land borders.

The deletion of the "urban offensive" and "urban defense" army campaigns and the "coastal raid" navy campaign, on the other hand, seems unlikely to have hampered the preparedness of the Chinese military for plausible contingencies. The elimination of purely naval and air blockades in favor of joint island blockades seems reasonable as well, as a coercive blockade against Taiwan or attempt to enforce China's territorial claims in the South China Sea and East China Sea would at a minimum involve both the PLA Navy and the PLA Air Force, as well as the Second Artillery Force.

Match between Doctrine and Capabilities

Whether the match between the PLA's doctrine and its military capabilities improved between 2000 and 2010 is more difficult to assess, as little information is available on the specific content of the doctrinal documents that have been issued since 2004. The 1999 campaign guidance documents were said to be based on capabilities the PLA would acquire over the next ten to fifteen years. If the doctrinal publications that were issued after 2004 were also based on capabilities, the PLA was expected to acquire ten to fifteen years from the issuing of the publications, then it is possible that PLA doctrine in 2010 was still ahead of current PLA capabilities. The capabilities of the PLA had certainly improved since 2000, however, particularly in the areas of weaponry, personnel, and training. Thus, the PLA's overall ability to implement a doctrine of maneuver and indirection, as the doctrine of 2010 presumably continued to be, had unquestionably improved. Nonetheless, as detailed in the subsequent chapters of this book, critical shortcomings remained in the areas of organizational structure, logistics, and organizational culture.

The doctrinal publications issued in 1999 were said to have accounted for the likelihood of conflict with adversaries that possessed an advantage in high-technology weapons.[51] In the years after 1999, the PLA continued to follow developments in foreign militaries, particularly the U.S. military, very closely. Meanwhile, beginning in 2004, the U.S. military became increasingly preoccupied with developing capabilities, such as armored vehicles that were resistant to roadside mines, of use primarily in counterinsurgency warfare. Few fundamentally new capabilities that would have been relevant to a conflict with China were developed and fielded between issuing of the 1999 doctrinal publications and 2010. Thus, it seems likely that PLA doctrine in 2010 was still well matched to the capabilities of potential adversaries, including the U.S. military.

Integration of the Capabilities of Different Services and Branches
As noted above, a major weakness of the 1999 doctrinal principles was that they did not adequately integrate capabilities across services. Addressing this weakness appears to have been a major focus of the post-2004 doctrinal revisions. "Integrated joint operations" is also said to have been an important emphasis of the new training guidelines issued in 2009, which presumably reflected the new doctrinal developments. Thus, there seems little doubt that China's military doctrine did a better job of integrating the capabilities of the different services in 2010 than it did in 2000. Without detailed information about the content of the new doctrine, however, it is difficult to assess whether China's doctrine had reached U.S. levels of "jointness" or whether there continued to be shortcomings in the degree to which it enabled the services to support and interoperate with each other.

THE CHINESE MILITARY'S DOCTRINE IN 2020

The PLA will undoubtedly make further refinements to its doctrine between 2010 and 2020. Since the founding of the PRC, the PLA has issued a new set of doctrinal publications every eight to fourteen years.[52] Although the PLA will apparently no longer issue entire sets of doctrinal publications simultaneously, by 2020 as many as sixteen years will have elapsed since the drafting of the current set of publications was begun. Thus, it seems likely that many of the publications in use today will at least be under revision by 2020, if they have not actually been replaced. This will be particularly true in areas where new capabilities appear or new domains of warfare emerge. For example, the PLA does not currently have doctrinal regulations for military operations in space. Given the space warfare capabilities that it is acquiring (see Chapter Four), it seems likely that by 2020 the PLA will want to have promulgated principles for the use of those capabilities. More generally, Xi Jinping, who took over from Hu Jintao as chairman of the CMC (and as secretary-general of the CPC) in late 2012, moved quickly to put his own imprimatur on the PLA by declaring the importance of being "able to fight and win battles" (能打仗，打胜仗). Although Xi continued to refer to the requirement to perform "diversified military missions," the emphasis on fighting and winning battles appeared to signal an intention to increase the focus on combat operations and deempha-size "nonwar military actions."[53]

Although it is not possible to predict the precise changes the PLA will make to its doctrine between now and 2020, we can describe some of the general features its doctrine will likely possess in 2020. First, it will likely be based on a PLA whose weaponry has been thoroughly updated to early twenty-first-century standards. The PLA leadership has identified 2020 as an important modern-ization milestone. China's official 2006 defense white paper stated that the PLA's goal was to have made "major progress" in the modernization of China's armed forces by "around 2020".[54] And, as will be seen in Chapter Four, it appears that by 2020 or so the PLA will indeed have replaced most of its weaponry that is based on 1950s-era Soviet designs with modern systems comparable to those that make up the vast majority of the U.S. military today (along with, like the U.S. military today, a small number of more-advanced systems, such as stealth fighters). Nonetheless, as detailed in Chapter Three and Chapter Eight, if PLA doctrine in 2020 continues to be based on maneu-ver and indirection, its organizational structure and organizational culture will likely continue to be hindrances to its ability to implement such a doctrine.

The PLA's doctrine in 2020 will likely continue to take into account the types of capabilities a potential adversary, most particularly the U.S. military, might possess in the 2020s. Most major U.S. defense programs are a matter of public record and take years to complete, so it will not be difficult for those responsible for revising the PLA's doctrine to identify most of the capabilities the U.S. military will possess in 2020 and the years that follow.

Finally, it is likely that China's military doctrine in 2020 will have made further progress in the area of joint operations. The Chinese military leadership clearly recognizes that joint operations are a weakness of the Chinese military. The U.S. military of today has nearly thirty years of experience, beginning with its operation in Panama in 1988, in conducting joint combat operations using modern weaponry. The PLA only began acquiring modern weaponry in the 1990s and as of today has conducted no actual combat operations using it (indeed, the only triservice combat operation the PLA has *ever* conducted was the invasion of a small Taiwanese-held offshore island in 1955). Thus, it seems likely that, even with the revisions that occurred after 2004, the PLA's doctrine today still has shortcomings in the area of joint operations and that this will be a continued focus of doctrinal revisions between now and 2020.

The overall quality of China's military doctrine in 2020 will depend on decisions that are made about what types of conflicts and capabilities the doctrinal publications should be designed around, the quality of the individuals, organizations, and processes involved in drafting them, and the way in which they are interpreted and implemented in contingency planning and preparation. Over the past decade, however, the PLA appears to have put a priority on developing modern doctrinal principles that are applicable to China's particular circumstances and that take account of the recent experiences of other militaries, particularly the U.S. military. Thus, it seems likely that, assuming improving the PLA's capabilities remains a priority for China's leadership, China's doctrine in 2020 will correspond well with the types of contingencies the PLA is likely to become involved in, will be at least as well matched to the capabilities both China and its likely adversaries would possess in such a conflict as it was in 2010, and will do a better job of integrating not only the capabilities of the different branches and specialties within each service, but also the capabilities provided by different services. The question, therefore, is whether the PLA will have the organizational structure, weaponry, personnel, training, logistics capabilities, and organizational culture needed to implement this doctrine. These questions are examined in the next six chapters of this book.

3

Organizational Structure

Warfare is a contest between organizations. A well-organized force would be expected to defeat a similarly skilled and equipped but disorganized aggregation of soldiers. Indeed, much military training is focused not on individual skills but on how the individual should perform as a member of a larger organization. Beyond this basic recognition, however, there is little literature on what the characteristics of more or less effective military organizations are. Assessing the quality of the PLA's organization, therefore, requires first identifying what the characteristics of effective military organizations are. This, in turn, requires an understanding of the basic features that can be used to characterize all organizations and why particular types of organizations are best suited for different purposes.

TYPES OF ORGANIZATIONAL STRUCTURE

Organizations can be characterized by five basic features: the amount of *horizontal* and *vertical differentiation* in the organization, the degree of *centralization* of the organization, the degree of *integration* within the organization, and the extent of *standardization* of activities within the organization.

Horizontal differentiation refers to the distinct roles established within an organization and how those roles are grouped into departments and divisions at each level within the organizational hierarchy. The basic principle for horizontal differentiation is that each role should correspond to a unique set of task-related behaviors that can be performed by a single person, and that the roles should be grouped together into departments and divisions based on shared characteristics such as function, product, customer, or location.[1]

Vertical differentiation refers to how the roles of managers at different levels within the organizational hierarchy are distinguished. The basic principle for vertical differentiation is that an organization should have the minimum

37

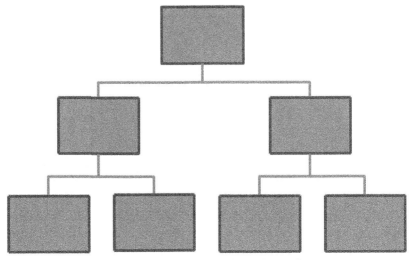

FIGURE 3.1 Optimal Organizational Structure When Span of Control Is Narrow

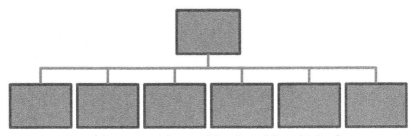

FIGURE 3.2 Optimal Organizational Structure When Span of Control Is Broad

number of hierarchical levels needed to ensure effective control of its operations. Organizations with greater than the minimum number of levels are less efficient and agile. The minimum number of hierarchical levels needed is determined by the maximum span of control of managers within an organization, that is, the maximum number of subordinates each manager can effectively supervise. In two organizations of similar size, one in which the maximum span of control of managers is wider will require fewer organizational levels than the one in which the maximum span of control is smaller. See Figures 3.1 and 3.2.

The maximum span of control of a manager is a function of the similarity and complexity of subordinates' tasks. When subordinates' tasks are complex and dissimilar, the maximum span of control is small. When subordinates' tasks are routine and similar, the maximum span of control is larger.

In addition, the more closely interrelated subordinates' tasks are, the greater the challenge coordination and control present to the manager, and the smaller the maximum span of control.[2]

The degree of *centralization* of an organization is the extent to which the authority to make decisions is reserved for managers at the top of the hierarchy as opposed to delegated to managers at lower levels of the organization. Excessive centralization can result in slow decision making and a failure to respond to newly appearing opportunities or challenges. Excessive decentralization can result in inappropriate decisions by managers lower down in the hierarchy who lack visibility into how their decisions affect other parts of the organization and can make planning and coordination difficult.[3]

The degree of *integration* in an organization is affected by various factors. One is the degree to which personal relationships and professional contacts exist between people in different hierarchies of the organization. Some organizations increase integration by rotating managers between hierarchies over the course of their careers, or at least occasionally assigning them to work outside of their usual hierarchy, so that their personal relationships and professional contacts are not limited to people within a single hierarchy. Another integrating mechanism is to formally designate one or more members of each hierarchy to act as liaisons to other hierarchies. A third type of integrating mechanism is to create a temporary or permanent cross-hierarchical teams of members from different hierarchies to address problems that affect multiple hierarchies. A fourth integrating mechanism is to establish a manager or even an entire department whose sole function is to facilitate communication and information sharing between different hierarchies. None of these mechanisms is costless, however. All of them increase the amount of time members of the organization spend communicating and coordinating with other members of the organization. Excessive integration can be wasteful and may inhibit the organization's ability to make timely and appropriate decisions.[4]

The degree of *standardization* of activities in an organization is the extent to which they conform to written and unwritten rules and norms as opposed to being performed based purely on the judgment of the specific individuals involved. Standardization makes actions of individuals predictable and consistent and, to the extent to which the rules and norms are based on known best practices, generally ensures that they are efficient and effective. Excessive standardization, that is, rigid implementation of rules and norms, however, can inhibit appropriate responses to situations that deviate from the situations for which the rules and norms were developed.[5]

Although the organizational features described above define five independent dimensions that can be used to characterize an organization's structure, many organizations can be arrayed along a spectrum between two ideal types: those with *mechanistic* structures and those with *organic* structures. Mechanistic structures have high degrees of horizontal and vertical differentiation and are highly centralized and highly standardized but have low levels of integration. Organic structures have low degrees of horizontal and vertical differentiation, are decentralized, have low levels of standardization, and are highly integrated. Whether a mechanistic or organic organizational structure is more effective depends on the type of environment the organization faces. Studies have found that when an organization faces a stable, predictable environment, mechanistic structures are more efficient. When an organization faces an unstable, unpredictable environment, an organic structure is more effective.[6]

IMPLICATIONS FOR MILITARY ORGANIZATIONS

For business organizations, the environment consists primarily of the company's suppliers, customers, and competitors. For a military organization in wartime, the organization's environment includes the political leadership to whom the military reports, the civilian organizations that support the military, the geographical and meteorological conditions within which operations are being conducted, and the adversary with whom the war is being fought.[7]

How stable and predictable the environment a military organization faces depends in part on the type of doctrine it employs. As noted in Chapter Two, military doctrines can be characterized as falling along a spectrum, with doctrines based on direct engagement at one end and doctrines based on indirection and maneuver at the other. In a doctrine based on direct engagement, the aim is to attack the adversary's main forces with one's strongest forces and, because of the quantitative and/or qualitative superiority of one's own forces, destroy those of the adversary. In a doctrine of maneuver, the aim is to defeat the adversary not by directly attacking its main forces but rather by destroying their logistical support or command and control capabilities, or by attacking them from directions or in locations where they are unable to properly defend themselves.[8] No military, of course, employs a pure direct engagement or pure indirection and maneuver doctrine, but some military organizations tend toward the direct engagement end of the spectrum whereas others tend toward the maneuver end. The U.S. and Soviet militaries during World War II are viewed as having employed doctrines that were primarily focused on direct engagement, but the German military during the early years of World War II and the Israeli military during the Arab-Israeli wars employed doctrines that emphasized maneuver and indirection.[9]

If a military employs a direct engagement-based doctrine, its environment, particularly at the operational level, can be relatively stable and predictable, especially if its opponent also employs such a doctrine.[10] Field officers (battalion, regiment, and brigade commanders) under such a doctrine will not often need to make decisions on their own initiative. Thus, militaries with doctrines focused on direct engagement, for example, the majority of the Soviet army during World War II, can be effective with a mechanistic structure. Indeed, one observer states that, for Soviet infantry divisions and armies, "the highest military virtue was to act with cog-like uniformity and predictability in the great machine of war."[11]

If a military employs a doctrine of maneuver and indirection, on the other hand, organization theory strongly suggests that it needs to adopt an organic structure to be most effective. Maneuver-based doctrines require the exploitation of unexpected and transitory opportunities while avoiding and countering actions of the adversary. The same observer quoted in the previous paragraph, for example, states that unlike officers in ordinary infantry divisions, officers in the Soviet tank and mechanized corps, which, unlike the bulk of the Soviet army, employed a doctrine of indirection and maneuver, "had to think on their feet and ... adapt their battles to changing circumstances."[12] As this quotation indicates, doctrines of maneuver and indirection will tend to create unstable, unpredictable operational environments for which an organic structure is better suited.

China's military doctrine since 1999 has clearly been a doctrine of maneuver and indirection. According to one analyst, "the starting point of [a doctrine of maneuver and indirection] is the avoidance of the enemy's strengths, followed by the application of some particular superiority against presumed enemy weaknesses, be they physical, psychological, technical, or organizational."[13] This is almost an exact description of the central tenets of the PLA's doctrine since 1999, which, as noted in Chapter Two, has been based on avoiding direct engagement with an adversary's combat forces and instead focusing the PLA's best forces on attacks against "key points" – vulnerable but critical elements of the adversary's overall combat system. To effectively implement this doctrine, therefore, the PLA would need an organic structure.[14]

Based on the tenets of organization theory reviewed at the beginning of this chapter, a military with an organic structure would be decentralized and highly integrated and have a low degree of standardization. In a completely decentralized military, the authority to make decisions would be delegated to officers at all levels of the organization. Thus, platoon commanders could make decisions for their platoon without needing to consult their company commanders, company commanders could make decisions for their company without needing to consult their battalion commanders, and so on. Such an extreme degree of decentralization would be undesirable in any military. Company commanders generally are more experienced and have more information available to them than platoon commanders, and battalion commanders are more experienced and have more information available to them than company commanders. Consulting with a more experienced superior on important decisions should result in better quality decisions in most cases, provided a decision is not needed before the superior's approval can be received (including the possibility that communications with the superior may be interrupted during combat). If that superior must then receive the approval of his or her *own* superior, however, or if the superior officer is burdened with too many requests for direction or approval from his or her subordinates, then the organization will not be able to respond rapidly to changing conditions, and the quality of decisions may degrade because of higher-ranking officers having to make so many decisions that they do not have enough time to give adequate consideration to the truly important decisions. In a relatively static situation, such as the Western Front during World War I, more centralized decision making may be more effective. In dynamic, rapidly changing circumstances, as implied by China's doctrine of maneuver and indirection, however, more decentralized decision making is required.

A high degree of integration would be manifested in multiple ways. One would be personnel policies that either regularly rotated officers (commissioned and noncommissioned) between hierarchies or at least occasionally placed them in positions outside of their "home" hierarchy over the course of their careers. Another way in which a high degree of integration would be manifested could be the existence of formal liaisons between organizations in one hierarchy and parallel organizations in other hierarchies.

Another element of a high degree of integration would be the existence of permanent cross-hierarchical teams or the frequent creation of temporary teams of members of different hierarchies to address problems that affect multiple hierarchies. An example would be if a team drawing on representatives from each Army, Navy, and Air Force base and Second Artillery brigade in a given military region were created to address a problem of frequent interruption of fuel supplies to military units in the region. Another example would be if a group army established a task force drawing on elements from several different divisions and brigades underneath it to perform a specialized mission.

Finally, a high degree of integration would be reflected by the existence of staff organizations whose sole function was to facilitate communication and information sharing between different hierarchies. At the national level this would mean the existence of an independent joint staff whose role was to coordinate the activities of the different services (as opposed to simply being the personal staff of the top commander of the PLA). Within military regions it might mean the existence of a joint integration department whose role was to coordinate the activities of the different services with the military region.

In a military with a high degree of standardization, the regulations, doctrine, and other rules and norms are followed closely. The advantage of this is that rules and norms are usually based on procedures that have been shown to be most effective (although in some cases they may be based on knowledge that is outdated or theories that have not been tested in action). Standardization also makes coordinated action easier, as the course of action each unit should take to be in conformance with doctrine and regulations will generally be apparent to all parties involved. The disadvantages of standardization are that it may inhibit troops and commanders from taking courses of action that are better than the standard courses of action in particular situations, and that the standard courses of action will become obvious and predictable not only to one's own forces but also to the adversary, and thus the adversary can take action to exploit this predictability. If a military has a doctrine based on direct engagement, these disadvantages may be outweighed by the advantages of standardization. If a military has a doctrine based on maneuver, which entails exploiting unique features of a situation and acting in ways that are unpredictable to the adversary, however, an excessive degree of standardization will limit its ability to implement that doctrine.

THE ORGANIZATIONAL STRUCTURE OF CHINA'S
MILITARY IN 2000

The horizontal differentiation of the PLA throughout the period of study did not significantly change and was similar to that of most militaries. Like most armed forces, the PLA was divided into an army, a navy, and an air force. Like most armies, the PLA Army was divided into platoons, companies, battalions, regiments, brigades, and divisions. Also like most armies, PLA Army units generally belonged to a single branch (e.g., armor, infantry, artillery, etc.) up through the battalion level, but became combined armed formations above that level. Similarly, the PLA Navy, like the U.S. Navy, was divided into major fleets (two in the case of the U.S. Navy, three in the case of the PLA Navy), each of which comprised aircraft, surface ships, and submarines. Within each fleet, moreover, all ships of a given type (e.g., destroyers, frigates, attack submarines) were under a single commander, and ships of a given type (e.g., frigates) were further broken down into squadrons. When they put to sea, however, task forces generally were created by combining individual vessels of different types (e.g., destroyers, frigates, submarines, and support vessels). Finally, the aircraft of the PLA Air Force, like those of the U.S. Air Force, were organized into smaller units (called "regiments" [兵团]in the PLA Air Force and "squadrons" in the U.S. Air Force) that generally consisted of a single model of aircraft (e.g., J-8s) and larger units (called "divisions" [师] in the PLA Air Force and "wings" in the U.S. Air Force) that generally consisted of a single *type* of aircraft (e.g., bombers). Unlike the U.S. military, the PLA's land-based long-range surface-to-surface missiles were operated by an independent branch, the Second Artillery Force, whereas in the U.S. military land-based long-range surface-to-surface missiles are operated by the traditional services (now only the U.S. Air Force, since the U.S. Army eliminated its long-range surface-to-surface missiles in 1991). The Russian military, however, like the PLA, has a separate branch, called the Strategic Missile Troops, that operates Russia's land-based long-range surface-to-surface missiles. Also unlike the U.S. military, the PLA Air Force operated long-range surface-to-air missiles and anti-aircraft artillery, whereas in the U.S. military all land-based surface-to-air missiles and anti-aircraft artillery are operated by the ground forces (the U.S. Army and U.S. Marine Corps). In other militaries (e.g., Japan's Self-Defense Force), however, it is common for land-based surface-to-air missiles to be operated by the air force. Overall, therefore, the horizontal differentiation of the Chinese military does not differ significantly from that of other militaries and, as noted already, did not significantly change during the period of study. As a result, horizontal differentiation will not be considered further in this chapter. Instead, attention will be focused on vertical differentiation, centralization, standardization, and horizontal integration.[15]

Vertical Differentiation

Exactly how PLA forces would have been structured in wartime in 2000 is not completely clear, but evidence suggests that, unless the forces involved were predominantly from a single service, a joint force commander would have been designated in each military region involved in the conflict. Below each joint force commander would have been commanders of the PLA Army, Navy, Air Force and, probably, conventional Second Artillery forces in each military region. (If more than one military region was involved in the conflict, the military region joint force commanders would have reported to a higher-level overall commander for the conflict.)[16] In the case of the PLA Army, there would have been as many as seven organizational layers between an individual soldier (the lowest-level organizational entity in most army units) and the overall commander of the PLA Army forces in a military region: a squad leader, a platoon leader, a company commander, a battalion commander, a regiment commander, a division commander, and a group army commander.[17] Similarly, in the U.S. Army in 2000, there would also have been as many as seven organizational layers between an individual soldier and the overall commander of army forces in a combat theater: squad leader, platoon leader, company commander, battalion commander, brigade commander, division commander, and corps commander. The number of soldiers under this structure in the U.S. case would have ranged from about forty thousand to at most about two hundred thousand, however, whereas each military region in China contained between 180,000 and 300,000 soldiers in 2000.[18] Thus, it appears that, in a conflict in 2000, the overall organization of PLA Army forces would have been a relatively flatter than that of the U.S. Army, with significantly more soldiers accommodated by the same number of organizational layers. Whether this means that the U.S. Army combat structure in 2000 was excessively tall or that the number of subordinates overseen by some leaders within the PLA Army would have exceeded their effective span of control in a conflict is unclear, but the PLA Army in 2000 was not obviously better or worse than the U.S. Army in terms of organizational height or span of control.

In a conflict involving the PLA Navy in 2000, there would have been three layers of officers between the captain of a major ship and the overall commander of PLA Navy forces in a military region: squadron commander, flotilla commander, and base commander.[19] By comparison, in a conflict involving the U.S. Navy in 2000, there would have been at most either two or three layers of officers between an individual ship captain and the overall commander of U.S. naval forces in a theater: squadron commander, battle group commander, and possibly a numbered fleet commander.[20] A U.S. numbered fleet commander could have been in charge of fifty or more major combat ships (submarines, frigates, destroyers, cruisers, aircraft carriers, etc.), with at most two organizational layers between him[21] and the captain of an individual ship, whereas the overall commander of PLA Navy forces in a military region would also have had command of at most forty to fifty major combat ships but would have had three organizational layers between him[22] and an individual ship captain. As a result, the organization of PLA Navy forces in the event of a conflict in 2000 would likely have been taller than optimal.[23]

In a conflict involving the PLA Air Force in 2000, there would have been five layers of officers between an individual pilot and the overall commander of PLA Air Force forces in a military region: element commander (中队); flight commander (大队); regiment commander; division commander; and air corps, base, or command post commander.[24] Similarly, in a conflict involving the U.S. Air Force in 2000, there also would have been five layers of officers between an individual pilot and the overall commander of U.S. air forces in the conflict: element lead, flight lead, squadron commander, group commander, and wing commander.[25] The overall commander of PLA Air Force forces in a military region would likely have had command over fewer than one thousand aircraft in a conflict, but he would also have had responsibility for surface-to-air missile and anti-aircraft gun units in the military region.[26] In comparison, the overall commander of U.S. air forces in a conflict could have had commanded two thousand or more aircraft.[27] Thus, as with the PLA Army, the overall organization of PLA Air Force forces would not have been obviously better or worse than that of its U.S. counterpart in terms of organizational height and span of control.

The Second Artillery Force in 2000 was known to control at least six missile "bases," each with several launch brigades. Beneath each launch brigade were several battalions (typically six), and beneath each battalion were two companies, with the company apparently being the lowest organizational level in the Second Artillery Force. For China's nuclear intercontinental ballistic missiles (ICBMs) each battalion may have been in charge of a single missile, but, in the case of SRBMs (estimated to be approximately forty launchers with at least 335 missiles allocated across three brigades in 2000), each battalion was subdivided into two launch companies, with each company in charge of one or more launchers and several missiles.[28] Thus, there were probably two layers of officers between the commander of an individual missile launcher and the overall commander of the Second Artillery Force forces in the theater: battalion commander and brigade commander.[29] This suggests a relatively flat operational organization, although the U.S. military does not have similar organization to which the Second Artillery could be compared.

Centralization

By all reports, the PLA was a highly centralized organization in 2000. According to one study, "the order to move any but the smallest military units for operational purposes must originate in the [GSD] at the direction of the [CMC]."[30] Another indicated that in combat situations the PLA allows "minimal leeway for independent interpretation of orders."[31] According to a third study, compared to the U.S. military, "the PLA relies less on lower-level initiative and interservice coordination and more on centralized command."[32]

Indeed, although organization theory suggests that the PLA would need a decentralized, organic organizational structure to effectively implement its doctrine of maneuver and indirection, as noted in the previous chapter, PLA leaders apparently believed that a unified and tightly centralized command system was required to implement the carefully synchronized and coordinated operation needed to defeat a militarily superior adversary.

Standardization

The PLA in 2000 was an organization with a high degree of standardization. Tactics (战术) were developed by the command academies or test bases of the different services, and specific combat techniques (战法) were developed by designated combat units. Once approved, they would be promulgated throughout the force, and all units were expected to train using the officially approved approaches. If the leadership of a unit felt that officially approved tactics or techniques were flawed or could be improved upon, they were allowed to communicate their views up the chain of command and, if the higher leadership agreed, then the tactics or techniques would be revised. In the meantime, however, units were expected to continue to train according to the officially approved approach.[33]

Horizontal Integration

At the macrolevel, the PLA employed a matrix organization in 2000.[34] That is, it was organized both according to broad functional areas – combat, political work, logistics, and equipment – and according to geographic location (i.e., military region, group army, division/brigade, etc., in the case of the PLA Army). This organizational structure provided an intrinsic degree of integration down to the regimental level. For example, a logistics unit within an Army division was under the chain of command of both the logistics system and the division to which it belonged. This prevented the logistics unit from being organizationally isolated either from the combat and equipment units in its division that it supported or from the functional expertise and standardization that the logistics system provided. It should be noted, however, that this type of integration came at a price, as the existence of two lines of authority in matrix organizations creates ambiguity and uncertainty for individuals within the organization. This, in turn, can cause leaders to try to strengthen their control, resulting in a more rigid, less flexible organization.[35]

Personnel Policies

Aside from its matrix structure, the PLA was lacking in other aspects of horizontal integration. One example is in personnel policies. The U.S. military has a long-standing policy of rotating its active duty personnel across organizational hierarchies and between geographic locations. In the PLA, by contrast, people tended to stay within a single organizational hierarchy throughout their careers. If an NCO or officer belonging to a given platoon was assigned to a company headquarters position, it would be the headquarters of the company to which that platoon belonged. If they were sent to a battalion headquarters, it would be the battalion to which that company belonged, and so on, with the result that most would spend their entire career within a single division or even a single regiment. Only when they reached the group army level or higher would officers be transferred out of the organizational hierarchy in which they had begun their careers.[36]

This insularity applied to the functional dimension of the matrix as well. Early in their careers officers would be assigned to one of five developmental tracks: command, political, logistics, equipment management, or technical. Once assigned to a track, all future assignments would be within the designated track. Thus, officers in the command track would never receive assignments as political officers, logistics officers, equipment officers, or technical officers, and the same applied to officers in the other tracks. Officers in different functional tracks enrolled in separate courses when participating in advanced education and training and even ate in different mess halls.[37]

Although these policies promoted close-knit units based on career-long relationships and deep expertise within functional areas, they prevented officers and NCOs from developing an understanding of the roles and functions of their counterparts in other functional tracks and hierarchies. Most critically, they prevented officers and NCOs from developing relationships with people outside of their organizational and functional hierarchies. This undoubtedly hindered the flow of information about best practices within the PLA and made more difficult the coordination of the activities of units from different organizational hierarchies.

Cross-Hierarchical Teams

Other horizontal integration mechanisms were lacking as well in the PLA in 2000. Much PLA Army training, for example, was conducted by units of battalion size and smaller, meaning not only that soldiers did not regularly have contact with soldiers outside their own battalion (roughly five hundred people), but they also did not regularly have exposure to different service arms and branches, as each battalion was constituted entirely from a single service arm (e.g., infantry, armor, artillery, or engineers). In the U.S. Army, by contrast, battalions have permanent liaisons with the other battalions in their brigade, and even battalion-sized units frequently train and exercise with units outside their brigade as combined-arms "battalion task forces." On those occasions when combined arms training did occur in the PLA Army, more-over, it tended to be with units from the same regiment, brigade, or division. Units rarely trained with units outside their own division, much less with units from other group armies or military regions. Analogous characterizations applied to the PLA Navy, Air Force, and Second Artillery Force. As a result, the ability of the PLA to "task organize," that is, to temporarily create units tailored for a specific mission by combining previously unrelated units, was highly limited. Joint training – that is, training by units from different services, not just different branches within a service – was also rare and when it did occur, it was generally joint only at the group army level (and its organiza-tional equivalent in the other services). Below the group army level the units of the participating services operated independently of each other.[38]

Joint Staff Organizations

The PLA also lacked a joint staff in 2000. One source claims that the CMC had a Joint Operations Bureau whose responsibility was "to balance the demands of the individual services and promote integration among them" and which would send groups of officers to form joint operations staffs within the military regions, but the existence of this bureau is not mentioned in other sources and there is no evidence of standing joint operations staffs in the military regions.[39] In any case, the CMC as a whole was dominated by the PLA Army (all eight uniformed CMC members were from the PLA Army in 2000) as were the four general departments – the GSD, GPD, GLD, and GAD – which, although they nominally performed their functions for the entire PLA, in practice primarily served the PLA Army. Their directors and subordinate department heads were always Army officers, and the majority of their staff came from the Army. In addition, the Navy, Air Force, and Second Artillery had their own headquarters, each with four departments that repli-cated the functions of the GSD, GPD, GLD, and GAD. The Army, by contrast, did not have a separate headquarters organization. Instead the GSD, GPD, GLD, and GAD collectively acted as the headquarters for the PLA Army, further indication that they were not true joint organizations.[40]

The military region headquarters, nominally joint headquarters, were also essentially Army organizations. Although the MRAF commander and (in military regions in which a fleet was headquartered) fleet commander were deputy commanders of the military regions in which they were based, the military region commander himself and the directors of the primary staff departments below him were all Army officers, as were the majority of the headquarters staff. The MRAF commander and fleet commander, moreover, although deputy commanders of the military regions in which they were based, were not actually subordinate to the military region commander. A MRAF, for example, was under the "dual leadership" (双重领导) of both the PLA Air Force and the military region, but was *subordinate* (隶属) only to the PLA Air Force. The only units specified as subordinate to the military regions were group armies, service branch units, logistics support units, military districts, and garrison commands. The primary function of the military region headquarters staff, therefore, appears to have been to supervise the activity of PLA Army units in the military region. Second Artillery units, moreover, were apparently not even under the "dual leadership" of the military region, as the commanders of Second Artillery missile "bases" (基地 – the organizational level just below Second Artillery headquarters) were *not* deputy commanders of the military regions in which they were located.[41]

THE ORGANIZATIONAL STRUCTURE OF CHINA'S MILITARY IN 2010

As noted in the previous section, PLA organizations in 2000 already had what appeared to be a largely appropriate degree of vertical differentiation for combat operations. Between 2000 and 2010, further improvement was made by removing one organizational layer in both the PLA Navy and the PLA Air Force. Centralization and standardization in the PLA, however, despite marginal improvements, remained excessive, and the PLA still did not have a sufficient degree of horizontal integration to effectively implement its doctrine.

Vertical Differentiation

In 2010, the PLA Army had reduced its overall size from an estimated 1.6 million soldiers in 2000 to approximately 1.25 million.[42] These were still apportioned across seven military regions, meaning that the average military region in 2010 had about 180,000 soldiers in peacetime. In addition, many divisions had been eliminated and replaced by brigades. The number of organizational layers did not change, however, so that, in a conflict, there would still have been as many as seven layers of leader between an individual soldier and the overall commander of the PLA Army forces in a military region: squad leader, platoon leader, company commander, battalion commander, regiment commander, brigade or division commander, and group army commander.[43] Over this period the U.S. Army had also put increased emphasis on brigades rather than divisions as the basic operational unit, but brigades still reported to division headquarters in the U.S. Army. Thus, in a large-scale conflict involving the U.S. Army in 2010, there also still would have been as many as seven organizational layers between an individual soldier and the overall commander of U.S. army forces in a combat theater.[44] As a result, particularly since the PLA Army in 2010 was smaller than it had been in 2000, in the event of a conflict in 2010, there would not have been a significant difference between the PLA Army and the U.S. Army in terms of organizational height and span of control.

Between 2000 and 2010, the PLA Navy eliminated a major organizational layer, the naval base, from its operational chain of command. As a result, in a conflict involving the PLA Navy in 2010, there would have been just two layers of officers between the captain of a major combat ship and the overall commander of PLA Navy forces in a military region: squadron commander and flotilla commander. The number of major combat ships in the PLA Navy in 2010 had increased somewhat in comparison to 2000, moreover, so that the overall commander of PLA Navy forces in a military region could have had command over fifty or so combat ships at a time in a conflict.[45] By comparison, in a conflict involving the U.S. Navy in 2010, there would still have been at most either two or three layers of officers between an individual ship captain and the overall commander of U.S. naval forces in a theater: squadron commander, strike group commander, and/or numbered fleet commander.[46] If a numbered fleet commander had been designated the overall commander of U.S. naval forces in a theater in a major conflict in 2010, then, like his[47] PLA Navy counterpart, he would have had at most two layers of officers between him and an individual ship captain and could have had command over fifty or more ships.[48] Thus, it appears that the organizational heights and spans of control in the PLA Navy and U.S. Navy in the event of a conflict in 2010 would have been comparable.

Similar to the PLA Navy, the PLA Air Force eliminated a major organizational layer, in this case the air corps, from its operational chain of command between 2000 and 2010. Thus, in a conflict involving the PLA Air Force in 2010, there would have been at most four layers of officers between an individual pilot and the overall commander of PLA Air Force forces in a military region: element commander, flight commander, regiment commander, and division commander.[49] By comparison, in a conflict involving the U.S. Air Force in 2010, there would still have been five layers of officers between an individual pilot and the overall commander of U.S. Air Forces in a conflict.[50] The overall commander of PLA Air Force forces in a military region would likely have had command over five hundred or so aircraft in a conflict, along with ground-based air defences, whereas the overall commander of U.S. air forces in a conflict could have had command up to two thousand aircraft.[51] Thus, it appears that the organizational heights and spans of control in the PLA Air Force and U.S. Air Force in the event of a conflict in 2010 would have been roughly comparable.

The basic organizational structure of the Second Artillery Force did not change between 2000 and 2010. The number of missiles operated by the Second Artillery, however, expanded significantly between 2000 and 2010, as a result of the deployment of large numbers of conventionally armed SRBMs and ground-launched land-attack cruise missiles (GLCMs). In 2000, the PLA maintained an estimated 150 to 170 nuclear-armed missiles and more than three hundred conventionally armed SRBMs.[52] In 2010 the number of nuclear-armed missiles was largely unchanged (although older missiles had been phased out in favor of more-modern models), but the number of SRBMs had grown to more than a thousand, and between two hundred and five hundred GLCMs had been fielded as well. These missiles were controlled by at least five SRBM brigades and an estimated two or three GLCM brigades. In the case of SRBMs, each brigade controlled six launch battalions and each launch battalion controlled two launch companies, each with three launchers. Thus, there would have likely been three layers of officers between the officer in charge of an individual missile launcher and the overall commander of the Second Artillery Force forces in the theater: company commander, battalion commander, and brigade commander. This appears to have been an increase in organizational height relative to 2000 but seems reasonable given the increase in the number of missiles and launchers. [53]

Centralization

There is no evidence to suggest that PLA became a less-centralized organization between 2000 and 2010. Indeed, some observers believed that the growth of modern sensor and communication technology caused the PLA to become more centralized, as it gave commanders both the means to directly control lower-level units and the illusion that they had as much situational awareness as front-line commanders.[54] This problem was not limited to the Chinese military, of course, but U.S. combat experience in Iraq and Afghanistan had caused the U.S. armed forces, particularly the U.S. Army, to increase their level of decentralization, rely more on the judgment of junior officers, and rediscover the concept of "mission command" in which officers and enlisted personnel are expected to achieve their commander's overall intent, rather than simply execute his orders verbatim.[55] In the PLA, however, decision making remained highly centralized in 2010.[56]

Standardization

The degree of standardization in the PLA does not appear to have diminished between 2000 and 2010. Individual units were allowed to experiment with different tactics and techniques during exercises to find the best approach to solving a problem, and innovative and effective approaches that were discovered through this process were shared throughout the PLA. Once an actual conflict began, however, units would have been expected to strictly follow orders. According to one PLA officer, the sayings were that "military orders are like a mountain falling (on you)" (军令如山倒) and "what you understand, you should do, and what you don't understand you should also do" (理解的要执行, 不理解的也要执行). Although deviations were possible in special circumstances, even those deviations would have had to be first approved by higher authorities.[57]

Horizontal Integration

Only marginal improvements to horizontal integration were made in the PLA between 2000 and 2010.

Personnel Policies
Military personnel still tended to stay within a single organizational hierarchy and functional track throughout their careers. They had at least begun taking classes with personnel from unit types different than their own during the course of their professional military education, but still only with personnel from the same service. By comparison, only about half of the students at the U.S. military service war colleges are from the host service; the remainder are from other services or foreign militaries, or are U.S. government civilian employees.[58]

Cross-Hierarchical Teams
The degree to which military personnel had contact with people from other organizational hierarchies had increased somewhat, but still fell well short of U.S. standards. PLA Army units, for example, were beginning to investigate how to conduct combined arms operations at the battalion level (something the U.S. Army has been doing since World War II) and PLA Air Force units were beginning to practice air operations that combined more than one type of aircraft into a single "package." In addition, many PLA Air Force bases had

created special detachments whose mission was to host and service aircraft visiting from other units. The PLA had also begun experimenting with units from more than one service being controlled by a division-level or brigade-level headquarters, whereas ten years earlier joint operations had always been controlled by a group army-level headquarters. Moreover, during joint operations, commanders of the forces from the different services could be collocated in a single headquarters, whereas in the past the forces from the different services would simply dispatch midlevel liaison officers to each other's headquarters. The frequency of joint training had increased as well, with forces of a given group army frequently working with air and naval units based in the same area. Much training that was labeled "joint" training, however, was not truly joint, as the forces from different services were actually training in opposition to each other (e.g., PLA Air Force ground-attack aircraft practicing against PLA Army air defense forces).[59]

Joint Staff Organizations

The PLA still lacked a true joint staff in 2010, although the representation of the non-Army services in the CMC, GSD, and GPD had increased. In September 2004, the commanders of the PLA Navy, PLA Air Force, and Second Artillery Force were added to the CMC and, except for a fourteen-month interlude in 2006–2007 when the newly appointed PLA Navy commander was not a member of the CMC (probably because, then still a vice-admiral, he lacked the rank to be a CMC member), have remained there since. However, the other uniformed positions on the CMC included the two vice-chairmen and the Minister of Defense, who generally came from the PLA Army, and the directors of the four general departments – the GSD, GPD, GLD, and GAD – who were always members of the PLA Army. Thus, only three of the ten uniformed members of the CMC in 2010 were from services other than the PLA Army, and the CMC staff continued to be dominated by PLA Army personnel.[60]

Similarly, although the GSD had had one deputy chief of the general staff each from the PLA Navy and Air Force since 2004, and from the Second Artillery beginning in 2010, the chief of the general staff had always been from the PLA Army, as had been the directors of the highest-level subdepartments within the GSD, and the GSD staff as whole continued to be dominated by PLA Army personnel. Likewise for the GPD, which had had a deputy director from the PLA Air Force since 2005 and from the PLA Navy since 2009. The GLD, moreover, had had only one non-Army deputy director, Air Force Lieutenant General Li Maifu from 2006 to 2009, in recent years, and the GAD (established in 1998) had never had a non-Army deputy director.[61]

No significant changes to the organization of military region headquarters appear to have occurred between 2000 and 2010. Thus, although nominally joint organizations, their primary function appears to have remained as supervising the activity of PLA Army units in the military region, and only secondarily coordinating the activities of Army, Navy, and Air Force units in the region.

THE ORGANIZATIONAL STRUCTURE OF CHINA'S MILITARY IN 2020

Fundamental changes to the PLA's organization would be needed before it would have the type of organic structure needed to effectively implement its maneuver and indirection–based doctrine. The overall organizational height appears to be reasonable – comparable to that of the U.S. military and relatively flat compared to a corporation – suggesting that there are few advantages to be gained by further flattening the organization. Otherwise, however, the PLA is a highly centralized, poorly integrated, and highly standardized organization – the precise opposite of the characteristics needed to implement a doctrine based on maneuver and indirection. To become the type of organic organization that could effectively implement its doctrine, therefore, the PLA would have to become less centralized, better integrated, and less standardized.

Centralization

Decentralization would likely be the most difficult adjustment for the PLA to make. Becoming a decentralized organization in which lower-level officers are allowed greater latitude for independent decision making would require the PLA leadership to have a greater degree of trust in their junior officers than they currently appear to have. During a multination exercise involving both the United States and China in 2014, for example, the executive officer of a U.S. aircraft carrier observed that, on Chinese ships, either the commanding officer or his executive officer has to be on the ship's bridge at all times, whereas on U.S. ships the bridge is usually commanded by a junior officer.[62]

What might increase this level of trust is not entirely clear, but one contributor could be improving the quality of information available to lower-level units. As one PLA officer has noted, an individual or small unit only sees a limited part of the picture, whereas a central organization is responsible for the whole.[63] The PLA's sensor and communication technology, however, are improving rapidly. Thus, in the future a lower-level officer could in theory have available to him the same information as is available to his commander and higher-level officers, enabling him to make better-quality decisions than he could in the past. As noted earlier, however, the growth of modern sensor and communication technology so far is actually tending to cause the PLA to become more centralized, as it also gives commanders both the means to directly control lower-level units and the illusion that they have as much situational awareness as front-line commanders.

Another possible contributor to an increased level of trust in the judgment of junior officers would be recruiting new officers with greater innate capabilities. As will be detailed in Chapter Five, graduates of the PLA's military academies are generally regarded as less capable than graduates of China's civilian universities, and the proportion of new officers who are civilian university graduates is increasing. Officers assigned to the PLA's command track, however, are still largely graduates of the military academies. Graduates of civilian universities tend to be channeled into technical areas such as equipment or logistics, suggesting that, if anything, the PLA leadership trusts them even less to make command decisions than it does the graduates of military academies.

In addition, regardless of the innate capabilities of junior officers, becoming a decentralized organization would require tolerance for the mistakes that inexperienced officers will inevitably make. Increasing the degree of decentralization in the PLA would thus require not just change in organizational structure, it would also require a change in the organizational culture of the PLA to become more risk-tolerant. The organizational culture of the PLA will be addressed in Chapter Eight.

Standardization

Reducing the degree of standardization in the PLA will likely also be difficult for the PLA leadership. The desire to enforce a universal set of tactics and techniques again reflects in part a lack of trust in the judgment of individual officers. Instead, following generic principles reflecting the collective wisdom of the PLA leadership is apparently regarded as preferable to following the situation-specific judgment of individual leaders (even if those leaders are versed in those principles).

The desire to enforce a universal set of tactics and techniques may be in part a legacy of a military that traditionally had poor communication equipment. If commanders have difficulty communicating with their counterparts on either side of them, then it is better if everyone follows a standardized set of procedures. Otherwise their actions may be out of sync with each other's and collectively less effective than if they had all taken the same approach.

For example, if one regiment prepared for an assault by following official doctrine that prescribed first ordering an artillery barrage but the regiment next to it identified an opportunity to achieve surprise by launching an assault without a preliminary artillery barrage, the first regiment's artillery barrage might alert the defenders opposite the second regiment that an attack was imminent, with the result that the second regiment's assault enjoyed neither the advantage of surprise nor the benefit of a preliminary artillery barrage. The ineffectiveness of the second regiment's attack in turn, could allow the defender to focus its efforts on the first regiment's assault, rendering it less effective as well. If the regiment commanders were able to stay in continuous communication with each other and their division commander, on the other hand, then they could more effectively deviate from official doctrine while nonetheless coordinating their actions with each other. Put another way, in the absence of high-quality, reliable communications, strictly following official doctrine acts as a coordinating and integrating mechanism.

This being the case, it is possible that the improved communications equipment the PLA now possesses will enable a loosening of the degree to which official doctrine is expected to be followed. As noted earlier, however, this improved communications equipment is instead apparently encouraging higher-level commanders to increase their degree of control over lower-level commanders, as it now gives them a greater ability to communicate precisely what they want lower-level units to do. Thus, a greater capability for mutual adjustment, which is called for by a doctrine of maneuver and indirection, has instead resulted in greater centralized control, which is at odds with such a doctrine.

Horizontal Integration

Improving the degree of horizontal integration would probably be easier for the PLA than reducing its centralization and standardization, but there are few indications that this will be accomplished by the end of this decade. Adopting a policy of rotating people between organizational hierarchies, for example, would entail considerable expense, as the PLA would have to pay the cost of frequently relocating its personnel and their dependents from one base or headquarters to another. More significantly, it would entail a major change in PLA culture, as people would no longer work with the same peers, subordinates, and superiors for much of their careers, as they currently do.

Similarly, although the degree to which PLA personnel had contact with people from other organizational hierarchies increased somewhat between 2000 and 2010, for it to reach U.S. standards would require a significant increase in the frequency of training with unrelated units. In addition to the considerable expense involved in transporting personnel and equipment so that they could train together, this would also entail commanders having to work with counterparts with which they did not have longstanding personnel and professional relationships and a correspondingly increased risk of mis-communication, misunderstandings, and friction.

Finally, the PLA could create a true joint staff by 2020. In late 2013 and early 2014, reports in the Chinese media suggested that the PLA was planning on setting up a "joint operational command system," although no timeline was provided.[64] As of 2014, however, despite some marginal changes, the CMC, general departments, and military region headquarters were still dominated by PLA Army personnel. For them to become truly joint organizations would probably require the creation of separate Army-only counterparts for each of the general departments and military region headquarters. That is, a PLA Army headquarters with its own command, political, logistics, and equipment departments would need to be created, as well as separate Army headquarters for each of the seven military regions. Otherwise, the general departments and military region headquarters functioning as both Army headquarters and joint headquarters will inevitably result in an underemphasis on the non-Army services. It should also be pointed out that the PLA as a whole is still dominated by the Army, with roughly two-thirds of all PLA personnel belonging to the Army. The resulting much larger number of Army personnel available to staff joint organizations is another source of Army bias within those organizations. Creating joint organizations without an Army bias would either require drawing a disproportionate number of staff officers from the non-Army services, to the detriment of those services' ability to staff their own organizations with capable officers, or a reduction of the overall size of the Army compared to the other services.[65]

Conclusion

Although the PLA has recently acknowledged a need to adjust its organizational structure,[66] there is no indication that PLA leaders recognize the changes needed to effectively implement its current doctrine, which emphasizes maneuver and indirection. Creating such an organization would require a decision by the PLA leadership to fundamentally transform the PLA into an organization that was decentralized, had a low degree of standardization, and had a high degree of horizontal integration. This would be reflected by policies that regularly rotated personnel between different vertical hierarchies, frequent training with unrelated units, and the creation of a true joint staff and true joint headquarters. Although some of these changes, such as frequent training with unrelated units and the creation of a true joint staff and true joint headquarters, are conceivable between now and 2020, others will entail fundamental and difficult changes to PLA culture. A decision to transform the PLA into the type of organic organization needed to effectively implement its doctrine would be a profound and highly consequential one, and for that reason is unlikely to occur between now and 2020.

4

Weaponry

Although the other contributors to military capability assessed in this study are important, quality and quantity of weaponry cannot be ignored. In 2013, for example, the U.S. Defense Department spent 31 percent of its budget developing and acquiring new weapon systems.[1] Even if one regarded this proportion as excessive, few would argue that developing and acquiring new weapon systems was completely unjustified.[2]

The challenge is to develop a methodology for assessing the quality of a military's weaponry in aggregate. One approach would be to simply total the numbers of each type of major weapon system a military possesses. The disadvantage of such an approach would be that it would not account for qualitative differences between different of weapon systems. Using this system, a 1950s-era main battle tank would be regarded as equivalent to late-twentieth-century main battle tank.

During the Cold War, the U.S. Army developed a system called Weapon Effectiveness Index/Weighted Unit Value (WEI/WUV). This system calculated an overall Weapon Effectiveness Index (WEI) for each weapon based on its technical characteristics (rate of fire, maximum effective range, thickness of its armor, road speed, ground pressure, etc.). For each unit, an aggregate value, called the Weighted Unit Value (WUV), could then be calculated by multiplying the WEIs of each type of weapon the unit possessed by the number of that type of weapon the unit possessed and computing a sum weighted according to the category of each weapon (small arms, tanks, antitank missiles, artillery, armed helicopters, etc.).[3] This approach had several drawbacks, including the apparent subjectivity involved in assigning the weights for different technical characteristics of a weapon system as well as to different categories of weapons, and the fact that it only applied to ground forces, not air forces or naval forces.[4] In any case the U.S. government does not appear to have released WEI/WUV scores since 1979, before many of the weapon systems in use in the PLA in 2000 and later entered service.

The approach taken in this chapter falls between simply counting numbers of each type of major weapon system and the WEI/WUV system in its complexity. Each major category of weapon (e.g., main battle tanks) is subdivided into a small number of subcategories that can be regarded as qualitatively different from each other. China's main battle tanks, for example, are divided into those based on the Soviet 1950s-era T-54 (the Type 59, Type 69, Type 88, etc.), the more-modern Type 96, and the fully modern Type 98/99 (comparable to the U.S. M1A1 Abrams, the German Leopard II, etc.). The number of weapons in each subcategory is determined for the years 2000 and 2010 and estimated for 2020. These numbers are then compared to the number of weapons in equivalent categories in the U.S. military for those years. This approach enables an assessment of both the quantity and quality of China's weaponry in a way that is capable of highlighting differences between services and combat arms without getting bogged down in excessive detail.

Although the U.S. military is used as a point of comparison, the comparisons should not be taken as somehow representing the "military balance" between China and the United States. First, the fundamental premise of this book is that weaponry is just one of several elements of military capability. Thus, a comparison of the hardware of China and the United States, by itself, tells us relatively little about the relatively capability of the two militaries. In any case, military conflicts occur at specific times and places, and, in general, nations do not utilize their entire arsenal of military hardware in a conflict. For example, it is extremely unlikely that a conflict would occur between the United States and China in which all of the main battle tanks operated by both sides were involved. The comparisons are simply intended to illustrate the relative abundance and modernity of the China's military hardware as compared to that of the nation with the most abundant and modern military hardware, the United States.

THE CHINESE MILITARY'S WEAPONRY IN 2000

In 2000, the Chinese military was equipped almost exclusively with obsolescent weaponry.[5] The PLA Army possessed approximately seventy-six hundred main battle tanks in 2000, roughly the same number as the U.S. Army. Seventy percent of China's tanks, however, were Type 59s, based on the 1950s-era Soviet T-54. Another 20 percent were Type 79s and Type 88s, essentially upgraded versions of the Type 59 design. Fewer than 10 percent were modern Type 96s or Type 98/99s and, of these, only about sixty, less than 1 percent, were Type 98/99s, comparable in capability to the U.S. M1A1. In contrast, the U.S. Army

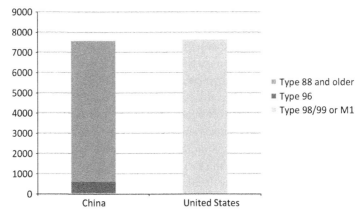

FIGURE 4.1 Main Battle Tanks, 2000

also possessed seventy-six hundred main battle tanks in 2000, but all were either M1A1s or even more advanced M1A2s.[6] Figure 4.1 show the numbers of each type of main battle tank in the PLA Army and U.S. Army in 2000.

The PLA Army's artillery force in 2000 was also largely obsolescent. Although artillery technology has changed less rapidly than tank technology in recent decades, and thus the basic designs of the PLA Army's artillery cannons were still serviceable, fewer than 10 percent of them were self-propelled, whereas in the U.S. Army roughly 60 percent of its four thousand artillery pieces were self-propelled.[7] Towed artillery are preferable in some situations, being lighter and more easily transportable than self-propelled artillery, but self-propelled artillery are more mobile on the battlefield and provide armor protection for their crews, and thus are less vulnerable to counterbattery fire than towed artillery. Figure 4.2 shows the numbers of each major type of artillery system in the PLA Army and U.S. Army in 2000.

The PLA Army also lacked armored infantry vehicles. In total it possessed only about fifty-three hundred such vehicles, and, of these, only about eight hundred WZ501s, copies of the Soviet BMP-1, which first entered service in the 1960s, were infantry fighting vehicles. The remainder were armored personnel carriers. By contrast, the U.S. Army operated more than twenty-two thousand armored infantry carriers. Of these, moreover, sixty-seven hundred were M-2 and M-3 Bradley modern infantry fighting vehicles.[8] Figure 4.3 shows the numbers of each type of armored infantry vehicles in the PLA Army and U.S. Army in 2000.

Finally, the PLA Army in 2000 was severely lacking in helicopters, possessing fewer than three hundred transport helicopters and only thirty armed

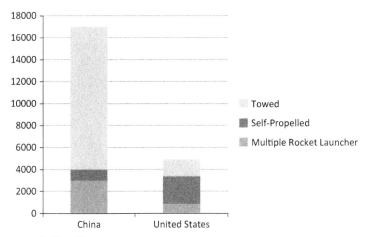

FIGURE 4.2 Artillery Pieces, 2000

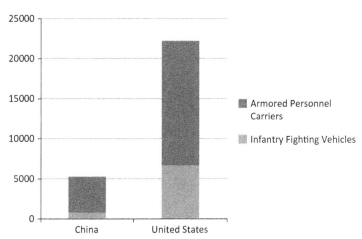

FIGURE 4.3 Armored Infantry Vehicles, 2000

helicopters based on the Z-9 light utility helicopter. The U.S. Army, in comparison, operated twenty-six hundred transport helicopters along with more than eleven hundred AH-1 and AH-64 dedicated attack helicopters and more than 220 other armed helicopters.[9] Figure 4.4 shows the numbers of each type of helicopter in the PLA Army and U.S. Army in 2000.

Thus, the PLA Army in 2000 was a largely unmechanized force. Despite being more than three times the size of the U.S. Army in 2000 (1.6 million soldiers vs. 480,000), it operated roughly the same number of main battle tanks, only half as many self-propelled artillery cannons, a quarter as many

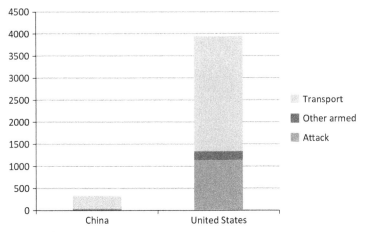

FIGURE 4.4 Helicopters, 2000

armored personnel carriers and infantry fighting vehicles, and a tenth as many transport helicopters.[10] In other words, the PLA Army in 2000 was essentially a light infantry force that would have had limited mobility on the battlefield.

The PLA Navy was similarly obsolescent in 2000. Of its sixty or so major surface warships (destroyers and frigates), for example, none were equipped with long-range surface-to-air missile defenses, only two were equipped with medium-range surface-to-air missiles, and nearly three-quarters of China's destroyers and frigates had no surface-to-air missiles at all. In comparison, of the 116 cruisers, destroyers, and frigates in the U.S. Navy in 2000, more than half were equipped with long-range surface-to-air missiles, and another 30 percent were equipped with medium-range surface-to-air missiles, with the remainder at least equipped with short-range surface-to-air missiles.[11]

The antiship cruise missiles of most of China's major surface warships, moreover, were based on 1950s-era Soviet P15 "Styx" design. These missiles had a large radar signature and flew at an altitude of at least three hundred feet above the sea surface, making them relatively easy to detect and shoot down. Only about a third of China's destroyers and frigates were equipped with the YJ-8 or YJ-82 missile, which were comparable, respectively, to the French Exocet and U.S. Harpoon. These missiles had smaller radar signatures than the P15-based missiles and flew at lower altitudes, making them more difficult to shoot down. China did have, however, two Russian-built Sovremenny-class destroyers, which were equipped with the 3M80 "Moskit" (SS-N-22) supersonic antiship cruise missile, more capable than any antiship cruise missile in the U.S. inventory. In comparison, all U.S. cruisers, destroyers, and frigates in

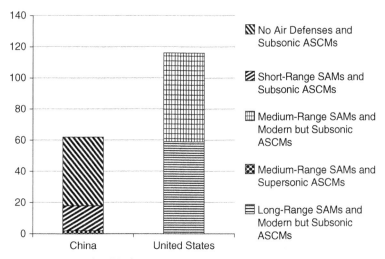

FIGURE 4.5 Major Surface Warships, 2000

2000 were armed with the modern albeit subsonic Harpoon.[12] Figure 4.5 shows the number of major surface warships in the PLA Navy and U.S. Navy in 2000 according to the capabilities of their air defenses and antiship cruise missiles.

Similarly, of the sixty-seven attack submarines in China's inventory in 2000, only about five, two Russian-made Type 636 Kilo-class boats and three domestically developed Song-class submarines, were modern and at least relatively quiet designs. These submarines were driven by diesel-electric engines, however, meaning that their ability to intercept ships on the open ocean (as opposed to restricted waters such as straits or close to ports) was limited. The Kilo class, moreover, were armed only with torpedoes, meaning that they could only attack ships that approached to within about ten miles of them. The three Song-class submarines, along with one modified older Romeo-class boat, were the only Chinese submarines capable of launching antiship cruise missiles. The remainder of China's attack submarine fleet consisted of five domestically developed Han-class nuclear-powered submarines that were too noisy to approach within torpedo range of a ship without being detected and fifty-six obsolete diesel-electric designs (1950s-era Soviet-designed Romeo class, the slightly larger and quieter Chinese-designed Ming class, and two Type 877 export versions of the Kilo class) that were both too noisy and too slow to close to within torpedo range of an alert adversary. By comparison, all but one of the fifty-five attack submarines in the U.S. Navy inventory in 2000 were modern Los Angeles–class or even more advanced Sea Wolf–class

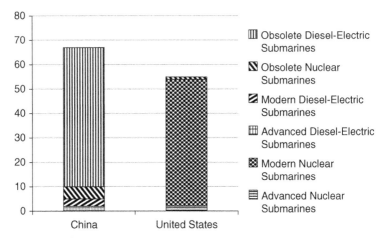

FIGURE 4.6 Attack Submarines, 2000

boats, all were nuclear powered, and all were capable of launching antiship cruise missiles.[13] Figure 4.6 shows the number of each type of attack submarine in the PLA Navy and U.S. Navy in 2000.

China's naval aviation capabilities in 2000 were very limited. The PLA Navy possessed no aircraft carriers, and thus its ability to employ naval aviation was limited to those areas within range of land-based aircraft. China's naval strike aircraft consisted of fewer than one hundred light bombers and attack aircraft, based on the Soviet 1950s-era Il-28 and MiG-19, capable only of delivering torpedoes or unguided gravity bombs, along with twenty-five medium bombers based on the Soviet 1950s-era Tu-16 and ten more-modern, Chinese-designed JH-7 fighter-bombers, both of which were capable of carrying antiship cruise missiles. The 330 fighter aircraft operated by the PLA Navy were all based on the 1950s-era Soviet MiG-19 and MiG-21 designs, and naval surveillance capabilities were limited to four Y-8X airborne early warning aircraft and a handful of reconnaissance aircraft. In comparison, the U.S. Navy in 2000 operated twelve aircraft carriers, each of which could carry fifty F-14 and F/A-18 fourth-generation fighter aircraft and four E-2C airborne early warning aircraft, along with electronic warfare aircraft and helicopters. Total U.S. Navy and Marine Corps inventory included nearly two hundred F-14s, nearly nine hundred F/A-18s, more than one hundred A/V-8 short takeoff/ vertical landing attack aircraft, nearly seventy E-2Cs, more than two hundred P-3 long-range maritime patrol aircraft, and 120 EA-6B electronic attack aircraft.[14] Figure 4.7 shows the numbers of each category of naval strike aircraft in the PLA Navy and U.S. Navy in 2000, and Figure 4.8 shows the

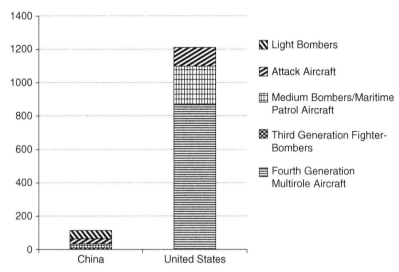

FIGURE 4.7 Naval Strike Aircraft, 2000

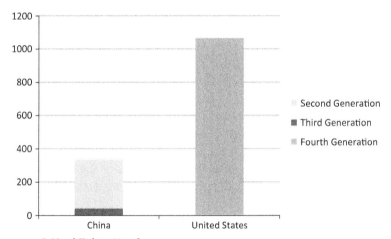

FIGURE 4.8 Naval Fighter Aircraft, 2000

numbers of each generation of fighter aircraft in the PLA Navy and U.S. Navy in 2000 (note that the multirole U.S. F/A-18s are included in both figures).

The weaponry of the PLA Air Force was similarly out of date in 2000. Of the approximately twenty-four hundred fighters PLA Air Force operated, twenty-three hundred were based on the 1950s-era MiG-19 or MiG-21. Only about ninety PLA Air Force fighters, less than 4 percent of the total inventory, were modern, fourth-generation Su-27s and Su-30s purchased from Russia.

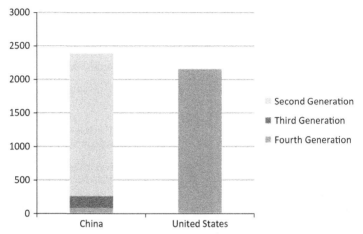

FIGURE 4.9 Air Force Fighter Aircraft, 2000

PLA Air Force ground attack capabilities were provided primarily by about three hundred Q-5 attack aircraft (based on the MiG-19), forty H-5 light bombers (based on the Il-28), and 110 H-6 medium bombers (based on the Tu-16), all of which were capable only of delivering unguided gravity bombs; the PLA Air Force in 2000 possessed none of the precision-guided munitions that the U.S. Air Force had employed so dramatically in the 1991 Gulf War with Iraq. The PLA Air Force did not operate any heavy bombers or stealth aircraft, and did not possess any airborne early warning aircraft; its combat aircraft were dependent on their organic radars and voice communications from ground-based radar operators for information about the locations of enemy aircraft.

By comparison, the U.S. Air Force operated approximately 2,150 fighter aircraft in 2000, fewer than the PLA Air Force, but all of the U.S. Air Force fighters were fourth-generation F-15s and F-16s. Ground-attack capabilities were provided by sixteen hundred of those fighter aircraft (F-16s and F-15Es) along with fifty stealthy F-117 strike fighters, ninety B-52 heavy bombers, ninety B-1 supersonic heavy bombers, twenty B-2 stealth bombers, and 390 A-10, OA-10, and AC-130 close air support aircraft. These aircraft, moreover, were capable of delivering a wide range of precision-guided munitions. Surveillance and reconnaissance in the U.S. Air Force was provided by multiple types of platforms including more than thirty E-3 Airborne Warning and Control System (AWACS) aircraft, nine E-8 Joint Surveillance and Target Attack Radar System ground surveillance aircraft, and more than thirty U-2 recon-naissance aircraft.[15] Figure 4.9 shows the numbers of each generation of fighter aircraft in the PLA Air Force and U.S. Air Force in 2000 and Figure 4.10 shows the numbers of each type of ground attack aircraft in the

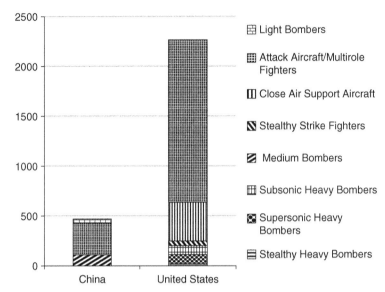

FIGURE 4.10 Air Force Ground Attack Aircraft, 2000

PLA Air Force and U.S. Air Force in 2000 (note that the multirole Chinese Su-30s and U.S. F-16s and F-15Es are included in both figures).

The PLA's ground-based air defenses were also outdated in 2000. The PLA Air Force possessed more than five hundred medium- or long-range surface-to-air missile launchers, but the bulk of these were the HQ-2 system that was first fielded in the 1960s and was based on the 1950s-era Soviet System-75 Dvina (known in the West by the designator "SA-2"). The PLA Air Force had, however, acquired from Russia sixty-four launchers of the modern, long-range S-300 ("SA-10") system. Short-range surface-to-air missiles, mostly operated by the PLA Army, included more than two hundred examples of the relatively modern HQ-7, based on the French Crotale system, along with two dozen of the highly capable Russian-made Tor M1 ("SA-15") system. The PLA also possessed an uncertain number of shoulder-fired very short-range surface-to-air missiles. In addition, the PLA Air Force and Army operated more than twenty thousand anti-aircraft guns of calibers ranging from twenty-three to one hundred millimeters. By comparison, the U.S. Army in 2000 operated a much larger inventory of long-range surface-to-air missiles, consisting of 480 Patriot long-range missile launchers. Other than the very short-range Stingers (some of which were mounted on various light armored vehicles), however, the U.S. military did not operate any ground-based short-range surface-to-air missiles nor did it have any dedicated anti-aircraft guns, although the twenty-five

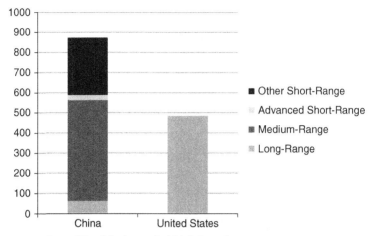

FIGURE 4.11 Ground-Based Surface-to-Air Missile Launchers, 2000

millimeter gun on Bradley fighting vehicles could be used in an anti-aircraft role.[16] Figure 4.11 shows the numbers of each category of ground-based surface-to-air missile launcher (other than very short-range systems) in the PLA and U.S. military in 2000.

One capability that was essentially unique to the PLA in 2000 was its conventional SRBMs, operated primarily by the Second Artillery Force. These consisted of an estimated 175 DF-11s, which had a range of 175 miles, and more than 160 DF-15s, which had a range of 370 miles. By contrast, the longest-range conventional ballistic missile in the U.S. inventory was the 185 mile-range ACTAMS Block 1A.[17] Although the total amount of high-explosive that could have been delivered by China's ballistic missiles was a fraction of the amount the fighter aircraft of the U.S. Air Force alone could have dropped in a single day, and far less accurately, the missiles did provide certain advantages for China. Ballistic missiles are extremely difficult to shoot down. Unlike aircraft, moreover, which must operate from large, immobile airfields or potentially sinkable aircraft carriers, the DF-11 and DF-15 are launched from mobile transporter-erector-launcher vehicles, which are extremely difficult to locate and attack before they have fired their missiles. Thus, any fixed targets within range of China's SRBMs were effectively indefensible. It should be noted, however, that the U.S. Air Force also had a capability to deliver high-explosive ordnance for which there was virtually no defense using its stealth fighters and bombers (although one stealth fighter was shot down over Serbia in 1999), a capability, moreover, that was more flexible and longer-range than China's and, unlike China's, could have been sustained for weeks on end.[18]

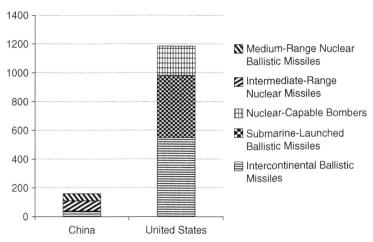

FIGURE 4.12 Strategic Nuclear Delivery Systems, 2000

China had a small nuclear force in 2000, consisting of ballistic missiles controlled by the Second Artillery. These included approximately twenty DF-5 ICBMs capable of hitting targets anywhere in the United States, a similar number of DF-4 ICBMs theoretically capable of reaching targets in Alaska but probably targeted at European Russia, and a few dozen shorter-range missiles capable of reaching most of Asia. The PLA Navy had built a nuclear-powered ballistic missile submarine, but it had never conducted a deterrent patrol and was assessed by the U.S. Defense Department as not operational in 2000. In comparison, in 2000 the U.S. military maintained 550 operational land-based ICBMs, eighteen nuclear ballistic missile submarines with a total of 432 submarine-launched nuclear ballistic missiles, and more than two hundred nuclear-capable long-range heavy bombers.[19] Figure 4.12 shows the number of each type of strategic nuclear weapon delivery system in the PLA and U.S. military in 2000.

China's military space capabilities in 2000 consisted of one relatively low-resolution optical reconnaissance satellite and one medium-capacity military communications satellite.[20] In comparison, U.S. reconnaissance satellite capabilities included an estimated three improved "Crystal"-type electro-optical imagery satellites, with a resolution of approximately six inches; an uncertain number of "Lacrosse" radar imaging satellites, with a resolution of three to six feet; and three sets of Naval Ocean Surveillance System electronic ocean imaging satellites. Other military satellites included twenty-four Global Positioning System (GPS) satellites, seven electronic intelligence and signals intelligence satellites, and numerous dedicated military communications satellites.[21]

Cyber warfare was a growing area of interest in China in 2000. The PLA was said to be studying how cyber warfare, such as inserting computer viruses into foreign information systems, could be used against foreign economic, logistics, and command-and-control systems, but its current capabilities were regarded as lacking depth and sophistication and capable of penetrating only poorly defended computer systems. A higher priority was assigned to defending China's own information systems against potential adversary cyber attacks.[22]

THE CHINESE MILITARY'S WEAPONRY IN 2010

Between 2000 and 2010, China's defense industries completed development of a variety of modern weapon systems, including modern infantry fighting vehicles, amphibious assault vehicles, self-propelled artillery, attack helicopters, submarines, destroyers, fighter aircraft, surface-to-air missiles, cruise missiles, and satellites. The numbers of each type of system that had been produced by 2010, however, were relatively small. As a result, although the Chinese military's weaponry had improved by 2010, it was still only partially modernized.[23]

The proportion of modern (Type 96 and Type 98/99) tanks had increased from less than 10 percent of the PLA Army's main battle tank force to about 28 percent, and the proportion of the most-capable model, the Type 98/99, which was comparable to the U.S. M1A1, had increased from less than 1 percent to more than 6 percent. As in 2000, however, all of the U.S. Army's tanks in 2010 were either M1A1s or even more-advanced M1A2s (although the total number of tanks in the U.S. Army inventory had fallen from seventy-six hundred in 2000 to fifty-eight hundred in 2010, probably because of combat losses and wear and tear during operations in Iraq and Afghanistan).[24] Figure 4.13 show the numbers of each type of main battle tank in the PLA Army and U.S. Army in 2010.

The PLA Army fielded two new types of self-propelled cannons between 2000 and 2010: the PLZ-07 122 millimeter self-propelled howitzer and the PLZ-05 155 millimeter self-propelled gun-howitzer.[25] The PLZ-07 was a significant improvement over some of the earlier 122 millimeter self-propelled cannons in the PLA inventory, as some of the older models provided little armor protection for the crew from small arms fire and shell splinters. The PLZ-05 was an improvement over the 152 millimeter self-propelled cannons already in the PLA inventory as it was longer-range, fired more-effective ammunition (including laser-guided projectiles), and had a higher rate of fire. In addition to laser-guided projectiles, new ammunition types included extended-range full-bore, base-bleed, and rocket-assisted projectiles (all of which have greater range than conventional projectiles), and projectiles that carried multiple armor-penetrating bomblets. About six hundred PLZ-07s and

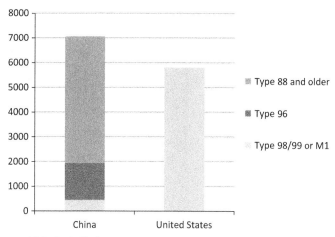

FIGURE 4.13 Main Battle Tanks, 2010

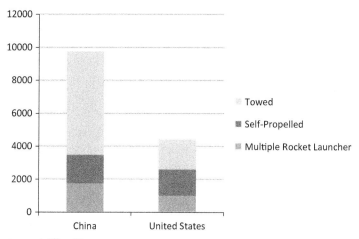

FIGURE 4.14 Artillery Pieces, 2010

one hundred PLZ-05s appear to have been built between 2000 and 2010. As a result of the production of these two systems, the proportion of self-propelled cannons in the PLA Army artillery force increased from less than 10 percent in 2000 to more than 20 percent in 2010, but that was still significantly less than in the U.S. Army, where nearly 50 percent of artillery cannons were self-propelled in 2010.[26] Figure 4.14 shows the numbers of each major type of artillery system in the PLA Army and U.S. Army in 2010.

The PLA Army also fielded two new types of infantry fighting vehicles between 2000 and 2010. One was the ZBD-04, which could carry up to seven

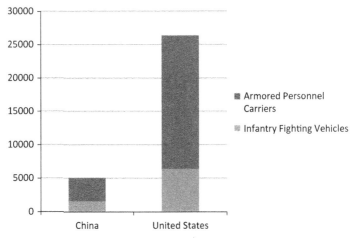

FIGURE 4.15 Armored Infantry Vehicles, 2010

infantrymen in addition to the vehicle crew and was armed with a one hundred millimeter gun, capable of firing laser-guided as well as conventional ammunition, and a thirty millimeter cannon. Another was the ZBD-05 amphibious assault vehicle, similar to the Expeditionary Fighting Vehicle that the U.S. Marine Corps was developing at the time but subsequently canceled. In addition, the PLA Air Force's airborne forces had acquired the ZBD-03 airborne assault vehicle, a nine- or ten-ton air-droppable infantry fighting vehicle. The numbers acquired of each of the new types were small, however. The PLA Army acquired roughly nine hundred new infantry fighting vehicles between 2000 and 2010, doubling the number of infantry fighting vehicles in the PLA to about sixteen hundred (the PLA Navy's marines acquired another 120 or so ZBD-05s and the PLA Air Force's airborne forces acquired an estimated forty ZBD-03s). The number of armored personnel carriers in the PLA Army, however, fell by more than a thousand between 2000 and 2010. By comparison, the U.S. Army, which was less than half the size of the PLA Army in 2010, operated four times as many infantry fighting vehicles and nearly six times as many armored personnel carriers as the PLA Army.[27] Figure 4.15 shows the numbers of each type of armored infantry vehicle in the PLA Army and U.S. Army in 2010.

In addition to new types of artillery and infantry fighting vehicles, the PLA Army in 2010 had also fielded a modern new attack helicopter, the WZ-10. Only about ten examples had been built, however, whereas the U.S. Army operated more than twelve hundred AH-64 attack helicopters in 2010. Although the total number of armed helicopters in service in the PLA Army had more than quadrupled since 2000, to 130 or so, this was less than a tenth as

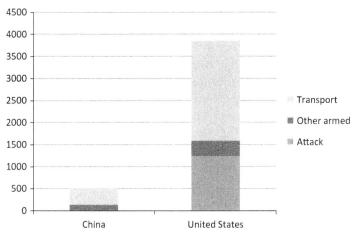

FIGURE 4.16 Helicopters, 2010

many as the nearly sixteen hundred armed helicopters that were operated by the U.S. Army in 2010. Almost all of the PLA Army's armed helicopters, moreover, were based on the Z-9 (Eurocopter AS 365N) light utility helicopter, whereas the majority of the U.S. armed helicopters were AH-64 dedicated attack helicopters.[28] Figure 4.16 shows the numbers of each type of helicopter in the PLA Army and U.S. Army in 2010.

Overall, the PLA Army in 2010 remained a largely unmechanized force. Despite being roughly twice the size of the U.S. Army in 2010 (1.2 million soldiers vs. 640,000, when activated U.S. Army reserves and Army National Guardsmen are included), the PLA Army operated only 20 percent more main battle tanks (7,000 vs. 5,800), only slightly more self-propelled artillery cannons (1,700 vs. 1,600), and, most tellingly, a fifth as many armored infantry vehicles (5,100 vs. 26,000) and a sixth as many transport helicopters (370 vs. 2,300).[29] The PLA Army thus still consisted primarily of light infantry that would have had limited mobility on the battlefield.

Like the PLA Army, the PLA Navy fielded a number of modern new systems between 2000 and 2010. Destroyers from three new classes, for example, were built between 2000 and 2010. The first to be completed were two Luyang I–class destroyers, the first domestically built ships to have more than short-range surface-to-air missile defenses. These ships were equipped with the Russian-made eighteen-mile-range Shtil-1 system. Shortly afterward, two Luyang II–class ships were completed. These ships were equipped with the domestically produced, long-range (at least sixty-two miles) HHQ-9 system. The missiles for this system were vertically launched and supported by phased array radars that could reportedly simultaneously track a hundred targets and engage fifty of them. Thus, the air defense capabilities of these ships were comparable to those of U.S. cruisers and destroyers equipped with the Aegis system (although they had only half as many vertical launch cells as the U.S. destroyers and less than 40 percent as many as the U.S. cruisers). These ships were also equipped with the 175-mile-range YJ-62 antiship cruise missile, which is about 50 percent larger (and, therefore, more destructive) than the Chinese YJ-83 or U.S. Harpoon.[30]

The third new class of destroyer were two Luzhou-class ships. These ships were equipped with the Russian-made, vertically launched ninety-three-mile-range Rif-M (SA-N-20) system, and thus, like the Luyang II-class, their air defense capabilities were also comparable to those of U.S. ships equipped with the Aegis system.[31]

Two new classes of frigates were also built between 2000 and 2010. The first were two Jiangkai I–class ships, which were about 50 percent larger than the previous Jiangwei class and were the first Chinese frigates to be equipped with towed sonar arrays and antisubmarine torpedo launchers, giving them a greatly increased antisubmarine warfare capability. These were followed by the Jiangkai II–class, which were equipped with vertically launched, twenty-miles-or-more-range HHQ-16 surface-to-air missiles, making them China's first frigates to be equipped with more than short-range surface-to-air missile defenses. Once initiated, construction of these ships proceeded rapidly, with an estimated eleven laid down and seven completed between 2005 and 2010.[32]

Despite these acquisitions, the overall capabilities of the PLA Navy's major surface ships remained outdated. Of the PLA Navy's nearly eighty major surface warships (destroyers and frigates), for example, only one-twentieth of them were equipped with long-range surface-to-air missile defenses, another sixth were equipped with medium-range surface-to-air missiles, a quarter were equipped with short-range surface-to-air missiles, and more than half were still not equipped with any surface-to-air missiles at all. In comparison, in 2010, nearly 80 percent of the U.S. Navy's more than a hundred major surface warships were equipped with long-range surface-to-air missiles, with the remainder equipped with either medium-range or short-range air defenses. As another point of comparison, although the air-defense capabilities of China's new Luyang II– and Luzhou-class ships were comparable to those of the U.S. Aegis-equipped ships, the PLA Navy acquired four such ships between 2000 and 2010, while the U.S. Navy acquired twenty-nine.[33]

Similarly, the offensive armament of nearly half of China's major surface warships in 2010 still consisted of antiship cruise missiles based on the 1950s-era Soviet P15. In comparison, roughly 80 percent of the U.S. Navy's major

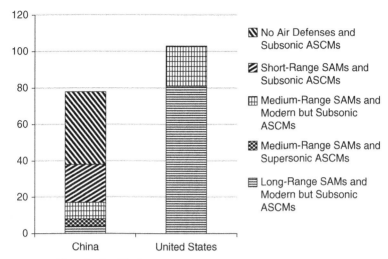

FIGURE 4.17 Major Surface Warships, 2010

surface warships were equipped with the modern Harpoon antiship cruise missile. China did, however, have four Russian-built Sovremenny-class destroyers equipped with the SS-N-22 supersonic antiship cruise missile. The six Luyang- and Luzhou-class destroyers and seven Jiangkai II–class frigates in operation in 2010, moreover, were equipped with the advanced Russian MR331 Mineral-ME fire-control radar, which may be capable of targeting ships beyond the normal radar horizon.[34]

Antisubmarine warfare was the weakest aspect of China's surface ships. Apparently only the nine Jiangkai I– and Jiangkai II–class ships were equipped with towed sonar arrays, which, by distancing the sonar from the noise caused by the ship's machinery, propellers, and passage through water, significantly improves its capability to detect submarines. Fewer than half of China's destroyers and frigates were equipped with helicopters, another important antisubmarine warfare system, and fewer than a third were equipped with antisubmarine torpedoes.[35]

A final weakness of many of China's surface ships was in their command and control capabilities. More than half of China's destroyers and frigates lacked a combat information center, a key facility for coordinating the sensors and weapon systems of a modern warship.[36] Figure 4.17 shows the numbers of each type of major surface ship in the PLA Navy and U.S. Navy in 2010.

In the area of small surface warships, the PLA Navy had acquired at least sixty Houbei-class fast attack missile craft. These ships employ a wave-piercing catamaran design that enables them to achieve a top speed of up to fifty knots and incorporates measures to reduce their radar signature. Each is equipped with eight modern YJ-83 antiship cruise missiles. The small size of these ships limits how far out to sea they can range as well as how far away they can detect surface targets (the maximum detection range of a surface-search radar is generally a function of its height above the surface of the ocean). However, their missiles could be provided with over-the-horizon targeting information by aircraft or, via satellite relay, other ships. Their lack of onboard defenses makes them essentially defenseless against antiship cruise missiles, but attacking in large numbers combined with their reduced radar signatures might allow for an acceptable rate of survivability. Any adversary, including the U.S. Navy, would be reluctant to send surface ships to within range of these craft. The overall number of fast attack missile craft in the PLA Navy did not increase significantly between 2000 and 2010, but the Houbei class replaced slower craft armed with less-capable missiles.[37]

The PLA Navy acquired three new types of attack submarines between 2000 and 2010. One consisted of eight Kilo-class conventionally powered submarines. Although the PLA Navy already possessed four Kilo-class submarines in 2000, the new batch were equipped with the Novator Alfa Klub supersonic antiship cruise missile system, which has a range of more than 130 miles. This system provided a qualitative improvement in the offensive capability of the Kilo-class, as it gave them the ability to engage surface ships on the open ocean at long ranges with a missile that was very difficult to intercept. Given their slow cruising speed, diesel-electric submarines would normally have difficulty closing to within torpedo range of their targets, except in restricted waters.[38]

The second new type of attack submarine acquired by the PLA Navy between 2000 and 2010 was the Yuan class, four of which had been commissioned by 2010. These submarines were almost as quiet as the most-recent Kilo-class boats and were believed to be equipped with an air-independent propulsion system that significantly extended the amount of time they could cruise submerged before needing to approach the surface to snorkel. Although not equipped with the Klub system, they were equipped with the twenty-five-mile-range YJ-82 subsonic antiship cruise missile, which at least enabled them to engage targets at up to three times torpedo range.[39]

The third new type of attack submarine consisted of two Shang-class nuclear-powered submarines. These submarines were apparently not a dramatic improvement over the Han class in terms of quieting, but they were significantly faster (top speed of thirty knots vs. twenty-five knots), improving their capability to intercept surface ships and launch missile or torpedo attacks on them.[40]

Besides the new classes of attack submarines, an additional thirteen of the relatively modern Song class were built between 2000 and 2010. Although not

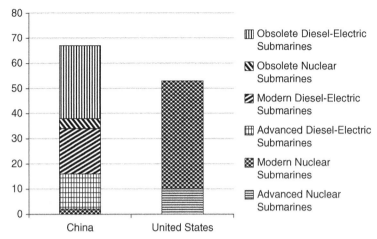

FIGURE 4.18 Attack Submarines, 2010

as quiet as the Kilo or Yuan class, the Song class were significantly quieter than the Romeo or Ming class and, like the Yuan class, were equipped with the YJ-82 antiship cruise missile.[41]

Nonetheless, significant numbers of Romeo- or Ming-class submarines remained in the PLA Navy inventory in 2010. Despite reports in the Western media that China's attack submarine force was expanding, the PLA Navy had roughly the same number of attack submarines – sixty-seven – in 2010 as it had in 2000. More than 40 percent of this force, moreover, consisted of obsolete diesel-electric submarines that were armed only with torpedoes. Another approximately 30 percent consisted of diesel-electric submarines armed with relatively short-range antiship cruise missiles. Only sixteen of China's attack submarines consisted of either diesel-electric boats armed with long-range antiship cruise missiles or (relatively noisy) nuclear submarines. By comparison, the U.S. Navy in 2010 operated fifty-three nuclear-powered attack submarines that were significantly quieter than any of China's nuclear submarines, including ten advanced Sea Wolf– and Virginia-class ships.[42] Figure 4.18 shows the number of each type of attack submarine in the PLA Navy and U.S. Navy in 2010.

China's naval aviation capabilities in 2010 were still very limited. The PLA Navy still did not possess any aircraft carriers, and thus its ability to employ naval aviation was limited to areas within range of land-based aircraft. One squadron of twenty-four advanced Su-30MKK2 fourth-generation naval strike fighters had been acquired since 2000, but the remainder of the fighter aircraft operated by the PLA Navy were based on the 1950s-era MiG-21 design. The greatest improvement appeared to be in the area of naval strike aircraft, where the estimated number of JH-7 supersonic fighter-bombers increased from ten in 2000 to eighty-four in 2010. In addition, the estimated number of PLA Navy antiship cruise missile-carrying H-6s increased from approximately twenty in 2000 to an estimated thirty in 2010. The remainder of China's naval strike aircraft, however, consisted of an estimated twenty torpedo-carrying H-5 light bombers and thirty Q-5 attack aircraft capable only of delivering gravity bombs. In theory the gravity bombs delivered by the Q-5 could have been laser-guided, as China had acquired such ordnance by 2010, but the combat radius of the Q-5 was only about 350 miles, meaning that only ships within 350 miles of a Chinese air field (i.e., less than 350 miles from China's coast) were vulnerable to attack by it. Approaching a ship closely enough to drop gravity bombs on it, moreover, would have been extremely hazardous for the Q-5 against any ship armed with modern surface-to-air missiles. Maritime surveillance capabilities had improved slightly since 2000, with four Y-8J improved airborne early warning aircraft added to the four Y-8Xs the PLA Navy operated in 2000, as well as two to four Y-8JB electronic intelligence aircraft.[43]

In comparison, the U.S. Navy in 2010 operated eleven aircraft carriers, each of which could carry fifty-five F/A-18 Hornet or improved Super Hornet fourth-generation naval strike aircraft along with four E-2C airborne early warning aircraft and various other aircraft. Total U.S. Navy inventory in 2010 (including Naval Reserve and Marine Corps aviation) comprised 610 F/A-18 Hornets, more than 430 F/A-18E/F Super Hornets, 130 A/V-8 short takeoff/ vertical landing attack aircraft, and 150 P-3 long-range maritime patrol aircraft. U.S. maritime surveillance capabilities included more than seventy-two E-2C airborne early warning aircraft, and eleven EP-3 electronic intelligence aircraft.[44] Figure 4.19 shows the number of each type of maritime strike aircraft in the PLA Navy and U.S. Navy in 2010, and Figure 4.20 shows the number of each generation of fighter aircraft in the PLA Navy and U.S. Navy in 2010 (note that the Chinese Su-30s and U.S. F/A-18s are included in both figures).

The PLA Air Force acquired significant numbers of modern fighter aircraft between 2000 and 2010. In 2006 it officially unveiled the J-10, a domestically designed (albeit with Israeli assistance) single-engine fighter comparable in capability to the U.S. F-16; more than 140 of these aircraft had entered service by 2010. In addition, in the late 1990s China had begun assembling Russian-designed Su-27s from knock-down kits at the Shengyang Aircraft Corporation and, in 2008, began producing its own version, designated the J-11B, entirely from Chinese-made components except for the engines. Roughly 130 Su-27s

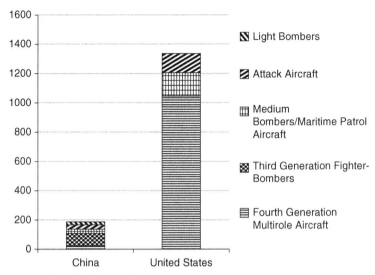

FIGURE 4.19 Naval Strike Aircraft, 2010

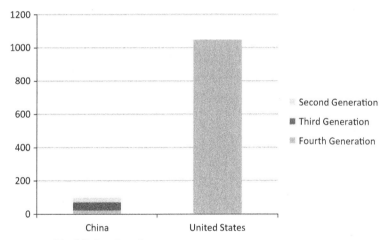

FIGURE 4.20 Naval Fighter Aircraft, 2010

were acquired from Russia or manufactured in China between 2000 and 2010, along with another seventy or so more-advanced Su-30s, and at least one squadron of J-11Bs was believed to be in service by 2010. The PLA Air Force had also acquired two different types of airborne early warning aircraft (including one, the KJ-2000, that was at least as capable as the U.S. E-3 AWACS), as well as dedicated electronic warfare aircraft. In addition, PLA Air Force had acquired several different types of modern air-to-air and

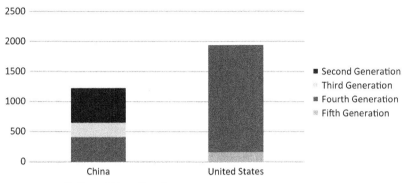

FIGURE 4.21 Air Force Fighter Aircraft, 2010

air-to-ground munitions, including active radar-guided air-to-air missiles, laser- and satellite-guided bombs, electro-optically guided air-to-surface missiles, and passive radar-homing antiradiation missiles.[45]

Despite these advances, much of the weaponry of the PLA Air Force was still outdated in 2010. The number of fighters operated by the PLA Air Force had fallen from approximately twenty-four hundred in 2000 to an estimated eleven hundred in 2010, largely because of the phasing out of obsolete J-6s (MiG-19s). Nonetheless, more than half of the remaining fighters were based on the 1950s-era MiG-21. Only about four hundred of the PLA Air Force's fighters were modern, fourth-generation designs. Aircraft capable of striking ground targets included 120 or so obsolescent Q-5s (down from three hundred in 2000), eighty or so H-6s (down from 110 in 2000), seventy-some JH-7 fighter-bombers, and roughly one hundred Su-30s and J-11Bs. The PLA Air Force in 2010 did not operate any heavy bombers or stealth aircraft and had a total of only eight or so airborne early warning aircraft. In comparison, in 2010, the U.S. Air Force operated nearly eighteen hundred fourth-generation fighters, most of which were multirole aircraft capable of striking ground targets with precision-guided munitions; more than 160 fifth-generation F-22s; more than 140 heavy bombers, including more than sixty that were supersonic and twenty that were stealthy; and more than thirty E-3 AWACS airborne early warning and control aircraft.[46] Figure 4.21 shows the number of each generation of fighter aircraft in the PLA Air Force and U.S. Air Force in 2010, and Figure 4.22 shows the number of each type of ground attack aircraft in the PLA Air Force and U.S. Air Force in 2010 (note that the Chinese Su-30s, J-10s, and J-11Bs and U.S. F-16s and F-15Es are included in both figures).

The PLA acquired three new types of surface-to-air missile systems between 2000 and 2010. One was the KS-1A medium-range (thirty-one-mile) system,

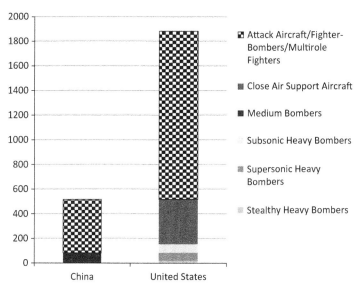

FIGURE 4.22 Air Force Ground Attack Aircraft, 2010

a modernized version of the venerable HQ-2. A second new type was the HQ-9, an advanced, long-range missile based on the Russian S-300 system that the PLA began acquiring in the 1990s (and possibly on U.S. Patriot technology supplied by Israel). The most capable surface-to-air missile system that the PLA acquired between 2000 and 2010 was an advanced version of the S-300 series, the S-300PMU2, which has a range of more than 120 miles. The PLA acquired eight batteries (sixty-four launchers) of this system from Russia between 2000 and 2010.[47] As a result of these acquisitions, along with additional examples of an earlier version of the S-300 system, by 2010 the PLA had more than two hundred modern, long-range surface-to-air missile launchers, along with four hundred or so medium-range surface-to-air missile launchers, including at least sixty of the relatively modern KS-1A. By comparison, the U.S. Army in 2010 still operated 480 Patriot long-range missile launchers. Since the HQ-9 and S-300 launchers each hold four missiles (as do Patriot launchers), but the HQ-2 and KS-1A launchers each hold two missiles, roughly half of China's medium- and long-range surface-to-air missiles consisted of modern, long-range systems. In addition, the PLA had approximately three hundred short-range surface-to-air missile launchers, all relatively modern and including sixty of the highly capable Russian-made Tor M1 system, as well as an uncertain number of shoulder-fired very short-range anti-aircraft missiles. The PLA Air Force and Army also still operated an

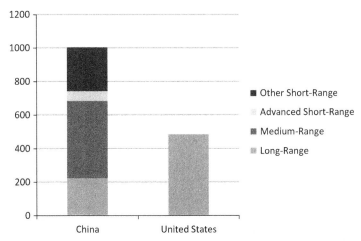

FIGURE 4.23 Ground-Based Surface-to-Air Missile Launchers, 2010

estimated more than twenty thousand anti-aircraft guns of calibers ranging from twenty-three to one hundred millimeters. In comparison, other than the very short-range Stinger, including those mounted on Avenger, Linebacker, and Light Armored Vehicle Air Defense vehicles, the U.S. military in 2010 still did not operate any ground-based short-range surface-to-air missiles, nor did it have any dedicated anti-aircraft guns.[48] Figure 4.23 shows the numbers of each category of ground-based surface-to-air missile launcher (other than very short-range systems) in the PLA and U.S. military in 2010.

The PLA's conventional surface-to-surface missile force expanded considerably between 2000 and 2010. The number of short-range (175 miles to 550 miles) ballistic missiles increased from three hundred or so in 2000 to more than a thousand in 2010, and the estimated accuracy of the warheads on the newest systems had improved from between one and two thousand feet to between fifteen and sixty feet, transforming them from what were essentially unguided rockets to near-precision weapons.[49] In addition, the PLA had begun fielding a conventionally armed medium-range ballistic missile, the eleven-hundred-mile DF-21C. An estimated thirty-six of these missiles had entered service by 2010. The PLA was also developing an antiship ballistic missile of similar range, the DF-21D, that was assessed in late 2010 to have an initial operational capability. Finally, by 2010 the PLA had fielded two hundred to five hundred GLCMs with ranges of at least nine hundred miles. Although these missiles were slower and theoretically easier to intercept than ballistic missiles, they provided China with a true precision strike capability without having to put manned aircraft at risk. And although the total amount of high explosive that could be delivered by China's conventional ballistic missiles was still less than the amount the aircraft of the U.S. Air Force could have dropped in a single day, there is very little defense against ballistic missile attack. If equipped with runway-penetrating submunition warheads, China's ballistic missiles could have been used, for example, to damage the runways at airfields in Taiwan or Japan, making it impossible for aircraft based at those airfields to take off until the runways were repaired. Cruise missiles or manned aircraft equipped with precision-guided munitions could then have been used to attack grounded aircraft and other key targets with relatively little risk of being intercepted by Taiwanese, U.S., or Japanese fighters. This could have resulted in Taiwanese and Japan-based U.S. air forces being defeated on the ground before they even had a chance to engage the PLA Air Force.[50]

China's nuclear forces had expanded somewhat by 2010, but remained small compared to those of the United States and Russia. ICBMs included the approximately twenty DF-5 ICBMs China possessed in 2000, along with two new types of road-mobile ICBM, the DF-31 and DF-31A. The DF-31 was capable of reaching targets throughout Eurasia as well as in Alaska and much of Canada. The DF-31A was capable of reaching targets anywhere in Eurasia, Canada, and the United States (as well as Africa and Australia). Fewer than ten DF-31s and between ten and fifteen DF-31As had been built by 2010, however. Between fifteen and twenty DF-4 ICBMs (albeit with only ten to fifteen launchers), capable of reaching targets in much of Eurasia as well as Alaska, were apparently still operational in 2010. In addition, the PLA operated roughly between fifty and one hundred shorter-range nuclear ballistic missiles capable of reaching targets in most of Asia. Finally, the PLA Navy had commissioned two new nuclear ballistic missile submarines, in addition to the one that existed in 2000, but the missile for the new submarines was still in development in 2010 and the operational status of the older submarine was uncertain. In comparison, the U.S. military in 2010 maintained 450 land-based ICBMs, fourteen nuclear ballistic missile submarines with a total of 336 submarine-launched ballistic missiles, and ninety nuclear-capable long-range heavy bombers.[51] Figure 4.24 shows the number of each type of strategic nuclear weapon delivery system in the PLA and U.S. military in 2010.

Perhaps the greatest improvement in China's military capabilities between 2000 and 2010 was in its space capabilities, especially its reconnaissance satellites. In 2000 China's military satellite capabilities had consisted of one relatively low-resolution optical reconnaissance satellite and one medium-capacity military communications satellite. In 2010, China had in orbit seven optical reconnaissance satellites, three synthetic aperture radar reconnaissance satellites, at least eight electronic intelligence satellites, a set of satellites that appeared to be similar in function to the U.S. Naval Ocean Surveillance

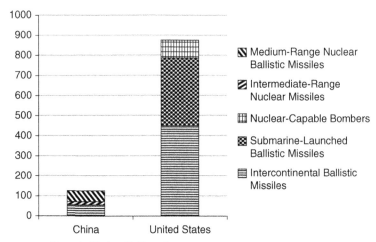

FIGURE 4.24 Strategic Nuclear Delivery Systems, 2010

System satellites (reportedly equipped with infrared sensors to detect ships as well as antennas to pick up electronic emissions), and a prototype missile launch early warning satellite. In comparison, in 2010 the United States operated only four optical reconnaissance satellites, although they were much more capable than China's optical reconnaissance satellites (e.g., resolution level estimated to be six inches as compared to two and a half feet for China's optical reconnaissance satellites) and the U.S. also had access to two World-view and one GeoEye commercial imagery satellites, all three with resolutions of about a foot and a half (i.e., better than China's best optical reconnaissance satellites, although China was also able purchase imagery with resolution as fine as twenty inches from the operators of these and other commercial imagery satellites). The U.S. also operated four radar reconnaissance satellites, four pairs of ocean reconnaissance satellites, and seven missile early warning and/or tracking satellites. China in 2010 had also begun to deploy a constellation of navigation satellites comparable to the U.S. GPS and Russian Glonass systems, with six of a planned thirty-five satellites in orbit. China remained relatively weak in communication satellites, however. It possessed only three dedicated military communications satellites of moderate capacity in 2010, although Chinese state-owned corporations did control another four or five civilian telecommunications satellites that presumably could have been appropriated for military purposes in a crisis. In comparison, the U.S. operated more than thirty dedicated high-capacity military communications satellites in 2010. The U.S. military required the capability to communicate with its forces throughout the world, however, whereas the PLA would have been fighting from Chinese territory in most plausible contingencies, and therefore had less need for military satellite communications.[52]

In addition to having deployed significant numbers of its own satellites, China was developing the capability to attack the satellites of other countries in 2010. This was dramatically demonstrated in January 2007, when China tested a ground-launched missile that destroyed one of its own weather satellites by directly colliding with it, creating what was called by some the worst single space debris event that had ever occurred to that date. The same missile was apparently tested again in 2010, this time against a medium-range ballistic missile as it traveled along the space portion of its trajectory. (Since ballistic missiles follow a trajectory that returns them to earth, little or no space debris was created by this second test.) The United States is the only other country to have demonstrated the capability to directly collide with a satellite using a missile launched from the earth's surface. In addition, in August 2010 a Chinese satellite conducted an in-space rendezvous with another satellite. Although this may have been a test of the rendezvous technology used the following year, when China used an unmanned space capsule to dock with a small space station, it could also have been a test of co-orbital antisatellite technology, in which a satellite closes in on another satellite and either destroys it by exploding or uses other means to interfere with its functioning.[53]

The PLA's interest in cyber warfare had only increased since 2000, and it was said to have established specialized information warfare units to develop viruses to attack enemy computer systems and networks along with tactics and measures to protect its own computer systems and networks. The PLA's actual capabilities in these areas, however, were unclear. The commander of U.S. Strategic Command stated that a cyber attack "could" have effects comparable to those of a weapon of mass destruction, and one prominent analyst assessed that one particular type of cyber attack, a denial-of-service attack, had the "potential" to cause cataclysmic harm to critical U.S. infrastructure or military command and control capabilities. Neither of these individuals, however, provided their assessment of the likelihood that China would actually succeed in carrying out such attacks.[54]

A 2012 study by the Northrop Grumman Corporation focused on the vulnerability of the computer networks that would support the deployment of forces and supplies to the western Pacific region in the event of a conflict with China. More than 90 percent of the communications associated with these deployments were said to be handled by unclassified commercial and Department of Defense networks. Penetration of these networks was said to have the potential both to provide detailed intelligence on U.S. force movements and, through the deliberate corruption of the data on these networks, to cause "serious delays" in the deployment of troops and equipment in the event of a crisis or conflict. This study, however, acknowledged that it did not "consider in detail possible countermeasures and network defense capabilities that the U.S. military and government may employ." The PLA itself, while acknowledging that it possessed "certain virus software and technology stockpiles" (有一定病毒软件和技术储备), assessed that the development of its network warfare forces lagged behind that of "the military powers" (军事强国).[55]

THE CHINESE MILITARY'S WEAPONRY IN 2020

It is of course impossible to predict with precision the numbers of each different type of weapon the PLA will possess in 2020. However, based on the trends over the decade 2000–2010, it is feasible to make rough estimates of how many new weapon systems the PLA will acquire between 2010 and 2020.

The Chinese government published figures for how much the Chinese military spent on weaponry (装备) for most years between 1998 and 2010. Most Western analysts believe that this figure does not include some or all expenditures on research and development, nor does it include expenditures on imported weapon systems (e.g., from Russia). It also does not account for any government subsidies to China's defense industries.[56] Knowing the true value of China's weapons expenditures, however, would not by itself be useful for estimating China future defense production, as the prices the PLA pays for domestically produced military systems are also unknown. Nonetheless, if we assume that the published procurement expenditure figures represent roughly the same *proportion* of the PLA's total procurement expenditures from one year to the next, then it is possible to calculate the approximate *rate* at which the PLA's procurement expenditures grew between 2000 and 2010. If we also have an estimate of the rate at which the PLA's procurement expenditures are likely to grow between 2010 and 2020, moreover, it is then possible to estimate the amount of new weaponry the PLA will acquire between 2010 and 2020 based on the amount it acquired between 2000 and 2010.

Since weapon systems generally take at least a year from the time they are ordered to when they enter service, the systems the PLA acquired between 2000 and 2010, therefore, are largely the result of its weaponry expenditures in the period 1999–2009.[57] Similarly, systems the PLA will acquire between 2010 and 2020 will primarily be determined by its procurement expenditures between 2009 and 2019. The published figure for PLA weapons procurement expenditures grew at an average annual rate of 12.37 percent (after accounting for inflation) between 1999 and 2009. This was virtually identical to the growth rate of China's defense expenditures as a whole, which grew at a 12.40 percent rate during this period (personnel expenditures grew more rapidly while maintenance and operations expenditures grew less rapidly), and was higher than the growth rate of China's economy as a whole, which grew at a 10.3 percent annual rate during this period.[58]

China has not published procurement expenditure figures for the PLA for any year after 2010. However, as noted, the rate at which the PLA's published procurement expenditures grew in the period 1999–2009 was virtually identical to the rate at which the PLA's overall published budget grew during that period, and China has continued to publish annual expenditure figures for the PLA as whole. Since 2009 the PLA has continued to receive attention for annual announcements of "double-digit" increases in its budget, but the announced increases are always in current-year *yuan* and do not account for the effects of inflation, which averaged more than 4 percent a year between 2009 and 2014. In addition, actual spending in 2013 fell nearly 3 percent short of the amount announced at the beginning of the year. Consequently, official PLA expenditures actually increased by an average annual rate of about 5.5 percent between 2009 and 2014.[59] This study assumes that China's defense expenditures will continue to grow at approximately this rate for the remainder of the decade and, therefore, that PLA procurement expenditures will also grow at an overall average annual rate of 5.5 percent between 2009 and 2019.[60]

Estimates of the numbers of each different type of weapon the PLA will possess in 2020 were made by assuming that it will continue to devote roughly same proportion of its procurement expenditures to each major category of weapon system in the period 2010–2020 as it did in 2000–2010. In reality, the PLA's procurement priorities in the period 2010–2020 are likely to differ from those during the period 2000–2010, and thus projections of the number of any individual type of weapon system acquired during the period 2010–2020 are not likely to be correct. Nonetheless, since procurement resources are finite, increases in the procurement of one type of weapon system will require decreases in the procurement of other types of weapon system. Thus, the resulting picture of the overall level of capability of the PLA's weaponry should be roughly accurate in aggregate.

With a few exceptions noted below, most major weapon systems that the PLA will acquire by 2020 had already entered production during the period 2000–2010. The numbers of these systems that will be acquired between 2010 and 2020, therefore, were estimated by determining the number acquired in the period 2000 to 2010 and multiplying that number by the ratio of the total of the PLA's announced procurement spending in the period 2009–2019 to its total estimated procurement spending in the period 1999–2009, assuming a 5.5 percent annual growth rate between 2009 and 2019.[61]

In a few cases (e.g., aircraft carriers, fifth-generation fighters, solid-fuel intermediate-range missiles), the PLA appears likely to acquire by

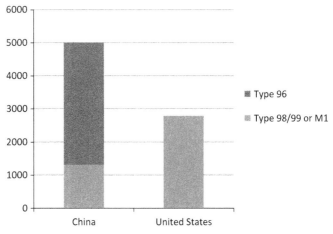

FIGURE 4.25 Main Battle Tanks, 2020

2020 fundamentally new weapon systems that had not yet entered operation as of 2014. In these cases, a key issue is whether China's defense industries are in fact capable of developing and manufacturing the system in question by 2020. In that regard this study has largely relied on published estimates by the U.S. government and other reliable sources to make a plausible estimate of whether the system is likely to be in service by 2020 and, if so, the number of examples that will be in operation by then. In cases where production of the new system was likely to take the place of production of an older system, moreover, estimated production of the older system was reduced by an appropriate amount. Since newer, more-capable systems are generally more expensive than older, less-capable systems, each example of the new system produced was assumed to result in some multiple of that number of older systems not being produced.

In the area of main battle tanks, the PLA acquired approximately one thousand Type 96s and four hundred Type 98/99s between 2000 and 2010. If the acquisition rate for these tanks grew at 5.5 percent a year between 2010 and 2020, the PLA would acquire another twenty-two hundred and 850, respectively, of these types, resulting in a total inventory of thirty-seven hundred Type 96s and thirteen hundred Type 98/99s in 2020. This would give China five thousand modern main battle tanks, more than the twenty-eight hundred M1A1s and M1A2s the U.S. military (Army and Marine Corps) will operate in 2020, although the Type 96 is less capable than the M1A1 and the Type 98/99 is probably less capable than the M1A2.[62] Figure 4.25 shows the estimated number of each type of main battle tank in the PLA and U.S. military in 2020.

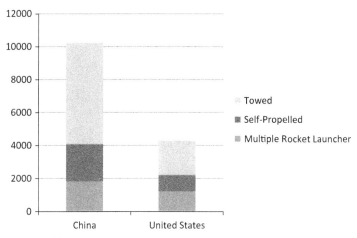

FIGURE 4.26 Artillery Pieces, 2020

The PLA appears to have acquired approximately six hundred PLZ-07 122 millimeter and one hundred PLZ-05 155 millimeter self-propelled howitzers between 2000 and 2010.[63] If the acquisition rate for these systems grew at 5.5 percent a year between 2010 and 2020, another thirteen hundred and two hundred, respectively, would be acquired between 2010 and 2020. Assuming that older 122 and 152 millimeter self-propelled howitzers were phased out during this period, the PLA would have a total of 2,250 modern self-propelled howitzers in 2020, significantly more than the 970 that will be operated by the U.S. military in 2020. Information on the number of towed howitzers and multiple rocket launchers the PLA acquired between 2000 and 2010 was not available. The numbers of these systems in 2020 are therefore assumed to be unchanged from 2014. Figure 4.26 shows the estimated number of each type of artillery piece in the PLA and U.S. military in 2020.[64]

The PLA acquired roughly five hundred ZBD-04 infantry fighting vehicles and 450 ZBD-05 amphibious assault vehicles, which can also function as infantry fighting vehicles, between 2000 and 2010. If the acquisition rate for these vehicles grew at 5.5 percent a year between 2010 and 2020, it would acquire another eleven hundred and one thousand respectively, for a total of approximately sixteen hundred and fourteen hundred of each type. In comparison, the U.S. Army will operate a total of 4,560 Bradley infantry fighting vehicles in 2020.[65]

Data on armored personnel carriers are less clear than on infantry fighting vehicles and amphibious assault vehicles, but the PLA appears to have acquired roughly one thousand armored personnel carriers between 2000 and 2010. If the acquisition rate for armored personnel carriers grew at

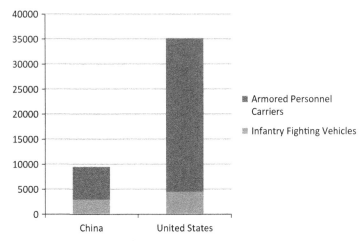

FIGURE 4.27 Armored Infantry Vehicles, 2020

5.5 percent a year between 2010 and 2020, then the PLA would acquire another twenty-one hundred between 2010 and 2020. Assuming that all of the armored personnel carriers in operation in 2010 remained in service in 2020, this would give China a total of about sixty-five hundred armored personnel carriers in 2020, as compared to more than thirty thousand in the U.S. military in 2020.[66] Figure 4.27 shows the estimated number of each category of armored infantry carriers in the PLA in 2020 and in the U.S. military in 2020.

The PLA acquired about one hundred armed helicopters between 2000 and 2010. Most of these were based on the Z-9 light utility helicopter, but, by the end of the decade, China had begun producing the WZ-10 dedicated attack helicopter. If the acquisition rate for armed helicopters grew at 5.5 percent a year between 2010 and 2020, then the PLA would acquire approximately three hundred new armed helicopters, for a total of more than four hundred. This would be about a third as many armed helicopters as will be operated by the U.S. military in 2020, which will have nine hundred dedicated attack helicopters and 350 other armed helicopters.[67]

The PLA Army also acquired about 125 transport helicopters and fifty or so light utility helicopters between 2000 and 2010. If the acquisition rate for these types of helicopters grew at 5.5 percent a year between 2010 and 2020, then it would acquire another 270 and 120, respectively, of these types, for totals of about 450 and 250. By comparison, the U.S. military will have nearly twenty-eight hundred transport helicopters and nearly seven hundred other helicopters in 2020.[68] Figure 4.28 shows the estimated number of each category of helicopter in the PLA in 2020 and in the U.S. Army in 2020.

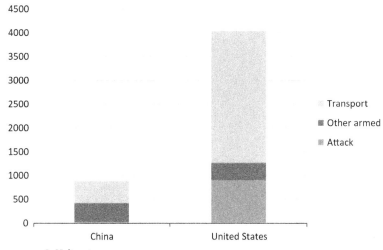

FIGURE 4.28 Helicopters, 2020

Overall, unless it radically downsizes, the PLA Army is likely to remain a largely unmechanized force in 2020. Although it will probably have more modern main battle tanks and self-propelled howitzers than the U.S. Army will in 2020, it will likely have only about half as many infantry fighting vehicles, a third as many armored personnel carriers, and a fifth as many transport helicopters for a force that will likely still be roughly twice the size of the U.S. Army.[69]

The PLA Navy acquired eight new destroyers between 2000 and 2010. If the acquisition rate for destroyers grew at 5.5 percent a year between 2010 and 2020, then it would acquire an additional sixteen between 2010 and 2020, giving the PLA Navy a total of about twenty-six modern destroyers in 2020.[70] The PLA Navy also acquired twelve frigates between 2000 and 2010. If the acquisition rate for frigates grew at 5.5 percent a year between 2010 and 2020, then it would acquire an additional 23 frigates between 2010 and 2020, for a total of forty-two frigates, thirty-two of them modern designs, in 2020.[71] In comparison, the U.S. Navy will operate eight-one modern cruisers and destroyers in 2020 (but no frigates). Thus, the PLA Navy would have about two-thirds as many modern surface warships as the U.S. Navy in 2020.[72] Figure 4.29 shows the estimated number of each category of major surface warship in the PLA Navy and U.S. Navy in 2020.

The PLA Navy acquired at least sixty Houbei-class fast attack missile craft between 2000 and 2010. If the acquisition rate for these craft grew by an average of 5.5 percent a year between 2010 and 2020, then, the PLA Navy

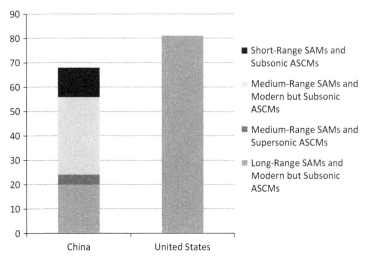

FIGURE 4.29 Major Surface Warships, 2020

would acquire another 140 by 2020. In fact, however, as of December 2013, no additional Houbei-class appeared to have been constructed since 2009. Instead, the PLA Navy appears to have switched to constructing a new type of ship, the Jiangdao-class corvette. These ships are armed with four YJ-83 antiship cruise missiles identical to those carried by the Houbei class but are several times the size of the Houbei-class, displacing about 1,650 tons as compared to 250 tons, and are also equipped with a seventy-six millimeter gun, two thirty millimeter guns, an eight-cell FL-3000N short-range surface-to-air missile launcher, six lightweight antisubmarine torpedo tubes, and a bow-mounted sonar, and are capable embarking a helicopter, although they lack a helicopter hanger. These ships, with a top speed of only twenty-five knots, lack the offensive power of the Houbei class, which carry twice as many antiship cruise missiles and have a top speed of fifty knots, but are able to operate in heavier seas and have a much greater cruising range than the Houbei class. In addition, with their greater size and surface-to-air missiles, they are more survivable against attack, and their sonars, antisubmarine torpedoes, and ability to embark a helicopter give them a modest antisubmarine capability. At least eighteen of these ships were laid down at four different shipyards between 2010 and 2013, with a total of at least thirty expected to be constructed. Since each shipyard appeared to be capable of working on at least four such ships simultaneously, and the construction time for each ship appeared to be about three years, it would be entirely feasible for thirty such ships to have been completed and commissioned by 2020.[73]

The PLA Navy acquired twenty-five diesel-electric and two nuclear-powered attack submarines between 2000 and 2010. If the acquisition rate for attack submarines grew at 5.5 percent a year between 2010 and 2020, then it would acquire an additional fifty-four diesel-electric and four nuclear-powered submarines. If this actually occurred, the new acquisitions alone would exceed the size of the entire Chinese submarine fleet in 2013. This seems improbable. A more plausible scenario, therefore, might be that the PLA Navy would acquire a greater number of nuclear-powered submarines, which are more expensive, along with enough diesel-electric submarines to ensure that all of the attack submarines in China's fleet are modern designs, while capping the overall size of the force at no more than sixty submarines.[74] The cost of a building a nuclear submarine in China is not known. A U.S. Virginia-class submarine costs about $2.5 billion but the Virginia-class boats are probably significantly more capable than the improved Type 093 and Type 095 nuclear attack submarines that China is currently developing. The Type 093 and 095 class, therefore, are assumed to cost approximately $1 billion each, less than half of what a Virginia-class submarine costs ($2.5 billion). Since China paid $200 million for each of the eight Kilo-class submarines it acquired between 2000 and 2010,[75] this suggests that a Chinese nuclear submarine might cost about five times as much to build as a diesel-electric submarine. Thus, if the PLA Navy's acquisition budget for attack submarines grew at 5.5 percent a year between 2010 and 2020, rather than building four nuclear-powered and fifty-four diesel-electric attack submarines, China could instead build about twelve nuclear attack submarines and fourteen advanced diesel-electric submarines. If China retained only the ten most-capable of its twelve Kilo-class submarines along with all of the Type 093, Song-, and Yuan-class boats that were in service in 2010, then in 2020 China would have an attack submarine force that consisted of approximately fourteen modern nuclear-powered submarines and forty-four modern or advanced diesel-electric submarines. In comparison, the U.S. Navy will operate fifty-one modern or advanced nuclear-powered attack submarines in 2020.[76] Figure 4.30 shows the estimated number of each category of attack submarine in the PLA Navy and U.S. Navy in 2020.

The PLA Navy acquired twenty-four Su-30MKK2 fourth-generation naval strike fighters, seventy-four JH-7 fighter-bombers, and twelve naval antiship cruise missile-carrying H-6 bombers between 2000 and 2010. If the acquisition rate for these aircraft grew at 5.5 percent a year between 2010 and 2020, the PLA Navy would acquire an additional fifty or so Su-30MKK2s (although these would probably be indigenously built naval versions of the J-11B, known as the J-11BH, and carrier-capable aircraft based on the Su-33, known as the J-15),

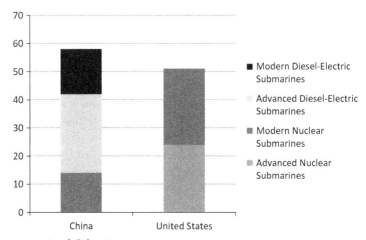

FIGURE 4.30 Attack Submarines, 2020

160 JH-7s, and twenty-five H-6s, for totals of about seventy-five, 250, and fifty-five, respectively. In comparison, the U.S. Navy inventory in 2020 (including Marine Corps aviation) will include approximately 130 F-35B and F-35C fifth-generation strike fighters, more than 950 F/A-18 Hornet and Super Hornet strike fighters, 125 A/V-8 short takeoff/vertical-landing attack aircraft, and approximately one hundred P-8 long-range maritime patrol aircraft.[77] Figure 4.31 shows the estimated number of each type of maritime strike aircraft in the PLA Navy and U.S. Navy in 2020, and Figure 4.32 shows the number of each generation of fighter aircraft in the PLA Navy and U.S. Navy in 2020 (note that the Chinese Su-30s, J-11BHs, and J-15s and U.S. F/A-18s and F-35s are included in both figures).

The PLA Navy also acquired six to eight Y-8J airborne early warning aircraft and Y-8JB electronic intelligence aircraft between 2000 and 2010. If the acquisition rate for these aircraft grew at 5.5 percent a year between 2010 and 2020, it would acquire an additional fifteen or so of these aircraft for a total of twenty to twenty-five. In comparison, the U.S. Navy in 2020 will operate ninety E-2C airborne early warning aircraft.[78]

In 2012 the PLA Navy commissioned its first aircraft carrier, the Liaoning, built on the hull of an incomplete Soviet Admiral Kuznetsov–class aircraft carrier acquired from Ukraine. In January 2014 the CPC secretary of Liaoning province was quoted as saying that a domestically built aircraft carrier was under construction in the city of Dalian, and other reports suggested that the PLA Navy would acquire as many as four "medium-size [i.e., like the Liaoning] aircraft carriers." Thus, it seems plausible that the PLA Navy will have at

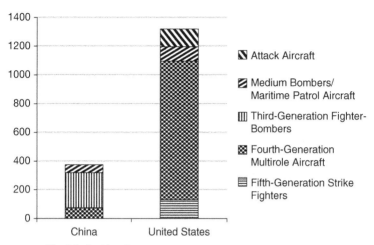

FIGURE 4.31 Naval Strike Aircraft, 2020

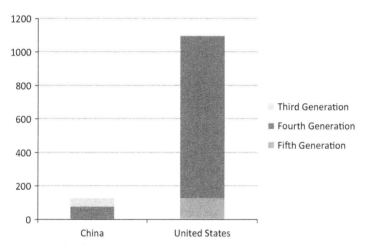

FIGURE 4.32 Naval Fighter Aircraft, 2020

least two and possibly more operational aircraft carriers by 2020. The normal complement for carriers of the Admiral Kuznetsov–class is apparently twenty-two fixed-wing combat aircraft and seventeen helicopters. In comparison, the U.S. Navy in 2020 will operate eleven "super carriers," each of which will normally carry fifty-five to sixty fixed-wing combat aircraft.[79]

The PLA Air Force acquired approximately 140 J-10s and 160 Su-27/Su-30/J-11Bs between 2000 and 2010. If the acquisition rate for these aircraft grew at 5.5 percent a year between 2010 and 2020, it would acquire another

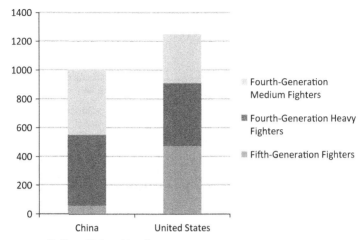

FIGURE 4.33 Air Force Fighter Aircraft, 2020

approximately 310 J-10s and 340 J-11Bs. In 2011, however, China test-flew a prototype of a fifth-generation stealth fighter known as the J-20, and in 2012 a second stealthy aircraft (often called the "J-31," although whether this is its official designator is not clear) was test-flown. The U.S. Department of Defense estimates that at least one of these types of aircraft could reach initial operational capability by 2018. If we assume that the PLA Air Force begins acquiring J-20s in place of J-11Bs for the last three years of the decade, and that each J-20 costs twice as much to produce as a Su-27/Su-30/J-11B, then in 2020 it would have about 450 J-10s, about 490 Su-27s, Su-30s, and J-11Bs, and about sixty J-20s. In comparison, the U.S. Air Force in 2020 will operate approximately 340 F-16s, which are comparable to the J-10, 435 F-15s, which are comparable to the Su-27/Su-30/J-11B, and 475 F-22 and F-35A fifth-generation stealth fighters.[80] Figure 4.33 shows the estimated number of each type of fighter aircraft in the PLA Air Force and U.S. Air Force in 2020.

The PLA Air Force acquired seventy-two JH-7 fighter-bombers between 2000 and 2010. If the acquisition rate for these aircraft grew at 5.5 percent a year between 2010 and 2020, then it would acquire another 155 by 2020, for a total of about 230.[81] The number of H-6 medium bombers in the PLA Air Force apparently fell from about 110 to about eighty between 2000 and 2010. However, new versions of this aircraft were still being developed and entering service throughout this period, so that many of the aircraft in service in 2010 had probably been newly built since 2000. The newest version of the H-6 is the H-6K, equipped with Russian-made Saturn D-30KP-2 turbofan

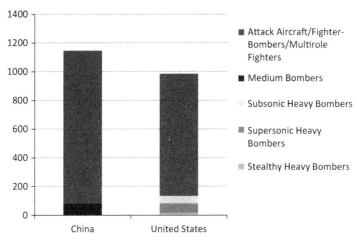

FIGURE 4.34 Air Force Ground Attack Aircraft, 2020

engines, which, with their greater power and fuel efficiency than the WP8 turbojets that power earlier versions of the aircraft, undoubtedly increase the H-6's range and payload by a significant amount.[82] Given the continuing development and production of new versions of the H-6, it seems likely that a substantial number of these aircraft will remain in service in 2020, but what that number will be is not clear based on the trend from 2000 to 2010. The number of H-6s service in 2020, therefore, was assumed to be the same as the number in service in 2010. The Q-5 attack aircraft, based on the 1950s-era MiG-19, will presumably have been phased out by 2020. Figure 4.34 shows the estimated number of each type of ground attack aircraft in the PLA Air Force and the U.S. Air Force in 2020 (note that the Chinese Su-30s, J-10s, J-11Bs, and J-20s, and U.S. F-16s and F-15Es are included in both Figure 4.34 and Figure 4.33).

The PLA Air Force acquired at least four each of two different types of airborne early warning aircraft between 2000 and 2010 – the KJ-2000, believed to be at least as capable as the U.S. E-3 AWACS, and the presumably less-capable KJ-200. If the acquisition rate for these aircraft grew at 5.5 percent a year between 2010 and 2020, the PLA Air Force would acquire another nine of each type, giving it a total of thirteen of each. In comparison, the U.S. Air Force will operate approximately thirty E-3 AWACS airborne early warning and control aircraft in 2020.[83]

The PLA acquired approximately 220 modern, long-range surface-to-air missile launchers between 2000 and 2010. If the acquisition rate for these systems grew at 5.5 percent a year between 2010 and 2020, the PLA would acquire another 480, for a total of about seven hundred. In comparison, the

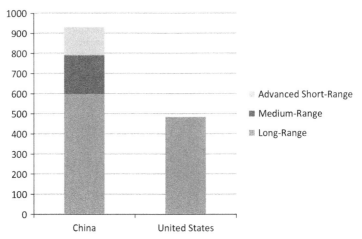

FIGURE 4.35 Ground-Based Surface-to-Air Missile Launchers, 2020

U.S. Army in 2020 will operate approximately 480 Patriot long-range surface-to-air missile launchers. In addition, the PLA acquired sixty KS-1 medium-range surface-to-air missile launchers and thirty-six Tor M1 short-range surface-to-air missile launchers between 2000 and 2010. If the acquisition rate for these systems grew at 5.5 percent a year between 2010 and 2020, then the PLA would acquire another 130 and eighty, respectively, for a total of 190 KS-1 launchers and 140 Tor M1 (or, more likely, a Chinese equivalent believed to be under development) launchers. Along with shoulder-fired very short-range anti-aircraft missiles and anti-aircraft guns, these systems would provide China with a highly capable and dense, layered air defense system. As in 2010, the U.S. military in 2020 will not operate any short-range ground-based surface-to-air missiles, nor will it have any dedicated anti-aircraft guns.[84] Figure 4.35 shows the estimated number of each category of surface-to-air missile launcher in the PLA and U.S. military in 2020 (older PLA surface-to-air missile systems are assumed to have been phased out by 2020).

The PLA acquired approximately 550 DF-11 and two hundred DF-15 SRBMs and thirty-six conventionally armed DF-21 medium-range ballistic missiles between 2000 and 2010. If the acquisition rate for these missiles grew at 5.5 percent a year between 2010 and 2020, the PLA would acquire another 1,200, 470, and eighty, respectively. The total number of SRBMs in the PLA's inventory appears not to have significantly increased after 2008, however. Instead, as new missiles with improved ranges, accuracies, and payloads have been delivered, older missiles have been removed from service. This probably reflects an assessment by the PLA that it now has sufficient numbers of short-range missiles to strike all the important targets that are within range of them (i.e., all of

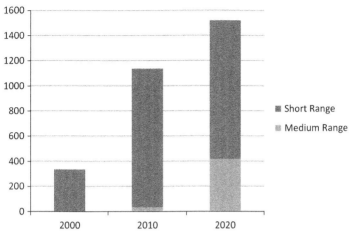

FIGURE 4.36 Chinese Conventional Ballistic Missiles, 2000–2020

the targets on Taiwan for which ballistic missiles are the optimal form of attack), and that future increases in the PLA's ballistic missile inventory will consist of missiles capable of reaching more-distant targets, such as U.S. bases on Okinawa and elsewhere in Japan. If we assume that only about two hundred DF-11 and 170 DF-15 missiles enter the PLA's inventory after 2010 and are used to replace the older versions that were in the inventory in 2000, then the resources to produce an additional one thousand DF-11s and three hundred DF-15s would be available for producing longer-range missiles. Everything else being equal, the cost of producing a ballistic missile is roughly proportional to its range. Since the conventional DF-21 has a range of about eleven hundred miles, as compared to 170 to 220 miles for the DF-11 and 370 to 560 miles for the DF-15, each DF-21 probably costs roughly five or six times as much to produce as a DF-11 and two or three times as much as a DF-15. This suggests that one thousand DF-11s and three hundred DF-15s would cost about as a much to produce as 250–350 DF-21s. If China used the resources that would have been required to produce additional DF-11s and DF-15s to instead produce DF-21s, therefore, then it could produce a total of approximately 380 conventional DF-21s between 2010 and 2020. This would result in a total inventory of about 420 DF-21s by 2020.[85] Figure 4.36 shows the estimated numbers of each category of conventional ballistic missile in the PLA military in 2000, 2010, and 2020.

The PLA acquired approximately 350 CJ-10 GLCMs between 2000 and 2010. If the acquisition rate for these missiles grew at 5.5 percent a year between 2010 and 2020, then it would acquire another 750 or so by 2020, for a total of about eleven hundred. Some of this production would likely be in air- or ship-launched variants of this missile.[86]

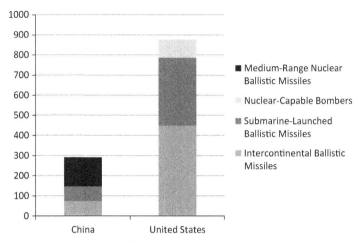

FIGURE 4.37 Strategic Nuclear Delivery Systems, 2020

The PLA acquired fewer than ten DF-31 and between ten and fifteen DF-31A nuclear ICBMs between 2000 and 2010, as well as roughly thirty nuclear-armed DF-21 medium-range ballistic missiles. If the acquisition rate for these missiles grew at 5.5 percent a year between 2010 and 2020, then China would acquire another thirteen or so DF-31s, twenty-five or so DF-31As, and sixty or so nuclear DF-21s. Assuming that China retained its roughly twenty silo-based DF-5 ICBMs but phased out its older DF-4 ICBMs and DF-3 intermediate-range ballistic missiles, this would give it a total of approximately twenty DF-5, twenty DF-31, and thirty-five to forty DF-31A ICBMs, along with 140 DF-21 medium-range ballistic missiles. This would represent a rough doubling of the size of China's land-based nuclear ballistic missile force.[87]

The PLA Navy acquired two new nuclear ballistic missile submarines between 2000 and 2010. If the acquisition rate for these submarines grew at 5.5 percent a year between 2010 and 2020, then China would acquire four additional examples, for a total of six. This would potentially give China a survivable sea-based nuclear strike capability, which it currently does not possess.[88] Figure 4.37 shows the estimated number of each type of strategic nuclear weapon delivery system in the PLA and U.S. military in 2020.[89]

Extrapolating China's military space capabilities in 2020 based on the systems deployed between 2000 and 2010 is problematic, as China in 2010 already possessed more of some types of systems than did the United States. In 2010, for example, China had in orbit seven optical reconnaissance satellites while the United States operated only four. Thus, it seems unlikely that China would have three times as many optical reconnaissance satellites in orbit in 2020 as it did in 2020. A more likely scenario might be that China would maintain the same rough number of optical reconnaissance satellites while replacing the current ones with more-capable designs when the current satellites reach the end of their operational lifetimes (typically about six years) and increasing the numbers of other types of satellites. If China maintains its current numbers of optical reconnaissance and electronic intelligence satellites, completes its constellation of navigation satellites by 2020 as expected, and deploys radar reconnaissance, ocean reconnaissance, and missile launch early warning satellites in numbers similar to the United States, in 2020 China would have: seven optical reconnaissance satellites, four radar reconnaissance satellites, eight electronic intelligence satellites, four groups of ocean reconnaissance satellites, seven missile launch early warning satellites, and thirty-five navigation satellites. The number of military communications satellites China might operate in 2020 is difficult to project, but if the average number in orbit grows at 5.5 percent a year between 2010 and 2020, then by 2020 China might have half a dozen dedicated military communication satellites.[90]

China's antisatellite capabilities in 2020 are even more difficult to project than its satellite capabilities, but it has continued to test systems believed by Western observers to be antisatellite weapons, including, in May 2013, what appeared to be the rocket component of a new ground-launched antisatellite missile designed to hit satellites in medium earth orbit, highly elliptical orbit, and geostationary Earth orbit, where most navigation satellites, missile early-warning satellites, and communications satellites reside.[91] Thus, by 2020 the PLA will probably possess some number of operational ground-launched antisatellite missiles and co-orbital satellite interceptors. China may also have ground-based antisatellite lasers or particle beam weapons capable of temporarily or permanently blinding optical reconnaissance satellites and potentially of destroying other types of satellites in low earth orbit, along with high-power microwave beams capable of disrupting or destroying the electronics of satellites in low earth orbit.[92]

Since so little information was available about China's cyber warfare capabilities as late as 2014, it is difficult to project how capable they will be in 2020. Revelations beginning in 2013 of the extent of the U.S. National Security Agency's electronic surveillance activities, however, suggest that U.S. capabilities in this area were extremely robust. Although it is possible that China's cyber warfare capabilities in 2020 might be comparable to those of the United States, it seems unlikely that they would surpass them.

5

Personnel

Differences in personnel quality can have dramatic effects on military capability. This is illustrated by an experiment that was conducted at the U.S. Army's National Training Center (NTC) a few years ago. The NTC maintains a dedicated "Opposing Force" that, in simulated battles, routinely defeats the visiting units that deploy to the NTC for training, largely because of its familiarity with the terrain, scenario parameters, and so on. When a visiting commander was allowed to create a battalion entirely out of high-performing soldiers and officers, however, his unit was able to defeat the Opposing Force in every simulated battle.[1]

Personnel quality is a function both of the innate abilities of individuals (intelligence, intuition, work ethic, etc.) and of the knowledge they acquire through experience, formal training, and so on.[2] Studies of the U.S. military have found that personnel who are above average in innate ability (as measured by Armed Forces Qualification Test scores) perform significantly better in a variety of military tasks – such as tank and air defense simulations, making communications systems operational, and maintaining equipment – than personnel who are below average in innate ability, even when controlling for other factors such as training and experience.[3] Training and experience are important, too, however. Multiple studies have found that experienced personnel are anywhere from 25 percent to ten times more productive than first-term personnel in a variety of different military specialties. Studies of naval pilots showed that those with the most lifetime flying hours (forty-five hundred to fifty-five hundred hours) were three times less likely to make an unsatisfactory landing attempt on an aircraft carrier, up to twice as accurate in marine bombing exercises, and only a fifth as likely to be "killed" in simulated air-to-air combat as compared to pilots with the least lifetime flying hours (five hundred hours).[4]

Thus, quality of personnel is an important aspect of any military. Since the late 1990s, however, its importance for the PLA has steadily increased, for two main reasons. First, the modernization of the weaponry of the PLA is transforming it from a force in which the only piece of equipment many of its personnel needed to know how to operate was a rifle, into one in which growing numbers of personnel must be capable of operating and maintaining a variety of modern vehicles, weapon systems, computers, communications devices, and sensors. Second, the PLA's doctrine of indirection and maneuver requires personnel at all levels that are capable of understanding complex, rapidly changing circumstances and independently devising flexible, innovative responses. This implies personnel who are intelligent, open-minded, creative, and broadly knowledgeable.

A historical example of the importance of personnel quality to the implementation of a doctrine of indirection and maneuver can be seen in the development during the nineteenth century of light infantry, or "skirmishers," which were mobile forces that moved quickly on the battlefield and used terrain features, dispersion, and accurate fire to achieve effects, as opposed to the massed musket volleys and bayonet charges of standard infantry units. According to one student of military affairs, unlike the members of traditional infantry units, a light infantryman, "needed a number of qualities which the traditional line infantryman had not … [In particular], he had to be able to make his own decisions. He was no longer under the close control of a solid rank of NCOs and officers: He was on his own. This meant that ways had to be found for developing the intelligence and understanding of every single skirmisher."[5]

Another example of the particular importance of personnel quality in maneuver warfare can be seen in the Soviet Army in the latter part of World War II. The bulk of the Soviet Army was made up of infantry units that employed a doctrine of direct engagement. Part of the Soviet Army, however, consisted of tank, mechanized, and horsed cavalry maneuver units whose role was to conduct breakthrough and exploitation operations. The best officers were deliberately concentrated in these mobile forces because, as noted in Chapter Three, unlike officers in the ordinary infantry divisions, the officers in these units needed to be able to think on their feet and adapt their battles to changing circumstances.[6]

The challenge in assessing the quality of an organization's personnel is identifying objective, measurable attributes that reveal the quality of those personnel. Assessments of personnel quality in the U.S. military have used, among other indicators, Armed Forces Qualification Test scores, education level, years of service, rank, and training hours.[7] Unfortunately, systematic information on the PLA is not available for many of these measures. For example, the PLA does not appear to administer a standardized aptitude test for its recruits that is comparable to the U.S. Armed Forces Qualification

Test.[8] Similarly, the PLA does not publish systematic data on the numbers of personnel at each rank or the amount training personnel receive over the course of their careers.

The measures of PLA personnel quality used in this chapter, therefore, consist of estimates of the education level of officers and enlisted personnel, estimates of the average amount of experience of officers and enlisted personnel, and, in the case of officers, whether their education was received at a civilian university or a military academy. This last measure is used because, according to many studies of the PLA, by the late 1990s the PLA itself had concluded that its military colleges and academies were not capable of producing the type of officers it needed.[9] According to a 2003 article in a journal published by the GAD, for example, PLA officers' lack of understanding of the capabilities of the modern weaponry that the PLA was acquiring meant that it was often not possible to make full use of the capabilities of those systems.[10] Doubts about the quality of education provided by PLA academies are reinforced by reports that only 15 percent of instructors in those academies had degrees higher than bachelor's degrees, as compared with 90 percent reportedly having advanced degrees in U.S. military academies.[11] The low educational level of PLA instructors, moreover, was not because of an emphasis on field experience over academic training among instructors, as most academy faculty became instructors early in their careers and had no subsequent experience in operational units.[12] In response to concerns about the quality of students and instruction at its academies, and in the belief that the students and instruction in China's civilian colleges were better, beginning in the late 1990s the PLA began to commission increasing numbers of officers who were graduates of civilian universities, with the goal of having 60 percent of newly commissioned officers come from civilian universities by 2010.[13] The analysis in this chapter, therefore, assumes that officers who are graduates of civilian universities in China are more capable than officers who are graduates of military academies.

CHINESE MILITARY PERSONNEL QUALITY IN 2000

The PLA operated a conscription system in 2000 in which all males between eighteen and twenty-two were obligated to provide military service if requested by the government. Nearly ten million men turned eighteen each year in China, however, whereas only a few hundred thousand recruits were needed for the PLA each year, so in practice only a small fraction of men enlisted in the PLA (women were allowed to enlist in the PLA, but were not obligated to provide military service and represented only about 5 percent of the PLA in 2000).[14]

Before 1999, conscripts in the PLA Army served for three years, whereas those in the Navy and Air Force served for four years. Beginning in 1999, however, the term of conscription was reduced to two years for all services.[15]

Before 1999, the PLA also did not officially have NCOs. Instead, at the end of their initial terms, conscripts could volunteer to stay on for a longer period. Those who were accepted were referred to as "volunteer soldiers" (志愿兵, sometimes called "long-term conscripts" in Western writings on the PLA). The maximum length of service for volunteer soldiers, including their conscription period, was sixteen years. In 1999, however, the PLA formally instituted an NCO system, and the maximum length of service was raised to thirty years.[16]

Under the new system, at the end of their term of conscription, conscripts could volunteer to become NCOs. The precise overall numbers of conscripts, NCOs, and officers in the PLA in 2000 are not known. However, one source estimates that roughly half of the PLA Army, which represented approximately two-thirds of the PLA as a whole, consisted of conscripts in 2000.[17] If we assume that only one-third of the PLA Navy, Air Force, and Second Artillery, which were believed to have a higher proportion of NCOs than the PLA Army, consisted of conscripts, then about four-ninths of the PLA as a whole would have consisted of conscripts in 2000. About a third of the PLA as whole was believed to consist of officers in 2000, which would imply that NCOs constituted about two-ninths of PLA military personnel.[18]

Education Level

Educational requirements for conscripts were minimal in the PLA in 2000. Conscripts from rural areas were required to have only a middle school education although those from urban areas were required to have a high school education.[19] Education was only universal through middle school in China in 2000, so most recruits from the countryside probably indeed had only middle school educations. Those few who had high school educations were probably counterbalanced by conscripts who had not actually completed middle school, as in some cases unqualified candidates would use bribes to be conscripted into the PLA.[20] Roughly 70 percent of conscripts in the PLA came from the countryside in 2000, so probably about 70 percent of conscripts had only a middle school education, whereas most of the other 30 percent had high school educations (full-time college students were exempt from being conscripted).[21] There were no additional educational requirements for NCOs in 2000, but the proportion of NCOs with high school educations was probably higher than amongst conscripts.[22]

Education levels for PLA officers were improving rapidly in 2000. As recently as 1980, less than 10 percent of PLA officers had had college degrees.[23] By 2000 this number had risen to somewhere between 65 percent and 80 percent.[24] Nonetheless, this meant that a fifth to a third of all officers still did not have college degrees in 2000. Approximately 90 percent of the college degrees, moreover, were three-year technical degrees, rather than four-year bachelor's degrees.[25] In addition, PLA officers had only been required to have high school diplomas since 1983, so it is possible that some officers who did not even have high school diplomas remained in the force in 2000, although most had probably been required to receive a high school equivalency education at a PLA academy.[26] At least 90 percent of the college degrees, moreover, had been conferred by PLA academies.[27] As discussed above, graduates of PLA academies were regarded as less capable than graduates of civilian colleges.[28] Although these officer education levels are low by Western standards, officers represented a much larger proportion of the PLA than officers do in most Western militaries. As noted earlier, officers are believed to have constituted about a third of the PLA as whole in 2000. In comparison, only about 15 percent of active duty U.S. military personnel were officers in 2000.[29]

Using the figures above, it is possible to estimate the overall education level of the PLA in 2000. If we assume that half of NCOs had middle school educations and half had high school diplomas (as compared to 70 percent and 30 percent for conscripts), that the percentage of officers who did not have at a least a high school diploma was negligible, and that 72.5 percent (the midpoint between 65 percent and 80 percent) of officers held college degrees, then approximately 42 percent of PLA personnel in 2000 had only a middle school education, 33 percent had high school diplomas, and 24 percent had college degrees, 90 percent of which were three-year technical degrees and 10 percent of which (i.e., about 2 percent of the whole PLA) were four-year college degrees.[30] Of the college degrees, moreover, at least 90 percent were from PLA academies, as opposed to civilian colleges. By comparison, in the U.S. military, only about 1 percent of personnel did not hold at least a high school diploma or General Educational Development (GED) certificate, about 79 percent had only a high school diploma or GED, about 6 percent had a two-year associate's degree, and 14 percent had at least a four-year bachelor's degree. Nearly 7 percent, moreover, had advanced degrees (master's degrees or doctorates).[31]

Education levels in the PLA and U.S. military in 2000 are compared in Figure 5.1. As can be seen, the principle differences are the large numbers of personnel in the PLA (more than half of the enlisted force) who had not graduated from high school, and the small percentage of PLA personnel who

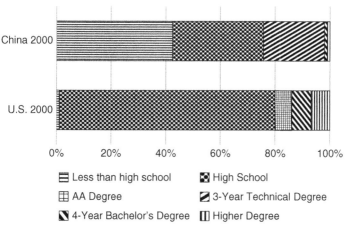

FIGURE 5.1 Education Levels in the U.S. and Chinese Militaries, 2000

had graduated from four-year colleges (2 percent, compared to 14 percent in the U.S. military). Looked at another way, although about 10 percent of the PLA was nominally better educated than their counterparts in the U.S. military (the proportion of PLA personnel who had received at least a three-year college degree was 10 percentage points larger than the proportion of U.S. military personnel who had received a four-year college degree or higher), more than 50 percent of U.S. military personnel were better educated than their counterparts in the PLA (the proportion of PLA personnel who did not have a high school education was approximately 41 percentage points greater than in the U.S. military, and the proportion of officers who had a four-year college degree, as opposed to a three-year degree, was approximately 12 percentage points larger in the U.S. military than in the PLA). In addition, 7 percent of the U.S. military had advanced degrees, whereas at most 1 percent of the PLA had advanced degrees.[32]

Experience

The PLA does not publish statistics indicating the average experience levels of its officer and enlisted corps. However, it is possible to estimate the average experience level of the enlisted corps based on what is known about maximum term lengths and the composition of the force. As noted above, before 1999, PLA Army conscripts were required to serve three years and PLA Navy and Air Force conscripts were required to serve four years. In mid-2000, therefore, one-third of PLA Army conscripts had presumably been conscripted in late 1997 under the old conscription rules and were half way through their third year of conscription (all conscripts for a given year entered the PLA at the same time, in December of their year of conscription), another third had been conscripted in late 1998 and were half way through their second year (of three) of conscription, and one-third were half way through their first year (of two) of conscription. In the PLA Navy and Air Force, which combined comprised about a third of the PLA, a quarter of conscripts were half way through their fourth year of conscription, another quarter were half way through their third year, a quarter were half way through their second year, and a quarter were half way through their first year. Thus, the average PLA conscript in 2000 had about one and two-thirds years of experience.

Before 1999 the maximum length of service for enlisted personnel (including their conscription period) was sixteen years. In 1999 this limit was raised to thirty years, but, since only one year had gone by since the cap was raised, the longest any NCO could have served in 2000 was seventeen years.[33] It is not clear what the attrition rate for "volunteer soldiers" was before 1999 but, if we assume that the preponderance served their entire sixteen years and that only a small number were demobilized as a result of the implementation of the new NCO system in 1999, then in 2000 the average PLA Army NCO would have had at most 10.5 years of experience (three years as a conscript, six and a half years of a maximum possible thirteen years as a volunteer soldier before 1999, and one year since then) and the average PLA Navy or Air Force NCO would have had at most eleven years of experience (four years as a conscript and six of a maximum possible twelve years as a volunteer soldier before 1999, and one year since then). If we assume, as estimated at the beginning of this chapter, that only one-sixth of the PLA Army (i.e., a quarter of the PLA Army enlisted force) consisted of NCOs in 2000, and that a third of the PLA Navy and Air Force (i.e., half of the PLA Navy and Air Force enlisted force) consisted of NCOs, and that the PLA Army represented roughly two-thirds of the PLA in 2000, with the PLA Navy and Air Force representing the remaining third, then the average enlisted person in the PLA in 2000 had about four and a half years of experience. In comparison, the average enlisted person in the U.S. military had a bit over seven years of experience in 2000.[34]

Information from which the average amount of experience of PLA officers in 2000 could be estimated is not publicly available. The PLA in 2000 practiced a strict "up-or-out system" for its officers, however, with mandatory retirement ages based on the grade (级) of their position (not rank), from a maximum age of thirty years old for a platoon leader to a maximum age of sixty-five years old for a military region commander.[35] This suggests that the age and experience distribution of PLA officers was probably similar to that for the U.S. military, in which 80 percent of officers were of the rank of major (lieutenant commander in the U.S. Navy) or below. If we assume, therefore, that the average PLA officer had the same amount of experience as the average U.S. military officer – eleven years – then the average member of the PLA as a whole had about six and a half years of experience, only somewhat less than the average of seven and a half years in the U.S. military in 2000. This was because officers constituted roughly a third of PLA personnel in 2000, however, whereas they constituted only 15 percent of U.S. military personnel in 2000.[36] Thus, the distribution of experience in the PLA in 2000 was probably not ideal, with roughly 40 percent of the force consisting of conscripts having fewer than two years of experience balanced by a disproportionately large number of officers with an average of ten or more years of experience.

CHINESE MILITARY PERSONNEL QUALITY IN 2010

Significant changes to the quality of Chinese military personnel occurred between 2000 and 2010. The PLA still operated a conscription system and the educational requirements for recruits remained middle school graduation for those from rural areas and high school graduation for those from urban areas, and two-thirds of conscripts still came from rural areas, but the proportion of conscripts with high school educations increased significantly during this period. By 2007, 67 percent of incoming conscripts had high school educations and that number presumably continued to increase in following years.[37] Some reports from the middle of the decade suggest difficulty meeting conscription quotas, particularly in urban areas. The worldwide economic downturn that began in 2008 and affected China, albeit to a lesser extent than the United States or Europe, however, along with the growing prestige of the PLA, appears to have made enlisting in the military an increasingly attractive option for young men in China, so that by the end of the decade, the PLA's "conscripts" were largely, if not entirely, volunteers.[38]

Undoubtedly related to this was a huge influx of full-time civilian college students enlisting in the PLA at the end of the decade. Full-time students were officially exempt from conscription, but in 2001 the PLA began recruiting current college students to serve in the PLA for a period before returning to school to complete their studies, and college students were given preference over other conscription candidates. The numbers were initially small, just two thousand or so a year for the first few years, but began to increase after the middle of the decade. Thirty-eight thousand college students (of about four hundred thousand conscripts taken each year) were recruited in 2008 and in 2009 the number surged to 130,000, roughly a third of all conscripts inducted that year, and more than 100,000 college students were enlisted in 2010.[39]

What is clear is that the PLA experienced significant difficulties assimilating such large numbers of college students into its conscript force. These students were presumably, like college students in general in China, disproportionately from the more developed and cosmopolitan parts of China, whereas traditionally the PLA's enlisted personnel predominantly came from China's poorer rural areas. Problems involving college student recruits were said to include refusal to take orders from superiors (who often were less educated than the college student recruits), poor physical fitness, lack of mental preparation for hardship, inability to deal with frustration, lack of real-life experience, self-centeredness, unwillingness to sacrifice themselves for national defense, and poor discipline. College students were also said to be of "low political quality," meaning that they liked to gossip, tended to notice too many shortcomings in the Communist Party, and were "not vigilant enough about cultural infiltration by hostile forces," presumably an insinuation that they were susceptible to believing in Western political ideals such as democracy and human rights. In addition, college students were said to have unrealistic ideas about their chances of being promoted to officer or getting into a military academy, or to have other ulterior motives for enlisting. Interestingly, however, the theme of the articles in Chinese periodicals about these problems in 2010 and 2011 was not that it had been a mistake to recruit so many college students as conscripts but rather how to make their transition into military life easier.[40] This suggests that the decision to recruit such large numbers of full-time college students into the PLA was one to which the PLA leadership remained committed, even if there were pains associated with it. Consistent with this, more than 100,000 college students enlisted each year from 2009 to 2014, with the number reaching 150,000, more than a third of all new recruits, in 2014.[41]

These changes in the conscript force were mirrored by changes in the NCO and officer corps. Before 2003 all NCOs came from conscripts who volunteered to reenlist after their term of conscription ended. Beginning in 2003, however, the PLA began recruiting civilian college graduates to become enlisted personnel, allowing them to become NCOs directly without having to first spend two years as a conscript.[42] The educational requirements for NCOs were increased as well. Beginning in 2008, all NCOs were required to have at least a high school education, and senior NCOs (NCOs in the fifth through seventh of seven grades) were required to have at least a three-year college degree.[43] In addition, the overall size of the NCO corps increased relative to the conscript force and officer corps. Whereas NCOs represented about 20 percent of the PLA in 2000, by 2009 they had increased to about 35 percent, even as the overall size of the PLA decreased from 2.5 million to 2.3 million.[44] In addition to reducing the number of conscripts from about

1.1 million in 2000 to about eight hundred thousand by 2009, this was accomplished by turning over to NCOs about seventy thousand positions formerly held by officers or civilian officials (who are counted as part of the 2.3 million personnel in the PLA). These included positions such as vehicle unit commander, small boat commander, radar operator, sonar operator, mess officer, medic, or club manager.[45]

A final change in the nature of the PLA's NCO corps between 2000 and 2010 was an attempt to improve the quality of training that they received. Early in the decade, operational units were complaining that the graduates of the PLA's NCO schools were unable to function in their jobs and that the NCO schools focused too much on theory and not enough on practical application.[46] By the end of the decade, however, the education provided by the PLA's NCO schools was said to be more practical than it had been in the past.[47]

Changes in the PLA officer corps between 2000 and 2010 included a decrease in its size and an increase in its education levels. Whereas the officer corps were believed to represent about a third of the PLA in 2000, by 2008 it had fallen to less than 30 percent of a PLA that had itself been reduced from 2.5 million to 2.3 million.[48] Meanwhile, whereas less than 80 percent of officers in 2000 had held college degrees, by 2010 all but "a minority of older officers" held college degrees. And although, in 2000, 90 percent of those officers who held college degrees had degrees from three-year technical colleges, by 2010, 61 percent of officers were said to hold degrees from four-year colleges.[49]

The change in the PLA officer corps that occurred between 2000 and 2010 with potentially the greatest long-term implications, however, was a turn to civilian universities as the principle source of new officers. Before 2000, civilian college graduates were allowed to join the PLA as officers, usually after spending a year at a PLA military academy. In the years before 2000, thirty-five thousand to fifty thousand college graduates joined the PLA and became officers this way. Beginning in 2000, however, the PLA formally instituted a National Defense Student program similar to the U.S. Reserve Officer Training Corps (ROTC) program. Under this program, students who had been admitted into civilian colleges could apply to be provided with college tuition and a stipend in return for eight years' service obligation upon graduation.[50] In 2003, the first thousand National Defense Students (who had been sophomores when the program began) graduated from college and entered the PLA.[51] They were followed by another eighteen hundred in 2004, and the program grew steadily thereafter.[52] By 2010, roughly forty-two thousand officers had joined the PLA this way.[53] Although graduates of civilian universities probably represented less than 25 percent of the PLA officer corps in 2010, the PLA's stated goal was for 60 percent of all new officers to be graduates of civilian universities in the future.[54]

The PLA also began using civilian universities to provide advanced training for its officers. Although officers had previously been allowed to train for advanced degrees (master's and doctorates) at the PLA's military academies, beginning in 2002 the PLA began sending officers to civilian universities for advanced training, with about eighteen hundred a year being enrolled in three-year programs. In addition, graduates of civilian universities who had advanced degrees were allowed to be commissioned as officers, with those holding master's degrees being given the rank of captain (first lieutenant in the PLA Navy) upon commissioning and those holding doctorates being made majors (lieutenant commander in the PLA Navy).[55]

As was the case with assimilating students from civilian colleges into the enlisted ranks, however, there were problems assimilating the graduates of civilian colleges into the officer corps. First, there appeared to be an effort to channel the graduates of civilian colleges into support areas rather than operational units. As noted in Chapter Three, in the PLA all officers belong to one of five tracks: command (formally referred to as "military affairs" 军事), political affairs, logistics, armaments management, or technology. Officers in the last category, technical officers (技术军官), are distinguished from ordinary officers by special collar insignia and play roles in some ways similar to those of warrant officers in the U.S. military, except that they hold ranks identical to those of commissioned officers.[56] The majority of graduates of civilian universities were designated as technical officers or assigned to the other two support tracks, logistics and armaments management.[57] Moreover, officers in the PLA rarely transfer from one track to another.[58] Thus, with some exceptions, the graduates of civilian universities were not being incorporated into the ranks of those officers who commanded operational units.

Aside from their deliberate segregation into certain functional areas, there were other ways in which the graduates of civilian universities encountered difficulty assimilating into the PLA officer corps. As was the case with undergraduate students who enlisted, one was meeting the PLA's physical fitness requirements. More significantly, civilian college graduates were said to find it difficult to communicate with fellow soldiers, to have a hard time accepting criticism, to not be sufficiently interested in "politics," and to not have a strong sense of group solidarity. Conversely, officers who were graduates of civilian universities were also said to chafe at arbitrary regulations and orders, to learn faster, to be more creative thinkers, and to be more concerned with efficiency than the graduates of military academies.[59] In other words, civilian college graduates were precisely the type of independent-thinking soldier the PLA needed to implement its doctrine of maneuver and indirection. However, given that they were relegated to support functions rather than command roles, they were not in a position to contribute to the effective implementation of this doctrine, and the PLA in 2010 continued to be led by the less-independent-thinking products of its military academies.

Education Level

As noted above, by 2007, 67 percent of incoming conscripts had at least a high school education, and from 2008 all NCOs were required to have at least a high school education. Senior NCOs, moreover, meaning those of the fifth through seventh ranks, were required to have a technical college degree. If we assume that the attrition rate for NCOs was such that only half of them would eventually make it to the senior ranks, this would imply that at least 28 percent of NCOs had degrees from technical colleges in 2010.[60] If we assume that the "minority of older officers" who did not have college degrees represented 1 percent of the total PLA officer corps, then 38 percent of PLA officers would have had three-year technical degrees and 61 percent would have had four-year college degrees. At least 7 percent of PLA officers, moreover, had advanced degrees.[61]

By 2008, enlisted personnel represented 1.6 million of the 2.3 million people in the PLA and by 2009 more than half of them were NCOs.[62] This suggests that by 2010 more than 35 percent of the PLA consisted of NCOs, less than 35 percent consisted of conscripts, and at most 30 percent consisted of officers (less than 30 percent if a significant number of the seven hundred thousand non-enlisted personnel were civilian officials). Based on these figures, we can estimate that by 2010 less than 12 percent of the PLA had only a middle school education, about 49 percent had a high school education, about 21 percent had three-year technical degrees, 18 percent had at least a four-year bachelor's degree, and 2 percent had advanced degrees. By comparison, in the U.S. military in 2010, about 1 percent of personnel did not hold at least a high school diploma or GED certificate, about 78 percent had only a high school diploma, about 6 percent had a two-year college degree, and about 15 percent had at least a four-year bachelor's degree. Nearly 7 percent, moreover, had advanced degrees (master's degrees or doctorates).[63]

Education levels in the PLA and U.S. military in 2010 are compared in Figure 5.2.

As can be seen, the principle differences are the roughly 11 percentage points more people who had not graduated from high school in the PLA than

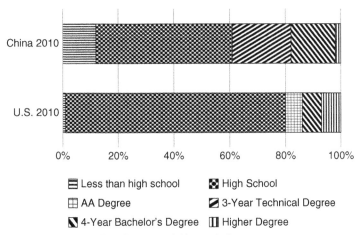

China 2010

U.S. 2010

0%   20%   40%   60%   80%   100%

⊟ Less than high school   ▨ High School
⊞ AA Degree   ◪ 3-Year Technical Degree
◣ 4-Year Bachelor's Degree ▥ Higher Degree

FIGURE 5.2 Education Levels in the U.S. and Chinese Militaries, 2010

in the U.S. military, the 21 percent of people in the PLA who had three-year college degrees as compared to the 6 percent in the U.S. military who had two-year college degrees, and the 7 percent of the U.S. military who held advanced degrees as compared to only 2 percent in the PLA. Perhaps most surprisingly, a higher proportion of the Chinese military in 2010 held bachelor's degrees than in the U.S. military (18 percent vs. 14 percent). Overall, average education levels in the U.S. and Chinese militaries in 2010 were roughly equal, with 19 percent of the PLA being better educated than their counterparts in the U.S. military (those in the PLA who had three-year degrees but whose counterparts in the U.S. military had only high school educations or two-year degrees, along with some in the PLA who held four-year college degrees but whose counterparts in the U.S. military held only two-year degrees), and about 16 percent of the U.S. military being better educated than their counterparts in the PLA (the proportion of PLA personnel who did not have a high school education was 11 percentage points greater than in the U.S. military, and the proportion of U.S. military personnel who had advanced degrees was five percentage points larger than in the PLA).

A key difference, however, was in the proportions of officers who had received their college educations from civilian universities. In the U.S. military, approximately 80 percent of officers receive their education at civilian universities.[64] In the PLA in 2010, only about 20 percent of officers had received their educations at civilian universities, which, despite a loosening of admissions standards at civilian universities and reported improvements in the quality of instruction at the PLA's academies, were still considered to produce graduates intellectually superior to those of the PLA's academies.[65] The graduates of China's civilian colleges, moreover, were largely excluded from operational command positions, which remained monopolized by the graduates of PLA military academies. Thus, the PLA was also not receiving the full benefit of the intellectual capabilities of those officers who had come from civilian universities.

Experience

Since there were no longer any three- or four-year conscripts serving in the PLA in 2010, the average conscript in mid-2010 had one year of experience (half of them had half a year of experience and the other half had a year and a half of experience). If we assume that the attrition rate for NCOs in 2010 was such that half of them would eventually make it to the senior ranks, and we assume that the average NCO had two years of experience before becoming an NCO (former three-year or four-year conscripts would have had three or four years of experience before becoming an NCO, but from 2003 growing numbers of college graduates were recruited to become NCOs without first serving as conscripts), then the average NCO in 2010 had about 11 and a half years of experience. Since the PLA enlisted force in 2010 was about half conscripts and half NCOs, this means that the average enlisted person in the PLA in 2010 had a bit more than six years of experience, a significant increase over the four and a half year average in 2000 and almost as much as the nearly seven years of experience that the average enlisted person in the U.S. military in 2010 had.[66]

Assuming, as in 2000, that the average PLA officer in 2010 had roughly the same amount of experience as his U.S. counterpart – eleven years – then the average PLA member had about seven and a half years of experience, the same as the average member of the U.S. military.[67] Since officers still constituted about 30 percent of the PLA in 2010, this average, however, disguised the fact that roughly a sixth of the PLA consisted of conscripts with less than one year of experience.[68]

CHINESE MILITARY PERSONNEL QUALITY IN 2020

The trends in PLA personnel quality described above are likely to continue through 2020. The PLA reportedly plans to continue to increase the size of the NCO corps and decrease the size of the commissioned officer corps at least until the PLA reaches a force consisting of eight hundred thousand conscripts, nine hundred thousand NCOs, and six hundred thousand officers.[69] Education levels are likely to continue to increase as well. High school education, moreover, is becoming near-universal in China: Of the 18.5 million students who graduated from middle school in China in 2009, about 88 percent enrolled in some sort of high school.[70] These numbers will likely be reflected in the future conscript force. Education levels for officers will also increase. In 2000 a fifth to a third of PLA officers did not have college degrees, and only about 6 percent had four-year bachelor's degrees. By 2010 virtually all officers had college degrees, and 61 percent of them had four-year bachelor's degrees. At least 60 percent of officers commissioned between 2010 and 2020, more-over, are likely to have received their degrees from civilian universities. The proportion of officers holding advanced degrees is likely to increase as well, as the proportion of PLA officers holding advanced degrees increased from about 2 percent in 2000 to about 7 percent in 2010. And, although the average conscript will still only have one year of experience in 2020 and the average amount of experience of PLA officers is unlikely to increase, the average amount of experience of an NCO in the PLA will continue to increase, as there will now be NCOs with more than twenty-seven years of experience and possibly as much as thirty-seven years. (In 2009 the previous thirty-year service limitation on NCOs was lifted.)[71]

Based on these trends, it is possible to estimate education and experience levels in the PLA in 2020 using some reasonable (but conservative) assumptions. The proportions of conscripts, NCOs, and officers in the PLA in 2020 are assumed to be comparable to the numbers cited in the previous paragraph, although the overall size of the PLA may be smaller than 2.3 million people by then. Based on the educational trends in the broader Chinese population also mentioned in the previous paragraph, 88 percent of conscripts are assumed to have high school educations in 2020. All senior NCOs are assumed to have three-year technical degrees.[72] Since the percentage of officers with four-year bachelor's degrees increased from 6 percent in 2000 to 61 percent in 2010, by 2020, 90 percent of officers are assumed to have four-year degrees. Assuming that PLA officers continue to receive advanced degrees at the same rate between 2010 and 2020 as they did between 2000 and 2010, by 2020 about 14 percent of PLA officers will hold advanced degrees.[73] Finally, attrition rates for NCOs are assumed to be the same as was assumed for 2000 and 2010. Based on these assumptions, in 2020, 4 percent of the PLA will have less than a high school education, 59 percent will have a high school education, 14 percent will have three-year technical degrees, 20 percent will have four-year college degrees, and 3 percent will hold advanced degrees. By comparison, in the U.S. military in 2010, about 1 percent of personnel did not have at least a high school education, about 78 percent had only a high school diploma, about 6 percent had a two-year college degree, about 8 percent had a

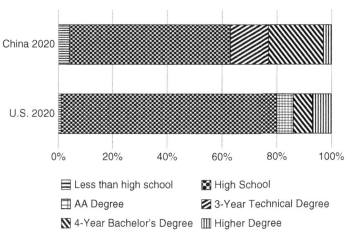

FIGURE 5.3 Projected Education Levels in the U.S. and Chinese Militaries, 2020

four-year bachelor's degree, and about 7 percent had advanced degrees. Assuming that these proportions do not change significantly between now and 2020, then the PLA will have nine percentage points more personnel who have four-year college degrees than the U.S. military and 17 percentage points more personnel who have any kind of postsecondary degree. The U.S. advantage will be that three percentage points more of the PLA will have less than a high school education than is the case in the U.S. military, and three percentage points more of the U.S. military will hold advanced degrees. Thus, if current trends continue, by 2020 the PLA will on average be a better-educated force than the U.S. military. A significant proportion of PLA officers, moreover, will have received their degrees from civilian colleges in 2020. Projected education levels in the PLA and U.S. military in 2020 are shown in Figure 5.3.

In terms of experience, the average PLA conscript will still have only one year of experience, but the average NCO will have about twelve and a half years of experience in 2020, so the average enlisted person in the PLA will have about seven years of experience in 2020, about the same as the average enlisted person in the U.S. military in 2010. Assuming that the average PLA officer in 2020 has roughly the same amount of experience as his U.S. counterpart (eleven years), then the average PLA member will have about eight years of experience, about the same as the seven and a half years of the average member of the U.S. military in 2010. This will primarily be because of the disproportionately large size of the PLA officer corps, however, and, assuming the PLA continues its conscription system, a sixth of PLA personnel will still have less than one year of experience in 2020.

6

Training

The centrality of unit training to military effectiveness is widely recognized. As has been demonstrated repeatedly throughout history, a well-trained military unit will almost always outperform a poorly trained unit in battle, no matter which side is more numerous or better equipped.[1] The challenge for the researcher is identifying objectively measurable characteristics that distinguish a well-trained military from a poorly trained one. The most obvious and commonly used measure is the amount of time spent training. Without question, for a unit or individual to reach a given level of proficiency, a certain minimum amount of training time will be required. However, simply logging a specified amount of training time does not guarantee that a given level of proficiency will be achieved. More important than the amount of time spent training is the *quality* of the training that occurs during that time. As one example, number of flying hours is a commonly used measure of aircraft crew proficiency. But a training mission that consists simply of an aircraft navigating to a fixed point, conducting a single action (e.g., a simulated bombing run or fighter engagement), and then returning to base does not provide nearly as much training as a mission of shorter duration that presents a flight crew with multiple challenging situations in the course of a single flight.

A review of the extant literature on military training did not uncover any explicit generalizations about the characteristics of effective training. Analysis of publications of the U.S. military and related sources, however, reveals a number of implicit beliefs about the characteristics of an effective training regime. According to these publications, effective military training has the following characteristics:

- *Unit commanders have primary responsibility for training.* Armed forces exist to conduct military operations. When not actively conducting military operations, their primary mission is to be prepared to conduct such operations when called upon. Ensuring that the unit is prepared, therefore, must be the primary responsibility of the unit commander. If a unit's commander is not the person with ultimately responsibility for the unit's training, it is unlikely that the unit will be well trained.[2]

- *Training is intensive.* The more actual training and the less idle time that occurs during a training period, the more effective the training period will be. One U.S. Army publication, for example, calls for "multiechelon" and "concurrent" training. "Multiechelon training" refers to multiple levels within an organizational hierarchy being simultaneously engaged in training. An example of multiechelon training would be if, while a battalion's headquarters staff was engaged in a brigade-level chemical warfare command post exercise, the individual companies within the battalion were engaged in chemical warfare field drills. Concurrent training refers to different portions of the same unit being simultaneously engaged in different types of training. An example given in the U.S. Army publication is of the howitzer section of an artillery battery conducting gunnery training while the battery's fire direction center and fire support officers are supporting an infantry battalion in a nonfiring maneuver exercise.[3]

- *Units are trained to conduct operations according to doctrine.* Doctrine represents the official view of a military on how to most effectively conduct military operations of different types. Training units in the tactics, techniques, and procedures described in doctrine ensures that they are learning to conduct operations in the way that the military leadership believes to be most effective. It also ensures that all units employ the same set of tactics, techniques, and procedures for a given type of operation, improving the ability of commanders to coordinate the actions of different units and reducing the chances of miscommunication and misunderstanding between units and echelons.[4]

- *Training is focused on priority skills.* The range of possible activities that a military unit might be called upon to perform is too broad for it to be proficient in all of them. Training must therefore be focused on skills associated with the most important activities. The U.S. military refers to these as "mission-essential tasks." These are tasks that the unit would be required to perform in the course of carrying out any of its assigned missions. Only after the skills necessary for proficiently performing mission-essential tasks have been acquired should time and effort be allocated to acquiring other skills.[5]

- *Training is progressively more complex and difficult.* Units first ensure that they have mastered basic individual and small-unit skills, then move to increasingly complex and larger-scale training, including combined arms and joint operations. Training that was not progressive would either engage units in complex, large-scale activities before fundamentals had been mastered, or, alternatively, would never move beyond small scale and a low level of complexity.[6]

- *Training is realistic.* To be effective, training should reflect the physical, military, sociocultural, and political parameters within which operations may be conducted. These parameters include the capabilities of potential adversaries, the different types of terrain on which operations might be conducted, night operations, adverse weather, simulated equipment breakdowns, conditions of stress and fatigue, and potential limitations on the ways in which force may be employed. Since warfare is an inherently unpredictable activity involving a noncooperating opponent, realistic training correspondingly includes presenting units with unpredictable environmental and military circumstances, and simulated adversaries acting in ways that are not known beforehand. This is particularly important for countries, such as China, that employ doctrines of maneuver and indirection in which the goal is to take advantage of potentially fleeting opportunities created by the adversary's actions. Realistic training also includes training in the logistics requirements of military operations such as maintaining and repairing equipment in the field and sustaining units away from their bases for extended periods.[7]

- *Units train until defined performance standards are achieved.* Effective training regimes do not specify a fixed amount of time or the performance of specified activities as the standard for having been trained in a given skill; they require the achievement of a specific performance standard. Ideally, these standards consist of criteria that are defined in terms of measurable units such as time (e.g., to complete a mission), percentage, distance, and number of occurrences. For example, a bombing proficiency standard might require that a certain percentage of bombs dropped land within a specified distance of their targets. Ideally units will be subject to periodic independent proficiency assessments, but on a day-to-day basis commanders and training officers are responsible for evaluating individual and unit proficiency. An efficient training regime assesses proficiency before training begins, so that training can be concentrated on skill areas in which the individual or unit is not yet proficient, then again after a training period ends. If proficiency has not been achieved in certain skill areas, then additional training is provided until the proficiency standard is achieved.[8]

At least as valuable as peacetime training, of course, is actual warfighting experience. Real-world military operations always deviate from standardized training scenarios, generally occur on unfamiliar terrain, and usually involve adversaries whose choices of actions are fundamentally different from those that would be selected by a member of one's own military (even a dedicated "opposition force"). In addition, real-world military operations are attended by pressure from civilian authorities, physical dangers, and consequences of failure that are unlike those of peacetime training. As a result, real-world military operations, even low-intensity conflict or noncombat operations, prepare militaries for future combat operations in ways that peacetime training cannot replicate.

Assessing the quality of training in the Chinese military is challenging, as comprehensive, detailed information about PLA training is not publicly available. The GSD periodically issues a set of training guidelines that stipulate the specific training subjects, the total amount of time to be spent in training each year, and performance standards for the entire PLA (including reserve units). In addition, each year it issues training directives specifying particular areas of emphasis for the year. None of these documents are publicly available, however, so analysis of Chinese military training must be based on incomplete information revealed in Chinese media reports, conversations with Chinese military personnel, and other sources.[9]

CHINESE MILITARY TRAINING QUALITY IN 2000

Military training was in a period of transition in China in 2000. The latest set of training guidelines had been issued in 1995, but, as described in Chapter Two, a fundamentally new doctrine had been promulgated in 1999. Meanwhile, in 1998 then-Chairman of the CMC Jiang Zemin had issued a call for the PLA to "use science and technology to train troops" (科技练兵) that had prompted a three-year period of exploration and experimentation with new training principles. The results of this period of exploration and experimentation as well as the new doctrinal principles were incorporated into a new set of training guidelines that was issued in June 2001.[10] Nonetheless, although some of the principles embodied in the 2001 guidelines were already being implemented in 2000, training in 2000 was probably largely similar to training in the late 1990s, before the period of experimentation and issuance of the new doctrinal guidelines.

Responsibility of Unit Commanders for Training

Leadership in Chinese military units is less unitary than in the U.S. military. In addition to its unit commander, each unit at the company level and above has a political instructor or commissar, and leadership duties are the joint responsibility of the commander and political commissar. Each unit at the company level and above also has a Party committee that includes all Party members and Communist Youth League members in the company (or within the unit headquarters for higher-level units), and many important decisions are made collectively by the Party committee. Nonetheless, by regulation, for squads and platoons the unit leader is responsible for all unit activities including training and for company-level and higher units the unit commander and political instructor or commissar are jointly responsible for the work of the entire unit, with the unit commander having primary responsibility for individual and unit training and other military (as opposed to political) issues within the unit, and the political instructor or commissar has primary responsibility for political training and morale.[11] Thus, Chinese military units in 2000 largely conformed to the principle of the unit commander being responsible for training.

Intensity of Training

The training guidelines issued in 1995 and still in force in 2000 specified the amount of time units were to spend on each training subject. The total amount of training time stipulated by the guidelines is not known, but evidence suggests that PLA training in 2000 was not particularly intensive.[12] Indeed, although commanders in the Chinese military were the people with primary responsibility for training in their units in 2000, whether unit training was a priority of unit commanders is less clear. A 2002 interview with then-Chief of the General Staff Fu Quanyou notes that some of the areas in which a new set of military training regulations 《军事训练条例》 issued that year differed from the previous set were in emphasizing that training was a "critical link" (关键环节) in preparations for military struggle, in requiring that the entire PLA make training a regular central task, and in requiring that Party committees and leaders at all levels be responsible for ensuring the centrality of training. The regulations were said to have "for the first time" (首次) made clear the training duty of military personnel and required that military personnel participate in military training.[13] Such revisions would only have been made, and emphasized by the chief of staff, if before 2002, training had *not* been a regular central task throughout the PLA and if significant numbers of military personnel had *not* consistently participated in training.

In addition to training in general apparently not having been a central task throughout the PLA in 2000, it appears that *unit* training in particular was not the focal point of training efforts. The 2002 interview with General Fu notes that one of the "basic considerations" (基本考虑) behind revising the military training regulations was to make unit training, as opposed to individual drill or classroom education, the "center of gravity" (重心). This emphasis is repeated in a 2003 article describing the GSD's training tasking for that year.[14] The emphasis on the importance of unit training after 2001 again suggests that, in prior years, unit training had *not* been the focus of training efforts in the PLA.

A third piece of evidence suggesting that unit training in 2000 was not particularly intensive is the involvement of military units in numerous nontraining activities. As noted above, each unit at the company level and higher had a political instructor or commissar whose duties included political training. The precise amount of time that units spent in political training each year in 2000 is not known, but it probably represented 20 to 30 percent of total training time. Indeed, as late as 1995, then-Chief of the General Staff Zhang Wannian and editorials in *PLA Daily* were stating that ideological and political development were the main task of the PLA and took precedence over all other tasks.[15]

In addition to political training, moreover, up until 1998 military units were heavily involved in a variety of commercial activities such as running hotels or providing transport services (using military trucks, ships, and aircraft). In 1998 the PLA was ordered to divest itself of most of its businesses, but this process was still ongoing in 2000. Also, even after the PLA's divestiture from commerce, PLA soldiers continued to work part-time on PLA-run farms where they grew their own crops and raised pigs, ducks, fish, and other animals for their own consumption.[16]

Degree to Which Training Corresponded to Doctrine

When the PLA's new doctrinal publications were issued in January 1999, as described in Chapter Two, multiple articles emphasized that all future training was to be based on the new doctrine. However, the amount of print devoted to making this point, and the use of phrases such as "*resolutely* use the new doctrine to guide combat training" (emphasis added) or "conduct training and education *strictly* in accordance with the new doctrine" (emphasis added) indicates a concern that commanders would not conduct training according to the new doctrinal principles but rather continue to train as they had before the issuance of the new doctrine.[17] Assuming that this concern was justified, it seems likely that at least some units were not training in accordance with the new doctrine in 2000. Nonetheless, in principle, at least, training in 2000 was supposed to be conducted in accordance with the new doctrine.

Focus of Training on Priority Skills

The amount of time PLA units spent training in different skill areas in 2000 is not known, but evidence suggests that training was not necessarily focused on priority skills. One of the changes associated with the 2001 *Military Training and Evaluation Guidelines* 《军事训练与考核大纲》was that, although the guidelines specified the total amount of annual training time and the amount of time to be allocated to each phase of training, they did not stipulate specific amounts of time for each training subject. Instead, each unit from the military region level down was directed to allocate training time according to the priority (and difficulty) of the training subjects for that unit. In particular, the new guidelines required that training be driven by a unit's operational missions, and units were instructed not to train to the same degree in all areas. In 2002 articles in *PLA Daily* began referring to the importance of "mission topic training" (使命课题训练), with the term "mission topic" similar to the U.S. concept of "mission-essential tasks." This implied that training should be focused on topics that were directly associated with a unit's assigned missions.[18] These changes to the *Military Training and Evaluation Guidelines* and annual training directives imply that, before they were issued in 2001, each unit of a given type (e.g., each infantry battalion) spent the same amount of time training on each subject area as every other unit of that type did, regardless of whether or not that training subject was associated with the unit's assigned missions, and, therefore, that training in 2000 was not necessarily focused on priority skills.

Progressiveness of Training

PLA training in 2000 clearly followed a progressive pattern, beginning with individual and small unit training early in the calendar year, shifting to increasingly larger units and more complex operations over the following months and peaking in the fall. Evidence suggests, however, that the maximum scale and complexity of training in 2000 was limited. Each service branch was said to spend most of its time training separately from the other branches, with combined arms and joint training only occurring during major exercises at the end of the year. For the PLA Army, training above the company level did not begin until April, and most training was at the battalion level and below. Part of this was the result of the heavy dependence of the PLA on conscripts, as described in Chapter Five, many of whom were in their first year of service. Approximately a quarter of all enlisted personnel in the PLA Army in 2000, for example, were in their first year of military service. This meant that Army units could not easily build on skills acquired in previous years but needed to devote significant time to training the new soldiers in basic and small-unit skills. Over the course of the year, training and exercises progressed up to the regimental and division level for most units, but exercises involving more than one division were apparently rare. In the case of the PLA Navy, large-scale, complex training was also hindered by the limited amount of time ships spent at sea, about twenty-four days per year, as compared to at least 120 days a year for most U.S. Navy ships. In the words of one observer, "A warship's crew … that has to spend the first 25 to 50 percent of each underway training period ensuring that its crew remains proficient at individual and single-ship level tasks, will have considerable difficulty establishing crew proficiency at a level of complex, integrated joint operations."[19]

Joint exercises involving units from different services were even rarer than high-level combined arms operations, and many of them were joint in name only – more than one service would be present at the exercise, but each service would train separately. The limited amount of joint training in 2000 is implied by the emphasis put on the importance of joint training in the GSD's annual training directives beginning in 2001.[20]

Realism of Training

Increasing the realism of training was a clear area of emphasis in the PLA in 2000. This was reflected in efforts to conduct opposing force exercises in which units would have to respond to the actions of a thinking, adapting adversary, instead of simply following a pre-scripted plan against an imaginary opponent. It was also reflected in a greater emphasis on training at night and in bad weather, on training in the presence of jamming and other forms of electronic warfare, and on live fire exercises. These efforts were building on a very low baseline, however, and, despite the rhetorical calls, the amount of realistic training actually conducted was probably quite limited. In a 2002 article in *PLA Daily*, for example, confrontational training was said to still be infrequent, small-scale, and oversimplified. As noted above, in 2001, PLA Navy surface ships were observed to only spend about twenty-four days underway each year, a very low number by Western standards, and PLA air defense exercises were said by the U.S. Defense Department to be "highly scripted and the scenarios lacked realism." Tellingly, when the 2001 training guidelines were issued, a key difference from the previous guidelines was said to be the 2001 guidelines' emphasis on the "uniformity between training and combat" (训战一致), implying that such a uniformity had not been embodied in the guidelines previously in force. Even in 2002, moreover, a *PLA Daily* article noted that, although the new guidelines had created the *conditions* for organizing training according to the requirements of actual warfare, "a relatively large shortfall still exists" (还存在较大差距). According to the article, some units did not know how to conduct training according to the requirements of actual warfare because of insufficient understanding of the new guidelines; some were unwilling to do so because of the limitations imposed by "traditional thinking" (传统思想); and some were afraid to do so out of concern for accidents. The existence of resistance to realistic training after the 2001 guidelines were issued suggests that the amount of realism in training in 2000 was even more limited.[21]

One area in which training does appear to have been relatively realistic for the PLA Army in 2000 was in including training in the logistics requirements of military operations. Logistics and armament support units, in addition to conducting their own separate training, were routinely included in large-scale exercises. Areas in which logistics capabilities were exercised included deploying units to exercise areas; feeding, resupplying, and providing medical support to units in the field; and conducting forward maintenance and on-site repair. It is not clear, however, that the services other than the PLA Army also incorporated logistics training into operational training and exercises. In the case of PLA Navy, for example, logistics and maintenance training was typically not incorporated into vessel training at sea.[22]

Standards-Based Training

Training in the PLA in 2000 was primarily time-based, rather than standards-based. Although the training guidelines in effect in 2000, which dated from 1995, included proficiency goals, they also specified the precise amount of time to be spent on each subject, and units apparently considered training on a given subject to be complete when the designated amount of time to be spent training on it had been expended, regardless of whether an associated proficiency goal had been achieved. In at least some cases, moreover, units did not even expend the mandated amount of time on training. Articles published after the issuance of the 2001 guidelines, by contrast, emphasize that the 2001 guidelines did *not* specify a fixed amount of time to be spent on each training topic (although they did specify minimum and maximum training times) and were the first to provide a comprehensive set of training standards for each service and branch of the PLA. The revised training guidelines issued in 2001, moreover, were the first to be titled "*Military Training* and Evaluation *Guidelines*" (emphasis added), as opposed to simply "*Military Training Guidelines*"《军事训练大纲》, indicating that evaluation of unit proficiency relative to defined standards became an important basis for training after 2001. The implication of these changes, of course, is that the training guidelines before 2001 did *not* include a comprehensive set of standards and that evaluation of unit proficiency relative to specified standards was *not* an important basis for training before 2001.[23]

Operational Experience

The Chinese military in 2000 had not engaged in a major combat operation since China's brief invasion of Vietnam twenty-one years earlier. Occasional border clashes and artillery duels with Vietnam had continued into the mid-1980s, however, and in 1988 the PLA Navy had fought a battle with the Vietnamese Navy in the area around Fiery Cross Reef in the South China Sea. In addition, since 1990 more than a thousand PLA personnel had participated in United Nations (UN) peacekeeping operations, with a handful having been killed and several dozen wounded during those deployments.[24] Nonetheless, given the sixteen-year limitation on enlisted service in effect until 1999, by 2000 there would have been very few enlisted personnel along with a relatively small number of senior officers (mostly colonels or generals) in the PLA who had ever participated in combat operations.

CHINESE MILITARY TRAINING QUALITY IN 2010

Despite the changes to training that were implemented after the issuance of the 2001 guidelines, by the mid-2000s several shortcomings in the current training regime had been identified. One, reflecting the weakness of the 1999 doctrinal publications in the area of joint operations as discussed in Chapter Two, was a lack of joint training. Another was that the majority of training was focused on common training subjects with not enough attention to specialized training topics. A third shortcoming was insufficient emphasis on "informationization," the term that started to be used in 2003 to describe the dominant characteristic of future wars. This was said to be reflected in particular by a lack of training in "complex electromagnetic environments" (复杂电磁环境下), a reference to battle environments characterized by intensive use of the electromagnetic spectrum both for surveillance and reconnaissance and for communications, along with extensive electronic jamming and deception measures, cyber warfare, and other conditions that could affect the smooth collection, processing, and dissemination of battlefield information. A fourth shortcoming was said to be the total amount of time devoted to training each year as well as the amount of time devoted to specialized training, such as night training and large-scale combined arms and joint training. A final shortcoming was said to be that performance and evaluation standards were not rigorous enough.[25]

In addition, in December 2004, then-Chairman of the CMC Hu Jintao gave a speech in which he called on the PLA to be prepared to carry out "historical missions for the new stage of the new century." These missions required performing "diversified military tasks" including a variety of "nonwar military actions" such as counterterrorism, stability operations, or disaster relief.[26]

In June 2006, at a PLA-wide training conference, Hu Jintao called on the PLA to transform the focus of PLA training from mechanized warfare to informationized warfare. The CMC issued a *Decision of the CMC Regarding Strengthening Military Training in the New Period of the New Century* 《中央军委关于加强新世纪新阶段军事训练决定》, and the four general departments issued a set of recommendations on how to implement the *Decision*. The drafting of a new set of *Military Training and Evaluation Guidelines* began, and, after two years of testing and validation, the revised Guidelines were issued in July 2008.[27]

The new Guidelines were said to be more closely tied to the missions, tasks, and requirements of real war; to incorporate joint operations at all levels of training; to include greater emphasis on nonwar military actions; to put more emphasis on opposition force training; and to put more emphasis on performance standards. They were also said to incorporate training in a complex electromagnetic environment into basic unit training and tactical training, to increase the emphasis on training of command organizations (as opposed to just field units), and to increase the amount of time spent training under unfavorable and complex natural conditions.[28]

Responsibility of Unit Commanders for Training

Unit commanders remained the people having primary responsibility for individual and unit training in 2010.[29] According to an article in *PLA Daily*, the principle was "whoever is in charge of combat organizes training (谁主战谁组训)."[30]

Intensity of Training

By all reports, training in 2010 was significantly more intensive than in 2000. The military training regulations issued in 2002 for the first time made clear the training duty of military personnel and the requirement that military personnel participate in military training. The new *Military Training and Evaluation Guidelines* issued in 2008 were intended to further increase the amount of time spent training each year as well as the intensity of that training. Nonetheless, there are indications that training in 2010 was still not as intensive as it could have been. A 2010 article in *PLA Daily*, for example, notes a problem of going too easy on joint training, and a 2011 article reports as news that members of the political department of the Beijing Military Region headquarters had that year started being required to participate in physical training, formation drills, and firearms training.[31]

Units remained involved in activities other than military training, although less so than in 2000. Units still spent 20 to 30 percent of total training time on political and ideological instruction and, although the PLA had largely divested itself of business interests by 2010, units at the brigade and regimental level continued to raise crops and animals for their own consumption. Any time spent on political training and farming activities obviously reduced the amount of time that could be devoted to military training.[32]

Degree to Which Training Corresponded to Doctrine

In April 2008, an article in *PLA Daily* stated that the training reforms underway at the time were employing the approach of simultaneously revising doctrine, training guidelines, and related teaching materials so as to cause them to be organically unified. However, although the new training guidelines were issued in July 2008, as described in Chapter Two, the new doctrinal publications were not issued until late 2009. Thus, for at least one year, the training guidelines were based on doctrine that had not yet officially been issued and therefore training presumably did not correspond to the doctrine that was still official at that point, which would have been doctrine that had been promulgated in 1999. Reflecting the awkward situation this created, a *PLA Daily* article from November 2009 refers to the "urgent need (迫切需要)" to revise and issue the joint campaign guidance. This problem was presumably rectified in 2010, however, after the new doctrinal publications were finally issued.[33]

Even if the training guidelines corresponded to the official doctrine in 2010, if units were not training according to the guidelines, then their training did not correspond to doctrine. Articles from 2011 to 2013 note ongoing problems that include an improper training ethos (训风不正), not following training regulations (有法不依), or not strictly enforcing regulations (执法不力).[34] This suggests that not training according to doctrine remained a problem in the PLA.

Focus of Training on Priority Skills

The 2008 training guidelines were said to emphasize carrying out the PLA's "historical missions for the new stage of the new century" as announced by Hu Jintao in 2004, including responding to new security threats and performing "diversified military tasks." Accordingly, the guidelines called for training for nonwar military actions such as counterterrorism, stability maintenance, "responding to sudden [incidents]" (处突, i.e., domestic disturbances), border control, and humanitarian assistance and disaster relief to be expanded. Although winning informationized local wars was said to be the PLA's "core military capability" (核心军事能力), given that the amount of time available for training is finite, preparation for nonwar military actions could only have come at the expense of training for high-intensity combat operations. A 2010 article in *PLA Daily* acknowledged this tension, noting that "some" (一些) officers and enlisted personnel were confused about the priority that should be accorded to the "diversified military tasks" relative to warfighting requirements. The article, however, made clear that preparing to conduct "diversified military tasks" was not an optional activity.[35]

Since conducting diversified military tasks was an official assigned mission of the PLA, it could be argued that any training to conduct those tasks was in fact focused on priority skills. With respect to the warfighting capability of the PLA, however, it seems unlikely that the skills required to perform "nonwar military actions" represented priority skills. That said, the amount or proportion of time actually devoted to training for diversified military tasks is unclear. Even after the 2008 training guidelines were issued, articles in *PLA Daily* emphasized that priority was to be given to raising the PLA's core military capabilities. Training for diversified military tasks was apparently included in the category of "elective" (选训) training topics, moreover, implying that, although the diversified military tasks were not truly optional, mastery of the "required" (必训) training topics had to be achieved before training in the elective topics began. And although the amount of time devoted to training for nonwar military actions may have increased with the 2008 training guidelines, any negative effect on actual warfighting capability may have been mitigated by an increase in the *total* amount of time spent in training each year that was also mandated by the 2008 guidelines.[36]

Regardless of the amount of time spent on training for nonwar military actions, the 2008 training guidelines were said to be more focused on training in specialized skills and the tasks and requirements of actual war. This suggests that actual combat training, at least, was more focused on priority skills in 2010 than it had been in 2000. Nonetheless, articles appearing in late 2010 and 2011 suggest that the PLA leadership was still not satisfied with the quality of training in the PLA including the problem of "one size fits all" (一刀切) training, indicating that, in the opinion of the PLA leadership at least, training in 2010 was still not adequately focused on the skill needs of individual units.[37]

Progressiveness of Training

PLA training in 2010 still followed a progressive pattern, beginning with individual and small unit training early in the calendar year, shifting to increasingly larger units and more complex operations over the following months, and peaking in scale and complexity in the fall. Unlike a decade earlier, however, units apparently continued to do at least some training from December through February, after the previous year's second-year conscripts had been demobilized (or sent for NCO training, in the case of those conscripts staying on to become NCOs) and before the current year's new conscripts had completed their basic training. As discussed in Chapter Five, moreover, the average recruit in 2010 was significantly better educated than in 2000. Thus, units in 2010 not only maintained a higher level of proficiency during the winter than they did in 2000, the better education level of recruits presumably meant that units were able to more quickly build upon that level of proficiency. In addition, the 2008 training guidelines put particular emphasis on joint training. Although joint training occurred before 2008, the 2008 training guidelines were the first to explicitly mandate it, with even basic unit training supposedly including joint training. However, some of what was described as "joint" training was in fact opposition force training (e.g., PLA Army air defense units practicing against PLA Air Force aircraft) and the amount of truly joint training appears to still have been quite limited in 2010, for reasons that were said to include a lack of understanding by officers and enlisted personnel of the operations of services other than their own, a lack of joint command organizations, and the noninteroperability of communications equipment. In a 2010 interview, the director of the GSD's Military Training and Service Arms Department forecast that in five years' time combined arms training by combat units would have been "universally initiated" and that joint training involving all systems and all force elements would have achieved a "preliminary level of integration." This reveals that, as of 2010, combined arms training had in fact *not* been universally initiated and that joint training involving all systems and all elements had not yet achieved even a preliminary level of integration. Consistent with this, one U.S. Air Force analyst noted that "The most glaring [deficiency in PLA Air Force training] is the limited joint training [it] conducts." Nonetheless, despite these acknowledged shortcomings, it is clear that training in 2010 was reaching greater scale and higher levels of complexity than it had been in 2000. In the case of the PLA Air Force, according to the U.S. Air Force analyst, "One strength of [PLA Air Force] training includes the number and scope of their exercises, and recent years have seen the PLAAF executing increasingly large and complex training events."[38]

Realism of Training

The realism of training significantly increased between 2000 and 2010. The 2001 training guidelines had strongly emphasized realistic training, and this emphasis was apparently further strengthened in the 2008 guidelines. Particular areas of focus in the 2008 guidelines were opposing force training (with some units creating permanent opposition forces organized, trained, and equipped to simulate military units of potential foreign adversaries), night training (with approximately a quarter of training time to occur at night), training in bad weather, training under stressful psychological conditions, and training "in complex electromagnetic environments." The 2008 training guidelines also emphasized field training away from home bases, so that troops would become used to the living conditions of actual combat. All ground force units were required to spend at least four months away from home each year and some spent as many as eight months, with the average being half a year. The living conditions while in the field were made more realistic as well. Apparently in the past, when units deployed to the field for training, they would pull up the weeds, build roads, put up light poles, string clothes lines, build shops, and so on, but after 2008 an attempt was made to more accurately simulate the rigors of actual battlefield living conditions. Whether the requirement to spend four months "in the field" also applied to the Navy, Air Force, and Second Artillery units is unclear, but Navy ships were spending substantially more time at sea each year, and Second Artillery units were frequently deploying away from their bases for training and exercises. In addition, most major exercises involved not only training in combat operations but also emphasized the logistical requirements of rapid mobilization and deployment to the exercise area and sustainment of units in the field during the exercise. Despite these efforts, however, the aforementioned U.S. Air Force analyst noted that "most [PLA Air Force] training events remain heavily scripted, with little autonomy save for an elite cadre of pilots." Consistent with this, the PLA leadership was apparently not satisfied with the realism of training in 2010, as articles from that and subsequent years were still noting the need to strengthen training for "real war" (实战) and a continued lack of realism in exercises.[39]

Standards-Based Training

Between 2000 and 2010, training in the PLA was transformed from a time-based system to a standards-based one. The training guidelines in effect in 2000 had specified the precise amount of time to be spent on each subject. The 2001 guidelines, by contrast, were the first to provide a comprehensive set of training standards for each service and branch and allowed each unit to determine the actual amount of time (within limits) to be spent in training to meet that standard. The 2008 guidelines, which were in effect in 2010, continued the focus on standards and put even greater emphasis than the 2001 guidelines on assessing whether units had actually achieved those standards.[40]

Despite the increased emphasis on rigorous assessment in the 2008 guidelines, however, problems with the assessment process continued in 2010 and after. A 2009 article in *PLA Daily* noted an urgent need make the standards for joint training more specific and more quantitative. Also, under the 2008 guidelines, units were apparently responsible for creating their own standardized assessment and evaluation systems, but as of 2010 many had not yet done so. Many had failed to create independent assessment and evaluation organizations and assessments were reportedly often subjective judgments based on visual observation rather than on detailed quantitative data. In addition, in a typical bureaucratic pathology, assessments were apparently often based simply on whether a training program had been implemented rather than on whether the goals of the program had been achieved.[41]

Operational Experience

By 2010 it had been more than thirty years since the PLA's last major combat operation and more than twenty years since the minor border and naval clashes with Vietnam of the 1980s. China's participation in UN peacekeeping operations had markedly increased over the past decade, however, with about sixteen thousand PLA personnel participating in various operations between 2000 and 2010. By 2010 nine of these people had lost their lives in UN peacekeeping operations. In addition, beginning in December 2008 China began deploying naval ships to the Western Indian Ocean to protect merchant vessels there from attacks by pirates based in Somalia. Each deployment generally consisted of two surface warships and a supply ship, with each task force remaining on station for an average of four months before being relieved by a new task force.[42] Although they did not involve actual combat (the pirates preferring to attack ships not guarded by naval vessels), these deployments provided the PLA Navy with invaluable operational experience both in the physical and psychological rigors of remaining at sea for long periods and in providing the supplies, maintenance, and repairs needed to sustain naval forces away from their home ports for several months. Nonetheless, less than 1 percent of the individuals in the PLA in 2010 would have directly participated in any of these operations and only a tiny proportion would have had actual combat experience.

CHINESE MILITARY TRAINING QUALITY IN 2020

As noted in the previous section, despite the significant improvements in training between 2000 and 2010, the PLA leadership was clearly still not satisfied with the quality of the PLA's training in 2010. Articles published in that and subsequent years pointed out weaknesses in the assessment and evaluation system, the need for improvements in combined arms and joint training, units' failure to follow training regulations, inconsistency in applying effective training technique, a lack of realism in exercises, and other shortcomings in PLA training. In October 2010 the CMC issued an "Opinion Regarding Deeply Advancing the Transformation of Military Training"《关于深入推进军事训练转变的意见》, and, based on it, in 2011 the GSD issued an "Overall Plan for Military Training Reform during the 12th Five Year Plan Period [2011–2015]"《"十二五"时期军事训练改革总体方案》, indicating an intention to further improve the quality of training in coming years.[43]

In 2020 PLA unit commanders will almost certainly still be the people with primary responsibility for individual and unit training, and the intensity of training will likely further increase between 2010 and 2020. Given the Chinese leadership's concern about maintaining the PLA's loyalty to the CPC, however, a significant amount of time will probably still be devoted to political and ideological training in 2020, and this will still constrain the amount of time that can be devoted to military training. Training will undoubtedly continue to be expected to be based on doctrine, and compliance with this principle will presumably improve between 2010 and 2020. Starting in 2010, annual training directives began emphasizing mastering "core military capabilities" (核心军事能力) and the 2011 plan for military training reform sought to further improve the fit between training requirements for specific units and the assigned missions of that unit. Nonetheless, the ongoing requirement for units to be prepared to perform nonwar military actions and "diversified military tasks" will limit the amount of time they can spend on improving their actual combat capabilities.

Training will continue to begin with basic individual and small unit skills and build up to larger scale and higher levels of complexity over the course of a year, but the decreasing proportion of new recruits and higher education levels of all PLA personnel will enable units to increase their skills more rapidly. In addition, the growing emphasis on combined arms and joint operations, as well as the increasing availability of funding to pay for the costs of large-scale, integrated training, will allow the ultimate scale and complexity of training reached each year to steadily increase. As noted earlier, the PLA

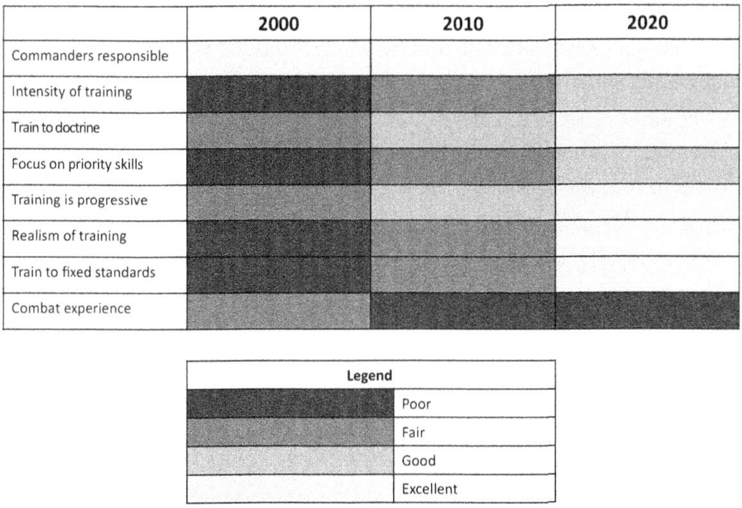

	2000	2010	2020
Commanders responsible			
Intensity of training			
Train to doctrine			
Focus on priority skills			
Training is progressive			
Realism of training			
Train to fixed standards			
Combat experience			

Legend	
	Poor
	Fair
	Good
	Excellent

FIGURE 6.1 Changes in Training Quality, 2000 to 2020

leadership is currently especially concerned with increasing the realism of training, and thus the realism of training will likely reach higher levels by 2020. Similarly, the growing emphasis on training to defined standards, and, particularly, rigorous assessment of whether units are actually reaching those standards, will likely result in a largely standards-based training regime by 2020.[44]

The one glaring area of weakness in the PLA's training in 2020 will likely be its lack of significant experience in real-world military operations. UN peacekeeping operations and counterpiracy patrols are unlikely to engage a significant proportion of PLA personnel and, although they provide valuable organizational and operational experience for the PLA as a whole, are no substitute for actual combat. It is possible, however, that the PLA will have engaged in actual combat by 2020. Aside from a major war, such as one over Taiwan, conflicts that China could plausibly become involved in include naval clashes over competing island claims in the East China Sea or South China Sea, counterterrorist operations along China's Inner Asian borders, and stability operations in North Korea following a collapse of or split in its government. As the United States learned from its operations in Grenada and Panama in the 1980s, even a very small scale conflict can provide invaluable experience that has a significant effect on the readiness of a military for a larger-scale conflict, such as the U.S. military's operations against Iraq in 1991.

Figure 6.1 illustrates the changes in the different elements of training quality that occurred in the PLA between 2000 and 2010 and will likely occur between 2010 and 2020.

As the figure suggests, with the exception of actual combat experience, by 2020 training in the PLA will likely have progressed from being an area of weakness to one of relative strength.

7

Logistics

The term *logistics* covers a wide range of activities and capabilities, some of which are more closely related to each other than others. They may be grouped into the following categories:[1]

1. *Supply.* Supply entails providing combat forces with the fuel, ammunition, spare parts, equipment, food, water, and other materials they need to operate. It also entails providing other logistics organizations, such as those responsible for repair and maintenance, mobility, engineering, and health care, with the tools, equipment, spare parts, blood, and other materials they need to perform their functions.

2. *Repair and maintenance.* Repair and maintenance entails keeping weapon systems, vehicles, and other equipment in good working condition as well as repairing them, either in the field or at rear area depots, when they become damaged.

3. *Mobility.* Mobility refers to moving combat and support units from one location to another (when such movement involves other than the organic movement capabilities of the moving units, such as the ability of a tracked vehicle to move cross-country or the ability of a soldier to walk). Note that many of the assets used for mobility can also be used for performing other logistics functions, such as delivering supplies, moving damaged equipment to rear area depots for repair and returning it when repaired, and evacuating injured and dead personnel to medical facilities and morgues.

4. *Engineering.* Engineering includes activities such as constructing and repairing roads, railroads, bridges, airfields, seaports, base camps, and other facilities.[2]

5. *Health services.* Health services include both keeping personnel healthy (through vaccinations, regular examinations, etc.) and treating the wounded, injured, and sick.

6. *Other logistic services.* Other logistic services include preparing food, providing hygiene services, operating base camps, and so on.

A common saying in military circles is that "Amateurs talk about strategy and tactics; professionals talk about logistics." Thus, the importance of logistics to the success of military operations is well recognized. As in the case of training, however, students of military affairs do not appear to have developed a general theory of the characteristics of good logistical support. The issue is further complicated by the diversity of activities included under the rubric of logistics. The approach taken in this chapter, therefore, is simply to attempt to assess the principal factors that can affect the PLA's capability to conduct each of the five main types of logistics support listed above (supply, repair and maintenance, mobility, engineering, and health services). Factors that can be used to assess these capabilities are listed below:

- The locations and amounts of existing stocks of fuel, ammunition, spare parts, blood, and other key supplies
- The nation's capability to produce or purchase additional fuel, ammunition, spare parts, food, and other supplies
- The distance between where operations might be conducted and
  - Where forces are based in peacetime
  - Where supply sources, repair depots, and medical facilities for those forces are (these locations are sometimes, but not always, the same as where forces are based in peacetime)
- The terrain types and transportation infrastructure (roads, railroads, airfields, seaports, etc.) that exist at and between all of these locations
- The quality of routine maintenance performed by the military
- The military's capabilities for repairing damaged equipment in the field
- The military's capabilities for repairing damaged equipment at rear area depots
- The military's ability to keep its personnel healthy
- The military's capabilities for treating wounded, injured, and sick personnel
- The military's capabilities for building and repairing roads, railroads, bridges, airfields, seaports, base camps, and other facilities
- The transport capabilities available to the military including military and civilian trucks, trains, ships, and transport aircraft as well as specialized systems such as underway replenishment ships, aerial refueling aircraft, and amphibious assault ships

- The efficiency with which all of the above are managed. Such efficiencies can have dramatic effects. For example, between 1995 and 1998 the U.S. Army halved the average time it took to deliver a spare part.[3]

Logistics requirements are not invariant but are dependent on, among other things, the type of doctrine a military employs and the kinds of weaponry it operates. A doctrine of direct engagement imposes more predictable and more slowly changing (albeit not necessarily less-demanding) logistics requirements, as forces move forward (or backward) at a steady rate. A doctrine of indirection and maneuver such as the PLA has employed since 1999, on the other hand, requires a logistics system that is more agile and responsive, as forces are redeployed quickly to create opportunities, then must move to rapidly exploit them.[4] Similarly, low-tech, simple equipment such as trucks, rifles, and artillery pieces is easier to repair and maintain than modern armored vehicles, jet fighters, and missile destroyers.

Publicly available information about PLA logistics capabilities is incomplete.[5] Reports on China's military capabilities by the U.S. government and other organizations generally have little to say about the PLA's logistics capabilities, and accounts in PLA publications generally describe the qualities of new equipment items or the accomplishments of individual units without providing any information on how widespread those equipment items or accomplishments are within the PLA. Nonetheless, enough information is available to make informed estimates of the main elements of the PLA's logistics system.

CHINESE MILITARY LOGISTICS CAPABILITIES IN 2000

The PLA's logistic system was originally designed to support defensive positional warfare, not the mobile offensive actions required by the "high-technology local war" doctrine adopted in 1999. These capabilities were sufficient to support defensive military operations at or near China's border, but were not adequate for supporting mobile offensive operations beyond China's borders, as was discovered during China's invasion of Vietnam in 1979. Apparently little improvement was made in the subsequent twenty years, moreover, as, in the late 1990s, China's logistics capabilities were still assessed as "woefully inadequate" and "plagued by chronic inefficiency," with the inability to "sustain large forces in intense, fast-moving combat operations" said to be among the PLA's greatest weaknesses. In recognition of these shortcomings, in 1998 the PLA had initiated a ten-year logistics reform program to create a more agile and efficient system. However, this program was only in its initial stages in 2000. Overall, the PLA's logistics system would not have been capable of projecting and sustaining forces in the event of a conflict outside of China's borders in 2000.[6]

Supply

Consistent with being originally designed to support defensive positional warfare, the PLA's supply system in 2000 was based primarily on stockpiling materials in a system of fixed depots of various levels, rather than on delivering supplies directly to units in the field on an as-needed basis. Strategic reserves of war material, for example, were concentrated at several national-level logistics bases in China's inland areas, each military region controlled multiple storage depots of its own, and depots were associated with lower-level organizational units as well. In the case of the PLA Air Force, there were three levels of supply depot: The first (strategic) level was controlled by PLA Air Force headquarters. Second-level depots were controlled by the seven MRAF headquarters. The third level consisted of supply depots colocated with the operational units they supported. In the event of a conflict, supplies would have been moved to and concentrated at depots as close to the involved units as possible, but would have had to follow the progression from strategic-level depots to MRAF-level depots to operational-level depots, rather than being delivered directly from a central depot to an operational unit.[7]

No information is publicly available about the actual quantities of the PLA's stocks of fuel, ammunition, spare parts, blood, and other key military supplies in 2000. Given the PLA's tradition of stockpiling materials at fixed depots, it seems likely that the stocks of most key military supplies were substantial, but whether they would been sufficient to support sustained operations is unclear. In the late 1990s PLA logistics planners were stating that war materials stockpiles needed to be increased and, as part of the logistics reform program initiated in 1998, warehouse capacities were being expanded, suggesting that PLA leadership judged that existing stocks might have been inadequate in the event of a major contingency.[8]

In any case, in the event of significant combat operations, the PLA's primary supply challenge initially would have been moving supplies from their storage locations to the units actually conducting operations.[9] Under the 1998 reform program, efforts were underway to improve the speed with which supplies could be delivered to operational units. Forklifts and containers for the movement of material were being introduced; fuel trucks and portable bladders were being issued; mobile pipeline units were being created; and the efficiency of supply operations was being enhanced by the use of computers, bar codes and scanners, improvements in communications between units in garrison and the field, and the implementation of modern management techniques. These efforts had only just begun in 2000, however, and the head of the GLD admitted that the PLA's supply efficiency was "low" at the time these reforms began.[10]

Moving supplies from their storage locations to the units conducting operations, moreover, would have been hampered by the fact that major maneuver units lacked organic capabilities for transporting stockpiles of fuel and other supplies. A U.S. mechanized brigade, for example, has more than two hundred medium and heavy cargo trucks to support its 233 combat vehicles. In the PLA in 2000, on the other hand, supplies would have had to be provided by "emergency support units" created specifically for the contingency. In the case of the PLA Army, each group army, division, brigade, and regiment involved would have established "field service centers" and "field armament centers" to provide supply support to their units.[11] Aside from the operational and coordination problems that such ad hoc organizations undoubtedly would have created, this approach suggests that the PLA as a whole had insufficient organic resupply capability to support a large-scale commitment of force.[12] In the event of a major contingency, therefore, the PLA would likely have had to requisition civilian trucks to supplement its organic capabilities to transport supplies. The PLA, however, did not appear to exercise such operations in peacetime, suggesting that an attempt to conduct them during a contingency could easily have resulted in massive coordination problems.[13]

It is also not clear whether China's transportation infrastructure would have been able to support the supply requirements of a major military operation, even one that occurred within China's borders. A Chinese army division engaged in heavy combat would have required roughly thirteen hundred to fourteen hundred tons – meaning 150 to 250 truckloads (assuming each truck carried five to ten tons) – of supplies a day.[14] Although many major civilian highway and railway projects in China in the 1990s had been constructed to military specifications, the total length of China's highway system in 2000 was less than 40 percent of that of the United States, a country of similar geographic size. Similarly, the total length of China's railways was less than 30 percent of the United States', the total length of China's petroleum pipelines was only 5 percent of the United States', and China had only 20 percent as many commercial airports as the United States.[15] In the event of a major conflict, this underdeveloped transportation infrastructure could have limited the PLA's ability to move supplies from their storage depots to the locations at which units were conducting combat operations and, as new supplies were produced, from the producing factories to supply depots. If a conflict had occurred across or near one of China's land borders, supply challenges would have been increased by the particularly weak transportation infrastructure in the areas of China near most its land borders (which are generally sparsely populated) and the rugged or mountainous terrain of most of these areas.[16]

Combat operations at sea within a few hundred miles of China's coast would have presented relatively few supply challenges for the PLA. Ships would have been able to put into port for supplies and then return to the area of combat operations within a day or two, and aircraft would have been able to reach their targets without needing to be refueled en route. If a conflict had occurred farther out at sea, however, the PLA would have had difficulty sustaining naval and air forces in the area of combat operations. The PLA in 2000 had only three ships capable of transferring supplies (fuel, fresh water, food, etc.) to naval vessels while at sea, as compared to more than thirty such ships in the U.S. Navy that year, and only a dozen or so aircraft capable of refueling other aircraft while in flight, as compared to more than seven hundred such aircraft in the U.S. military.[17]

If the PLA had deployed significant ground forces across water for combat operations, in an invasion of Taiwan, for example, keeping those forces supplied would have entailed further challenges. China being one of the world's largest trading nations, its commercial ports had extensive freight handling capacity, loading and unloading an average of nearly four million tons of freight a day in 2000 (the top fifty U.S. ports handled six million tons of freight a day that year).[18] China also had one of the largest merchant fleets in the world in 2000, with more than fourteen hundred ships that displaced one thousand tons or more registered in China,[19] so there is little question that the Chinese government could have requisitioned sufficient numbers of civilian cargo ships to supplement its military supply ships if needed. However, transferring supplies from standard military or civilian cargo ships to land would have required access to usable port facilities not just in China but also in the territory where combat operations were being conducted. In the case of an amphibious invasion, such facilities might not have been available initially. Smaller boats and helicopters could have been used to bring supplies to shore from larger ships, but this would have been a highly inefficient and difficult-to-organize operation. China did have more than fifty landing ships with a total transport capacity of about twenty thousand tons that theoretically could have been used for unloading supplies directly onto beaches, but in an invasion of any scale those ships would have been in high demand for bringing reinforcements to the landed forces. The landing ships, moreover, would have been a priority target for the defending country (and any other countries, such as the United States, contributing to its defense).

In terms of airlift capabilities, the PLA Navy and Air Force had 160 or so medium and large transport aircraft capable of carrying a total of about twenty-five hundred tons of cargo. Assuming that all of these aircraft were available and dedicated to supply operations, that none were shot down, and that each was able to make one round trip per day, they would have been able to convey enough supplies to support at most two divisions in heavy combat operations. China did have more than five hundred civilian transport aircraft in 2000, but the vast majority of them were undoubtedly configured for passenger transport and thus would not have been an efficient way of transporting supplies. Nonetheless, after the December 2004 tsunami in the Indian Ocean, when the PLA deployed supplies for disaster relief in the stricken areas, it used civilian aircraft to fly them, possibly suggesting a lack of confidence in the reliability of the PLA's transport aircraft for operations outside of China at that time.[20]

Repair and Maintenance

PLA repair and maintenance capabilities in 2000 were poor. Although incremental improvements had been made over the 1990s and each military region contained multiple repair depots, major force elements lacked organic first- or second-line maintenance elements as well as capabilities for evacuating and repairing battlefield equipment casualties. In the PLA Navy, crews did not generally train in maintaining equipment at sea. In a contingency, repair support for PLA Army units would have been provided by emergency support units created specifically for the contingency at field service centers and field armament centers. These emergency support units were still at the experimental stage in 2000, however, and few units would have had the capability to conduct rapid repairs on the battlefield or during movement. Instead, in most cases damaged equipment would have had to be evacuated to rear area repair depots or even to the producing factories. Similarly, PLA Navy ships at sea had to return to port or a shipyard for even minor repairs. Much of the PLA's weaponry, moreover, based as it was on 1950s Soviet designs, had high maintenance requirements. The engines of the J-6 (MiG-19), J-7 (MiG-21), and J-8, for example, the PLA Air Force's primary fighter aircraft, needed to be overhauled after every one hundred to three hundred hours of operating time, as compared to once every two thousand hours or so for a modern Western jet engine.[21]

China's military, having not fought a war for more than twenty years, also had no recent experience with maintaining its equipment under the high operational tempo of actual combat. Modern high-intensity military operations put a premium on conducting routine but required maintenance with speed and efficiency so that equipment and the personnel who use it can spend the maximum amount of time in actual operational activities. This is a skill that the U.S. military has mastered as a result of the requirements of the Cold War and the frequent military operations it has conducted since then, but that does not come automatically to militaries that have not recently experienced the pressures of actual military operations. During a period of heightened tensions over Taiwan in July and August 1999, for example, the PLA Air Force units in the area still flew an average of only thirty sorties per day.[22]

Contingencies that required significant redeployment of forces would have created repair and maintenance problems for the PLA as well, even if the redeployment occurred entirely within China. Things like stock numbers, requisition procedures, and inventory standards were not standardized between military regions. Air bases were generally only capable of supporting the single type of aircraft normally stationed there, and in 2000 the PLA Air Force was only beginning to experiment with mobile support detachments to support aircraft operating from other than their home airfields, including from dispersal airfields and highway airstrips. The first time a full PLA Air Force aviation division (the equivalent of an air wing in the U.S. Air Force) deployed away from its home bases was in 2000.[23]

Mobility

PLA Army and Air Force units in 2000 lacked the organic transportation elements needed for long-distance deployments. In a contingency, road transportation would have been provided by emergency support units created specifically for that contingency. For strategic movements within China, moreover, rail transport would have been the primary modality. As noted in the section on supply, however, the areas of China near most of its land borders had weak transportation infrastructure and rugged or mountainous terrain. If the contingency had required the deployment of significant forces into these regions, therefore, the infrastructure and terrain would likely have substantially slowed the rate of deployment. If the contingency had involved a significant proportion of PLA Army units, moreover, the PLA would not have had enough organic ground transportation assets to reposition the involved units and would have had to requisition civilian trucks and trains, potentially causing further delays.[24]

Deployments across water would have been reliant on sea and air transport. The PLA Navy's organic sealift capabilities in 2000 were modest, consisting of thirty relatively small cargo ships capable of transporting twelve thousand to fifteen thousand tons of soldiers and equipment along with about fifty landing ships capable of transporting another twenty thousand tons. Collectively these ships could have carried a total of about two light infantry divisions or one understrength armored division at a time. PLA Navy and Air Force aircraft could have carried one infantry regiment at a time. As noted in the subsection on supply, given the size of China's merchant fleet, the Chinese government could easily have requisitioned significant numbers of civilian cargo ships to help transport PLA Army forces, but the process of doing so would likely have been slower than if the ships were PLA-owned assets to begin with. As also noted in the subsection on supply, China had more than five hundred civilian transport aircraft in 2000, although the vast majority of them were undoubtedly configured for passenger transport and thus would have been useful mainly for transporting personnel, not supplies or equipment.[25]

An amphibious assault would have been particularly challenging for the PLA's transport capabilities. The PLA Navy's landing ships were collectively capable of carrying less than one partly mechanized division at a time and the PLA Air Force had the capacity to airdrop one airborne regiment at a time. In comparison, Taiwan's military in 2000 comprised the equivalent of about fifteen divisions. Even though only a portion of Taiwan's forces would have been close to any given landing site, and the redeployment of additional Taiwanese forces to the landing site(s) could have been hampered by air and missile strikes, the Chinese landing ships would have required at least two days for each round trip (including transit and loading and unloading times), and the transport aircraft would likely have been able to conduct at most one airlift each day. Thus, it would have taken the PLA over a week, with minimal losses in transit, to build up even a localized preponderance of force on Taiwan. During this time, moreover, assets used to bring additional forces to Taiwan would not have been available for delivering supplies to them.[26]

Engineering

Very little information is publicly available about the engineering capabilities of PLA logistics forces in 2000. At a minimum, however, the PLA was said to lack port-opening and airfield-opening packages as well as construction engineers to build the land-based transportation infrastructure that would have been required to support combat operations outside of China.[27]

Health Services

Each military region in 2000 contained multiple PLA hospitals, and personnel from PLA hospitals were reported to frequently deploy to the field for training exercises. Portable modular field hospitals and air-droppable medical support packages were also being developed. In the event of a contingency, field service centers would have been established to provide medical support to the engaged units. In addition, the PLA Navy operated two small (twenty-four-hundred-ton) hospital ships. Otherwise little information is publicly available about the medical and health service capabilities of the PLA in 2000.[28]

CHINESE MILITARY LOGISTICS CAPABILITIES IN 2010

The PLA made a wide range of efforts to improve its logistics capabilities between 2000 and 2010. Indeed, according to one observer, by 2010 logistics modernization was the highest priority it had been in at least thirty years.[29] One major initiative was the establishment of joint logistics departments in each military region in 2000. Before 2000, the three services and the Second Artillery had each managed their logistics separately. The creation of joint logistics departments eliminated duplicate logistics facilities and services and simplified and rationalized the logistics system. The result was increased efficiency, higher standards in the materials and services provided, an increase in the responsiveness of logistics support, and significant economic savings through a reduction in transportation mileage and the consolidation of rear area warehouses. In 2004 this approach was taken one step further in the Jinan Military Region by completely eliminating the PLA Navy, PLA Air Force, and Second Artillery logistics organizations within the region and giving the region's Joint Logistics Department responsibility for all logistics activities in the region.[30]

Another major initiative within the PLA's logistics system in the period 2000 to 2010 was the outsourcing of many services, such as transportation and food preparation, formerly performed by military personnel. Procedures were also formally put in place for the PLA to be able to employ civilian transportation assets and facilities, such as railway platforms and shipping wharves, in the event of a crisis. As a result, although the PLA would still have been dependent on civilian personnel, material, and transportation assets to support any extended operation inside or outside China, the speed and ease with which it could have employed those capabilities had improved.[31]

For the PLA Navy, a major change to its logistics system occurred in 2003, when its ten or so bases were removed from the operational chain of command and made responsible solely for logistical functions, including provisioning, repair and maintenance, medical care, and support of technical systems on naval units afloat and ashore. At the same time, the logistics departments of the three PLA Navy fleets (North Sea Fleet, East Sea Fleet, and South Sea Fleet), which had previously overseen these activities, were eliminated, thus keeping the total organizational height of the PLA Navy's logistics system unchanged. In addition, in 2004 the PLA Navy created separate combat support vessel flotillas to improve the efficiency of logistics provision at sea, and shore-based organizations began training together with vessels in logistics provision.[32]

Other measures to improve the performance of the PLA's logistic system that were implemented between 2000 and 2010 included improved communications systems; the application of bar codes, scanners, and computer tracking and management systems; and the production of mobile medical facilities and mobile repair vans and shelters equipped with spare parts and heavy machinery. A variety of other personnel, organizational, training, and procedural improvements were made as well.[33]

All these changes undoubtedly resulted in a more efficient and responsive logistics system for the PLA. In the words of one observer, the PLA's logistics moved "steadily" toward a higher degree of support capacity over the period from 2000 to 2010.[34] Logistics improvement was still secondary to other PLA priorities, however, such as the purchase of advanced arms and equipment. These advanced arms and equipment, moreover, often had greater logistics requirements than what they replaced. Funding for logistics reform was insufficient and logistics reforms were not quickly disseminating throughout the armed forces, as the PLA leadership apparently lacked either the will or the ability to mandate rapid change. Overall, the rate at which China's military logistics system was modernized between 2000 and 2010 did not appear to reflect a high level of urgency.[35]

Of the specific shortcomings that remained in China's logistics system, one was the lack of a corps of professional logisticians sufficient to support an organization the size of the PLA, and the best and brightest personnel were said to not go to logistics units. Another weakness was low levels at which information technology such as optical storage cards, bar codes, and radio frequency tags for tracking materials were actually being implemented. Inventory visibility and management, standardization, tracking of materials and equipment throughout the distribution process, and information management in general were regarded as weaknesses within the PLA as well as in China's commercial logistics structure.[36]

Another shortcoming was the excessive number of organizational levels within the logistics chain of command, which delayed support to end users. This problem was further complicated by the organizational separation between the GAD and GLD chains of command. The GAD was responsible for the provision of weapon systems and ammunition as well as their maintenance and repair. Meanwhile, the GLD was responsible for the delivery of all other supplies and services such as fuel, food, clothing, transportation, and health services. How these two separate organizations would have coordinated and prioritized their respective demands on transportation assets and infrastructure in a major military contingency is unclear. In addition, further logistics challenges would have been created by the many disparate models of equipment in the force. The PLA Army, for example, operated at least five different models each of tanks, armored infantry carriers, and artillery pieces, and the PLA Navy operated five different classes of submarine, nine different classes of destroyers, and nine different classes of frigates.[37]

Another major problem faced by the PLA's logistics system in 2010 was high levels of corruption. Involvement in the procurement and delivery of supplies and transportation services offered extensive opportunities for what PLA journals politely refer to as "rent seeking" (寻租), a temptation that was probably not lessened by the growing practice of contracting with commercial providers for services. The result was, in the words of one analyst, "a persistent tradition of abuse of military logistics for personal gain."[38] Indeed, in January 2012, a deputy director of the GLD was detained, reportedly on suspicion that he had received hundreds of millions of yuan in cash and gifts.[39]

The massive earthquake in Sichuan in May 2008 exposed many of the shortcomings of the logistics capabilities of the PLA, which was called on to provide emergency relief to the stricken areas. As one example, the PLA set up a number of command posts, each with its own zone of responsibility, to oversee relief efforts. These command posts, however, lacked the equipment needed to effectively coordinate their operations. In particular, the destruction of terrestrial communications networks forced units to rely on satellite communications capabilities, which were unavailable in the required quantities. The earthquake also demonstrated the PLA's shortfalls in large transport aircraft capable of landing at small, unimproved airfields and in heavy-lift helicopters capable of transporting construction equipment. After the earthquake, the Chengdu Military Region, in whose area of responsibility the earthquake and relief efforts had occurred, assessed that the PLA logistics system needed better information, decision making, planning, organization, coordination, and control, particularly for units on the move.[40]

A test of the PLA Navy's logistics capabilities occurred beginning in December 2008, when it began deploying three-ship task groups off of the coast of Somalia in the Gulf of Aden to conduct antipiracy patrols. Each task group consisted of two combat ships and one underway replenishment ship and lasted for an average of four months. China had no naval bases outside of its own territory, but was able to quickly put in place arrangements for food, fresh water, fuel, and spare parts to be provided for the ships on patrol. The size of this deployment was small, and the PLA Navy experienced challenges in keeping its ships supplied and in helicopter maintenance. Nonetheless, by 2014 it had been able to maintain a continuous naval presence several thousand miles from the nearest Chinese port for more than five years. The Gulf of Aden deployments, therefore, along with naval exercises in the late 2000s, indicated that significant progress had been made in naval logistics capabilities, and Western analysts assessed the PLA Navy to be generally capable of supporting its operating forces.[41]

Overall, however, the net improvement in China's logistics capabilities since 2000 appears to have been limited. One analyst described PLA logistical systems as having been "somewhat" modernized, logistical processes as having been "somewhat" rationalized, and the PLA to have "gradually" improved its ability to support operations in the field and missions of increasing complexity and ambition. Consequently, the PLA's logistics modernization program remained "a work in progress ... still lacking effective application to the operational level."[42] Overall, PLA logistics remained an area of weakness that continued to confront significant challenges in all areas, and one that lagged well behind the capabilities of other militaries. Support for mobile operations was an area of particular weakness, and, in a contingency, forward and deployed units would still have been dependent on "emergency support units" that had been formed on an ad hoc basis. China's ability to apply military power beyond its borders would have been particularly limited.[43]

Supply

The PLA's supply system in 2010 was still primarily based on stockpiling materials at fixed depots of various levels, rather than on delivering supplies directly to units in the field on an as-needed basis. In the Xinjiang Military District, for example, the first time repair parts were delivered directly from a factory to distribution centers within the district, rather than to a central warehouse, was in 2009. Numerous supply depots were located throughout China. Two national-level strategic logistics bases under the control of the GLD were still maintained, one in Wuhan and the other in the Qinghai-Tibet area. In addition, each of the seven military regions had two to six logistics subdepartments, each of which controlled multiple storage depots. Finally, each military district also oversaw logistics depots and bases. As a result, the majority of PLA units were based within a few tens of miles of a warehouse or other material facility.[44]

No information is publicly available about the actual quantities of the PLA's stocks of fuel, ammunition, spare parts, equipment, blood, and other key military supplies in 2010. In the event of significant combat operations, however, the PLA's primary supply challenge initially would have been moving supplies from their storage locations to the units conducting operations. Depending on how substantial initial stocks were, however, if the conflict was protracted, then the challenge would have been the ability of PLA and civilian defense industry factories to produce additional materials and deliver them either to supply depots of various levels or directly to operational units.

A variety of new supply equipment, including trucks, fuel tankers, and material handling equipment such as containers, pallets, forklifts, and cranes, had been issued to units since 2000. Information on the actual quantities of such equipment acquired is not publicly available, and thus it is difficult to assess the net improvement in the PLA's supply capabilities. That plans still involved the creation of emergency support units in a contingency, however, suggests that the organic supply-provision capabilities of individual units were still not sufficient to support high-intensity combat operations.[45]

If the organic transportation capabilities of the PLA as a whole had been insufficient to keep units supplied in a contingency, civilian transportation assets would have been used to supplement them. This was codified in a national mobilization law passed in 2003 and there were military representative offices at important civilian transportation facilities throughout China to oversee PLA use of civilian transportation assets in an emergency. Again, however, the PLA did not appear to exercise such operations in peacetime, suggesting that an attempt conduct them in a contingency could have been highly chaotic.[46]

China's national transportation infrastructure had undergone a significant expansion between 2000 and 2010, although it still significantly lagged that of the United States. The total length of China's highway system was about 60 percent of that of the United States; the total length of China's railways was about half that of those of the United States; the total length of China's petroleum pipelines was about a quarter of those of the United States; and there were about a third as many commercial airports in China as in the United States. Thus, in the event of a major conflict, particularly one across or near China's land borders, China's transportation infrastructure might still have inhibited the PLA's ability to keep combat units supplied.[47]

As in 2000, combat operations at sea within a few hundred miles of China's coast in 2010 would have presented relatively few supply challenges for the PLA. Ships would have been able to put into port for supplies and then return to the area of combat operations within a day or two, and aircraft would have been able to reach their targets without needing to be refueled en route. Also as in 2000, however, if a conflict had occurred farther out at sea, the PLA would have had difficulty sustaining naval and air forces in the area of combat operations. The PLA Navy's surface ships had adjusted the types and amount of food and water carried on board and developed plans for how to receive supplies if their port facilities were destroyed, and China's subsequent experience conducting patrols off of the coast of Somalia undoubtedly increased the PLA's capability to keep distant naval forces supplied. The number of underway replenishment ships in the PLA Navy, moreover, had increased from three in 2000 to five in 2010, and in 2009 the PLA Navy had demonstrated the ability to conduct certain replenishment-at-sea operations using civilian cargo ships, when two tons of vegetables were transferred from a ship operated by a Chinese shipping company to ships patrolling off of Somalia. The Somalia patrols were small-scale, however, involving only two combat ships at a time, and nonetheless experienced problems in areas such as preserving foodstuffs and other consumables. More generally, the PLA Navy's five underway replenishment ships for its nearly eighty major surface warships were still few in number compared to the U.S. Navy, which had more than six times as many underway replenishment ships for fewer than twice as major surface warships. Indeed, one of the conclusions PLA analysts drew from the Somalia patrols was the need for new and additional underway replenishment ships. The PLA's capability to sustain long-range air patrols, moreover, had not improved since 2000, because it still only operated a dozen or so aerial refueling aircraft, as compared to the nearly five hundred operated by the U.S. Air Force in 2010.[48]

If the PLA had deployed significant ground forces across water for combat operations, keeping those forces supplied would have entailed additional challenges. The freight handling capacity of China's major coastal ports, already extensive in 2000, had quadrupled since then, to an average of fifteen million tons of freight loaded and unloaded each day (the top fifty U.S. ports handled about six million tons of freight a day in 2010), and China's merchant fleet continued to be one of the largest in the world, with more than eleven hundred ships that displaced one thousand tons or more. The organic cargo transport capabilities of the PLA Navy, however, which had been modest in 2000, had actually diminished by 2010, to twenty-some mostly small and aging cargo ships with a total displacement of about sixty thousand tons and a total cargo capacity of perhaps ten thousand to twelve thousand tons. For an overseas deployment of any scale, therefore, the PLA would have had to supplement the Navy's organic cargo capabilities by requisitioning civilian cargo ships.[49]

Transferring supplies from standard military or civilian cargo ships to land would have required access to usable port facilities in the territory where combat operations were being conducted, and, in the case of an amphibious invasion, such facilities might not have been available, at least initially. As in 2000, in the absence of such facilities, smaller boats and helicopters could hypothetically have been used to bring supplies to shore from larger ships, but this would have been a highly inefficient and difficult-to-organize operation. The PLA Navy's amphibious landing fleet had increased to nearly ninety ships with a total transport capacity of about thirty thousand tons that theoretically could have been used for unloading supplies directly onto beaches, but in an invasion of any scale those ships would still have been in high demand for bringing reinforcements for the initially landed forces and would have been a priority target for the defenders. Meanwhile, the air transport capabilities of the PLA had actually fallen since 2000, as aircraft based on the 1950s-era Antonov-12 and Antonov-24 designs became too old to operate any longer and only a handful of new aircraft were acquired. As a result, the PLA's air transport capabilities in 2010 had diminished to 120 or so medium and large cargo aircraft capable of carrying total about twenty-two hundred tons of cargo. Assuming that all of these aircraft were available and dedicated to supply operations, that none were shot down, and that each was able to make one round trip per day, they would have been able to convey enough supplies to support less than two divisions in heavy combat operations.[50]

Repair and Maintenance

Since 2000 the PLA had been making efforts to improve the organic repair and maintenance capabilities of its units. Spare parts services were being centralized; PLA Army armaments personnel were teaching other soldiers proper techniques for the daily maintenance and operation of weapons and equipment; and a large assortment of new mobile repair vans had been issued to units. In the PLA Navy, ship and equipment maintenance had become high priorities, with shore-based organizations regularly training together with vessels on how to perform maintenance. Naval aviation field stations were transitioning from only being capable of supporting a single type of aircraft at their home stations to being capable of supporting operations for multiple types of aircraft both at home and at other airfields. Similarly, the PLA Air Force had been reorganizing its maintenance groups so that they could support multiple types of aircraft deploying into their home airfield or could send small teams (by rail, road, or air) to support aircraft from their home airfield that deployed to another airfield. Naval aviation and the PLA Air

Force were also practicing in the rapid repair of aircraft and other equipment that would be required following an enemy attack.[51]

Each of the logistics subdepartments and each military district within the military regions operated multiple repair depots, and each group army had armaments support units attached to it. Information on the repair and maintenance capabilities of units below the group army level is scarce, but they do not appear to have had significant organic repair capabilities. Instead, in a contingency, ad hoc field repair centers would have been created for each division, brigade, and regiment involved in operations. One of the goals of the PLA's logistics improvement efforts was to acquire the capability to repair equipment in the field, instead of having to bring it to rear area depots for repair. It appears, however, that any progress made toward this goal was marginal, and the PLA continued to be dependent on centralized repair facilities. Indeed, the increasingly sophisticated nature of the weaponry operated by the PLA seems to have made units less able, rather than more able, to repair equipment on site. PLA Air Force bases, for example, were able to conduct intermediate and overhaul maintenance on older aircraft designs, such as the J-7 (based on the MiG-21), but not on its newer designs, such as the J-8 and fourth-generation J-10, which had to be returned to the factory that produced them for overhaul. In the case of aircraft based on the Russian Su-27, including the Su-27, Su-30 and J-11, special facilities had been created in Dalian and Wuhu to conduct intermediate-level maintenance.[52]

The ability of the PLA to keep equipment serviceable when deployed away from its home base, moreover, was questionable. Although air force and naval aviation field stations were supposed to be able to support visiting aircraft and helicopters, for example, they could do so only for short periods. Similarly, the Somalia counterpiracy patrols revealed the PLA Navy's weakness in keeping its helicopters in working order at sea. For forces operating outside of China's borders, China's lack of overseas bases or other facilities at which routine maintenance and repairs could have been performed would have been an additional limitation on the PLA's ability to sustain its forces abroad.[53]

Mobility

The organic transport capabilities of the PLA do not appear to have increased dramatically from 2000 to 2010. For example, a "large assortment" of new trucks was said to have been issued to PLA Army units, and each PLA division was said to have been assigned an organic transportation regiment that included large cargo trucks, fuel tankers, and heavy equipment transport trailers for carrying tracked vehicles. However, there is little information available on exactly how much equipment was assigned to each unit. What information is available, moreover, suggests that the PLA Army continued to suffer from significant limitations in organic transport capabilities. In 2009, for example, the organic transport capability of an armored regiment (containing roughly twelve hundred soldiers and more than one hundred armored vehicles) in the Xinjiang Military District consisted of two trucks. In comparison, in the U.S. Army, a Heavy Brigade Combat Team (a unit roughly three times the size of a Chinese armored regiment), has more than two hundred medium and heavy cargo trucks and more than four hundred light utility trucks. Similarly, after the May 2008 Sichuan earthquake, the logistics department of the entire Chengdu Military Region, in which were based four full divisions and nine independent brigades not including border defense and reserve units, was able to spare a total of only three hundred vehicles for the rescue and recovery effort.[54]

As noted in the subsection on supply, the PLA Navy's organic sealift capabilities had also not dramatically increased since 2000, consisting in 2010 of about twenty cargo ships with a cargo capacity of perhaps ten thousand to twelve thousand tons and about ninety landing ships with a total transport capacity of about thirty thousand tons. Collectively these ships could have carried the equipment and personnel of one armored division or somewhat more than two infantry divisions at a time. PLA Navy and Air Force transport aircraft, whose total transport capacity had actually fallen since 2010, could have carried the equipment and personnel of about one infantry regiment at a time.[55]

Large-scale force deployments, therefore, either within China or abroad, would have required the mobilization of civilian transportation assets. Overland movements would have been primarily dependent on rail and road. Emergency logistics militia units existed throughout the country that could perform vehicle and ship transport, and, as noted earlier in this section, there were military representative offices at important civilian transportation facilities throughout China to oversee PLA requisitioning and operation of civilian transportation assets in an emergency. These were put to use in the 2008 Sichuan earthquake, when, although the Chengdu Military Region was only able to provide three hundred of its own vehicles, it was able to requisition more than twelve thousand civilian cars and trucks. Similarly, when the Chinese government decided to evacuate its citizens from Libya in the midst of domestic unrest there in 2011, although military aircraft participated in the evacuation operations, more than 90 percent of the evacuation flights were conducted by civilian aircraft (Chinese and foreign-owned) and all seventeen ships used to conduct evacuation operations were chartered commercial ships (though the Chinese frigate *Xuzhou*, redeployed from the waters off of Somalia, was present for protective purposes). These civilian assets were mobilized quickly, moreover, with the first chartered flight for Libya taking off just one day after the decision to evacuate was made.[56]

There were sixteen million civilian trucks as well as six hundred thousand freight railcars in China in 2010, so there was ample vehicle capacity in China for virtually any size force movement. Mustering these vehicles would have taken a certain amount of time, however, and, as noted earlier, was not exercised on regular basis, although the response to the 2008 Sichuan earthquake may have provided valuable experience in this regard. As noted in the section on supply, moreover, the areas of China near most its land borders still had relatively weak transportation infrastructure and rugged or mountainous terrain. If a contingency had required the deployment of significant forces into these regions, therefore, the infrastructure and terrain could have substantially constrained the rate of deployment. In the case of deployments across water, since there were more than eleven hundred civilian ships of one thousand tons or more registered in China, the Chinese government could easily have requisitioned sufficient numbers to transport a force of virtually any size although, again, it would undoubtedly have taken a certain amount of time to collect and prepare the needed ships. Once the deployment began, moreover, a more significant limiting factor would have been the offload capacity of the ports at which the forces were disembarked. China also had sixteen hundred civilian transport aircraft in 2010, although, as in 2000, the majority of them were undoubtedly configured for passenger transport and thus would have been useful mainly for transporting personnel rather than supplies or equipment.[57]

Although the PLA's amphibious fleet had expanded significantly since 2000, an amphibious invasion would still have been challenging for the PLA's transport capabilities. The PLA Navy's landing ships in 2010 were collectively capable of carrying about one full infantry division plus one armored regiment (or else three armored regiments without any division-level assets) at a time, while the PLA Air Force had the capacity to airdrop about one airborne regiment at a time. The actual operational capability of China's airborne troops, however, was apparently questionable. Out of sixty-five hundred paratroopers deployed to Sichuan in response to the May 2008 earthquake, poor weather conditions prevented all but fifteen from actually parachuting into the disaster zone. Although Taiwan's military had been downsized considerably since 2000, its army still comprised the equivalent of about thirteen divisions. Thus, it would have taken the PLA multiple return trips with minimal losses on each trip to deliver enough units to reach numerical parity with Taiwan's armed forces.[58]

Engineering

Relatively little information is publicly available about the engineering capabilities of PLA logistics forces in 2010. It is known that there were emergency logistics militia units throughout the country capable of performing road, railroad, and bridge repair. In addition, both the PLA Navy's aviation forces and the PLA Air Force regularly practiced rapidly repairing facilities and runways following an enemy attack. A significant weakness revealed by the 2008 Sichuan earthquake, on the other hand, was the lack of heavy-lift helicopters capable of moving large equipment items like bulldozers or removing large pieces of debris from collapsed buildings.[59]

Health Services

Little information is publicly available about the health services capabilities of PLA logistics forces in 2010. What is known is that each logistics subdepartment within a military region oversaw multiple hospitals, so that the vast majority of units in peacetime were within a few tens of miles of a hospital, and that each regiment and brigade had its own medical team. There were also mobile medical facilities along with emergency logistics militia units throughout the country capable of performing medical support. In addition, with the construction of a new, purpose-built twenty-six thousand ton hospital ship, as well as five small supporting hospital ships, the PLA Navy had substantially increased its capabilities to provide health services at sea, to deployed forces, and to disaster-stricken islands. Little other information is publicly available about the actual medical and health service capabilities of the PLA in 2010.[60]

CHINESE MILITARY LOGISTICS CAPABILITIES IN 2020

The reforms to China's defense logistics system since 2000 have been significant. The PLA is applying approaches and technologies similar to those used by the U.S. and other advanced militaries, and the establishment of a joint logistics system provides a basis for further improvements in efficiency and responsiveness. The PLA's experiences with the Sichuan earthquake relief, Somalia counterpiracy patrols, and Libya evacuation, moreover, have given it real-world opportunities to exercise its logistics capabilities while at the same time helping it identify important shortfalls. Meanwhile, Chinese military and civilian logistics researchers and military units are continuing to research, develop, and test new logistics capabilities and techniques. All of these activities are providing a foundation for the future development of the PLA's logistics capabilities.[61]

Nonetheless, the amount of progress made in this area between 2000 and 2010 appears to have been modest. The PLA in 2010 was still dependent on fixed depots for supplies, a system that, although satisfactory for static, positional defense, is not well suited for mobile, offensive, operations. China's transportation infrastructure was probably adequate to support most military operations within and near its borders, but the PLA's organic transportation capabilities had not markedly increased between 2000 and 2010. As a result, in the event of a conflict of any scale, the PLA would have been dependent on requisitioned civilian transportation assets and other ad hoc arrangements to keep its forces supplied. The lack of regular training and practice in performing military support operations on the part of civilian transportation providers, and the lack of long-term relationships between PLA logistics units and the combat forces they would have supported (because the logistics units would only be created in a contingency), would have made these operations inefficient and vulnerable to disruption. In addition, although efforts had been made to improve the organic repair and maintenance capabilities of units, the increasing complexity and sophistication of the weaponry operated by the PLA meant there was probably little net improvement in the ability of units to keep their equipment in working order. In a conflict of any duration, this would have meant a steadily diminishing proportion of weapons and equipment that were operationally functional.

Many military transport vehicles, such as trucks and transport ships, are relatively inexpensive and quickly built. Chinese shipyards, for example, delivered thirty new amphibious landing ships between 2003 and 2005.[62] Significantly increasing its organic transportation capabilities by 2020, therefore, is certainly physically and financially feasible for the PLA. Doing so, however, would require both a commitment to do so and an expansion of the PLA's logistic organization, neither of which is in evidence at present. The organizational changes required to implement a truly modern, responsive logistic system, moreover, like the Velocity Management system employed by the U.S. Army, would be even more disruptive.[63]

In the absence of such fundamental reforms, which in any case would take several years to implement, improvements in the PLA's logistics capabilities from 2010 to 2020 are likely to follow the pattern exhibited between 2000 and 2010. The PLA's supply system in 2020 will likely remain fundamentally based on fixed depots, although perhaps with incremental improvements in responsiveness and, in a contingency, supplemented by the ability to deliver some fuel, ammunition, food, and spare parts from factories and central warehouses directly to the units needing them. The organic transport capabilities of the PLA Army will likely increase, but keeping large-scale operations supplied will still require the mobilization of civilian transportation assets. The PLA Navy has not acquired any new cargo ships since the 1990s and therefore seems unlikely to have dramatically increased its cargo fleet by 2020. The ability of the PLA Air Force to transport supplies will also probably not dramatically increase by 2020. Total air transport capacity actually fell between 2000 and 2010, and production of the new turboprop Y-9 medium airlifter will be counterbalanced by the aging out of existing Y-8 transports (on which the Y-9 design is based). And, although the PLA has for several years expressed interest in acquiring additional Il-76 jet transports from Russia, it has not pursued this prospect vigorously, probably because China has been developing a comparable aircraft, the Y-20. The Y-20 is targeted for entry into service as early as 2017, but development delays are common in aircraft programs. It therefore seems unlikely that the PLA will have acquired significant numbers of additional jet transports by 2020. As a result of these limitations, keeping units supplied when deployed across water will continue to be dependent on the use of commercial shipping and aviation assets.[64]

The ability of the PLA Navy to keep ships at sea supplied while conducting operations far from China's shores will likely increase through the acquisition of additional underway replenishment ships and regularized access to foreign ports, although it is unlikely that China will have any formal overseas naval bases by 2020. Indeed, as of 2013, two additional underway replenishment ships had already been added to the fleet and one Western analyst had estimated that the PLA Navy will have a total eight underway replenishment ships by 2020. This expansion of naval supply capabilities will still not be enough for the PLA to be able to sustain large-scale naval operations outside of East Asia for a protracted period, however. The PLA has not increased the number of aerial refueling aircraft it operates over the past decade and probably will not do so until an aerial refueling aircraft based on a Chinese-built transport such as the Y-20 or perhaps the commercial C919 airliner has been developed. Given that it seems unlikely that China will acquire overseas air bases between now and 2020, air operations farther from China than the unrefueled combat radius of land-based aircraft, therefore, would require a third country to grant China temporary basing rights or else will be limited to the number that can be sustained by the PLA's small current fleet of aerial refueling aircraft along with aircraft carried by however many aircraft carriers the PLA Navy operates in 2020.[65]

The ability of PLA units to keep weapons and equipment operational, particularly when deployed away from their home bases, will also remain modest. Improvements in organic repair and maintenance capabilities will be counterbalanced by increased technical difficulty, as the PLA's relatively simple 1950s-era designs are replaced by sophisticated modern systems. As a result, the PLA will have difficulty sustaining protracted high-tempo operations, particularly when they entail the deployment of substantial forces away from their home bases.

Large-scale force movements, whether within China or outside its borders, will continue to require the requisitioning of civilian transportation assets. Amphibious invasions will remain particularly challenging. The PLA Army's amphibious forces currently consist of two mechanized infantry divisions and one armored brigade. The PLA Navy's amphibious fleet would have to roughly double in capacity to be able to transport the approximately sixty-five thousand tons that these forces weigh. Although the number of amphibious landing ships completed between 2003 and 2005 demonstrates that China's shipyards certainly have the capacity to build the required ships, the PLA Navy would also have to provide them with crews and then train the crews in conducting operations at this substantially enlarged scale if it were to have an effective capability to concurrently land both of its mechanized infantry divisions and the armored brigade. Since the PLA's airlift capability is unlikely to significantly increase between 2010 and 2020, moreover, the maximum size of any airborne operation will remain at about one regiment.[66]

In sum, although the PLA's capability to sustain and project combat forces will undoubtedly improve by 2020, logistics will remain a significant weakness. In the event of a large-scale contingency, the PLA would likely experience difficulty keeping its forces supplied if they were deployed at a significant distance from their bases, and that supply would be vulnerable to disruption and interdiction. The proportion of weapons and other equipment that were operable would diminish over time, as units would be unable to keep them in working order and they would have to be returned to rear area depots for repair and overhaul. Major force movements could be delayed by the need to mobilize civilian transportation assets including trucks, trains, ships, and aircraft, and, since the civilian operators of those assets would not have trained in operating while under threat of attack, would be vulnerable to interdiction. The maximum size force that could conduct an amphibious landing at one time in 2020 will probably be less than two divisions, and the PLA will be able to sustain only small amounts of force for extended periods outside of the East Asian region.

8

Organizational Culture

The importance of organizational culture to organizational performance has become widely recognized in recent years, and this relationship unquestionably applies to military organizations as much as to any other type of organization.[1] Theorists on organizational culture conceive of it as a multilayered phenomenon. At the surface level it is exhibited in observable behaviors and physical artifacts (such as the layout of an organization's facilities or how they are decorated). Underlying these observable behaviors and artifacts are norms and values that are shared by members of the organization. Underlying these norms and values, in turn, are a set of assumptions that are also shared by members of the organization but are often not consciously recognized.[2]

There is no universally recognized set of cultural characteristics that have been identified as key to organizational success. Indeed, which characteristics are most important depends on the specific circumstances of the organization – that is, its goals, the environment in which it operates, and so on.[3] Two widely used methodologies, however, one developed by Cameron and Quinn and one developed by Denison,[4] focus on the norms-and-values level of culture. Both methodologies group values that have been identified as associated with organizational effectiveness into four clusters. The four clusters represent the degree to which the organizational culture is internally focused or externally focused and the degree to which it emphasizes stability and control or flexibility and discretion.[5]

Although there are slight differences, the four clusters of values used by the two methodologies are largely similar to each other. One cluster consists of values associated with participation and collaboration in the organization. These include the importance of teamwork, of the welfare of individuals within the organization, of developing the capabilities of individuals within the organization, of the organization's mission, of involving all members of the organization to some degree in generating new ideas and making decisions, and of loyalty to the organization.[6] A second cluster of values consists of those associated with consistency and predictability. These include the importance of following established rules and procedures, of efficiency, of coordinating activities within the organization, of smooth operations, and of reliability and dependability.[7] A third cluster consists of values associated with mission accomplishment. These include the importance of producing results, of improving the capabilities of the organization, of having clear goals and objectives, of having a shared understanding of the function and purpose of the organization, and of having a vision of the future toward which the organization is advancing.[8] The fourth cluster consists of values associated with adaptability and innovativeness. These include the importance of creativity, of entrepreneurship, of flexibility, of taking chances, and of anticipating future challenges.[9]

Note that many of these values are in tension with each other. For example, values associated with adaptability and innovativeness may conflict with values associated with consistency and predictability, and values associated with participation and collaboration might conflict with values associated with mission accomplishment. Nonetheless, both methodologies assume that all organizational cultures contain values from all four clusters and that cultures differ from each other primarily in the relative importance they accord to the different clusters.

ASSESSING THE ORGANIZATIONAL CULTURE OF MILITARY ORGANIZATIONS

Both the Cameron and Quinn methodology and the Denison methodology postulate that organizational effectiveness is a function of the difference between the relative importance an organization's culture *actually* accords to each value cluster, and the relative importance the organization's culture *should* accord to each value cluster. However, organizational theorists have not developed a general theory about what relative importance different types of organization should ideally assign to different values. Lacking such a standard, the two methodologies apply two different approaches to identifying the preferred distribution of values for an organization. In the Cameron and Quinn methodology, this approach consists of simply asking the members of the organization to identify the relative importance they think their organization *ought* to assign to each of the four groups of values, and then asking them what relative importance their organization *actually* gives to each group of values. In the Denison methodology, it consists of asking the organization's members what relative importance their organization actually gives to each group of values, then comparing that to the average strength assigned to each value cluster by other organizations within the subject organization's field (e.g., other "global technology firms").

Neither of these two approaches appears to be feasible for analyzing the culture of the PLA. Although the two methodologies have been applied to a wide variety of organizations, including military organizations,[10] they were primarily designed for businesses. Not all of the values they measure apply to military organizations, and, conversely, there may be values that are uniquely important for military organizations that are not captured by these methodologies. In addition, it is unlikely that a representative sample of PLA members could be found that would be willing and allowed to give an accurate description of the PLA's organizational culture. As a result, a new culture assessment methodology was developed, modeled on the Cameron and Quinn and Denison approaches but adapted for the specific case of military organizations in which directly polling the organization members is not feasible.

Military-Specific Values

The methodology employed here emulates the Cameron and Quinn and Denison methodologies in focusing on the values-and-norms level of culture, but differs from it in using a set of values that are believed to be important specifically to military organizations. These values were identified by analyzing the official publications of military organizations themselves, as well as the writings of informed observers and commentators on military culture and ethos.

The three primary services of the U.S. military as well as some foreign militaries have, at various times in recent years, issued official statements of their "core values" along with other documents, such as "creeds" and "ethoses" for the services and their members, that explicitly or implicitly identify specific values that should be held by these organizations and the individuals who make them up. Regardless of whether the organizational cultures of these services and militaries are actually consistent with their espoused values, these documents presumably reflect the values that their leaderships believe are important to the success of their organizations.

Each U.S. service espouses a somewhat different set of values, and the values espoused by foreign militaries differ both from each other and from those of the U.S. military. The rationales underlying the specific values that are espoused, moreover, are often unclear and in some cases appear to be partly whimsical (e.g., the U.S. Army's "Army Values" were apparently chosen so that they spell out the acronym "LDRSHIP," raising questions about whether all of the values embodied in that acronym are truly important as well as whether important values might have been omitted because of not fitting the acronym).[11] Nonetheless, analysis of the espoused values of different services and militaries reveals several that are common to most of the U.S. services as well as several other Western militaries. These are the following:

- *Moral integrity.* Although different terms are used to refer to it – "integrity," "honor," "character," etc. – all three U.S. services as well as all of the foreign militaries examined emphasize the importance of the moral integrity of their members, meaning that their members must behave in ways that are legally, ethically, and morally acceptable, not just while "on the job," but in their personal lives as well.[12] The reason why moral integrity is so important to militaries is probably because of the unique nature of military organizations. Societies provide the members of military organizations with weaponry far more powerful and dangerous than ordinary citizens have access to. To prevent the individual or collective abuse of this power, societies expect that the people entrusted with those weapons to be of higher moral character than the average person. In addition, the core function of a military, killing people, is morally challenging for the individual who may be called upon to do so and may not be universally regarded as morally acceptable by the society within which he or she lives. Holding military service members to a high moral standard in all other areas of behavior may help compensate for a perceived moral deficiency in this one area, and motivate capable people, who might otherwise be deterred by a perceived immorality of the profession, both to join a military and to willingly perform its core function when asked to.
- *Discipline.* All three of the U.S. services as well as most of the foreign militaries and services examined for this study identify discipline as an important value.[13] Discipline is related to moral integrity in that it includes following laws and regulations, but it also represents the capability to follow laws and regulations and perform job functions under the extreme physical and psychological duress that combat can impose. Discipline also entails maintaining individual skills and physical fitness, as well as resisting appetites and temptations that might undermine them or the individual's moral integrity.
- *Responsibility.* All of the U.S. services and most of the foreign militaries and services examined for this study state the importance of their members performing all actions that are expected of them (often referred to by the term "duty") as well as being accountable for any failures that

occur under their purview.[14] Responsibility is particularly important to military organizations because, unlike in other organizations, in a military organization failure to behave responsibly can result not merely in delays, inefficiency, or loss of revenue, but death of members of the organization and even, potentially, defeat of the nation they are charged with protecting.

- *Loyalty.* Most U.S. services as well as most foreign militaries and services explicitly specify the importance of loyalty.[15] This generally includes both loyalty to the nation as a whole and loyalty to the service and its other members. The importance of loyalty to the nation as a whole is obvious – only organizations that pledge loyalty to the nation are likely to be entrusted with the most powerful weaponry in the nation. Loyalty to other members of the military, service, or other suborganization is also important, however, as it can be an additional and less-abstract motivatation for the individual sacrifices, including the ultimate sacrifice, that are sometimes required for the survival of a unit or the success of a military operation.

- *Self-sacrifice.* All three U.S. services call on their members to put the interests of others – other members of the service, the service as a whole, and the nation as a whole – before their own.[16] Similarly, the Canadian, British, and Australian militaries call for "unlimited liability" or "selfless commitment."[17] In addition, the "Warrior Ethos" of the U.S. Army's "Soldier's Creed" states that "I will never leave a fallen comrade" while the U.S. Air Force's "Airman's Creed" states that "I will never leave an Airman behind."[18] These promises make clear that, for members of these armed forces, self-sacrifice includes putting their own lives at risk for the sake of others.

- *Patriotism.* All three U.S. services as well as some foreign militaries state that they expect their members not only to behave in a morally upright way, but to do so at least in part because they believe in the nation whose interests they are defending (or, in the case of the United States, to principles that are proxies for the nation itself). The U.S. Army's "Soldier's Creed," for example, states "I am a guardian of freedom and the American way of life," and its "Army Values" define loyalty as including bearing "true faith and allegiance to the U.S. Constitution."[19] Similarly, the U.S. Navy's "Navy Ethos" states simply, "We are patriots," and the U.S. Air Force's "Airman's Creed" states "I am ... guardian of Freedom and Justice."[20] Of the espoused values of foreign militaries that were examined for this study, only the Israeli military's explicitly refers to patriotism ("Love of the Homeland").[21] Nonetheless, a belief in the inherent value of the nation that a military is created to defend seems likely to increase the willingness of the members of the military of that nation to effectively perform their duties even under circumstances where their lives are at risk.

- *Mission Accomplishment.* The U.S. Army's "Soldier's Creed" and the Navy's "Navy Ethos" both explicitly describe the accomplishment of missions as an important value.[22] The U.S. Air Force's "Core Values" refer to mission accomplishment less explicitly (and for some reason in the language of a business), when they say that "We must focus on providing services and generating products that fully respond to customer wants."[23] If the "customer" is understood to be the government of the United States, "services and products" are understood to be things such as destroying targets or transporting troops, and "customer wants" are understood to be the missions assigned by the U.S. government (or its agent, such as a joint force commander), then the U.S. Air Force can also be said to value mission accomplishment. The values of non-U.S. militaries are less clear on this point, but it stands to reason that mission accomplishment should be a value of all militaries that wish to be effective fighting forces. Militaries that are not focused on accomplishing the missions assigned to them may be effective in other areas, but probably not at winning wars. For those militaries that may be called on to fight wars, such as the PLA, an organizational culture that did not value accomplishing assigned missions would be a significant weakness.
- *Courage.* All three of the U.S. services and most of the foreign militaries and services examined for this study explicitly identify courage as an important value.[24] This is unsurprising given that, when performing their core mission – fighting wars – military organizations require their members to perform their job duties even while members of a rival organization are actively trying to kill them. It seems implausible that a military organization that did not to some degree value courage could be successful in the conduct of warfare.
- *Perseverance.* Perseverance in the face of adversity and difficulties (sometimes referred to as "determination," "tenacity of purpose," or "overcoming challenges") is clearly valued by all three U.S. services as well as the Israeli Defense Force.[25] The Canadian, British, Australian, and New Zealand militaries do not explicitly list perseverance or a synonymous term among their values, but it is possible that they consider perseverance to be an aspect of one of the values they do identify, such as "courage" or "commitment." The U.S. Army's "Army Values," for example, define "personal courage" as including facing physical or moral adversity.[26] In any case, given the extreme physical and psychological demands that

combat can place on individuals, it seems likely that a military that values perseverance will be more likely to succeed than one that does not.

- *Expertise.* Expertise in the performance of tasks is clearly valued by the U.S. services. The U.S. Army's "Soldier's Creed," for example, includes the statements "I am . . . proficient in my Warrior tasks and skills" and "I am an expert and I am a professional." Indeed, the U.S. Army has issued an entire white paper devoted to the importance of expertise and professionalism.[27] Similarly, the U.S. Navy's "Core Values" call on members of the Navy to "Exhibit the highest degree of . . . professional excellence, quality, and competence."[28] Most of the foreign militaries examined for this study also identify "professionalism" – which can be understood as comprising expertise, as well as moral integrity and discipline – as one of their core values.[29] Given the demonstrated importance of individual skill to performing military tasks (see Chapter Five), a military that values expertise would appear to be more likely to be successful than one that does not.[30]

- *Respect for Others.* Some might question whether respect for others is a value that contributes to the organizational effectiveness of an organization whose mission entails killing others, and consequently suspect that it, in the words of one observer, is included purely "as a genuflection to political correctness."[31] However, not only do all three U.S. services list it as part of their "core values," several foreign militaries do so as well.[32] Although all of the militaries examined belong to liberal democracies, its ubiquity suggests a belief that militaries that do not show respect for all people, including both those who are members of the organization and those who are not, are less organizationally effective than militaries that do. This could apply even to militaries that exist under authoritarian systems such as China's.

In addition to the above values, which are all espoused by at least two of the U.S. services and one foreign military, several other values are explicitly espoused only by the U.S. military or else only by foreign militaries, but appear to also be important for all militaries. These are the following:

- *Personnel Development.* All three of the U.S. services emphasize the importance of developing the capabilities of their personnel. The U.S. Army's Field Manual No. 1, *The Army,* for example, states that its officers and NCOs "are given considerable authority early in their careers" and "developed through a series of schools that equips them for greater responsibilities as they are promoted," and that "Military professionals personally commit to a career-long process of learning."[33] The U.S. Army's white paper on "The Profession of Arms" states that "Army leaders establish a professional identity and culture [that] sponsors continuous self-assessment, learning, and development."[34] Similarly, the U.S. Navy's "Core Values" call for its members to "Always strive for … personal improvement," and the U.S. Air Force's "Core Values" state that "Military professionals must seek out and complete professional military education."[35] Unofficial publications by members of the U.S. military also emphasize the importance of personnel development. A proposed "professional ethic" for U.S. Army officers by a professor at West Point, for example, calls on them to "develop and maintain the highest level of professional expertise" and to be "seeking continually to enhance my professional education."[36] Similarly, an assessment of the organizational culture of the U.S. Army by a researcher at the U.S. Army War College states that "the Army's professional culture should be one that is characterized by … a long-term commitment to professional growth."[37] Although the foreign militaries examined for this study do not explicitly identify personnel development as an important value, it would seem that any military that seeks to retain both officers and enlisted personnel for long periods does so because its leadership believes that capabilities of personnel improve over time and that these improved capabilities contribute to the effectiveness of the military. If this belief is correct, then a military whose culture values personnel development should be more effective than one that does not.

- *Trust.* Although the U.S. Army's "Soldier's Creed" and "Army Values" do not mention trust, the Army's white paper on "The Profession of Arms" lists it as one of five "key attributes" for the development and stewardship of the Army profession.[38] The U.S. Air Force's "Core Values" state that trust is "imperative in today's military" and go on to call for "faith in the system" and for Air Force personnel to give coworkers "the benefit of the doubt" as well as for "openness" (which requires trust).[39] The U.S. Navy's "Navy Ethos" and "Core Values" do not mention trust and none of the institutional values advocated by the foreign militaries examined in this study include trust, but it would appear that trust is an important element of effective military organizations. Whole-hearted participation in highly risky activities such as combat operations requires a belief that other members of the organization will perform the actions that are expected of them, whether those actions require bravery on the part of those other members, such as laying down suppressive fire on a machine gun nest, or mere diligence and attention to detail, such as making sure that the missiles mounted on an aircraft are properly attached and armed. A military in which members do not have trust in each other is unlikely to be an effective fighting force.

- *Teamwork.* Surprisingly, of the U.S. services, only the U.S. Navy mentions teamwork as an important value, in both its "Navy Ethos" ("We are a team") and its "Core Values" ("The day-to-day duty of every man and woman in the Department of the Navy is to join together as a team to ...").[40] Most of the foreign militaries and services examined for this study, however, explicitly list teamwork (or the related term "comradeship") as one of their core values[41] and, by the same logic as trust would seem to be an important value for all military organizations, teamwork would seem to be as well. With few exceptions, military operations are team operations. Individuals who do not coordinate their actions with those of other members of their unit and ensure that their actions support those of the other members will not only reduce the effectiveness of the other members of their unit, they themselves will not be effective.

- *Care for subordinates.* All three U.S. services explicitly call on their members to take care of their subordinates. The "Army Values" state that "selfless-service" includes putting the welfare of one's subordinates before one's own; the Navy's "Core Values" call on its members to "care for the personal and spiritual well-being of my people" (who "my people" are is not defined and could include all the members of one's unit – i.e., peers and superiors as well as subordinates – but the use of the possessive "my" suggests that this invocation applies particularly to subordinates); and the Air Force's "Core Values" state that "a good leader places the troops ahead of his/her personal comfort."[42] The foreign militaries examined for this study do not explicitly mention care for subordinates although, as with the U.S. Army, the value might be considered to be implied by concepts such as "selfless-service." In any case, the U.S. military services, at least, appear to believe that motivating capable people to join and stay in the service, and to perform dangerous actions when called upon, requires leaders to take responsibility for the personal well-being of their subordinates to a degree that would not be expected – indeed, might be considered inappropriate – in civilian organizations in America. Considering that the nature of military service is similar throughout the world, it seems likely that this value is important for non-U.S. militaries as well, even if they do not explicitly recognize it.

- *Efficiency.* Both the U.S. Navy and the U.S. Air Force, in their "Core Values" statements, mention the importance of efficiency. The Navy calls on its members to ensure that "the resources entrusted to me are used in an ... efficient way," and the Air Force states that "Military professionals have an obligation to ensure that all of the equipment and property they ask for is mission essential."[43] The U.S. Army, however, in its white paper on "The Profession of Arms," asks Army leaders to "establish a culture where effectiveness prevails over efficiency" and it certainly could be argued that, particularly in combat operations, effectiveness (mission accomplishment) is far more important than efficiency for military organizations.[44] Overwhelming success, moreover, is preferable to minimal success in most military operations, even though more people and material are required for overwhelming success than for minimal success, meaning that overwhelming success could be viewed as less "efficient" than minimal success. This does not mean that efficiency is not also important in combat operations, however. A military that conducts its operations more efficiently will be able to wring greater combat power out of the same amount of forces and, given that military forces are finite, they must be distributed in the most efficient possible way. Indeed, the U.S. Army's own basic doctrinal publication lists "Economy of Force" as one of nine basic "Principles of War and Operations."[45] One way to reconcile the Army's statement about effectiveness prevailing over efficiency, therefore, is to note that it does not imply that efficiency is not also important – it merely a provides a guideline to follow when the two different values are in tension with each other.

Several other values are not frequently mentioned by official publications of the U.S. services and other militaries but are mentioned by observers and commentators on military culture and ethos and seem to be important values for a military organization to hold. These are the following:

- *Obedience.* Of the official "core values," "creeds," and "ethoses" of the U.S. military, only the "Navy Ethos" explicitly mentions obedience (to orders) and, of the foreign militaries examined, only the Canadian Defence Forces mention it ("obey and support lawful authority").[46] Two U.S. military commentators, however, include obedience (to "lawful orders" and to "lawful and moral authority," respectively) within proposed ethics for the U.S. Army,[47] and it would seem that obedience is a key value for all military organizations. A military in which orders and higher-ranking personnel were not regularly obeyed would not be an effective fighting force.[48]
- *Initiative.* Initiative (making decisions and acting without explicit instructions to do so) would appear to be a valued attribute of most Western militaries, but, of the official "core values," "creeds," and "ethoses" of the U.S. and foreign militaries and services examined for this study, only the Australian Army's explicitly mentions it, although the U.S. Army's Field Manual No. 1 does refer to it.[49] Commentators on U.S. military culture and ethos, however, consistently identify initiative as important value,

and a strong culture of initiative is generally regarded as a key aspect of the most successful militaries in history, such as the German military during the early part of World War II and the Israeli military.[50]

- *Adaptability and Flexibility.* Although none of the official "core values," "creeds," and "ethoses" of the U.S. and foreign militaries and services examined for this study explicitly mention adaptability or flexibility, other publications of the U.S. Army clearly describe them as important attributes of soliders, as do other commentators on military culture and ethos.[51] For militaries, such as the PLA, that have a doctrine of maneuver and indirection that requires them to avoid direct confrontation with the enemy's strongest forces and to exploit unplanned opportunities, adaptability and flexibility would appear to be particularly important values.

- *Innovation and Creativity.* In the technologically dynamic and operationally fluid realm of warfare, innovation can provide a decisive advantage. New combat methods, employed first by the Germans and subsequently by the Allies, broke the trench stalemate on the Western Front in 1918. Twenty-two years later, it was again the German Army that first implemented the innovative methods that would enable it to defeat the numerically and materially superior French and British Armies in only ten days. Of the U.S. and foreign militaries services whose espoused values were examined for this study, only the U.S. Navy's "Core Values" explicitly refer to innovation ("I will . . . encourage new ideas"), but other publications of the U.S. military as well as commentators on U.S. military culture and ethos identify innovation and creativity as important attributes.[52]

- *Risk Taking.* None of the U.S. and foreign militaries and services whose espoused values were examined for this study identify risk taking as an important value, but at least one commentator on U.S. military culture does so, and military history seems to suggest that success on the battlefield requires taking chances. At Trafalgar, Nelson split his forces in two and allowed them to endure withering broadsides to penetrate the French battle line. Similarly, successful blitzkriegs during World War II required leaving the flanks of a spearhead lightly defended, and it was only when Stalin allowed his own generals to engage in bold, risky moves that the Soviets were able to implement blitzkrieg methods against the Germans.[53]

- *Decisiveness.* Surprisingly, of the U.S. and foreign militaries and services whose espoused values were examined for this study, only the U.S. Navy's "Navy Ethos" explicitly mentions decisiveness as an important value.[54] Nonetheless, given the extent to which decisiveness is perceived to be an important characteristic of military leaders, I have included it as a key military cultural value.

Data Collection

As noted above, assessing the importance of each of these values within PLA culture via the traditional method – asking key members of the organization to fill out a survey instrument – did not appear to be feasible. The approach used for this study, therefore, was to instead make use of the knowledge of U.S. military personnel who have had substantial interaction with the PLA, primarily those who have served in the U.S. Defense Attaché Office in Beijing. As a result of their frequent contact and interactions with PLA personnel, these individuals were assumed to have the best understanding of PLA culture of any readily available survey subjects. As members of the U.S. military, moreover, they were able to assess PLA culture in comparison to another military organization, rather than in the abstract or in comparison to nonmilitary organizations.

Accordingly, sixteen individuals who had served in the U.S. Defense Attaché Office in Beijing at different times were identified. Of them, twelve were successfully contacted, all of whom agreed to fill out a short questionnaire about the values of the PLA. Specifically, respondents were asked to provide their impression of the degree to which PLA culture supported each of the twenty-two values above in comparison to the degree to which U.S. military culture supported that value. They were asked to do so using a five-point ordinal scale where a "1" meant the PLA's culture supported the value *much less* than the U.S. military's culture, a "2" meant the PLA's culture supported the value *somewhat less* than the U.S. military's culture, a "3" meant the PLA's culture supported the value *about the same* as the U.S. military's culture, a "4" meant the PLA's culture supported the value *somewhat more* than the U.S. military's culture, and a "5" meant the PLA's culture supported the value *much more* than the U.S. military's culture.

This approach has a number of methodological shortcomings. The most obvious is that the questionnaire respondents were not actually members of the organization of interest (the PLA). Another is that the people in the PLA with whom the respondents had the most contact had undoubtedly been specially selected to handle interactions with foreigners, and thus may not have been representative of the PLA as a whole.[55] A third shortcoming is that the respondents themselves, those chosen to work in the defense attaché office in China, may not constitute a typical sample of U.S. military officers, and thus their understandings of U.S. military culture may not have been representative of the U.S. military as a whole. A fourth shortcoming is the likelihood of a systematic bias toward rating PLA culture as inferior to U.S. military culture, given the tendency of all people to view their own culture as "correct" and other cultures as flawed. A final weakness is the very small number of respondents.[56] Nonetheless, this approach appeared to be preferable to any of the available alternatives and, in aggregate, seems to have provided useful insights, even if the assessments of the importance accorded to any single organizational value cannot be considered to be statistically valid at high levels of confidence.

The ten people who actually filled out the questionnaire[57] were divided into two groups, depending on whether their average year of contact with the PLA was closer to 2000 or closer to 2010. This resulted in four of the sets of questionnaire responses being correlated with 2000 and five with 2010.[58] Based on the questionnaire responses, the minimum, median, and maximum rating for each of the twenty-two values was identified for each of the two time periods.

The results were surprisingly consistent between the two periods. Of the thirteen values for which the median response about the degree to which PLA culture supported that value compared to U.S. military culture was at most "somewhat less" ("2") in 2000, for twelve of these values the median response in 2010 was also at most "somewhat less."[59] Similarly, for five of the eight values for which the median response in 2000 was between "somewhat less" ("2") and "somewhat more" ("4"), in 2010 the median response was also between "somewhat less" and "somewhat more." Finally for the one value for which the median response in 2000 was that PLA culture supported this value at least "somewhat more" ("4") than U.S. military culture, the median response for 2010 was also that PLA culture supported this value at least "somewhat more." There were only two instances, moreover, in which the median response changed by more than one full category between 2000 and 2010.[60] This self-consistency suggests that, although the sample size is extremely small, there was a relatively high level of agreement among those who responded to the questionnaire in their assessments of the degree to which PLA culture supported the twenty-two values identified on the questionnaire, even across the two periods examined.

CHINESE MILITARY CULTURE IN 2000

The lowest, median, and highest responses for each value from questionnaire responders whose period of greatest contact with the PLA was closer to 2000 are shown in Table 8.1.

These responses revealed only one value ("obedience") that was viewed as more strongly supported by PLA culture than U.S. military culture in 2000, whereas there were thirteen values that the responses indicated were less

TABLE 8.1 *Lowest, Median, and Highest Assessment of Each Cultural Value, ~2000*

Value	Lowest Response	Median	Highest Response
Moral integrity	1	2	3
Discipline	3	3½	4
Responsibility	1	1½	2
Loyalty	3	3½	4
Self-sacrifice	1	2½	5
Patriotism	2	3	4
Mission accomplishment	2	2½	3
Courage	2	2½	3
Perseverance	2	3	4
Expertise	1	2½	4
Respect for others	1	2	3
Personnel development	1	2	2
Trust	1	2	3
Teamwork	2	2	3
Care for subordinates	1	2	3
Efficiency	1	2	2
Obedience	3	4	4
Initiative	1	1	2
Adaptability and flexibility	1	1	2
Innovation and creativity	1	1½	2
Risk taking	1	1	2
Decisiveness	1	2	3

strongly supported by PLA culture than U.S. military culture. Given the methodology used for obtaining this assessment, it is impossible to determine the extent to which this asymmetry reflects an overall weakness of PLA culture in supporting values associated with military success, as opposed to cultural bias on the part of the questionnaire responders. Attention, therefore, will be focused on those values that appear to be *relatively* strongly and *relatively* weakly supported by PLA culture.

The values that appeared to be relatively strongly supported by PLA culture (median response of "about the same" or better) in 2000 were *discipline, loyalty, patriotism,*[61] *perseverance,* and *obedience.* The values that appeared to be most weakly supported by PLA culture (median response of "much less" or between "much less" and "somewhat less") were *responsibility, initiative, adaptability and flexibility, innovation and creativity*, and *risk taking*.

The relative strengths of PLA culture in 2000 exhibit no obvious pattern. The five values that were identified as most strongly supported by PLA culture, for example, are associated with three of the four value clusters identified by Cameron and Quinn and Denison.[62] Of the five values that were identified as most *weakly* supported by PLA culture, however, four of them are associated with the value cluster that emphasizes adaptability and innovativeness (which is also the one cluster that none of the PLA's strongly supported values were associated with). The relative importance of this value cluster to military organizations as a general proposition is unclear. None of the values associated with this cluster are frequently mentioned in official publications of the U.S. services and other militaries, although they are frequently mentioned by observers and commentators on the U.S. military's culture and ethos.[63] Similarly, a study of the preferences of future U.S. Army leaders found that they regarded this cluster to be the third-most important of the four clusters.[64] However, as discussed in previous chapters, the PLA in 2000 had a doctrine that emphasized avoiding a direct confrontation with an enemy and instead exploiting vulnerabilities in the enemy's combat system. Since such vulnerabilities are likely to be situation dependent and in many cases transient, this requires operational commanders to take *initiative* and to be *innovative and creative, adaptable and flexible*, and *risk taking*, all of which were identified as relatively weak areas of PLA culture.[65] Combined with a similar inconsistency between its doctrine and its organizational structure, as found in Chapter Three, the fact that the PLA's culture was assessed as weakest in these values suggests that it would have experienced serious difficulties implementing its doctrine in 2000.

CHINESE MILITARY CULTURE IN 2010

The lowest, median, and highest responses for each value from questionnaire responders whose period of greatest contact with the PLA was closer to 2010 are shown in Table 8.2.

The responses to the questionnaire indicated that there were three values that were more strongly supported by PLA culture than by U.S. military culture in 2010, as compared to only one in 2000. There were, however, still thirteen values that the responses indicated were less strongly supported by PLA culture than by U.S. military culture in 2010.

The values that were said to be most strongly supported by PLA culture (median response of "about the same" or better) in 2010 were *discipline*,

TABLE 8.2 *Lowest, Median, and Highest Assessment of Each Cultural Value, ~2010*

Value	Lowest Response	Median	Highest Response
Moral integrity	1	1	2
Discipline	2	3	5
Responsibility	2	3	3
Loyalty	3	4	5
Self-sacrifice	3	4	5
Patriotism	1	3	4
Mission accomplishment	1	3	4
Courage	1	3	3
Perseverance	1	3	4
Expertise	1	2	4
Respect for others	1	2	3
Personnel development	1	1	2
Trust	1	1	4
Teamwork	1	2	3
Care for subordinates	1	1	3
Efficiency	1	1	4
Obedience	4	5	5
Initiative	1	1	2
Adaptability and flexibility	1	1	2
Innovation and creativity	1	1	2
Risk taking	1	1	2
Decisiveness	1	2	4

responsibility, loyalty, self-sacrifice, patriotism, mission accomplishment, courage, perseverance, and *obedience.* The values that were said to be most weakly supported by PLA culture (median response of "much less" or between "much less" and "somewhat less") were *moral integrity, personnel development, trust, care for subordinates, efficiency, initiative, adaptability and flexibility, innovation and creativity,* and *risk taking.*[66]

As in 2000, the relative strengths of PLA culture in 2010 exhibit no obvious pattern, with at least two values viewed as relatively strongly supported by PLA culture coming from each of the four clusters except for the cluster centered on adaptability and innovativeness.[67] In addition, the relative weaknesses of PLA culture in 2010 exhibited a less clear pattern than in 2000. The cluster

involving adaptability and innovativeness remained the most strongly represented, with all four of the values associated with that cluster identified as areas
of weakness. At least two values each from the cluster involving consistency
and predictability and from the cluster involving participation and collaboration were also identified as areas of weakness, however. The only cluster that
did not have any of the values associated with it identified as areas of weakness
was the cluster involving mission accomplishment. These results suggest that
the values associated with adaptability and innovativeness remained an area of
weakness within PLA culture. Indeed, some of the questionnaire responders
for this period provided verbal comments on the topic, with one noting that
"PLA culture is very risk averse, structured, and does not foster independent
thinking in general" and another stating that "a general fear of failure pervades
[PLA officers'] approach to work."[68] Adaptability and innovativeness, moreover, were as important to the PLA's doctrine in 2010, which was still a
doctrine of maneuver and indirection, as they were in 2000.

Values associated with mission accomplishment, on the other hand, may
have been emerging as an area of relative strength within PLA culture. Two of
the four values associated with mission accomplishment were identified as
areas of relative strength, and none was regarded as an area of relative
weakness. In the study of U.S. Army leaders referred to above, this cluster
was regarded as the second-most important value cluster (after the cluster
associated with participation and collaboration).[69]

CHINESE MILITARY CULTURE IN 2020

The overall change in Chinese military culture between 2000 and 2010 was at
best small. Although some values appeared to strengthen somewhat, others
weakened, without any clear pattern emerging. Based on the small amount of
change between 2000 and 2010, therefore, PLA culture does not appear to be
on a trajectory that will result in it being fundamentally different in 2020 than
it was in 2000. In particular, the values associated with adaptability and
innovativeness appear likely remain an area of weakness within PLA culture.
Given the importance of these values to implementing a doctrine of indirection and maneuver, unless the PLA's doctrine changes to one of direct
engagement between now and 2020, there will continue to be a fundamental
mismatch between the PLA's doctrine and the organizational culture that
would be required to effectively implement it (as well as with the PLA's
organizational structure, as discussed in Chapter Three).[70]

Rapid organizational culture change, such as would be required for the
PLA to develop a culture that emphasized adaptability and innovativeness by

2020, generally occurs as a result of a crisis or dramatic organizational failure.[71] As of this writing, there is a growing concern in China's political and military leadership about the extent of corruption in the PLA (as well as in China more generally).[72] However, using the model of culture described at the beginning of this chapter, the focus appears to be at the surface level – the behavior – rather than on the norms and values that underlie it (much less the assumptions that underlie those norms and values). The social science literature does not appear to have a precise understanding of the norms and values that contribute to corruption, but there is at least some evidence that corruption is correlated with a lack of trust (in other people and/or the legal system) and low levels of risk taking, both of which are values that the survey conducted for this chapter found to be relatively weak in the PLA. Corruption may also be associated with a high value placed on the importance of loyalty, an area in which the PLA appears to be relatively strong (see Tables 8.1 and 8.2).[73] China's civilian and military leadership, however, does not appear to recognize that, to eliminate corruption, the norms and value of the PLA must change. Thus, it would appear that the most likely cause of fundamental cultural change in the PLA by 2020 would not be in response to the corruption problem but rather a disastrous military failure of some sort. In the absence of such an event, it is unlikely that the organizational culture of the PLA will have significantly changed by 2020 and that corruption, along with adaptability and innovativeness, will continue to be areas of weakness.

9

Scenario Analysis

Assessing the overall military capabilities of a nation's military, as has been done in the previous seven chapters of this book, is valuable. It provides a way to compare the military power of that nation to that of the other nations of the world, and the overall military power of different nations affects the calculations and decisions of national governments and leaders. The actual outcomes of military conflicts, however, depend not just on the overall military capabilities of the combatants, but also on the specific nature and location of the conflict (as well as difficult-to-predict factors such as the competency of top military and civilian leaders, intelligence breakthroughs, and plain luck). Thus, in 1973 the world's most powerful military conceded defeat to a much less powerful military, in part because the nature of the conflict prevented the United States from bringing its full military capabilities to bear against the Democratic Republic of Vietnam. In addition to assessing a nation's overall military power, therefore, analyzing specific conflict scenarios in which that military power might be employed is also important. The purpose of such analysis is not to predict the outcome of a future conflict, but rather to provide a means of assessing how effectively the nation would be able to bring its military power to bear in a particular conflict. Such assessments can assist in understanding the calculus of different nations with regard to the issues over which the conflict could occur, as well as in understanding what changes to the capabilities of the participants in the conflict are likely to have the greatest effect on the outcome.

The number of imaginable conflict scenarios involving China is large, but it is not practical to analyze all of them. Instead, this chapter examines two scenarios that, at the time of this writing, appear to be among the more likely scenarios involving China.[1] The first scenario entails a Chinese attempt to invade and conquer Taiwan in the face of U.S. intervention on Taiwan's behalf. The second scenario entails a war over the Spratly Islands of the South

China Sea that involves China on one side and treaty allies the United States and the Philippines on the other.

The analyses in this chapter each examine one particular way the conflict in question could progress. The strategic choices made by each actor are those that seem to be the most logical in the circumstances of the scenario. However, not all possible alternative courses of action were considered in detail, and it is possible that other courses of action would produce preferable outcomes for the respective sides. Indeed, in an actual war each side would be vigorously seeking to identify courses of action that its adversary had not considered but that could provide an advantage. Thus, if one of the scenarios examined here actually occurred, it could play out very differently than analyzed here. Again, however, the purpose here is not to predict the outcome of an actual war, but rather to assess the overall balance of military capability that the two sides would bring to the conflict, as this balance is likely to affect what actions the nations involved will take with respect to the issue at stake and provide a guide to those nations about how to change that balance in a way more favorable to them.

The analyses also do not attempt to represent detailed technical differences between different weapon systems. Broadly comparable weapons in the hands of equally competent operators are assumed to produce roughly similar effects. Although in practice a Su-27 is probably not the exact equal of an F-15 in air-to-air combat, if a number of Su-27s go up against an equal number of F-15s and the pilots are equally skilled, the average result is not likely to be a lopsided victory for one side or the other. On the other hand, if one side has twice as many Su-27s as the other has F-15s or vice versa, the side with the more numerous aircraft is likely to win the encounter (again, assuming equally competent operators). Thus, for analytic purposes, Su-27s and F-15s are assumed to comparable. An F-22, however, an aircraft that is thirty years newer than the F-15 and far more technologically advanced, is assumed to be several times more effective than an F-15 or Su-27 (consistent with the fact that each F-22 was several times more expensive to produce than an F-15).

Another simplification is that the analyses break combat down into separate operational realms (air-to-air combat, air-to-ground combat, air-to-ship combat, etc.) and assess each realm independently. Although the analyses consider the effects of the outcomes of operations in one realm on the outcomes of operations in other realms, for analytical tractability they are analyzed sequentially. In a real war, however, multiple types of operations would occur simultaneously, with each operation being affected by the other operations that were going on.

Despite these simplifications, the broad conclusions that result from this type of analysis should be valid. That is, if one side or the other is likely to win a lopsided victory, the analysis should reflect that. If the sides are more closely matched, with the outcome likely to be either a costly stalemate or one in which victory will depend on luck and which side makes the right decisions at the right time, the analysis should reveal that as well.[2] The advantage of this simplified, disaggregated approach, moreover, is that the logic and calculations involved in the analysis are transparent and intelligible to anyone with a knowledge of high school mathematics. This allows the reader to examine and assess the assumptions and findings of the analysis in a way that is not possible when analysis uses a detailed computer simulation.

CHINESE INVASION OF TAIWAN

Analyzing a military scenario requires information about the political-military context of the conflict, the overall military capabilities of each of the combatants, the initial locations of the forces actually involved in the conflict (known as the "order of battle"), each side's objectives in the conflict, and their overall plans for achieving them.

Political-Military Context

The premise of this scenario is that, in 2020, the Chinese leadership launches an invasion of Taiwan to force its unification with the mainland under the PRC government. One way such a decision might come about would be if, for example, pro-independence political parties in Taiwan grew in power in the years leading up to 2020, culminating in pro-independence candidates winning not only Taiwan's presidency in 2020 but also, for the first time, control of Taiwan's legislature as well. Since this development could be interpreted as amounting to a tacit declaration of independence by the people of Taiwan, China's top leadership might therefore feel compelled, both by popular opinion and by criticism from lower-level leaders who wish to replace the top leadership in their positions, to demand that Taiwan explicitly renounce the possibility of independence for the island. If such a demand were rebuffed, China's leaders, to maintain their position of power within China, might conclude that they had no choice but to use military force to bring about Taiwan's unification. Such a decision might be particularly likely if the legitimacy of the PRC leadership was already under question at the time, such as because of a slowdown in China's economic growth, widening economic inequality, an environmental disaster, or other perceived failures of leadership.

Although China would derive many advantages from launching an invasion that came as a complete surprise to both Taiwan and the United States,[3] in practice an attack that was a complete surprise seems unlikely. If the invasion was a result of political developments such as those described above, Taiwan and the United States would have ample warning that a use of force was possible. In the run-up to Taiwan's 2020 elections, for example, as it became clear that the pro-independence parties had a significant chance of winning, the mainland would likely, as it has in the past, issue various public and private warnings to Taiwan's public, government, and military about the potential consequences of a pro-independence victory. And, as implied in the previous paragraph, even after the pro-independence parties won the election, if the victory was indeed interpreted in mainland China as a de facto declaration of independence, the Chinese government, rather than immediately deciding to launch an invasion, would probably first attempt to pressure Taiwan's government to specifically renounce the possibility of independence for Taiwan. For this demand to have any likelihood of being accepted, of course, it would have to be backed by an implicit or explicit threat to use force if it was not accepted. The resulting crisis atmosphere would undoubtedly cause Taiwan to put its military forces on alert and the United States to send forces to the areas around Taiwan, as it has in crises past. If Taiwan's leaders rejected (or simply ignored) the mainland's demand, Taiwanese and U.S. intelligence services would undoubtedly be watching extremely closely for any indications that the mainland was preparing for an armed attack.

Under such circumstances, the PLA could possibly covertly prepare and launch a sudden small-scale attack using forces operating out of their normal basing locations, but adequate preparations for a full-scale offensive would require major movements of forces that would almost certainly be detected by Taiwanese and U.S. intelligence assets. Thus, China's leadership would be faced with a choice of launching a small-scale surprise attack against partially mobilized and deployed Taiwanese and U.S. forces, launching a full-scale attack against fully mobilized and deployed Taiwanese and U.S. forces, or delaying for some time, perhaps several years, in the hopes of being able to achieve complete surprise with a full-scale attack at some later date. Since the premise of this scenario is that China's leadership feels compelled by popular opinion and internal criticism to use military force to bring about Taiwan's unification, however, the third option does not seem viable (that is, if the Chinese leadership felt able to delay the attack for such an extended period, then they most likely would not feel compelled to attack at all). A small-scale surprise attack could theoretically shock Taiwan's people and leadership into accepting unification with the mainland. If it failed to do so, however, China's leadership would be forced to choose between accepting the result, with the attendant blow to their legitimacy as China's leaders, or launching a full-scale attack against a now fully mobilized and deployed opponent. Thus, it seems unlikely that a full-scale Chinese attack would occur under circumstances such that it came as a complete surprise to Taiwan and the United States. A smaller-scale attack that came as a partial or complete surprise might present significant military challenges for Taiwan and the United States, but the purpose of the scenario analyzed here is to examine the effects of the PLA using its full military power against Taiwan. The South China Sea scenario that follows will examine a conflict involving a lesser use of force with a greater degree of surprise.

Combatant Capabilities

The principal combatants in this scenario are the aggressor, the subject of the aggression, and the nation pledged to aid the subject of aggression: China, Taiwan, and the United States. Two other nations, however, play important albeit less central roles. One is Japan. U.S. land-based combat aircraft would play a key role in a U.S. defense of Taiwan. The U.S. air bases closest to Taiwan, however, are in Japan. This scenario assumes that the Japanese government allows the United States to operate combat aircraft involved in the defense of Taiwan from bases in Japan (including from Japanese Self-Defense Force bases). Under the laws of war, however, this would make Japan a belligerent in the conflict. This has two implications. First, for China to subsequently launch attacks on Japan would not constitute an act of aggression, as Japan would already be at war with China. Second, *legally* there would be no difference between allowing the United States to fly combat missions out of Japanese territory against China and Japan doing so itself. Nonetheless, this scenario assumes that neither Beijing nor Tokyo wishes to expand the conflict to include direct combat between the two countries. For Beijing this is because it wishes to portray the conflict purely as a dispute between itself and U.S.-backed separatists in Taiwan, not as a war between China and other countries in Asia, and also because it does not wish to add Japan's military capabilities to those of the adversaries it is already facing. Tokyo similarly does not wish to be involved in direct conflict with China, because of a desire to minimize the risk and costs associated with supporting the United States in this conflict.[4]

Although neither Beijing nor Tokyo wishes to expand the conflict between each other, however, China is not assumed to allow U.S. combat aircraft to fly out of Japan with impunity. Beijing is assumed to be willing to launch missile attacks on any air bases in Japan at which U.S. combat aircraft are stationed, accepting the likelihood that some missiles will kill Japanese military and civilian personnel both on and outside these bases. For its part, Japan is assumed to defend its territorial waters and air space against incursions by Chinese ships, aircraft, or missiles, but not to retaliate for such attacks by attacking China or otherwise directly participating in the conflict unless China itself appears to be deliberately targeting Japanese forces or civilian facilities.[5]

The other nation that plays an important role is Australia. Australia is assumed to play a role similar to Japan: Canberra allows U.S. military aircraft, such as aerial refueling aircraft and maritime patrol aircraft, to operate from its territory, but does not send forces to participate in the conflict unless China launches attacks on Australian forces or territory. Despite such actions making Australia a belligerent in the conflict, however, as in the case of Japan, Beijing seeks to avoid direct conflict with Australia, and, therefore, refrains from attacking Australian forces or territory.[6]

China

China's military capabilities in 2020 have been estimated in the previous seven chapters of this book. As noted in Chapter Seven, however, the PLA Navy does not currently appear to be on a trajectory that will by 2020 provide it with the capacity to conduct a simultaneous landing of the PLA Army's entire amphibious force of two mechanized infantry divisions and one armored brigade. This scenario, therefore, modifies the amphibious lift estimate in Chapter Seven by postulating that the additional amphibious ships required have been built and that the PLA Navy has provided them with trained crews.[7] This is something could be accomplished within a few years (e.g., beginning after Taiwan's 2016 elections), is well within the industrial capacity of China's shipbuilding industry (as was demonstrated by the rapid construction of amphibious lift ships in 2003–2005) and the organizational capacity of the PLA Navy, and, being relatively low cost, would have little measurable impact on the other aspects of China's military capability in 2020.

In addition, China has been assessed to be developing an "intermediate range" conventional ballistic missile (i.e., one with a range between 1,860 miles and 3,110 miles). As the likely production rate for this missile is unclear, Chapter Four did not provide an estimate of the number of these missiles that would be produced by 2020. Since such a missile would be capable of attacking Guam, where U.S. forces important to this scenario would be based, however, this scenario assumes that some of the resources that in Chapter Four were assumed to be used to produce the DF-21 medium-range conventional ballistic missile are instead devoted to producing twenty-five of this longer-range missile. Because, as stated in Chapter Four, the cost of producing a ballistic missile is roughly proportional to its range, and this new missile would have roughly twice the range of the DF-21, China's projected inventory of conventional DF-21s is consequently reduced by fifty, to 370. Of these, approximately fifty are assumed to be DF-21D antiship ballistic missiles.

Finally, Chapter Four also noted that China is developing ground-launched antisatellite missiles, co-orbital satellite interceptors, ground-based antisatellite lasers, and high-power microwave beams, but did not attempt to estimate how many of each type of system it might have by 2020. For purposes of scenario analysis, however, China is assumed to have a small number of each type of system, including ten ground-launched antisatellite missiles, five co-orbital satellite interceptors, three ground-based lasers, and three high-power microwave beam generators.

Taiwan

Taiwan's military forces in 2020 are assumed to have a reasonably modern doctrine that is consistent with the performance capabilities of Taiwan's weapon systems, that takes into account the capabilities of its most likely adversary (the PRC), and that addresses the most likely conflict scenarios for Taiwan, including invasions, blockades, air and missile bombardments, and so on. The doctrine is assumed to integrate well the capabilities of the different branches of each service within Taiwan's armed forces but, as with many militaries in the world, to integrate capabilities between different services less well.

The organizational structure of Taiwan's military in 2020 in assumed to be largely appropriate in terms of organizational height and span of control, as appears to be the case today. Taiwan's armed forces are assumed to have implemented a planned reduction in their overall size from 215,000 active duty personnel in 2014 to between 170,000 and 190,000 by 2020.[8] Most of the cuts are assumed to come from Taiwan's army, bringing its total size down to about one hundred thousand active duty personnel and reducing the army's combat forces to five armored, one armored infantry, two special operations, and nine light infantry brigades.[9] The organizational structure and culture of Taiwan's military in 2020, however, is assumed to be like the PLA in being overly centralized in its decision making and lacking the flexibility needed to implement a doctrine of maneuver and indirection or to rapidly adapt to the actions of an opponent seeking to achieve surprise and exploit vulnerabilities in Taiwan's defenses.[10]

The weaponry of Taiwan's armed forces is assumed to remain largely the same as in 2014, with a few changes. In 2008 and 2010, the United States agreed to sell to Taiwan seven batteries of Patriot air defense missiles to be added to the three batteries Taiwan already possessed. These are assumed to have all been delivered by 2020. In 2010, Taiwan contracted with Boeing to purchase thirty AH-64E Apache Longbow attack helicopters, with deliveries beginning in 2014. These are also assumed to have all been received by 2020. Of Taiwan's 137 domestically designed and built F-CK-1 fighters, seventy-one are assumed to have been upgraded, according to a program announced in 2011, with the remainder having been retired. The sixty-six retired F-CK-1s are assumed to have been replaced by an equal number of Block 50/52 F-16s, which Taiwan has long requested from the United States, and the 145 Block 20 F-16s Taiwan currently possesses are assumed to have been upgraded to the Block 50 standard, as authorized by the U.S. government in 2011. Finally, all of the F-5 and Mirage-2000 fighters Taiwan currently operates are assumed to have been retired by 2020.[11]

Taiwan's military has been attempting to implement an all-volunteer system of enlistment. Although initial recruiting efforts were disappointing, as of late 2014 Taiwan's Ministry of National Defense expected to achieve its goal of an all-volunteer force by 2017.[12] Even if the goal of an all-volunteer military is not achieved by 2017, the scenario analyzed here assumes that it will have been by 2020. Taiwan's enlisted personnel in 2020, however, are assumed to be less–well educated and less experienced than their counterparts in both the U.S. and the mainland militaries.[13] The average quality of Taiwan's officers is assumed to be roughly comparable to that of the U.S. and mainland militaries.

The quality of training in Taiwan's military is assumed to be comparable to that of the PLA in 2020, but inferior to that of the U.S. military. Similarly, Taiwan's logistics capabilities are assumed to be adequate and comparable to those of the PLA in 2020, but inferior to those of the U.S. military.

United States
The U.S. military is assumed to have in 2020 a modern doctrine that is appropriate for scenarios that include a Chinese attack on Taiwan, that both is well designed for the capabilities of the U.S. military and accounts for capabilities of an adversary such as China, and that better integrates the capabilities of different services and branches than the doctrines of the PLA or Taiwan's military. This doctrine is assumed to be based primarily on maneuver and indirection, and the organizational structure and culture of the U.S. military in 2020 is assumed to be better than that of the PLA and Taiwan's military (although not perfect) in terms being decentralized and allowing the flexibility and discretion needed to implement this type of doctrine as well as to rapidly adapt to the actions of an opponent seeking to achieve surprise and exploit vulnerabilities in U.S. defenses.

The overall size of the U.S. military in 2020 is assumed to be as defined in the report of the 2014 Quadrennial Defense Review, with older weapons being taken out of service as new systems are acquired.[14] U.S. weapon systems in 2020 are assumed to include those planned for delivery by June 2020, as detailed in the defense budget documents issued in March 2014.[15] Estimates of the total numbers of all major U.S. combat systems relevant to this scenario in 2020 are shown in Table 9.1.[16]

TABLE 9.1 *Inventory of Major U.S. Combat Systems Relevant to Taiwan Scenario in 2020*

System	Type	Number
Patriot	Long-range surface-to-air missile	108 batteries (~6,000 missiles)
THAAD	Land-based missile defense system	6 batteries (~260 missiles)
Virginia class	Nuclear-powered attack submarine	21
Seawolf class	Nuclear-powered attack submarine	3
Los Angeles class	Nuclear-powered attack submarine	27
Ohio class	Nuclear-powered cruise missile submarine	4
Ford class	Nuclear-powered aircraft carrier	1
Nimitz class	Nuclear-powered aircraft carrier	10
Zumwalt class	Land-attack destroyer	3
Arleigh Burke class	Destroyer	70
Ticonderoga class	Cruiser	11[17]
Independence class, Freedom class	Littoral combat ship	24
America class	Amphibious assault carrier	2
Wasp class	Amphibious assault carrier	8
F-35C	Carrier-capable multirole stealth fighter	70
F/A-18E/F	Carrier-capable semistealthy multirole fighter	560
F/A-18A/B/C/D	Carrier-capable multirole fighter	405
EA-18G	Carrier-capable electronic warfare aircraft	135
F-35B	Short takeoff/vertical-landing multirole stealth fighter	60
AV-8	Short takeoff/vertical-landing ground-attack fighter	125
P-8	Land-based maritime patrol aircraft	100
E-2	Carrier-capable airborne early warning and control aircraft	90

System	Type	Number
MQ-4	Unmanned maritime surveillance aircraft	12
F-22	Land-based air superiority stealth fighter	175
F-35A	Land-based multirole stealth fighter	300
F-15E	Land-based multirole fighter	210
F-15C/D	Land-based air superiority fighter	225
F-16C/D	Land-based multirole fighter	340[18]
B-52H	Subsonic heavy bomber	54
B-1B	Supersonic heavy bomber	63
B-2A	Stealthy heavy bomber	19[19]
KC-10	Aerial refueling/transport aircraft	54
KC-46	Aerial refueling/transport aircraft	65
KC-135	Aerial refueling aircraft	325[20]
RQ-4	Unmanned reconnaissance aircraft	40
MQ-9	Unmanned reconnaissance/ground attack aircraft	320[21]
RQ-180	Stealthy unmanned reconnaissance aircraft	Unknown
RC-135	Electronic intelligence aircraft	17
E-3	Land-based airborne early warning and control aircraft	30
E-8	Ground surveillance aircraft	15[22]
EC-130	Electronic warfare aircraft	12
Various	Optical/infrared imagery satellites	4
Various	Synthetic aperture radar imagery satellites	4
Various	Passive signals intelligence maritime surveillance satellites	3 pairs[23]

Sources: "MIM-104 Patriot," 2013; Department of the Air Force, 2013a; Mayer, 2013; IISS, 2014, pp. 42-54; Department of Defense, 2014a; Department of Defense, 2014b; Department of the Navy, 2014a; Department of the Navy, 2014c.

Most of the systems listed in Table 9.1 were already in service in 2014, the primary difference between 2014 and 2020 being the numbers of the more modern types. However, several significant new types of weapons will have entered the U.S. inventory by 2020. One such system will be the USS *Gerald R. Ford*. This ship will be the first of a new class of aircraft carrier that will carry approximately seventy-five fixed-wing aircraft, as compared to roughly sixty fixed-wing aircraft on the current Nimitz class, and will be able to launch and recover 25 percent more aircraft per day than the Nimitz class.

Another new system will be the Zumwalt-class destroyer, all three of which will have been completed by 2020. Zumwalt-class ships will have an air defense radar that is superior to that of the current Arleigh Burke–class destroyers and Ticonderoga-class cruisers, a significantly reduced radar signature, and will be better able to survive strikes by antiship cruise missiles.[24]

A third new type of ship that will have entered wide service by 2020 will be two classes of Littoral Combat Ships. These are small, fast ships capable of being configured for antisurface warfare, antisubmarine warfare, or minesweeping. Their chief advantage over existing Oliver Hazard Perry–class frigates is their much higher maximum speed (forty knots vs. twenty-nine knots). Four such ships had been commissioned by 2014, but by 2020 approximately twenty-four should be in operation.[25]

Three important new types of aircraft will be in operation by 2020. The most important of these will be the F-35 Joint Strike Fighter, which will exist in three configurations: a conventional land-based variant (F-35A) for use by the U.S. Air Force, a carrier-capable variant (F-35C) for use by the U.S. Navy, and a short takeoff/vertical-landing variant (F-35B) for use on the U.S. Marine Corps' amphibious assault ships. As compared to the F-16s, F/A-18s, and AV-8s currently operated by the three services, the F-35 will have a significantly reduced radar signature. The F-35 program has experienced numerous delays, but, as of 2014, approximately three hundred of the U.S. Air Force version, seventy of the U.S. Navy version, and sixty of the Marine Corps version were planned to be in operation in 2020.[26]

Another new type of aircraft will be the U.S. Navy's P-8A land-based maritime patrol aircraft. This aircraft, based on the Boeing 737 airframe, will be faster than the aging propeller-driven P-3s it will replace and will carry more-advanced sensors, providing it with significantly improved antisubmarine and antisurface warfare capabilities. A total of about one hundred of these aircraft should have been acquired by 2020.[27]

A final important new type of aircraft will be the RQ-180, a long-range, long-endurance, stealthy, unmanned surveillance aircraft capable of operating within interception range of China's surface-to-air missiles and manned fighters. It reportedly could enter service as soon as 2015, although it is unclear how many will have been produced by 2020.[28]

Several significant new types of missiles will have entered service by 2020 as well. One will be the Terminal High-Altitude Area Defense (THAAD) system, a land-based missile defense system designed to intercept theater ballistic missiles at ranges of up to 180 miles and altitudes of up to seventy-five miles. At least six batteries with a total of about 260 missiles should be in operation by 2020.[29]

Another new missile system will be the SM-6, a ship-launched anti-aircraft missile that achieved initial operating capability in 2013. The SM-6 has a range of as much as 230 miles, as compared to 105 miles for the SM-2 missiles currently in use, and will have an active-radar seeker that will improve its ability to intercept targets that are highly agile or beyond the effective range of the illumination radars of the ship that launches the missile. At least nine hundred SM-6 missiles should be in service in 2020, roughly eleven for every cruiser and destroyer in the U.S. Navy.[30]

A third new missile system will be the Joint Air-to-Surface Stand-off Missile – Extended Range (JASSM-ER), a longer-range version of the Joint Air-to-Surface Stand-off Missile (JASSM), a stealthy, precision-guided, air-launched cruise missile of which more than fifteen hundred were already in service in 2014. The JASSM-ER will have a range of 700 miles, as compared to less than 300 miles for JASSM. Approximately sixteen hundred JASSM-ERs should be in service in 2020.[31]

The education and experience levels of U.S. military personnel in 2020 are assumed to be roughly the same as in 2010 and 2000. This means that enlisted personnel in the U.S. military will have about the same amount of experience as enlisted personnel in the PLA but be less–well educated on average, whereas officers in the U.S. military are assumed to have roughly the same amount of experience, on average, as their counterparts in the PLA but to be better educated.[32]

The quality of U.S. military training in 2020 is assumed to be comparable to that in 2000 and 2010, meaning that it will remain superior to that of the PLA, particularly in the area of recent combat experience.[33] Similarly, U.S. logistics capabilities are assumed comparable to those in 2000 and 2010, meaning that they will also remain significantly superior to those of the PLA.[34]

Order of Battle

Neither China nor the United States would fight a war over Taiwan with its entire inventory of forces. Both sides would intentionally hold some forces in reserve, as a hedge against new contingencies occurring or the possibility of new fronts opening up, and logistical constraints would limit, to different degrees, the amount of forces they could deploy to and support within the theater of conflict.

China

Although the PLA Army will still be extremely large in 2020, with the exception of some SRBMs and air defense systems operated by the PLA Army, only those Army forces that are successfully transported to Taiwan will be capable of engaging in combat (most ballistic missiles are operated by the Second Artillery Force, and long-range air defense systems are operated by the PLA Air Force). As noted earlier in this chapter, the PLA is assumed to begin the conflict with enough amphibious lift ships to simultaneously transport two mechanized infantry divisions and one armored brigade. As noted in Chapter Seven, moreover, the PLA will have enough air transport capacity to drop a single paratroop regiment at a time. In addition to the two mechanized infantry divisions and one armored brigade that are dedicated to amphibious operations, sufficient additional ground forces are assumed to be available to eventually overwhelm Taiwan's seventeen brigades, provided they can be transported to Taiwan. However, until the PLA seized control of a port or airfield in Taiwan, it would be dependent on its amphibious lift ships and transport aircraft to deploy forces to Taiwan and support them once landed. Since amphibious lift ships need approximately half a day to travel to Taiwan from the nearest ports on the mainland, they are assumed to be able to make the round trip at most once every two days, when loading and unloading times are included.[35] The PLA's transport aircraft are assumed to be able to conduct one paradrop per day. The ground forces committed to a Taiwan operation are assumed to be equipped with the most-modern amphibious assault vehicles, tanks, infantry fighting vehicles, helicopters, self-propelled artillery, and other weaponry in the PLA's inventory in 2020.

The PLA is assumed to commit approximately two-thirds of its modern naval and air forces to the Taiwan operation, and two-thirds of its modern air defense systems are assumed to be deployed along China's coast. Sufficient basing and supply capacity is assumed to be available to allow these forces to operate.[36] All of China's conventional ballistic and cruise missiles, as well as all of its space and counterspace assets, are assumed to be available for the conflict. China's land-based and sea-based nuclear forces are assumed to have been put on alert and (in the case of China's mobile land-based missiles and ballistic missile submarines) to have been deployed away from their bases, but this is assumed to be purely for self-preservation and deterrent purposes – China's leadership is assumed to have no intention of using its nuclear forces unless the United States first attacks China with nuclear weapons or attacks China's nuclear forces with conventional weapons. China's naval, air, conventional missile, and space forces available for this conflict are listed in Table 9.2.[37]

Taiwan

All of Taiwan's combat systems are assumed to potentially be available for the conflict, although the ability to actually employ them would depend on the mobility of the system and the location of PLA forces. For example, Taiwan is

TABLE 9.2 *PLA Naval, Air, and Conventional Missile Combat Systems Available for Taiwan Operation*

System	Type	Number
Modified Liaoning class	Aircraft carrier	1
Liaoning class	Aircraft carrier	1
Luyang III class	Destroyer	8
Luyang II class	Destroyer	4
Luyang I class	Destroyer	1
Luzhou class	Destroyer	1
Sovremenny class	Destroyer	3
Jiangkai II class	Frigate	20
Jiangkai I class	Frigate	1
Jiangwei II class	Frigate	7
Jiangdao class	Corvette	20
Houbei class	Guided missile fast attack craft	44
Type 093A/095 class	Nuclear-powered attack submarine	8
Shang class	Nuclear-powered attack submarine	1
Kilo class	Diesel-electric attack submarine	7
Yuan class	Diesel-electric attack submarine	12
Song class	Diesel-electric attack submarine	11
Multiple classes	Amphibious landing ships	180
J-15	Carrier-capable multirole fighter	44
Y-8J/Y-8JB	Maritime patrol/electronic intelligence aircraft	14
J-20	Multirole stealth fighter	40
Su-27/Su-30/J-11B	Air superiority/multirole fighter	325
J-10	Air superiority/multirole fighter	300
JH-7	Fighter-bomber	315
H-6	Subsonic medium bomber	90
KJ-2000	Airborne early warning and control aircraft	9
KJ-200	Airborne early warning and control aircraft	9
Y-8D/G	Electronic warfare aircraft	20
S-300/HQ-9	Long-range surface-to-air missile system	60 batteries (480 launchers)
KS-1	Medium-range surface-to-air missile system	30 batteries (120 launchers)

(continued)

Table 9.2 (*continued*)

System	Type	Number
Tor M-1	Short-range surface-to-air missile system	95 launchers
DF-11, DF-15	Conventionally armed SRBMs	220 launchers 1,100 missiles
DF-21C	Conventionally armed medium-range ballistic missile	320 missiles 25 launchers
DF-21D	Conventionally armed medium-range ballistic missile – antiship variant	50 missiles 12 launchers
Unidentified	Conventionally armed intermediate-range ballistic missile	25 missiles 25 launchers
CJ-10	Ground/air/ship-launched cruise missile	1,100
Various	Optical reconnaissance satellites	7
Various	Synthetic aperture radar satellites	4
Various	Ocean reconnaissance satellites	4 triplets
Unidentified	Ground-launched antisatellite missiles	10
Unidentified	Co-orbital satellite interceptors	5
Unidentified	Ground-based antisatellite lasers capable of permanently blinding optical reconnaissance satellites	3
Unidentified	High-power microwave beams capable of disrupting the electronics of satellites in low earth orbit	3

estimated to have more than one thousand towed howitzers in 2020, but their usefulness against PLA forces would depend on whether and where PLA forces were landed on Taiwan. Table 9.3 lists the major combat systems available to Taiwan for the conflict.

United States

Not all U.S. forces would be committed to a conflict over Taiwan. This scenario assumes that the United States would not deploy ground combat forces to either Taiwan or mainland China itself. Thus, the only ground forces involved would be those providing ground defense for U.S. bases in the region and those operating surface-to-air missile systems such as Patriot and THAAD. In 2020, at least 40 percent of U.S. naval forces will still be based in the Atlantic, and, given U.S. security interests outside of the Pacific as well as logistical limitations on sustaining large naval forces in the western Pacific

TABLE 9.3 *Major Combat Systems Available to Taiwan*

System	Type	Number
	Active duty army soldiers	125,000
M60	Main battle tank	200
M48	Main battle tank	365
M24	Light tank	230
M41	Light tank	625
CM-25	Armored infantry fighting vehicle	225
CM-32	Tracked armored personnel carrier	35
M113	Tracked armored personnel carrier	650
LAV-150	Wheeled armored personnel carrier	300
M110	8 inch self-propelled howitzer	70
M109	155 mm self-propelled howitzer	225
M44	155 mm self-propelled howitzer	50
T-69	155 mm self-propelled howitzer	45
M115	8 inch towed howitzer	70
M-59	155 mm towed howitzer	90
T-65 (M114)	155 mm towed howitzer	250
T-64 (M101)	105 mm towed howitzer	650
60 Kung Feng III/Kung Feng IV	126 mm multiple rocket launcher	60
RT 2000	126 mm multiple rocket launcher	150
Kung Feng VI	117 mm multiple rocket launcher	120
AH-64	Attack helicopter	30
AH-1	Attack helicopter	60
OH-58	Armed reconnaissance helicopter	40
Hai Lung (Zwaardvis) class	Diesel-electric attack submarine	2
Keelung (Kidd) class	Destroyer	4
Cheng Kung (Perry) class	Frigate	8
Chin Yang (Knox) class	Frigate	8
Kang Ding (La Fayette) class	Frigate	6
Jin Chiang class	Guided missile fast attack craft	12
Kwang Hua class	Guided missile fast attack craft	30
S-2	Antisubmarine warfare aircraft	20
S-70	Antisubmarine warfare helicopter	20
F-16	Multirole fighter	210

(*continued*)

Table 9.3 (*continued*)

System	Type	Number
F-CK-1	Multirole fighter	70
E-2	Airborne early warning and control aircraft	6
Patriot	Long-range surface-to-air missile	10 batteries 40 launchers
Hawk	Medium-range surface-to-air missile	13 batteries 100 launchers
Tien Kung	Long-range surface-to-air missile	10 batteries 60 launchers

Sources: "Taiwan > Army," 2012; IISS, 2013, pp. 335-337; "Boeing AH-64 Apache," 2013; Kan, 2013, p. 17.

area, this scenario assumes that no Atlantic-based naval forces are committed to the Taiwan conflict. Of the ships based in the Pacific, moreover, roughly 20 percent, including one of the six aircraft carriers to be based in the Pacific in 2020, are assumed to be undergoing long-term overhaul at the time of the conflict and unavailable for combat.[38]

As in the case of China's air forces, this scenario assumes that at most two-thirds of the total U.S. aircraft inventory is theoretically available for the defense of Taiwan, with the remaining one-third either being retained in the continental United States for training, testing, and other purposes or else deployed in other parts of the world. As will be discussed below, however, the number of fighter aircraft able to participate in this scenario would be further constrained by the capacity of the bases close enough to the locus of conflict for fighter aircraft to participate effectively. Similarly, in the case of the Patriot and THAAD land-based air- and missile-defense systems, the limitation is where they can be deployed such that they have operational utility. This scenario assumes that four Patriot batteries are deployed at each of three locations: at Kadena Air Base on Okinawa, near the Japanese Air Self-Defense Force (JASDF) base at Komatsu in central Japan, and on the island of Guam, and that one THAAD battery is deployed at each of four locations: on Okinawa, near the U.S. Air Force base at Misawa in northern Japan, near the JASDF base at Chitose on the northern Japanese island of Hokkaido, and on the island of Guam.[39]

Given the tensions before the beginning of actual military combat in this scenario, all U.S. ships available for the conflict are assumed to be on patrol at various locations around Taiwan and elsewhere in the western Pacific.[40]

Of the forty-eight carrier-capable F-35Cs available, one squadron of twelve aircraft each are assumed to be operating from the *Ford* and from three of the four Nimitz-class carriers. The *Ford* is also assumed to operate fifty-four F/A-18E/F multirole fighters, six F/A-18G jamming aircraft, and five E-2 airborne early warning and control aircraft. In addition to twelve F-35Cs, three of the Nimitz-class carriers are assumed to operate forty-two F/A-18E/Fs, four F/A-18Gs, and four E-2s. The fourth Nimitz-class carrier is assumed to operate fifty-four F/A-18E/Fs, four F/A-18Gs, and four E-2s. Finally, each of the five America-class and Wasp-class amphibious assault carriers is assumed to operate nine F-35B short takeoff/vertical landing multirole stealth fighters.[41]

As stated above, the availability of air bases is a major constraint on the number of land-based U.S. aircraft able to participate in a Taiwan scenario. The U.S. air bases closest to Taiwan are Kadena Air Base and Marine Corps Air Station Futenma, both on the island of Okinawa, approximately five hundred miles from the center of the Taiwan Strait. Both would also be within range of China's SRBMs, however, if these were deployed to the area of mainland China that is closest to Okinawa (the southeastern portion of Zhejiang province).[42] Kadena has only fifteen hardened aircraft shelters, moreover, and Futenma has none. The U.S. Air Force currently bases fifty-four F-15C/Ds, fifteen KC-135s, and two E-3s at Kadena.[43] No fixed wing combat aircraft are normally based at Futenma.[44] In this scenario, for political reasons, the F-15s are assumed to remain at Kadena throughout the period of rising tensions before the conflict, but, because of their vulnerability to ballistic missile attack, the KC-135s and E-3s are withdrawn to more-distant bases, and no additional fixed-wing aircraft are deployed to Kadena or Futenma.

After the bases on Okinawa, the usable U.S. air base that is next closest to the Taiwan Strait is Marine Corps Air Station Iwakuni, at the southwestern end of the main Japanese island of Honshu, approximately one thousand miles from the center of the Taiwan Strait.[45] However, Iwakuni is only about 630 miles from the Chinese mainland, well within range of China's DF-21 medium-range ballistic missiles (which have an estimated range of more than one thousand miles).[46] There are no hardened aircraft shelters on Iwakuni, and aircraft parked outside of hardened shelters are highly vulnerable to ballistic missiles that are equipped with small submunition warheads. About forty-five DF-21s with such warheads would likely be sufficient to destroy more than 80 percent of any aircraft parked on the ground at Iwakuni.[47] Given this vulnerability, it is unlikely that the U.S. would station significant numbers of aircraft at Iwakuni in a conflict with China over Taiwan.[48]

After Iwakuni, the next closest available U.S. air bases are Yokota Air Base and Naval Air Facility Atsugi, near Tokyo in central Honshu, approximately fourteen hundred miles from the center of the Taiwan Strait. However, like Iwakuni, Yokota and Atsugi do not have hardened aircraft shelters and are within DF-21 range of China. Fifty DF-21 missiles armed with small submunitions would be sufficient to destroy more than 80 percent of the aircraft parked on the ground at Yokota and ten such missiles would be sufficient to destroy more than 80 percent of the aircraft on the ground at Atsugi.[49] Thus, it is similarly unlikely that the United States would base significant numbers of aircraft at Yokota or Atsugi in a conflict with China over Taiwan.

The final U.S. air base in Japan is Misawa Air Base, in northern Honshu, about 1,650 miles from the center of the Taiwan Strait. Like other bases in Japan, Misawa is within DF-21 range of China. There are, however, approximately sixty hardened aircraft shelters at Misawa. This scenario, therefore, assumes that a full wing (72) of F-35As is stationed at Misawa. The two squadrons of JASDF F-2s normally based at Misawa are assumed to be redeployed to Matsushima, approximately 160 miles to the south, which normally hosts an F-2 training squadron and therefore would be capable of maintaining the redeployed F-2s. During the scenario, these aircraft are assumed to conduct combat air patrols over northern Honshu, including over Misawa.

In addition to U.S. bases in Japan, the United States has an agreement with the Japanese government for contingency access to the JASDF bases at Nyutabaru and Tsuiki on the island of Kyushu in southwestern Japan. Again, however, these bases are well within DF-21 range of China and have only a handful of hardened aircraft shelters each – insufficient to protect an operationally significant number of aircraft. A similar assessment applies to most other JASDF bases. The exceptions are Komatsu, in central Honshu, about thirteen hundred miles from the center of the Taiwan Strait, which has fourteen shelters, and Chitose, on the northern island of Hokkaido, about eighteen hundred miles from the center of the Taiwan Strait, which has twenty-eight shelters.[50] Using ballistic missiles to destroy aircraft parked in hardened aircraft shelters is much more difficult than aircraft parked in the open.[51] The U.S. military, therefore, would likely regard stationing aircraft at these bases as an acceptable risk (although, as will be shown later, they are still vulnerable to attack by cruise missiles). Since a third or more of the aircraft stationed at an air base could be kept in the air at any one time, moreover, a number of aircraft larger than the number of hardened shelters can viably operate out of an airfield. This scenario, therefore, assumes that the United States requests and receives permission from the Japanese government to station one squadron of twenty-four U.S. Air Force F-35As at Komatsu and two squadrons of (forty-eight) F-35As at Chitose. To make room for the U.S. aircraft and avoid Japanese aircraft being destroyed by attacks intended for the

U.S. aircraft, the two squadrons of JASDF F-15s normally based at Komatsu are assumed to be redeployed to other bases in central Honshu (such as Gifu, about seventy-five miles to the south and site of the JASDF's Development and Test Wing, which includes F-15s as well as an aircraft maintenance facility). The F-15s previously based at Komatsu are assumed to conduct combat air patrols in the airspace near the base, to protect the base and surrounding regions of Japan from possible attack by Chinese aircraft or cruise missiles. Similarly, the two squadrons of JASDF F-15s normally based at Chitose are assumed to be redeployed to Akita, in northern Honshu, about 230 miles south of Chitose, but to fly combat air patrols over Hokkaido.

The other U.S. air base of significance to this scenario is Andersen Air Force Base on the island of Guam, approximately eighteen hundred miles from the center of the Taiwan Strait. Andersen is a huge base with two twelve-thousand-foot runways and room to park more than two hundred aircraft.[52] There are no hardened aircraft shelters at Andersen, but in this scenario China has only twenty-five conventional ballistic missiles capable of reaching Guam. At least forty missiles with warheads the size of the DF-21 would be required to cover all of the parking areas at Andersen. In addition, in this scenario Andersen is defended by a battery of THAAD antimissile missiles and four batteries of Patriots. Given Andersen's relative safety from Chinese ballistic missiles – and the absence of better alternatives – the United States is assumed to station all 120 F-22s available to it in this scenario, along with one hundred KC-135 aerial refueling aircraft to support them, at Andersen. See Figure 9.1 for the locations of bases in the western Pacific from which U.S. aircraft operate in this scenario.

All other land-based U.S. aircraft in this scenario are assumed to operate from more-distant bases, such as the Royal Australian Air Force bases at Darwin, Tindal, Curtin, Sherger, and Learmonth in northern Australia, which are twenty-seven hundred to thirty-two hundred miles from the center of the Taiwan Strait.[53] These distances are too great for fighter aircraft to operate effectively, even if aerially refueled en route. However, large aircraft such as E-3 airborne early warning and control aircraft, RC-135 electronic intelligence aircraft, RQ-4 Global Hawk and MQ-4 Triton unmanned reconnaissance aircraft, P-8 maritime patrol aircraft, and aerial refueling aircraft (in addition to those operating from Andersen) could all operate over these distances, although some would also need to be aerially refueled en route.[54] Table 9.4 lists the numbers of each major U.S. combat system with the potential to participate in this scenario, recognizing that basing limitations would prevent some of them, particularly many of the fighter aircraft available, from actually doing so under most circumstances.

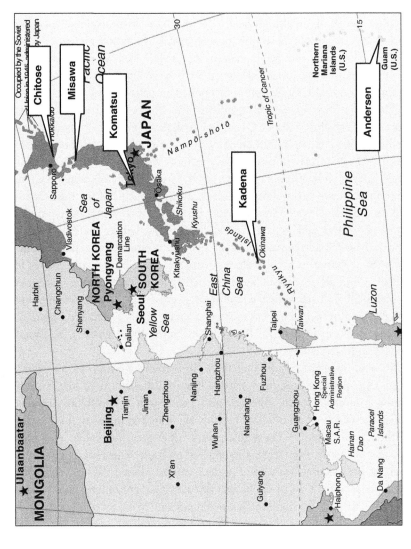

FIGURE 9.1 Locations of Bases from Which U.S. Aircraft Operate in Taiwan Scenario

TABLE 9.4 *Major U.S. Combat Systems Available for Taiwan Scenario*

System	Type	Number
Patriot	Long-range surface-to-air missile	12 batteries (~700 missiles)
THAAD	Land-based missile defense system	4 batteries (~180 missiles)
Virginia class	Nuclear-powered attack submarine	10
Seawolf class	Nuclear-powered attack submarine	2
Los Angeles class	Nuclear-powered attack submarine	13
Ohio class	Nuclear-powered cruise missile submarine	2
Ford class	Nuclear-powered aircraft carrier	1
Nimitz class	Nuclear-powered aircraft carrier	4
Zumwalt class	Land-attack destroyer	2
Arleigh Burke class	Destroyer	34
Ticonderoga class	Cruiser	6
Independence class, Freedom class	Littoral combat ship	11
America class	Amphibious assault carrier	1
Wasp class	Amphibious assault carrier	4
F-35C	Carrier-capable multirole stealth fighter	48
F/A-18E/F	Carrier-capable semistealthy multirole fighter	375
F/A-18C/D	Carrier-capable multirole fighter	270
EA-18G	Carrier-capable electronic warfare aircraft	90
F-35B	Short takeoff/vertical-landing multirole stealth fighter	40
AV-8	Short takeoff/vertical-landing ground attack fighter	85
P-8	Land-based maritime patrol aircraft	65
E-2	Carrier-capable airborne early warning and control aircraft	60
MQ-4	Unmanned maritime surveillance aircraft	8
F-22	Land-based air superiority stealth fighter	120
F-35A	Land-based multirole stealth fighter	200
F-15E	Land-based multirole fighter	140

(*continued*)

Table 9.4 (*continued*)

System	Type	Number
F-15C/D	Land-based air superiority fighter	150
F-16C/D	Land-based multirole fighter	225
E-3	Land-based airborne early warning and control aircraft	20
B-52H	Subsonic heavy bomber	36
B-1B	Supersonic heavy bomber	42
B-2A	Stealthy heavy bomber	12
KC-10	Aerial refueling/transport aircraft	36
KC-46	Aerial refueling/transport aircraft	45
KC-135	Aerial refueling aircraft	215
RQ-4	Unmanned reconnaissance aircraft	25
MQ-9	Unmanned reconnaissance/ground attack aircraft	215
RQ-180	Stealthy unmanned reconnaissance aircraft	Unknown
E-8	Ground surveillance aircraft	10
EC-130	Electronic warfare aircraft	8
RC-135	Electronic intelligence aircraft	11
Various	Optical/infrared imagery satellites	4
Various	Synthetic aperture radar imagery satellites	4
Various	Passive signals intelligence maritime surveillance satellites	3 pairs

China's Objectives and Overall Campaign Plan

The PLA's objective in this scenario is to force Taiwan to accept Beijing's rule over the island. Although the Chinese leadership would undoubtedly prefer that Taipei would capitulate before China invaded and conquered Taiwan, if Taiwan did not capitulate, forcing it to accept Beijing's rule would require an invasion and occupation of the island.[55]

A 2006 textbook on military campaigns, *Campaign Studies* 《战役学》, published by China's National Defense University, describes a generic approach for conducting amphibious invasions.[56] Although an invasion of Taiwan would undoubtedly differ in some of the details from the generic version described in *Campaign Studies* (especially since the PLA's doctrine for amphibious invasions will probably have been revised between 2006 and 2020), the overall approach described in *Campaign Studies* is probably largely accurate.

According to *Campaign Studies*, an amphibious landing campaign would consist of three main phases: (1) "initial operations" (先期作战), (2) "assembling & embarking and crossing the ocean" (集结上船和海上航度), and (3) "assaulting the beach and establishing a beachhead" (突击上陆和建立登陆场). The "initial operations" include seizing information superiority, air superiority, and sea control; neutralizing enemy defenses in the area where the landing will be conducted; and clearing mines and obstacles in the landing zone. Seizing information superiority, air superiority, and sea control, in turn, is said to entail neutralizing enemy command and control centers, communications hubs, information processing facilities, information warfare centers, radar emplacements, surface-to-air missile and anti-aircraft artillery batteries, air bases, navy bases and commercial ports, surface-to-surface missile emplacements, coastal defense missile emplacements, warships in port, munitions depots, aircraft, surface ships, and submarines. It also entails defending against such attacks from the adversary.[57]

Neutralizing enemy defenses in the area where the landing will be conducted entails attacks on many of the same targets as for seizing information superiority, air superiority, and sea control, but also involves attacks on transportation hubs, army bases, logistics facilities, artillery emplacements, other enemy ground forces, coastal defense guns, and fortifications. Clearing mines and obstacles in the landing zone entails attacks on a similar target set as well as finding and neutralizing enemy sea mines and destroying any natural or manmade obstacles in the water or on the landing beaches.[58]

Once initial operations are judged to be complete, the second phase, "assembling and embarking and crossing the ocean," begins. The invasion force moves to the embarkation ports, is loaded onto the amphibious transports, and sails to the invasion beaches. During this time the invader continues to maintain information superiority, air superiority, and sea control and to neutralize enemy defenses in the area where the landing will be conducted. Finally, when they arrive at the landing beaches, the third phase, "assaulting the beach and establishing a beachhead," begins. The invasion forces disembark, neutralize any enemy ground forces in the landing area, defeat any counterattacks on the beachhead, and expand the beachhead as rapidly as possible.[59] As additional forces are added to the beachhead, eventually the invasion force breaks out of the beachhead and seeks to conquer the entire enemy territory.

An amphibious invasion of Taiwan might well be accompanied by an airborne landing. Like an amphibious invasion, Chinese sources suggest that an airborne landing entails first seizing information and air superiority in the combat theater followed by the neutralization of enemy defenses in the area where the landing would be conducted. The airborne troops are then embarked onto their transport aircraft and flown to and dropped on the landing area, where they establish a defensive perimeter. Additional forces are brought in on subsequent airlifts.[60]

Assessment

Based on the description in *Campaign Studies*, therefore, a Chinese invasion of Taiwan would entail the PLA first attempting to seize information superiority, air superiority, and sea control in the area around Taiwan. Once these goals were achieved, they would be followed by efforts to neutralize Taiwanese defenses in the area where the amphibious and airborne landings would be conducted and to clear mines and obstacles in the amphibious landing zone. The invading forces would then be embarked, cross the Taiwan Strait, and attempt to land. Assuming they were successful and were able to hold off Taiwanese counterattacks, they would be reinforced by additional forces brought from the mainland until they were able to break out of their landing areas and conquer the rest of Taiwan.

Seizing Information Superiority and Air Superiority

Although *Campaign Studies* identifies seizing information superiority and seizing air superiority as two separate operations, in practice they would be closely interrelated. This is because many targets associated with the two different operations (e.g., radar stations) would be identical and because neutralizing some information superiority targets would require first neutralizing some air superiority targets and vice versa.

Specifically, the most effective and economical means of neutralizing many information superiority targets – such as command and control centers, communications hubs, information processing facilities, information warfare centers, and radar emplacements – would be with aircraft and cruise missiles. The ability of aircraft and cruise missiles to successfully attack those targets, however, would depend on the PLA first acquiring air superiority. Acquiring air superiority, on the other hand, would be facilitated by the existence of information superiority. This interrelationship between air superiority and information superiority implies, rather than one effort preceding the other, a prioritized sequencing of targets within both categories. Although the Chinese publications on military operations that have been analyzed are not specific about the order in which targets would be attacked and with what assets,[61] one logical approach that is consistent with those writing would be as follows:

Efforts to electronically infiltrate U.S. and Taiwanese military and civilian information systems would be underway well before the commencement of the attack. The actual attack would begin with the triggering of malware designed to disable, disrupt, or corrupt U.S. and Taiwanese information systems; the use of jammers and lasers to interfere with or blind U.S. and Taiwanese radars, surveillance satellites, and other sensors; the launching of antisatellite missiles against U.S. surveillance satellites; the launching of a barrage of ballistic missiles at U.S. and Taiwanese missile and air defense systems, air bases, and any warships within range of China's antiship ballistic missiles; and attacks on key targets – such as early warning radars, air traffic control facilities, underground cables and pipelines, and above-ground switching facilities and fuel manifolds – by covert operatives infiltrated in advance (potentially months or even years in advance) into Taiwan, Japan, and Guam.

Cruise missiles and aircraft with precision-guided munitions such as laser-guided and satellite-guided bombs and air-to-surface missiles would then be used to attack "point targets" that the ballistic missiles lacked the accuracy to directly hit with a high probability but were too robust to be vulnerable to ballistic missiles with small submunition warheads. Such targets would likely include hardened aircraft shelters, radar installations, command posts, communications hubs, aviation fuel storage and distribution facilities, aircraft repair and maintenance facilities, and munitions depots.

The PLA would also seek opportunities to attack U.S. aircraft carriers, another key element of achieving air superiority over Taiwan, whether with antiship ballistic missiles, submarine-launched torpedoes and antiship cruise missiles, land-based aircraft,[62] or even surface ships armed with antiship cruise missiles.

INITIAL INFORMATION ATTACKS Even experts on cyber warfare are uncertain as to how effective China's malware attacks might be.[63] Since this study has not determined that China's cyber warfare capabilities are likely to be dramatically better or worse than those of the U.S. or Taiwan in 2020, for purposes of this scenario, all three participants' cyber attacks are assumed to reduce the overall efficiency and effectiveness of each other's operations by a comparable amount and thus to largely cancel each other out. The net effect would likely to be to slow the overall pace and reduce the effectiveness of operations by interfering with the collection and dissemination of information about the locations of enemy forces, preventing units from receiving orders, disrupting supply flows, and so on.[64]

Given the limited number of direct-ascent antisatellite missiles China is postulated to have in this scenario (ten), they would probably be concentrated on the U.S. imagery satellites. If we assume that each antisatellite missile has a 50 percent chance of hitting a satellite, then, over the course of several days, China's ten antisatellite missiles would be expected to destroy about five of the United States' eight imagery satellites, leaving three operational.[65] The surviving satellites, as well as the six U.S. ocean surveillance satellites, would be subject to permanent or temporary blinding by lasers (in the case of optical/infrared satellites) and jamming (in the case of synthetic aperture radar and ocean surveillance satellites, the latter of which rely on passive collection of radio-frequency emissions from ships). All would be subject to attempts at disruption with high-power microwave beams.

Satellites in higher orbits, such as the GPS satellites, which orbit at an altitude of 12,500 miles (as opposed to about three hundred miles for imagery and ocean surveillance satellites), or communications satellites, which orbit at an altitude of twenty-two thousand miles above the earth's surface, would be relatively safe from ground-based lasers and high-power microwave beams, but their signals would still be subject to jamming.[66] In the case of communications satellites, whose function is to relay messages between two points on the earth's surface, the jamming would be directed into the satellites' receiving antennas, with the aim of preventing them from properly receiving the messages they are intended to relay. In the case of GPS satellites, such "uplink" jamming would not be effective, as the only signals they receive are occasional command signals and updates on their precise positions, all of which could be accomplished when the satellites were passing over the Western Hemisphere, away from China's jammers.[67] Instead, jamming would be focused on the terrestrial receivers of the relatively weak signals that come down from the GPS satellites. Such jammers would be ground-based, ship-borne, or airborne, depending on the application.

How effective all these efforts would be would depend on the numbers of antisatellite systems China possesses in 2020 and the technical characteristics of both the Chinese systems and the U.S. satellites, none of which is publicly available information. For purposes of this scenario, the net effect is assumed to be to substantially degrade, but not completely eliminate, U.S. ability to use its reconnaissance satellites, and to somewhat degrade the U.S. ability to use its military communications satellites. However, the U.S. would still have access to commercial satellite imagery, whose quality is continuously increasing, as well as to commercial communications satellites.[68] China's ability to disrupt or destroy these commercial satellites, owned by a variety of international consortia, would be limited both by their number and by the problem of attacking the assets of neutral nations in a conflict that China would wish to portray as involving only itself, the United States, and U.S.-backed separatists in Taiwan.[69]

Aside from satellites, the PLA would also attempt to degrade terrestrial sensors, most particularly radars. Radar jamming is a long-standing problem in warfare, and a variety of measures and countermeasures have been developed since the advent of radars. For purposes of this scenario, the net effect is assumed to be to degrade but not nullify the effectiveness of U.S. and Taiwanese ground-based, ship-borne, and air-borne radars.

INITIAL MISSILE ATTACKS The first target of the Chinese ballistic missile barrage would be U.S. and Taiwanese missile defenses. In the case of Taiwan this would include a long-range early warning radar system that became operational in early 2013[70] and Taiwan's ten Patriot PAC-3 batteries. Since the early warning radar has a diameter of about one hundred feet,[71] depending on the accuracy of China's SRBMs, a missile might possibly score a direct hit on the radar, which would probably destroy it.[72] If China's missiles lacked the accuracy to score a direct hit with a unitary warhead, a warhead that released runway-penetrating submunitions would probably be able to achieve multiple hits on the radar with its submunitions, severely damaging it. Using either method, two or three missiles aimed at the radar would be sufficient to put it out of action with a high probability.[73]

Each Patriot battery is apparently capable of intercepting two ballistic missiles at a time.[74] Assuming the locations of Taiwan's Patriot batteries were known at the time of missile launch, therefore, if five missiles were fired at each Patriot battery and timed to arrive nearly simultaneously then, even if one in five missiles failed or went off course, the battery would be able to intercept at most two of the remaining four. If the missiles were armed with small submunitions of the type described earlier in this chapter, key equipment items such as the Patriot's Engagement Control Station or radar system would likely be disabled. Thus, a total of fifty SRBMs should be sufficient to neutralize Taiwan's Patriot batteries.[75]

In this scenario, Kadena Air Base on Okinawa, in addition to hosting four batteries of Patriots, is also defended by a THAAD battery. THAAD is said to have a maximum intercept range of about 180 miles, as compared to about twelve miles for the Patriot's PAC-3 antimissile interceptor.[76] Thus, it is possible that THAAD could intercept as many as twenty-four missiles from the time they entered its engagement envelope until the time they impacted.[77] The four Patriot batteries at Kadena would each be able to intercept up to two additional missiles, once the missiles were close enough. This implies that at most sixty-five SRBMs would be needed to neutralize Kadena's ballistic missile defenses.[78]

The JASDF base at Komatsu in central Japan is defended by four U.S. Patriot batteries in this scenario. Thus, twenty ballistic missiles should be sufficient to neutralize Komatsu's ballistic missile defenses. However, Komatsu is out of range of China's SRBMs and would have to be attacked by medium-range ballistic missiles.

Misawa Air Base is defended by the Sixth Air Defense Missile Group of the JASDF,[79] which is assumed to operate three batteries of Patriots. In addition, as noted in the Order of Battle section, in this scenario a battery of THAAD is based near Misawa. Since China is assumed to avoid deliberately attacking Japanese military units in this scenario, only the THAAD battery would be attacked. Using the same logic as above, approximately forty ballistic missiles would be needed to ensure that it was put out of action.[80] These would again need to be medium-range ballistic missiles.

The JASDF base at Chitose on Hokkaido is similarly defended by the Third Air Defense Missile Group of the JASDF and, in this scenario, one THAAD battery. As at Misawa, approximately forty medium-range ballistic missiles would be needed to neutralize the THAAD battery at Chitose, with the JASDF Patriot batteries remaining untouched.

Simultaneously neutralizing the THAAD and U.S. Patriot batteries at Komatsu, Misawa, and Chitose would thus require a total of approximately one hundred medium-range ballistic missiles. However, in this scenario the PLA has only seventy-five DF-21C medium-range conventional ballistic missile launchers (not including twelve DF-21D launchers dedicated to launching antiship ballistic missiles). The PLA is therefore assumed to concentrate its initial medium-range ballistic missile salvo on Misawa and Komatsu.

Once the THAAD system at Misawa was neutralized, the PLA's goal would be to neutralize the aircraft based there. Since there are more than enough hardened shelters at Misawa to protect the seventy-two F-35As based there in this scenario from attack by ballistic missiles with small submunitions (assuming that at least twelve aircraft are in the air at any one time), the most effective ways to neutralize the F-35As would be either to damage the runways so that the aircraft could not take off or land or else to destroy their shelters. Damaging the runways would put Misawa out of action temporarily, but the runways could be made usable again in a fairly short amount of time. Destroying the shelters, on the other hand, would destroy any aircraft inside of them and force the U.S. Air Force to park any surviving aircraft in the open or in unhardened structures.

Since aircraft shelters are too small for even highly accurate ballistic missiles to hit directly with a high probability and small submunitions are ineffective against hardened aircraft shelters, the most effective way to attack the shelters at Misawa would be with land-attack cruise missiles or with manned aircraft armed with precision-guided munitions.. Manned aircraft, however, might be engaged by Japanese fighters defending Japan's air space and therefore need to fire back at them for self-preservation. Since this scenario assumes that China tries to avoid direct combat with Japanese forces, this suggests that China would more likely use CJ-10 land-attack cruise missiles to attack the shelters.

In this scenario the two squadrons of Japanese F-2s normally based at Misawa are operating from Matsushima, 160 miles to the south, but flying combat air patrols over northern Honshu. At that range, about eight F-2s would be flying near Misawa at any one time.[81] Each F-2 would carry four Japanese AAM-4s or U.S. AIM-120 AMRAAM air-to-air missiles.[82] The AAM-4 does not have a combat record but the AIM-120, which is similar in capability, has shot down approximately 60 percent (ten of seventeen) of the aircraft it has been fired at in combat.[83] If we therefore assume that each AAM-4 similarly has a 0.6 probability of successfully intercepting a cruise missile, then the eight F-2s on station would on average intercept about nineteen cruise missiles.[84] Since the three JASDF Patriot batteries at Misawa would not have been attacked by ballistic missiles, moreover, each cruise missile that was not shot down by an F-2 would also be subject to interception by the Patriots. Each JASDF Patriot battery consists of five quadruple launchers, so the three batteries would have a total of sixty missiles available to fire (it takes approximately an hour to reload Patriot launchers after firing).[85] If we assume that, like the AAM-4 and AIM-120, the Patriots have a 0.6 probability of successful intercept, they would be able to shoot down at most about thirty-six of the CJ-10s that survived intercept by the F-2s.[86] If the PLA simultaneously launched four CJ-10s at each shelter at Misawa, therefore (i.e., a total of 240 CJ-10s), then on average nineteen would be shot down by Japanese F-2s, another thirty-six would be intercepted by the Patriot batteries, and the surviving 185 CJ-10s would destroy most of the sixty shelters at Misawa,[87] along with approximately forty aircraft inside them.[88] Misawa would thus be reduced to about thirty F-35As and three usable shelters after this attack.

At Komatsu, as stated earlier, the two squadrons of F-15Js normally based there are in this scenario assumed to have redeployed to a nearby base in central Honshu but to be conducting combat air patrols in the area. As a result, at any one time an average of eleven F-15Js would be conducting combat air patrols in the airspace near Komatsu.[89] If each F-15J carried six AAM-4s,[90] then on average they would intercept about forty cruise missiles.

The four U.S. Patriot batteries positioned near Komatsu are assumed to have been neutralized by the initial DF-21 salvo and therefore unable to intercept any cruise missiles. If the PLA fired four CJ-10s at each of the fourteen shelters at Komatsu (a total of fifty-six), on average eight shelters, each with an F-35A inside, would be destroyed, leaving Komatsu with sixteen operational F-35As and six usable shelters.[91]

In this scenario the PLA also possesses twenty-five intermediate-range ballistic missiles capable of reaching Guam. Since Andersen Air Force Base is defended by a THAAD battery and four Patriot batteries, twenty-five missiles are probably not sufficient to neutralize the missile defenses at Guam with certainty while still reserving an operationally significant number for attacking the airfield itself. Instead, therefore, these missiles are assumed to all be launched directly at the parking areas at Andersen.

If 20 percent of these missiles fail or fly off course, half of the remainder are successfully intercepted by THAAD, and each of the four Patriot batteries successfully shoots down one of the remaining ten missiles, then a total of only six would reach their targets. Assuming that, in the crisis atmosphere leading up to the onset of hostilities, the F-22s at Andersen were flying continuous combat air patrols over Taiwan, only about 60 percent of the 120 F-22s and 100 KC-135s operating out of Andersen would be on the ground at any one time.[92] A total of forty missiles would be required to cover all of the possible parking areas at Andersen,[93] so six missiles arriving on target would only cover 15 percent of the parking areas and thus on average destroy eleven F-22s and nine KC-135s. If, more pessimistically for the United States, THAAD is assumed to successfully intercept only one or two of the incoming ballistic missiles and the Patriots do not intercept any (because of the extremely high speeds of an intermediate-range ballistic missile), then on average about thirty-two F-22s and twenty-seven KC-135s would be destroyed.

Altogether, the PLA's initial missile salvo would have used approximately 120 of its eleven hundred SRBMs, sixty of its 320 conventionally armed medium-range ballistic missiles, all twenty-five of its conventionally armed intermediate-range ballistic missiles, and three hundred of its eleven hundred land-attack cruise missiles. The results would be the neutralization of the missile defenses on Taiwan and at the air bases at Kadena, Komatsu, and Misawa, the destruction of most of the shelters at Misawa and Komatsu, and the destruction of approximately twenty F-22s, fifty-five F-35As, and twenty KC-135s.

SUBSEQUENT MISSILE AND AIR ATTACKS After the initial missile salvo, the PLA's best approach to achieving air and information superiority in the area around Taiwan would be to reload and reposition its missile launchers and launch a second round of ballistic missile attacks, which is assumed to be possible approximately eight hours later, followed by attacks by cruise missiles and manned aircraft.[94]

In the case of Kadena Air Base, roughly fifteen of the fifty-four U.S. F-15s based at Kadena would likely be in the air conducting combat air patrols at any one time.[95] Thus, about thirty-nine of them would be on the ground at the time of the second ballistic missile salvo. There are only fifteen shelters at Kadena, meaning that about twenty-four F-15s would be parked in the open or in unreinforced structures such as hangers and thus vulnerable to ballistic missiles with small submunition warheads. Kadena is a very large air base (the airfield and surrounding parking areas cover about three square miles). Thus, unless the PLA knew the specific location of each aircraft parked on the ground at Kadena (e.g., from very recent satellite imagery), about seventy SRBMs would be required to cover all potential parking areas for those aircraft. Such a missile barrage would destroy approximately 80 percent of the aircraft not parked in hardened shelters at Kadena (i.e., about twenty).

To destroy the aircraft protected by hardened shelters at Kadena (and render the shelters unusable by other aircraft) would require cruise missiles or manned aircraft armed with precision-guided munitions. Two squadrons of JASDF F-15Js will be based at nearby Naha air base,[96] however, and would presumably be flying combat air patrols to defend Okinawa's airspace. Since this scenario assumes that China avoids direct combat with Japanese forces, this suggests that China would therefore be more likely to launch a salvo of CJ-10 land-attack cruise missiles at the shelters.

The JASDF squadrons at Naha would be able to keep about eleven F-15Js airborne on combat air patrol at any one time.[97] If each carried six active radar-guided AAM-4 air-to-air missiles and the AAM-4s each had a 0.6 probability of successfully intercepting a cruise missile, then these aircraft could on average intercept about forty cruise missiles. If the PLA launched four CJ-10s at each shelter on Kadena (i.e., a total of sixty CJ-10s), therefore, on average about ten of the fifteen shelters would be destroyed, along with the aircraft inside of them.[98] This would leave Kadena with approximately twenty-five operational F-15s and five usable shelters. The small number of shelters would almost certainly deter the United States from deploying additional aircraft to Kadena, but this scenario assumes that the F-15s already at Kadena would continue to operate from there.

As noted earlier, although the air bases at Komatsu, Misawa, and Chitose are all within range of China's medium-range ballistic missiles, this scenario assumes that the PLA does not have enough medium-range ballistic missile launchers to simultaneously attack all three of them simultaneously and thus concentrates its initial attack on the two bases closest to Taiwan – Komatsu and Misawa. Chitose, therefore, would not be attacked until a second salvo of medium-range ballistic missiles could be fired. A salvo of approximately forty medium-range ballistic missiles would be sufficient to neutralize the THAAD battery at Chitose, and CJ-10 land-attack cruise missiles could be used to destroy the shelters at Chitose. In this scenario, the two squadrons of JASDF F-15Js normally based at Chitose have relocated to Akita but are flying combat air patrols over Hokkaido, which would result in approximately nine F-15Js on combat air patrol at any given time.[99] If, as before, four CJ-10s are launched at each of the twenty-eight shelters on Chitose (i.e., a total of 112 CJ-10s), then on average twenty of the twenty-eight shelters, each with an F-35A inside, would be destroyed, leaving Chitose with approximately twenty-eight F-35As and eight usable shelters.[100]

On Taiwan, its missile defenses having been neutralized by the initial ballistic missile attacks, its air bases would be essentially defenseless against subsequent ballistic missile attacks. However, Taiwan's air bases have an average of approximately fifty hardened aircraft shelters each, along with mountainside aircraft storage tunnels at Chia Shan and Taitung,[101] more than enough to protect all of the 280 fighter aircraft Taiwan possesses in this scenario. The PLA's best approach to defeating Taiwan's air force, therefore, would be to use its ballistic missiles to damage the runways at Taiwan's air bases, preventing Taiwan's aircraft from taking off, and use cruise missiles or manned aircraft with precision-guided munitions to attack the aircraft shelters.[102]

The number of missiles needed to damage the runways at Taiwan's air bases so that aircraft were unable to take off or land would depend on the accuracy of the missiles. A wide range of accuracies have been suggested for the PLA's SRBMs, depending in part on the type and model of missile, but it appears likely that a significant number have an accuracy of 150 feet or less and possibly as small as sixteen feet.[103] If we assume an intermediate value of about eighty feet for the accuracy of these missiles, then an attack on the runways at Taiwan's air force bases that used approximately seventy-five missiles would leave Taiwan with only one air base, on average, that had an operational runway.[104] And, until damaged runways at the other bases could be repaired, Taiwan would have only about sixty fighters available to respond to Chinese aircraft or cruise missile attacks.[105]

Any surviving U.S. fighters operating from Kadena, Komatsu, Misawa, Chitose, Andersen, and U.S. aircraft carriers would also be available to defend Taiwan against air and cruise missile attack. As described earlier in this section, the PLA's initial missile attacks on Guam would have destroyed approximately twenty F-22s and twenty KC-135s at Guam. Since a total of 215 KC-135s are available to the United States in this scenario and only one hundred are deployed to Guam initially, twenty KC-135s could be flown to Guam to replace those lost in the missile attack and would be able to begin operations within a day or so. All of the F-22s available to the United States in this scenario would already be operating from Guam, however, so any F-22s lost would have to be replaced with other aircraft. These are assumed to be the U.S. Air Force's next-most capable fighter, the F-35A. A squadron of 24 F-35As, therefore, is flown to Guam and begins operations on the second day of combat.[106] If we assume that 80 percent of the F-22s and F-35As on Guam are available for combat on any given day, that each available aircraft is able to perform one twelve-hour flight per day, and that the transit from Guam to Taiwan, including aerial refueling en route, requires roughly four hours each way,[107] then, once the F-35As began operations, at any one time there would be approximately thirteen F-22s and three F-35As from Guam flying over Taiwan, with a new group of thirteen F-22s and three F-35As arriving to replace the current group every four hours.[108] In addition, if the twenty-five surviving F-15s at Kadena were each able to conduct two flights a day, patrolling over Taiwan for four hours each time, then there would be about seven F-15s flying over Taiwan at any one time.[109] Similarly, Komatsu, Misawa, and Chitose would be able to keep three, four, and four F-35As, respectively, flying over Taiwan at any one time.[110]

As indicated earlier in this chapter, the five U.S. fleet aircraft carriers and five amphibious assault carriers in this scenario have a total of forty-eight F-35Cs, forty-five F-35Bs, and 234 F/A-18E/Fs (the carrier-based F/A-18G jamming aircraft, although combat-capable, are assumed to not directly engage in air-to-air combat). The U.S. Navy would have two main options regarding where to locate its carriers. One would be to have them operate fairly close to Taiwan, to maximize the number of aircraft it could keep over Taiwan at any one time. The disadvantage of this approach would be that the carriers would be subject to attack by a variety of means, including the PLA's antiship ballistic missiles and as well as land-based aircraft, submarines, and surface ships, all armed with torpedoes or antiship cruise missiles, some of them supersonic. Not only would locating the carriers so close to Taiwan risk them being put out of action by these attacks, the carriers' aircraft would be preoccupied with fending off such attacks and have a limited ability to contribute to the battle for air superiority over Taiwan. Consequently, the U.S. Navy is assumed to, at least initially, operate its carriers about twelve hundred miles away from China, out of range of the PLA's antiship ballistic missiles and land-based strike aircraft. Although they would still theoretically be subject to attack by China's submarines and surface ships at that range, most of China's submarines are diesel-electric-powered and thus cannot move quickly for long distances while submerged, and approaching the surface to snorkel would risk detection and attack. Any of China's surface ships attempting to engage the U.S. carriers would be vulnerable to attack by U.S. submarines and would be moving out beyond friendly air cover, making any survivors of the submarine attacks vulnerable to attack by U.S. aircraft. The surface ships and submarines escorting the U.S. carriers, along with the carrier aircraft assigned to protecting the carrier group, are therefore assumed to be able to manage PLA submarine and surface ship threats so that their effect on the air operations is minimal.

Each of the five fleet carriers is assumed to keep an average of four F/A-18E/Fs in the air flying self-protective combat air patrols over the carrier strike group at all times. The F-35Cs, the remaining F/A-18s, and all of the F-35Bs operating from the amphibious assault carriers are devoted to flying combat air patrols over Taiwan (the amphibious assault carriers are grouped together with fleet carriers and thus are protected from air attack by the self-protective combat air patrols from the fleet carriers as well as the air defense capabilities of the escorting cruisers and destroyers).[111] This would enable approximately six F-35Cs, six F-35Bs, and thirteen F/A-18E/Fs to be maintained on station over Taiwan at any one time.[112] Thus, U.S. Air Force, U.S. Navy, and U.S. Marine Corps fighters would together be able to maintain a total of approximately thirteen F-22s, twenty-three F-35s, seventeen F/A-18E/Fs, and seven F-15s on combat air patrol over Taiwan at the beginning of the conflict.[113]

In this scenario, China has a total of 665 fighter aircraft[114] and 155 JH-7 PLA Air Force fighter-bombers available to it for attacks on Taiwan.[115] Since the PLA would be choosing the day on which the war began, these aircraft are assumed to have an 80 percent readiness rate initially, despite the PLA's inferior repair and maintenance capabilities. This readiness rate, however, is assumed to fall by 3 percent per day throughout the conflict, as PLA finds itself unable to sustain such a high rate of readiness. In addition, maintenance and sortie-generation limitations are assumed to limit each of these aircraft to flying no more than two times a day, regardless of the length of the flight.[116]

One-third of the PLA's available fighters are assumed to be devoted to flying combat air patrols over Chinese territory to defend against potential U.S. counterattacks. This leaves about 360 fighters and 120 JH-7s for offensive operations (given an 80 percent initial readiness rate) on the first day of the air war.[117] Since coordinating this many aircraft in the air at the same time would be logistically and organizationally challenging for the PLA, rather than all of them taking flight together twice a day, instead a third of them –

120 fighters and forty JH-7s – are assumed to launch an attack on Taiwan every four hours.

Given the proximity of Taiwan's air bases to the locations where Taiwan's fighters would operate when engaging PLA aircraft (probably just off of Taiwan's coast), and the likely warning time Taiwan would have that a Chinese raid was developing,[118] the sixty fighters at Taiwan's one operational air base would not need to be kept in the air continuously. More likely about ten would be in the air at any one time while the remainder stayed on the ground on "strip alert," ready to take off on short notice. Assuming an 80 percent readiness rate, Taiwan could therefore send about forty-eight fighters to meet the initial Chinese raid.[119]

The initial air-to-air clash, therefore, would consist of 120 PLA fighters and forty PLA fighter-bombers against 108 U.S. and Taiwanese fighters. What would be the outcome of this engagement? Much would depend on the relative capabilities of the aircraft and the pilots flying them and the skill of the commanders on the ground orchestrating the conflict. The analysis here is not intended to be a detailed simulation of the capabilities of different types of aircraft or of air-to-air combat. As a first-order estimate, therefore, the air-to-air combat capabilities of all "fourth generation fighters" are assumed to be roughly comparable. This includes the F-16s, F-15s, F/A-18s, J-10s, J-11s, Su-27s, and Su-30s involved in the combat. As an aircraft that is essentially a modernized third-generation fighter, the F-CK-1 is considered to be about 75 percent as capable as the fourth-generation aircraft.[120] The fifth-generation F-22, F-35, and J-20, however, are qualitatively superior aircraft. Each F-22 is assumed to have the combat power of three fourth-generation fighters, and the F-35 and J-20 are each assumed to be equivalent to two fourth-generation fighters.[121] The superior training and command of U.S. aircraft, moreover, is assumed to mean that China and Taiwan's aircraft are only 80 percent as effective as their U.S. counterparts.

Based on these assumptions, the U.S. and Taiwanese forces would actually have a more than 50 percent advantage in combat power in the initial air-to-air clash.[122] If they pressed this advantage such that it resulted in 5 percent losses to the Chinese side – a high but not unprecedented attrition rate for air-to-air combat – then it would imply losses of about 2 percent on the U.S. and Taiwanese side.[123] In concrete terms this would mean that, in the initial clash, the PLA would lose about six fighters and two JH-7s, and the United States and Taiwan would each lose one fighter on average.

The role of the PLA's JH-7s would be to suppress Taiwan's Tien Kung and Hawk surface-to-air missile batteries (which, because they are housed in underground silos, in the case of Tien Kung, and mobile, in the case of

Hawk, would be relatively safe from ballistic missile attack) and to destroy aircraft shelters at Taiwan's air force bases. Of the forty JH-7s in the initial attack, ten are assumed to be devoted to suppressing surface-to-air missile batteries and thirty to destroying aircraft shelters. If we assume that, in addition to shooting down two JH-7s, the U.S. and Taiwanese fighter aircraft defending Taiwan cause half of the surviving thirty-eight JH-7s to break off their attacks or otherwise be unable to reach their attack locations,[124] then on average five JH-7s would succeed in attacking Taiwan's surface-to-air missile batteries and fourteen would succeed in launching attacks on aircraft shelters on Taiwan. For Taiwan's surface-to-air missile batteries to engage the incoming PLA aircraft, the batteries' radars would need to be exposed and radiating, which would make them vulnerable to attack by high-speed antiradiation missiles carried by the JH-7s.[125] For simplicity, therefore, most of Taiwan's surface-to-air missile batteries are assumed to either be destroyed or else choose not to turn on their radars, with the net effect that, although they cause the PLA to devote a quarter of its JH-7s to suppressing them, they do not cause significant attrition to the PLA's aircraft or missiles launched at Taiwan. As a result, the fourteen JH-7s that launch attacks on aircraft shelters would be able to destroy an average of approximately thirteen hardened shelters with a total of six aircraft inside them at Taiwan's air bases.[126]

Assuming the runway repair crews at Taiwan's air bases were able to restore flight operations at Taiwan's air bases (i.e., fill enough holes to create a straight surface at least five thousand feet long and fifty feet wide) in less than four hours, the PLA would need to launch another salvo of SRBMs at Taiwan's runways before the PLA's next aircraft raid arrived. As before, seventy-five missiles would on average shut down all but one of Taiwan's airfields.[127] Odds are, however, that the one airfield shut down would be a *different* airfield than before. After the second round of ballistic missile attacks on Taiwan's airfields, therefore, the one air base that was still operational would on average have only twenty-seven fighters.[128]

Consequently when the second wave of Chinese air attacks arrived, four hours after the first wave, Taiwan would only be able to get about twenty-two fighters into the air. As a result, the U.S.-Taiwan advantage in air-to-air combat power would be reduced to about 30 percent. If China's losses were again 5 percent, therefore, then U.S. and Taiwanese losses in air-to-air combat would be about 2.7 percent. Afterward, the PLA's JH-7s would destroy another thirteen shelters with six aircraft inside.

Meanwhile, assuming that it would take the PLA approximately eight hours to reload and reposition its ballistic missile launchers, after the second air attack on Taiwan, the PLA would be able to reattack Kadena and

Misawa in an attempt to further reduce the number of aircraft operating from there. Another seventy SRBMs and sixty CJ-10 land-attack cruise missiles at Kadena would likely destroy another eleven F-15s and three shelters, reducing it to fourteen F-15s and three usable shelters, and thus the number of F-15s in the air over Taiwan at any one time from seven to about four.[129] Similarly, launching seventy medium-range ballistic missiles at the parking areas and taxiways at Misawa would destroy about twelve more F-35As, leaving Misawa with nineteen.[130] Afterwards, Misawa would only be able to keep about two or three F-35As in the air over Taiwan at any one time. Finally, another salvo of 56 CJ-10s could be launched at Komatsu, destroying four more shelters, each with an F-35A inside, leaving Komatsu with twelve F-35As and two usable shelters, and able to maintain an average of only two fighters in the air over Taiwan at any one time. These attacks, combined with the additional Taiwanese aircraft destroyed on the ground, would mean that the U.S.-Taiwan advantage in air-to-air combat power in the third round of air-to-air combat would be reduced to about 20 percent. With plenty of SRBMs available, moreover, the PLA could continue to launch a salvo of seventy-five at Taiwan every four hours, disabling, on average, all but one of the Taiwan's air bases at any one time, while the PLA's fighters continued to do battle with the U.S. and Taiwanese fighters over Taiwan and the PLA's fighter-bombers continued to attack Taiwan's aircraft shelters.

After the fourth round of air-to-air combat, the PLA would be able to launch another salvo of medium-range ballistic missiles. Launching sixty-five medium-range ballistic missiles at the parking areas at Chitose, followed by four CJ-10 cruise missiles at each of the twenty-eight shelters on Chitose (a total of 112 CJ-10s), would destroy an average of thirteen more F-35As and six more shelters, leaving Chitose with fifteen F-35As and two usable shelters.[131] As a result, Chitose would only be able to maintain about two F-35As over Taiwan at any one time. In the meantime, however, the squadron of twenty-four F-35As that was deployed to Guam to replace the F-22s destroyed in the ballistic missile attack would begin operations, with the result that the U.S.-Taiwan advantage in air-to-air combat power would actually increase somewhat, to about 25 percent.

After a sixth round of air-to-air combat, the PLA would be able to launch a final salvo of DF-21 medium-range ballistic missiles at Misawa, where they would, on average, destroy another six F-35As on the ground, leaving Misawa with thirteen F-35As (and three usable shelters).[132] At this point, however, the PLA's inventory of land-attack medium-range ballistic missiles would essentially be depleted, and the United States and Taiwan would still enjoy a net advantage in air-to-air combat.

The PLA would still have four hundred CJ-10 land-attack cruise missiles, which could also be equipped with small-submunition warheads and used to attack unsheltered aircraft at U.S. air bases in Japan. The payload of the CJ-10 is estimated to be about half of the size of the DF-21C's,[133] meaning that a small submunition warhead on the CJ-10 would be able to cover about half the area of that a warhead on the DF-21C could cover. Thus, about 130 CJ-10s with small submunition warheads would be required to cover all of the parking areas at Chitose. If we assume that 260 such missiles are launched so as to be certain of overwhelming the fighters and Patriot batteries defending Chitose, then another six F-35As would be destroyed, leaving Chitose with nine F-35As.[134] If the remaining 140 CJ-10s were launched at Komatsu, they would destroy another five F-35As and one shelter, leaving Komatsu with seven F-35As and one usable shelter.[135]

The PLA would also still have more than three hundred SRBMs. It could thus launch four more salvos of seventy-five at Taiwan, one every four hours, while its fighters continued to do battle with the U.S. and Taiwanese fighters over Taiwan and its fighter-bombers continued to attack Taiwan's aircraft shelters. After two days of combat, however, the PLA would have expended nearly all of its SRBMs, and, because of the large number of aircraft shelters in Taiwan, much of Taiwan's air force would still be intact. As a result, the United States and Taiwan would likely still enjoy an advantage in air-to-air combat.

This advantage, moreover, would likely increase over time. This is because the United States has many more fighters than are able to participate in combat at any one time in this scenario, whereas is the PLA is assumed to be using all of the fighter aircraft it has committed to this conflict. Specifically, only 168 out of two hundred F-35As available to the U.S. Air Force and 234 out of 375 F/A-18E/Fs available to the U.S. Navy participate initially. As F-22s and F-35As flying out of Guam and off of the carriers are lost in air-to-air combat, they can be replaced by F-35As and F/A-18E/Fs, respectively. Although the F-35s are less capable than any F-22s lost and the F/A-18E/Fs are less capable than any F-35Cs that are lost, the net effect is that the air power generated by Guam and the carriers would diminish only gradually, as each aircraft lost could be replaced by another, albeit perhaps less-capable, aircraft.[136] For the PLA, on the other hand, all of the fighter aircraft available to it for this conflict are participating from the beginning. Each aircraft lost, therefore, is not replaced.[137] Over the long term, therefore, the U.S.-Taiwan advantage in air-to-air combat would continually increase and the PLA would be unable to achieve air superiority over Taiwan.[138]

The primary conclusion from this analysis, however, should not be that the U.S. and Taiwan can be confident of prevailing in a battle for air superiority with China in 2020. The multiple simplifications and approximations made in this analysis make such a conclusion unwarranted when the forces are in fact closely balanced. The conclusion, rather, should be that *neither* side can be confident of prevailing and that even the winning side is likely to sustain significant losses. War is a highly chaotic phenomenon in which seemingly small events can have decisive effects. Which side would actually prevail would depend on strategy, luck, and exactly how well the organizations, people, and equipment on the two sides actually performed. Given that an analysis of this scenario based on the forces available to the two sides in 2000 or even 2010 would almost certainly have predicted a lopsided victory for the United States and Taiwan, moreover, the trend appears to be running against them over the long run.

Amphibious Invasion of Taiwan

If, despite the findings of the preceding subsection, the United States and Taiwan began to lose the battle for air superiority, the best course of action for them would be to disengage their air and naval forces and hold them in reserve to interdict any attempted amphibious invasion of the island. In the case of Taiwan this would entail keeping its aircraft in the storage tunnels at Hualien and Taitung and putting its naval forces to sea out of range of China's land-based aircraft and missiles. In the case of the United States it would similarly entail keeping its naval forces well away from the Chinese mainland and keeping its aircraft on the ground or flying defensive combat air patrols over Japan and Guam. This would amount to conceding air superiority and sea control in the area around Taiwan and would give the PLA a free hand to conduct the other actions described in *Campaign Studies* as part of the initial operations in preparation for the invasion: attacking any targets associated with information superiority that had not yet been neutralized, attacking Taiwanese defenses in the area where the amphibious and airborne landings would be conducted, and clearing mines and obstacles in the amphibious landing zone. These unopposed attacks on Taiwan's infrastructure and defenses could potentially be sufficient to cause Taiwan to capitulate. Historically, however, populations under siege have not quickly capitulated, and the longer a conflict continued, the more international public opinion and possibly economic sanctions would be mobilized against China. Using air power to destroy ground forces in complex terrain such as Taiwan's highly urbanized west coast, moreover, would be a painstaking process,[139] and the PLA would fairly quickly reach a point of diminishing returns in that regard. For these reasons, the Chinese leadership would probably want to launch an amphibious invasion of Taiwan after a relatively brief period of bombardment – perhaps a few days or a week.

The amphibious landing ships involved in the invasion would likely depart from multiple points along China's southeast coast, both because of the sheer number of ships that would need to be loaded – roughly 180 – and to complicate and confuse any U.S. or Taiwanese attempts to intercept the invasion fleet.[140] PLA Navy surface ships would patrol the areas north and south of the Taiwan Strait, defending the landing ships from air and naval attack and searching for U.S. and Taiwanese submarines.

When the decision was made to initiate the landing operation, the landing ships would begin to converge toward one or two landing sites on Taiwan's coast. U.S. satellite surveillance of the waters surrounding China might be denied by laser dazzlers and jammers on board PLA Navy ships, and surveillance of the Taiwan Strait by conventional aircraft would be risky given the assumption that the United States and Taiwan have conceded air superiority in the area around Taiwan. MQ-4 unmanned maritime surveillance aircraft flying at fifty thousand feet, however, would be able to see into the Taiwan Strait from points well to the east of Taiwan, where they could be protected by fighter escorts.[141] In addition, the RQ-180 stealthy unmanned surveillance aircraft will be capable of operating within interception range of China's surface-to-air missiles and manned fighters, although it is unclear how many RQ-180s will be in service by 2020.[142] F-22 and F-35 stealth fighters, with their highly capable onboard radars, could also potentially act as reconnaissance aircraft.[143] If the United States and Taiwan succeeded in detecting the invasion fleet while it was still several hours away from landing its forces on Taiwan, then there would be an opportunity to launch attacks on the landing ships before they beached.

The most effective means for attacking the landing ships would be U.S. nuclear attack submarines, of which twenty-five are available in this scenario. Modern U.S. attack submarines are highly lethal against surface ships and very difficult to find and attack. If the U.S. attack submarines were positioned off of China's coast near the northern and southern ends of the Taiwan Strait, analysis suggests that they could sink as many as half or more of the amphibious landing ships.[144]

If significant numbers of landing ships survived the submarine attacks, the U.S. Navy would have the option of attacking the remaining ships using aircraft armed with long-range, stealthy antiship missiles.[145] When the remaining landing ships approached Taiwan, moreover, they would be subject to attack by Taiwan's coastal defenses.[146] These could include antiship cruise missiles launched from mobile, land-based vehicles;[147] long-range artillery positioned in advance to attack possible landing sites; and sea mines laid on the approach routes to the relatively few and small beaches on Taiwan's coast. The net effect of these U.S. and Taiwanese attacks would likely be to reduce the initially landed forces to the equivalent of less than one mechanized infantry division, significantly less than the amount of combat power in Taiwan's armed forces.[148] Given the assumption that the PLA has achieved air superiority over Taiwan, these forces might be sufficient to defeat Taiwan's ground forces or at least to break out of the beachheads and seize a port so that additional forces (and supplies) could be brought to Taiwan using conventional shipping. If not, however, the landing ships would have to return to China to bring additional ground forces, likely suffering additional losses on the second trip, with the result that at most the equivalent of one or two mechanized infantry brigades could be added to the already landed forces.[149] After two such trips the PLA could well be down to forty to fifty operational amphibious landing ships. A third trip, therefore, would be able to land at most one additional mechanized infantry brigade,[150] and a fourth trip, assuming additional losses, would be pointless. Thus, it appears that, even if China succeeded in achieving air superiority over Taiwan, something that would appear to be dubious in 2020, an amphibious invasion of the island would be a costly and highly risky operation. If China did *not* succeed in achieving air superiority over Taiwan, moreover, an amphibious invasion would likely be suicidal. Not only would even more ships likely be lost en route, but the landed forces would have to fight against an enemy able to freely use aircraft and helicopters in defending against the invasion.

Conclusions

Three main conclusions should be drawn from the above analysis. First, it does not appear that China in 2020 will have reason to be confident of successfully invading Taiwan if the United States intervenes on Taiwan's side. The forces involved would be, at best, roughly evenly matched, meaning that there would be a good chance that China would be defeated. Second, however, given how closely balanced the forces will be, although China's leadership could not be confident that an invasion of Taiwan in 2020 would succeed, it is nonetheless *possible* that it could succeed. Thus, if China's leadership were willing to gamble on success, or if China's military leaders had a more optimistic assessment of the probability of success than the above analysis would appear to warrant, then an attack might nonetheless be launched and, given enough luck, could actually succeed. Even a failed attempt, moreover, would likely be extremely costly to the United States and Taiwan.

A third conclusion is that, although China will probably not have the capability to successfully invade Taiwan in 2020, if its military capabilities continue to improve relative to those of the United States and Taiwan at the rate at which they have improved over the past two decades, it could well acquire the ability to do so at some point after 2020.

It is also important to keep in mind the assumptions on which the above analysis was based. If these assumptions are not born out, then the outcome could be very different. One assumption, for example, was that China will have only twenty-five conventional ballistic missiles capable of reaching Guam in 2020, as a result of which only about twenty F-22s and twenty KC-135 aerial refueling aircraft could be destroyed on the ground at Andersen Air Force Base, with the remaining aircraft able to continue to operate from Andersen. If China instead had two hundred conventional intermediate-range ballistic missiles available, however, it could effectively eliminate Andersen, which provides nearly half of the combined U.S.-Taiwanese air-to-air combat power in this scenario, as a viable location for basing aircraft. Coupled with the attacks on air bases in Japan, this would reduce the United States to relying largely on carrier aviation for contesting air superiority over Taiwan. Similarly, if China had a way of mounting effective attacks on U.S. aircraft carriers, then the carriers, which provide nearly 40 percent of the combined U.S.-Taiwanese air-to-air combat power in this scenario, might have to devote more fighters to self-defense and some of the carriers might even be put out of action. Either of these two developments would tip the balance in air-to-air combat toward China.

Another assumption is that sufficient aerial refueling aircraft are available for U.S. fighters from multiple locations to fly long distances and remain on patrol for four hours at a time. Analysis was not performed to determine whether the number of refueling aircraft available, flying out of Australia or even more-distant bases, would be sufficient to provide the aviation fuel needed to support the fighters as well as supporting aircraft such as E-3 early warning and control aircraft, RC-135 electronic intelligence aircraft, and P-8 maritime patrol aircraft (the last of which would be needed to help protect the carriers from submarine attack). Since some of the aerial refueling aircraft and other supporting aircraft (such as E-3s and RC-135s) would have to operate close to where the fighters were conducting their combat air patrols, moreover, a possible Chinese tactic would be for its fighters to attempt to evade the U.S. fighters and attack those supporting aircraft instead. If such attacks were successful, they could force the U.S. fighters to operate without E-3 and RC-135 support and to be able to remain on patrol over Taiwan for shorter periods of time, as subsequent refueling aircraft would have to operate at a greater distance from the patrol areas for self-preservation. Even unsuccessful attacks of this sort could force the U.S. to devote fighters to protecting the support aircraft, reducing the number of fighters able to patrol over Taiwan.

Yet another assumption is that the F-35, whose program has suffered from multiple delays and setbacks, is produced in the planned numbers and is indeed qualitatively superior to fourth-generation fighters in air-to-air combat. If the F-35's development is further delayed, then the U.S. fleet carriers might have to use F/A-18s, which in this analysis are regarded as half as effective as F-35s, in their place, and the amphibious assault carriers might only be able to carry aging AV-8s, an aircraft type with very limited air-to-air combat capabilities. The baseline F-35 design, moreover, has provisions for only two medium-range radar-guided air-to-air missiles and two short-range infrared-guided air-to-air missiles. Thus, although the F-35's small radar signature might make it superior to an older fighter design in a single air-to-air engagement, the number of adversary aircraft it could engage on a given mission would be limited by the small number of missiles it carried.

Multiple assumptions were also made with regard to the PLA, of course. The most important of these may be that the organizational, training, and cultural limitations that the PLA is likely to suffer from in 2020, as estimated in the preceding chapters, have the net effect of reducing its combat effectiveness by about 20 percent relative to how effective they would be if PLA organization, training, and culture were comparable to those of the U.S. military. Quantifying the effects of these dimensions of military capability on combat effectiveness is difficult, but, as noted in the first chapter of this book, history is replete with instances of decisive victories by materially inferior forces, so the impact of the PLA's inferiority in these dimensions could potentially be much larger than 20 percent. Conversely, it is possible that PLA shortcomings relative to the U.S. military in these areas by 2020 could have an impact smaller than 20 percent.

WAR IN THE SOUTH CHINA SEA

Given China's increased assertiveness toward its territorial claims in the South China Sea in recent years, concern has risen about the possibility of Beijing using military force to enforce those claims.[151] One scenario that could result in a U.S. military response would be if China used military force against the Philippines, a U.S. treaty ally. Such a conflict would require China to project military power to a distance more than five hundred miles from the nearest Chinese air and naval bases, but would also occur more than one thousand miles from the nearest U.S. bases and thus provides a different kind of test of the relative military power of the United States and China than the Taiwan scenario described in the previous section.

Political-Military Context

China claims many of the land features (islands, banks, and reefs) of the South China Sea as Chinese territory. Many of these features are also claimed by Vietnam, the Philippines, Malaysia, Brunei, and Taiwan. In particular, Vietnam, Malaysia, the Philippines, and Taiwan have military and/or civilian personnel stationed on features that are claimed by China.[152] In recent years there have been a number of incidents in which China has attempted to enforce its claims in the South China Sea. In March 2011 Chinese vessels interfered with a Philippine ship conducting a survey at Reed Bank, a submerged feature in the South China Sea. In April 2012, when a Philippine naval vessel (a decommissioned U.S. Coast Guard cutter) attempted to arrest Chinese fishermen operating around Scarborough Reef, a feature claimed by the Philippines, Chinese civilian law enforcement vessels interposed themselves between the Philippine naval vessel and the Chinese fishing boats. A protracted standoff ensued that eventually resulted in China taking effective control over Scarborough Reef, with Chinese maritime law enforcement vessels preventing Philippine ships from entering the waters around the reef. In May 2013 the Philippines reported that Chinese warships had begun circling a Philippine garrison that lives aboard a deliberately grounded landing ship at Second Thomas Shoal, and, in March 2014, Chinese coast guard ships prevented Philippine vessels from resupplying the garrison (they were later successfully resupplied). In response to these incidents, the Philippine military announced that it was initiating a five-year modernization plan that would include the purchase of, among other items, fighter aircraft and frigates.[153]

This scenario postulates that, by 2020, the Philippine military has succeeded in acquiring a decommissioned U.S. Oliver Hazard Perry–class frigate and twelve Korean-made FA-50 light fighter jets. In that year, the Philippines discovers construction underway on Scarborough Reef (which China, although it wrested control of the reef from the Philippines in 2012, is assumed not to have physically occupied before this time), just 140 miles from central Luzon, the largest of the Philippine islands and the site of the Philippine capital. Manila dispatches its frigate and several smaller vessels to blockade the reef and prevent resupply of the construction crews. Beijing announces that the blockade of what it considers Chinese territory is an act of war, and it attacks and sinks the Philippine frigate along with some of the smaller vessels. Beijing then announces that the Philippines has forty-eight hours to evacuate all of its personnel who are "illegally occupying Chinese territory" (i.e., the nine islands and reefs in the South China Sea that are occupied by the Philippines but claimed by China). Manila invokes the 1951 U.S.-Philippine

Mutual Defense Treaty and calls on the United States to help defend Philippine personnel stationed in the South China Sea.

The construction of facilities on Scarborough Reef was in fact a deliberate provocation by Beijing, which hoped to use a confrontation over the reef as a pretext to seize the other islands and reefs claimed by China but occupied by the Philippines. At the same time as the naval strike force that attacked the Philippine ships blockading Scarborough Reef left port, a separate naval task force including landing vessels also sailed from port and would be in position to conduct landings on all nine Philippine-occupied features shortly after the expiration of the forty-eight-hour evacuation period.[154]

Combatant Capabilities

Overall U.S. and Chinese capabilities are as described for the previous scenario, with the exception that, unlike in the Taiwan scenario, the PLA Navy is not assumed to have significantly increased its numbers of amphibious landing ships (the number of landing ships it possesses today being more than sufficient for the landing operations in this scenario). Philippine naval capabilities are assumed to be negligible, as its only significant warship is sunk in the initial clash. The twelve FA-50s could be based at Col. Antonio Bautista Air Base, at Puerto Princesa on the island of Palawan, about three hundred miles from the nine Philippine-occupied features. The FA-50s are capable of carrying AGM-65 Maverick air-to-surface missiles and have a combat radius of about 275 miles, and thus would be capable of conducting strike missions against ships near some of the Philippine-held features. The only air-to-air missile the FA-50 is capable of carrying, however, is the short-range AIM-9 Sidewinder, and thus the FA-50 does not have a significant anti-air capability.[155] Philippine maintenance capabilities are assumed to be such that on average eight of the 12 FA-50s are available for combat at any given time. FA-50 pilot skills are assumed to be mediocre.

Order of Battle

The goal of China's operation is to seize the Philippine-held features before the United States can muster significant forces to oppose the operation. Accordingly, to maintain the element of surprise, the PLA does not redeploy significant forces to bases in the southern part of China before the initiation of its operation. For its part, having had no advance indications of a potential crisis, the United States has available to it only those forces normally based in the region or that happen to be in the region at the time events occur.

China

One of the three aircraft carriers China is projected to have in 2020 is assumed to be available for this operation.[156] China's other naval forces in 2020 are assumed to be distributed between its three fleets in roughly the same proportions as they were in 2014, and 80 percent of these forces are assumed to be available for operations at the time the events in this scenario occur.[157] As of 2013, thirty-one landing ships, including three large (twenty-thousand-ton) Yuzhao-class "landing platform dock (LPD)" ships, were based in the South Sea Fleet.[158] At least this many landing ships are assumed to be based in the South Sea Fleet in 2020, with twenty-seven medium landing ships and tank landing ships – three for each of the nine features occupied by the Philippines – assumed to be available for the operation, along with two of the three LPDs. Sufficient forces are assumed to be available from the two marine brigades based in the South Sea Fleet to load out the twenty-seven smaller landing ships and the two LPDs.

The number of land-based aircraft available to China for this operation is constrained by the number of PLA Navy and Air Force bases within range of the Philippine-occupied features of the South China Sea, the nearest of which is more than 560 miles from Lingshui, the closest Chinese military air base.[159] This scenario assumes that 120 Su-27/Su-30/J-11 fighters, forty-eight JH-7 fighter-bombers, and twenty-four J-20 fighters are based within unrefueled combat range of the Philippine-occupied features of the South China Sea. In addition, the twenty-four J-10s currently based at Huiyang (745 miles from the nearest Philippine-held feature) could conduct combat operations over the Philippine-occupied features if refueled by the H-6U aerial refueling aircraft based at Lingshui.[160] Finally, roughly a third of the PLA's Y-8 maritime patrol aircraft and KJ-200 and KJ-2000 airborne early warning and control aircraft, which, with their longer ranges, are able to operate from more-distant bases, are assumed to be available for this operation.

A battery of six DF-21D antiship ballistic missile launchers with twenty-four missiles is assumed to have been covertly deployed to Hainan Island. In addition, a battery of six DF-21C medium-range conventional ballistic missile launchers with seventy-two missiles is assumed to have been deployed to southern Guangdong province, where they are within striking range of the northern part of the Philippines, along with a battery of six intermediate-range conventional ballistic missile launchers, each with two missiles capable of reaching targets anywhere in the Philippines. The naval, air, and conventional missile forces based in southern China that are available for this conflict are listed in Table 9.5.

Aside from forces based in southern China, it is possible that forces based in eastern China could participate in the conflict as well. Although, to keep the

TABLE 9.5 *PLA Naval, Air, and Conventional Missile Combat Systems Based in Southern China Available for South China Sea Operation*

System	Type	Number
Modified Liaoning class	Aircraft carrier	1
Luyang III class	Destroyer	5
Luyang II class	Destroyer	3
Jiangkai II class	Frigate	11
Jiangwei II class	Frigate	2
Jiangdao class	Corvette	8
Houbei class	Guided missile fast attack craft	18
Type 093A/095 class	Nuclear-powered attack submarine	3
Shang class	Nuclear-powered attack submarine	2
Kilo class	Diesel-electric attack submarine	3
Yuan class	Diesel-electric attack submarine	3
Song class	Diesel-electric attack submarine	3
Yuzhao class	Landing platform dock	2
Multiple classes	Amphibious landing ships	27
J-15	Carrier-capable multirole fighter	22
J-20	Multirole stealth fighter	24
Su-27/Su-30/J-11B	Air superiority/multirole fighter	120
J-10	Air superiority/multirole fighter	24
JH-7	Fighter-bomber	48
H-6	Subsonic medium bomber	24
Y-8J/Y-8JB	Maritime patrol/electronic intelligence aircraft	7
KJ-2000	Airborne early warning and control aircraft	5
KJ-200	Airborne early warning and control aircraft	5
DF-21C	Conventionally armed medium-range ballistic missile	72 missiles 6 launchers
DF-21D	Conventionally armed medium-range ballistic missile – antiship variant	24 missiles 6 launchers
n/a	Conventionally armed intermediate-range ballistic missile	12 missiles 6 launchers

conflict limited, the PLA will not attack U.S. forces while they are in Japan, it is willing to attack U.S. naval and air forces after they have departed Japan's territorial waters and airspace, if they appear to be headed toward the South China Sea. Thus, surface ships of the East Sea Fleet, as well as long-range

TABLE 9.6 *PLA Naval, Air, Conventional Missile, and Space Combat Systems Based in Eastern China Available for South China Sea Operation*

System	Type	Number
Luyang III class	Destroyer	2
Luyang II class	Destroyer	2
Sovremenny class	Destroyer	3
Jiangkai II class	Frigate	8
Jiangkai I class	Frigate	2
Jiangwei II class	Frigate	3
Jiangdao class	Corvette	8
Houbei class	Guided missile fast attack craft	18
Kilo class	Diesel-electric attack submarine	5
Yuan class	Diesel-electric attack submarine	6
Song class	Diesel-electric attack submarine	5
J-20	Multirole stealth fighter	10
Su-27/Su-30/J-11B	Air superiority/multirole fighter	160
JH-7	Fighter-bomber	105
H-6	Subsonic medium bomber	45
Y-8J/Y-8JB	Maritime patrol/electronic intelligence aircraft	7
KJ-2000	Airborne early warning and control aircraft	5
KJ-200	Airborne early warning and control aircraft	5
DF-21D	Conventionally armed medium-range ballistic missile – antiship variant	24 missiles 6 launchers

aircraft (Su-27/Su-30/J-11 fighters, J-20 fighters, JH-7 fighter-bombers, H-6 bombers, Y-8J/Y-8JB maritime patrol aircraft, and KJ-200 and KJ-2000 airborne early warning and control aircraft) operating from bases in eastern China, along with the other brigade of DF-21D antiship ballistic missiles, are potentially available as well. The naval, air, and conventional missile forces based in eastern China that are available for this conflict are listed in Table 9.6.

In addition, as in the previous scenario, the PLA operates multiple optical reconnaissance satellites, synthetic aperture radar, and ocean reconnaissance satellites. To limit the escalation of the conflict, the Chinese leadership does not authorize the use of destructive antisatellite weapons, but use of radio-frequency jammers and laser dazzlers is permitted. To avoid tipping off U.S. intelligence and, again, to limit the potential for escalation, China's land-based and sea-based nuclear forces are assumed to not have been put on alert.

United States

Since this scenario develops rapidly with little prior warning, the forces available to the United States are those that would be present in the region under normal conditions. As of 2014 approximately fifty-two U.S. Navy ships were based in the Asia-Pacific region (including in Hawaii but not including the West Coast of the United States). This scenario assumes that all ships currently based in the region are either still based there in 2020 or have been replaced by another ship of the same type and class. In addition, the U.S. Navy has announced plans to increase by ten the number of ships based in the region by 2020. In particular, it has stated that the number of littoral combat ships stationed in Singapore will be increased from one to four, the number of cruisers and destroyers based in Japan will be increased from eight to ten, and that the number of submarines stationed in Guam will be increased from three to four.[161]

Since the above ships constitute six of the ten additional ships to be based in the region by 2020, the four other additional ships are assumed to be based in Pearl Harbor, Hawaii, which in 2014 hosted thirty ships. The added ships are assumed to consist of one Arleigh Burke–class destroyer and three Virgina-class submarines (consistent with approximately one-third of the ships currently based at Pearl Harbor being cruisers or destroyers and two-thirds being submarines). The two additional ships based in Japan are assumed consist of one Ticonderoga-class cruiser and one Arleigh Burke–class destroyer. The additional submarine to be based in Guam is assumed to be a Los Angeles–class boat like the three currently based there, as it would be uneconomical to support submarines that belonged to two different classes if there were only four of them in total.

Even in peacetime, U.S. attack submarines spend approximately one-quarter of their time at sea patrolling. This implies that one of the four submarines based in Guam along with five of the twenty-one submarines based at Pearl Harbor would be patrolling somewhere in the Pacific or Indian Ocean at the time of the scenario. Of these six submarines, this scenario assumes that one Los Angeles–class boat is somewhere in the South China, another is in the East China Sea, and a Virginia-class boat is somewhere in the Philippine Sea. The other three submarines are assumed to be too far away to participate in the conflict (i.e., operating somewhere outside of the western Pacific).

In normal times, in addition to the U.S. Navy ships based in Japan, an aircraft carrier strike group is often present at sea somewhere in the western Pacific. This scenario assumes that a carrier strike group consisting of a Nimitz-class carrier, a Ticonderoga-class cruiser, two Arleigh Burke–class

destroyers, and a Virginia-class submarine (along with a Supply-class underway replenishment ship), all originating from the West Coast of the United
States, is operating in the vicinity of Guam at the time the Chinese fleet
begins sailing toward the South China Sea.[162]

Of the ships based in the Asia-Pacific region, approximately 80 percent are
assumed to be available for combat operations at the time of the scenario, with
the remainder undergoing repairs or long-term overhaul. The ships available
to the United States in this scenario are listed in Table 9.7.

The U.S. Air Force currently bases fifty-four F-15C/D fighter aircraft, fifteen
KC-135 aerial refueling aircraft, and two E-3 airborne early warning and
control aircraft at Kadena Air Base on Okinawa.[163] These aircraft are assumed
to still be based at Kadena at the time of the scenario. In addition, the U.S.
Navy operates a detachment of P-3 maritime patrol aircraft from Kadena.[164]
These aircraft are assumed to have been replaced by six more-modern P-8s at
the time of the scenario. Also, beginning in 2017, the U.S. Marine Corps will
operate a squadron of 16 F-35B short takeoff/vertical landing aircraft from
Marine Corps Air Station Iwakuni, at the southwestern end of the main
Japanese island of Honshu.[165]

As of 2014, no U.S. Air Force aircraft were permanently assigned to Guam.
However, at any given time, six B-52 bombers and three Global Hawk
unmanned reconnaissance aircraft are normally deployed to Guam.[166] This
is assumed to still be the case in 2020.

As of 2014, forty-eight F-16CJs were based at Misawa Air Base in northern
Honshu.[167] By 2020, however, they are assumed to have been replaced by
forty-eight F-35As. In addition, the U.S. Navy operates a detachment of P-3
maritime patrol aircraft from Misawa.[168] These aircraft are assumed to have
been replaced by six P-8s at the time of the scenario.

In addition to the above-mentioned aircraft, the air wing for the U.S. aircraft
carrier based in Japan is assumed to embark aboard the aircraft carrier when
the scenario begins. Both of the Nimitz-class carriers in this scenario are
assumed to carry twelve F-35C carrier-capable multirole stealth fighters,
forty-two F/A-18E/F fourth-generation fighters, twelve F/A-18G jamming aircraft, and four E-2 airborne early warning and control aircraft. The aircraft
initially available to the United States in this scenario are listed in Table 9.8.

However, although the ships available to the United States in this scenario
are limited to those in region at the time the scenario begins, the greater speed
of aircraft means that additional aircraft can be deployed to the region during
the scenario. Additional air forces potentially available to the United States in
this scenario are the same as those available in the Taiwan scenario and are
listed in Table 9.4.

TABLE 9.7 *U.S. Navy Ships Present in the Asia-Pacific Region at Time of South China Sea Scenario*

Location	Ship Type	Number
Singapore	Littoral combat ship	3
South China Sea	Los Angeles–class submarine	1
East China Sea	Los Angeles–class submarine	1
Philippine Sea	Virginia-class submarine	1
Guam	Los Angeles–class submarine	2
	Emory S. Land–class submarine tender	1
	Nimitz-class aircraft carrier	1
	Ticonderoga-class cruiser	1
	Arleigh Burke–class destroyer	2
	Virginia-class submarine	1
	Supply-class underway replenishment ship	1
Sasebo, Japan	Wasp-class amphibious assault carrier	1
	Denver-class amphibious transport dock	1
	Whidbey Island–class dock landing ship	1
	Mine countermeasures ships	3
Yokosuka, Japan	Nimitz-class aircraft carrier	1
	Ticonderoga-class cruiser	2
	Arleigh Burke–class destroyer	6
	Blue Ridge-class command ship	1
Pearl Harbor, Hawaii	Ticonderoga-class cruiser	2
	Arleigh Burke–class destroyer	8
	Los Angeles–class submarine	12
	Virginia-class submarine	5

Sources: "CNO's Navigation Plan, 2014-2018"; "Tenant Commands"; "FDNF Ships"; "Fleet Information"; "Aircraft Carriers – CVN"; "Amphibious Assault Ships – LHA/LHD/LHA(R)"; "Amphibious Transport Dock – LPD"; "Dock Landing Ship – LSD"; "Cruisers – CG"; "Destroyers – DDG"; "Attack Submarines – SSN."
Note that the ships listed in this table as being at a specific port are assumed to be either in port but ready to put to sea on short notice or operating at sea near that port.

China's Objectives and Overall Campaign Plan

The PLA's objective in this scenario is to evict all Philippine personnel from features of the South China Sea that are claimed by Beijing. To achieve this goal, the PLA plans to land its marines on all nine features occupied by the Philippines.

TABLE 9.8 *U.S. Combat Aircraft Present in the Asia-Pacific Region at Time of South China Sea Scenario*

Location	Aircraft Type	Number
Okinawa, Japan	F-15C/D land-based air superiority fighter	54
	KC-135 aerial refueling aircraft	15
	E-3 airborne early warning and control aircraft	2
	P-8 maritime patrol aircraft	6
Iwakuni, Japan	F-35B short takeoff/vertical landing multirole stealth fighter	16
Guam	B-52 subsonic heavy bomber	6
	RQ-4 Global Hawk unmanned reconnaissance aircraft	3
Misawa, Japan	F-35A land-based multirole stealth fighter	48
	P-8 maritime patrol aircraft	6
On board carriers	F-35C carrier-capable multirole stealth fighter	24
	F/A-18E/F carrier-capable semistealthy multirole fighter	84
	F/A-18G carrier-capable jamming aircraft	24
	E-2 carrier-capable airborne early warning and control aircraft	8

Campaign Studies describes a generic approach for "offensive campaigns against coral islands and reefs" (对珊瑚岛礁进攻战役), "coral islands and reefs" being a notably accurate description of the contested features of the South China Sea (implying that a seizure of features in the South China Sea was the exact scenario for which this campaign type was developed). According to *Campaign Studies*, such an operation would consist of three main parts: "seizing campaign control" (夺取战役控制权), occupying the islands and reefs, and solidifying defenses. Seizing campaign control is said to entail finding and destroying the enemy's main sea and air forces, cutting off the enemy's lines of communication with the islands and reefs, attacking the enemy forces occupying the islands and reefs with naval gunfire and aircraft, and sealing off the landing areas. Occupying the islands and reefs is said to entail transporting the invasion forces to sea areas near the islands and reefs, performing the landings, using fire support to suppress the enemy, maintaining control over the landing zone, and interdicting enemy reinforcements. Solidifying defenses once the islands and reefs have been seized entails redeploying the occupying forces into a defensive posture in case the enemy attempts to counterattack or retake the features.[169]

Assessment

The area of operations in this scenario is shown in Figure 9.2.

The PLA's goal in an operation like this would be to seize the Philippine-held features before the United States could intervene effectively. It would thus seek to prevent the United States and the Philippines from having any advance warning of its intentions. This scenario assumes that the Chinese believe (accurately) that the United States will not be able to detect the readying of the invasion fleet while it remains in port, but that once the strike group that will engage the Philippine frigate near Scarborough Reef leaves port, given the already existing tensions over Scarborough Reef, the United States will suspect that conflict is about to occur and begin deploying forces toward the South China Sea. Since Scarborough Reef is about six hundred miles from China's nearest naval bases at Sanya, Guangzhou, and Shantou, it will take about a day (at twenty knots steaming speed) for the strike group to reach the vicinity of Scarborough Reef, and the subsequent forty-eight-hour evacuation warning to the Philippines after the clash will give the United States another two days to react before China begins attacking the Philippine garrisons.[170]

Since "finding and destroying the enemy's main sea and air forces" is the first action listed in the description of offensive campaigns against coral islands and reefs in *Campaign Studies*, it seems likely that the PLA would attempt to intercept the U.S. ships as they approached the South China Sea. Given the slow transit speeds of diesel electric submarines and the uncertainty about the direction from which the U.S. ships would approach the South China Sea, the PLA is assumed to have covertly deployed, in advance, thirteen of the seventeen Song- and Yuan-class submarines available to it in this scenario (from both the South Sea Fleet and the East Sea Fleet) along a two-thousand-mile-long arc across the Philippine Sea between the southern tip of Taiwan and the northern tip of Sulawesi, with approximately one hundred miles between each submarine. In addition, six of the eight Kilo-class submarines available to the PLA in this scenario are deployed slightly behind the Song- and Yuan-class subs. Three of the five nuclear-powered attack submarines (Shang class and Type 093A/095) available to China in this scenario are then deployed behind the Kilo-class submarines. One Yuan-class submarine is deployed in the Makassar Strait (between Borneo and Sulawesi) to intercept any ships attempting to enter the Celebes Sea from the Java Sea. The remaining three Song-class and Yuan-class and two Kilo-class submarines are deployed along a five-hundred-mile long line between the southern tip of Vietnam and the northwestern end of Borneo, in case U.S. ships operating in the Indian Ocean attempt to enter the South China Sea from the southwest.

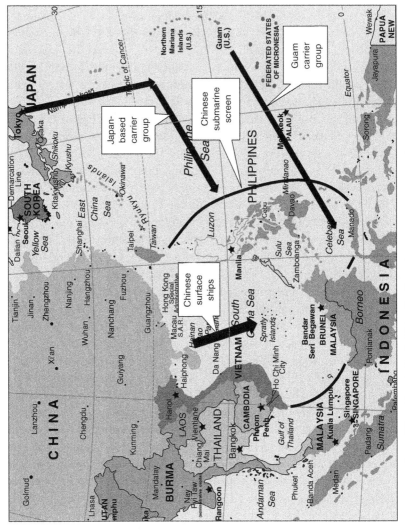

FIGURE 9.2 Area of Operations in South China Sea Scenario

Since the YJ-82 antiship cruise missiles carried by the Song- and Yuan-class have a range of only about twenty-five miles, there would be only a one-third chance that a given ship would pass within range of one of these submarines if the submarines did not move.[171] However, provided a U.S. ship group was detected far enough ahead of the picket line, the submarines could move to close any gap. In addition, the missiles carried by the six Kilo-class submarines have a range of 135 miles, and thus there would be a nearly 80 percent chance that a given ship group would pass within range of one of them, even if they did not move. Similarly, the greater cruising speed of the nuclear-powered submarines should enable at least one of them to intercept any approaching U.S. ship group.

The strike group that engages the Philippine frigate near Scarborough Reef consists of a Luyang III–class destroyer, a Luyang II–class destroyer, and three Jiangkai II–class frigates. At the same time as it leaves port, the Chinese landing fleet and carrier group also sets sail.

The Chinese landing fleet is divided into eight groups. Seven of these groups consist of either three or six landing ships – medium and tank landing ships escorted by a Jiangdao-class corvette. One group, with three landing ships, heads toward Commodore Reef, the southernmost of the Philippine-held features. A second group, also with three landing ships, heads toward Second Thomas Shoal, the eastern-most Philippine-held feature. A third group, with six landing ships, heads toward Flat Island and Nanshan Island, which are both part of a single atoll and represent the northeastern-most Philippine-held features. A fourth group, with three landing ships, heads toward Northeast Cay, the northwestern-most Philippine-held feature (only about two miles southwest of Chinese-held North Reef). A fifth group, also with three landing ships, heads toward West York Island, southeast of North-east Cay. A sixth group, again with three landing ships, heads toward Thitu Island, directly south of Northeast Cay and site of a three-thousand-foot airstrip. A seventh group, with six landing ships, heads toward Loaita Island and Lankiam Cay, which are only about ten miles apart from each other (and straddling a Chinese garrison located on Loaita Cay), southeast of Thitu Island. See Figure 9.3.

The eighth group consists of the two large Yuzhao-class LPDs, a Luyang III–class destroyer, a Luyang II–class destroyer, and six frigates. This group patrols approximately one hundred miles north of Northeast Cay, ready to reinforce any of the landing forces if needed.

The Chinese aircraft carrier and its escorts are positioned northeast of the Philippine-held features, between the Chinese landing ships and the most likely direction of approach of U.S. aircraft. The carrier's escorts consist of two

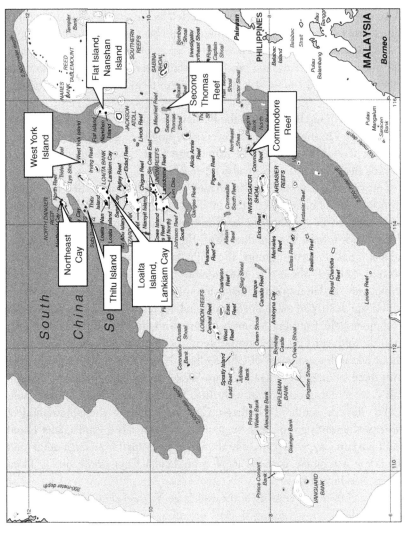

FIGURE 9.3 Philippine-Held Features in the South China Sea

Luyang III–class destroyers, one Luyang II–class destroyer, five frigates, and one Type 093A– or Type 095–class submarine.

The eighteen South Sea Fleet Houbei-class fast attack craft available to China in this scenario are spread out across the South China Sea, waiting to ambush any ships entering the sea. The final Type 095 submarine is also patrolling the South China Sea.

At the same time as the South Sea Fleet forces leave port, all available East Sea Fleet surface ships, consisting of three Sovremenny-class destroyers, two Luyang III–class destroyers, two Luyang II–class destroyers, eight Jiangkai II–class frigates, two Jiangkai I–class frigates, three Jiangwei II–class frigates, eight Jiangdao-class corvettes, and eighteen Houbei-class fast attack craft, begin steaming southeast from their ports near Shanghai, Hangzhou, and Ningbo toward the Philippine Sea, so as to be in position to intercept U.S. ships coming south from Japan.

On the U.S. side, the U.S. ships based at Yokosuka, when the Chinese ships are detected sortieing from port, immediately set sail. They head due south from Yokosuka for the first two days (the Wasp-class amphibious assault carrier based in Sasebo heads southeast and join up with the ships heading south from Yokosuka at the end of the first day), after which the ships then begin to head in a southwesterly direction, toward the central Philippines. This route will enable the ships to stay out of range of China's antiship ballistic missiles and land-based aircraft (except for the H-6 bombers, which would only be able to reach the U.S. strike group by flying unescorted and therefore highly vulnerable to being intercepted by U.S. fighters) after the first day (i.e., until after combat operations have started).[172] Another advantage of this approach is that it makes the East Sea Fleet surface ships extremely vulnerable to attack by the carriers' aircraft if they attempt to intercept the carrier group, as the carriers would not need to devote significant numbers of fighters to defending themselves. Although this approach will not bring the carrier aircraft to within unrefueled range of the Philippine-held features in the South China Sea for about four days, by the end of the third day the carrier group will be about twelve hundred miles away and able to launch strikes on the landing fleet with the assistance of aerial refueling aircraft.[173] Meanwhile, the carrier group operating near Guam at the beginning of the scenario begins steaming directly toward the Philippines as soon as the Chinese ships are detected sortieing from port.

While the ships in Japan begin sailing toward the Philippines, the F-35As based at Misawa Air Base in northern Japan deploy south to Kadena, where they are able to begin operations starting on the second day of the scenario. The P-8s at Misawa deploy to Andersen Air Force Base on Guam, so as to be better able to patrol the Philippine Sea. They are assumed to be able to begin patrols on the second day of the scenario. The United States also begins deploying F-22s along with aerial refueling aircraft and other supporting aircraft to Guam. Twelve of the F-35Bs stationed at Iwakuni are embarked aboard the Wasp-class amphibious assault carrier based at Sasebo.[174]

Although the sortieing of the Chinese fleet on the first day of the scenario signals that a crisis is developing, actual combat does not begin until the end of the first day, when the PLA sinks the Philippine frigate blockading Scarborough Reef. And, although U.S. ships also leave port and combat aircraft begin deploying to the region on the first day, this scenario assumes that the U.S. president would not authorize them to conduct combat operations against China without first publicly announcing his intention to do so. Accordingly, on the second day of the scenario, after the Chinese attacks on the Philippine ships near Scarborough Reef, the U.S. president calls on China to withdraw its military forces from the South China Sea and states that if China attempts further "unprovoked attacks" on Philippine territory, people, or military units, the United States will defend the Philippines with military force.

U.S. intentions regarding its willingness to intervene in the conflict having been made clear, the PLA is then authorized to attack U.S. forces, provided they are in international waters or airspace or on Philippine territory. However, by this time the U.S. ships departing from Japan are out of range of the PLA's antiship ballistic missiles and its Su-27/Su-30/J-11 and JH-7 naval strike aircraft.

By the end of the second day of the scenario, the carrier group that was operating near Guam at the beginning of the scenario would be close enough to launch strikes on the landing ships if supported by refueling aircraft operating out of Guam.[175] Before it did so, however, it would likely be attacked by some of the Chinese submarines screening the Philippines. If we assume that two Song- or Yuan-class submarines, one Type 093A– or 095–class boat, and one Kilo-class boat succeed in closing to within missile range of the carrier group, then they would be able to launch a total of eighteen YJ-82 subsonic antiship cruise missiles and six 3M-54E1 Novator Alfa Klub supersonic antiship cruise missiles at the carrier group.[176] On average one of the carrier's F-35Cs and six of its F/A-18s fighters would be on combat air patrol at the time.[177] Between them, these aircraft should carry enough AMRAAMS to engage each of the incoming antiship cruise missiles.[178] The surviving six YJ-82s and three 3M-54E1s[179] would then be engaged by the carrier group's long-range surface-to-air missiles and short-range defenses. As a result, on average a net of two YJ-82s and two 3M-54E1 would probably succeed in striking a ship in the carrier group.[180] The YJ-82 is a typical antiship cruise missile in its striking power and thus would probably not put any of the ships in the carrier group out of action unless both missiles struck the same ship.[181] The 3M-54E1 has at least several times the striking power of a typical antiship cruise missile and would almost certainly put out of action any ship it hit, including a Nimitz-class aircraft carrier.[182] Since there are five surface ships in this carrier strike group, however (the carrier, a cruiser, two destroyers, and an underway replenishment ship), there would be only a 0.36 probability of the carrier being hit by one of the 3M-54E1s.[183] Thus, it is likely that the carrier would still be operational when it reached a range such that it was able to launch an attack on China's landing ships.[184]

One approach to attacking the landing ships would be to launch all available F/A-18s, each of which can carry six Joint Standoff Weapons (JSOWs), stealthy glide-bombs that have a range of more than eighty miles when dropped from forty thousand feet.[185] The F/A-18s would be escorted by a squadron of F-22s based in Guam. The carrier's F-35Cs, along with any additional available Guam-based fighters, would provide defensive combat air patrols for the carrier group while the F/A-18s were on their missions. The landing areas are within range of China's land-based fighters but too distant for the fighters to maintain continuous combat air patrols over them. Assuming the incoming U.S. aircraft were not detected until they were less than six hundred miles away from the landing areas (the distance from the landing ships to the closest Chinese airfields), therefore, they would likely only have to contend with the twenty-two J-15s carried on board the Chinese aircraft carrier operating in the area (the closest Chinese air base being six hundred miles from the landing areas). The squadron of F-22s should be more than capable of driving off the J-15s,[186] allowing most or all of the F/A-18s to launch their JSOWs against the landing groups, with the quite likely result that none of the landing ships would be able to land a combat-effective force.[187] The Philippine FA-50s based on Palawan, if equipped with Maverick air-to-surface missiles, could supplement these attacks.

If, on the other hand, the PLA maintained its aircraft in a state of readiness at its airfields such that half of the operational fighters could be launched toward the landing areas as soon as a U.S. attack was determined to be developing, and detected the incoming attack shortly after the U.S. carrier aircraft began flying toward the landing ship groups (i.e., while the U.S. aircraft were still farther from the landing ship groups than China's closest airfields), then the U.S. aircraft would be faced with ten J-20s and a total of seventy-one J-10s, Su-27s, Su-30s, J-11s, and J-15s.[188] These aircraft would likely overwhelm the nineteen F-22s escorting the F/A-18s and prevent the F/A-18s from conducting an effective attack on the landing ships.

In either case, sometime during the third day, before the expiration of the forty-eight-hour evacuation notice, the Japan-based ships would also come close enough to launch strikes on the landing ships.[189] Like the carrier group that begins the scenario operating near Guam, however, it would likely first be attacked by some of the Chinese submarines screening the Philippines. If, as before, we assume that these include two Song-class or Yuan-class; one Shang class, Type 093A, or Type 095; and one Kilo-class submarines, then an average of two YJ-82 and two 3M-54E1 missiles would again hit ships in the carrier group. This group is much larger, however, consisting of eleven ships. Thus, there would be only a 17 percent probability that the fleet carrier was put out of action.

Assuming both carriers were still operational after passing through the submarine screen,[190] they could launch a combined total of 68 F/A-18s at the Chinese landing ships. If, moreover, by the third day of combat, two squadrons of F-22s had deployed to Guam, then the F/A-18s could be escorted by a total of 38 F-22s. If half of the operational PLA fighters were launched to intercept the U.S. aircraft, they would again consist of ten J-20s and a total of seventy-one J-10s, Su-27s, Su-30s, J-11s, and J-15s. In this case, the U.S. aircraft, when the F/A-18s are included, would actually outnumber the Chinese aircraft and have considerably more air-to-air combat power. Consequently, some of the F/A-18s would likely be able to evade interception and launch their JSOWs at the landing ships. If we assume that, on average, each F-22 was able to engage one intercepting Chinese aircraft and prevent it from reaching the F/A-18s, then approximately forty-three Chinese aircraft would evade the F-22s and reach the F/A-18s. If we similarly assume that each Chinese aircraft is similarly able to engage one F/A-18, either shooting it down or at least forcing it to jettison its JSOWs so as to be more maneuverable, then twenty-five of the sixty-eight F/A-18s would be able to evade interception and launch their JSOWs at the landing ships, with the likely result that only one or two landing ships would be able to land combat-effective forces.[191]

What would happen subsequently in this scenario is difficult to predict. Over time, the U.S. would be able to bring increasing amounts of combat force into the theater, as additional aircraft deployed into the region and ships began to arrive from Hawaii, the West Coast of the United States, and/or the Indian Ocean. Thus, particularly given the losses it would likely suffer in the first landing operation, it is unlikely that China would make further attempts to seize Philippine-held islands in the South China Sea.[192] On the other hand, to evict China's forces from the island(s) it had seized would require either a counterinvasion by the United States (or, perhaps, Philippine troops transported by U.S. amphibious landing ships), or else a blockade of the seized islands, which would almost certainly result in continued fighting with China. China could also attempt to blockade the remaining Philippine-held features, which would also likely result in continued combat.

The combat casualties suffered by the two sides up to this point would be significant. In the U.S. case these would probably include eight ships damaged or sunk by the Chinese submarine attacks, and at least several aircraft shot down. In China's case they could include thirty or so landing ships and corvettes damaged or sunk, a significant number of soldiers killed onboard the landing ships, and several aircraft shot down. Thus, even if a cease fire was negotiated at this point (for example, in which China was allowed to keep any features it had seized and the Philippines was allowed to continue to supply its personnel on the remaining features it held), the United States and China would likely remain in a confrontational stance toward each other long after the conflict was over. If the conflict continued after the initial clash, the casualties on both sides would likely become even more serious, making it even more difficult to bring about a ceasefire and increasing the likelihood of a serious and long-lasting confrontation between the United States and China.

Conclusions

The most prominent feature of this scenario is the sensitivity of its outcome to the ability of each side to acquire intelligence about the other side's actions. If there had been a prolonged build-up of tensions before the conflict, the United States would likely have positioned at least one and possibly two aircraft carrier strike groups in the Celebes Sea or Sulu Sea. From there the carriers could have remained out of range of China's land-based aircraft and antiship ballistic missiles and conducted multiple strikes against China's landing ships from distances too close for China's land-based fighters to have time to intercept the U.S. strike aircraft. As a result, probably none of the landing ships would have survived long enough to attempt a landing operation.[193]

Conversely, if the Chinese operation had come as a complete surprise to the United States, in which case the Japan-based carriers would likely not have been able to put to sea for the first day or two, and there had not been another carrier strike group operating close to the South China Sea, then the PLA would likely have succeeded in seizing most or all of the Philippine-held features before the United States had an opportunity to intervene (although U.S. attack submarines operating in the area would likely have exacted at least some losses on the invasion force). Then the United States would have been faced with a choice of attempting a counterinvasion, blockading the Chinese-seized islands, or simply accepting the fait accompli.

Other assumptions embedded in the analysis of this scenario should also be noted. For example, one assumption is that the intelligence capabilities of the United States and China are such that they are able to track the general locations of each other's ship formations. Finding ships on the open ocean is a difficult task. This assumption, therefore, gives both sides credit for having the surveillance satellites, over-the-horizon radars, submarines, and high-altitude manned and unmanned reconnaissance aircraft needed to accomplish this task, along with the capability to analyze the data that these assets collect and transmit it in a timely manner to the commanders who need it. If, for example, China had, long before the conflict, taken to routinely jamming and dazzling U.S. reconnaissance satellites passing over its ports and driving off U.S. reconnaissance aircraft attempting to approach China's coast, then the U.S. military might not have realized that China's ships had left port until the moment they began attacking Philippine forces, at which point it would have been too late to react. Conversely, if the U.S. ships based in Japan could have sailed directly to the area east of Luzon without being detected and attacked, then the Japan-based carriers would have been able to begin attacking the Chinese landing ships sooner and more frequently. A particularly key capability would be the PLA's ability to determine that the U.S. carriers had launched their aircraft toward the South China Sea. If the PLA was able to detect the incoming aircraft while they were still one thousand miles or more away from the landing ships, then it could potentially send large numbers of aircraft to intercept the U.S. aircraft. If the incoming aircraft were not detected until they were less than six hundred miles away, on the other hand, then only aircraft based on the Chinese carrier would be able to intercept the U.S. aircraft.

Other capabilities that could be acquired by the two sides could also alter the outcome. For example, if China developed and fielded a longer-range antiship ballistic missile, such as an antiship version of the intermediate-range conventional ballistic missile it is believed to be developing, or significant numbers of aerial refueling aircraft, then the Japan-based U.S. ships would be subject to attack even if they remained in the eastern part of the Philippine Sea. Conversely, if the United States possessed an antiship cruise missile of range significantly greater than those it currently employs, such as the Long-Range Anti-Ship Missile (LRASM) currently in development, then its aircraft would be able to launch attacks on China's landing ships from distances at which they could not be intercepted by China's fighters.[194] And if the LRASM were integrated onto P-8s or U.S. Air Force bombers, then these attacks could be launched by long-range land-based aircraft without carriers needing to be present at all.[195]

The sensitivity of the scenario outcome to the warning time and the availability of particular systems for the two sides is a reflection of how much

China's military capabilities will have improved by 2020. In 2010 China's capability to successfully conduct such an operation in the face of U.S. intervention would have been negligible. The acquisition of weapon systems capable of effectively operating at long ranges from the Chinese mainland, along with improvements in personnel and training by 2020, are what makes it possible for China to potentially succeed in this operation.

10

Conclusion

This study has proposed a seven-dimensional model of military capability comprising doctrine, organizational structure, equipment, personnel, training, logistics, and organizational culture. For each dimension it has identified a set of criteria by which the capability of a military in that dimension can be assessed. Using this model and these criteria, the capabilities of the Chinese military were assessed for two periods: the years around 2000 and the years around 2010. The amount of progress between 2000 and 2010 was then used to estimate the Chinese military's capabilities in each dimension in 2020.

The overall finding of the study is that the Chinese military has made progress in all seven dimensions, but that progress in some dimensions has been significantly greater than in others. Specifically, by 2020, the quality of the Chinese military's doctrine, equipment, personnel, and training will likely be approaching, to varying degrees, those of the U.S. and other Western militaries. Critical weaknesses, on the other hand, will remain in organizational structure, logistics, and organizational culture. In particular, although the Chinese military has adopted a doctrine of maneuver and indirection, it has neither the organizational structure nor the organizational culture required to effectively implement it. Thus, although the Chinese military may have what is on paper a modern and appropriate doctrine in 2020, it will likely be unable to implement its doctrine as written, thus weakening what would otherwise be an area of relative strength. As result, during a conflict, the Chinese military could find itself having to revert to a relatively static, direct engagement-based approach that would be unable to make full use of the capabilities of its equipment and personnel.

Despite the weaknesses that are likely to persist in the Chinese military in 2020, analysis of two plausible conflict scenarios involving China and the United States suggests that defeating China in these scenarios could nonetheless be difficult and costly for the United States. This is a result of the geographic advantages China would enjoy in such a conflict as well as the capabilities of specific systems the Chinese military has chosen to acquire, including short-range and medium-range ballistic missiles, supersonic anti-ship cruise missiles, and long-range fighter aircraft. If the equipment, person-nel, and training of the Chinese military continue to improve relative to those of the U.S. military in the years after 2020, moreover, prevailing in such scenarios is likely to become increasingly difficult and costly for the United States.

Viewed from a broader perspective, although China will not be the domin-ant military power in East Asia by 2020 or any time shortly thereafter, U.S. military dominance in the region will also no longer be unquestioned in the way it has been since the end of the Cold War. Unless China has undergone a fundamental transformation into a mature democracy at that point – some-thing that appears unlikely at the time of this writing – the end of unques-tioned U.S. military dominance in East Asia is likely to usher in an era of tensions and uncertainty. As long as the outcome of any military conflict with the United States was a foregone conclusion, no country in the region could credibly threaten to attempt to alter the prevailing status quo.[1] When the outcome of a military conflict is no longer a certainty, however, then China may begin to attempt to alter prevailing norms and assumptions. A possible early example of this, mentioned in the previous chapter, is Scarborough Reef. The dispute between China and the Philippines over this reef is longstanding. Only in 2012, however, did China move to assert effective control over the reef. Similarly, although Beijing long protested Japan's control over islands in the East China Sea that Tokyo calls the Senkaku and Beijing calls the Diaoyu, only in 2012 did China begin actively contesting that control by sending its coast guard and other civilian ships to patrol inside the territorial waters of the islands.[2]

As its military power grows, Beijing might begin to challenge other norms in the region, including those directly involving the United States. One example is U.S. reconnaissance patrols in China's exclusive economic zone (EEZ). Beijing has long argued that such patrols by ships and aircraft should not be allowed within another country's EEZ. In 2000 and 2001 it attempted to discourage U.S. intelligence-gathering flights along China's coast (outside of China's territorial airspace but inside its EEZ) by using fighter aircraft to harass the U.S. aircraft, resulting in a collision between a Chinese fighter and a U.S. EP-3 electronic intelligence aircraft in April 2001. Chinese harass-ment of U.S. aircraft became less aggressive for several years after that incident but resumed again in 2014.[3]

A related but less well-known incident occurred in March of 2001, when the U.S. naval survey vessel *Bowditch* was forced to leave China's EEZ in the Yellow Sea when confronted by a Chinese frigate. The ship later returned escorted by a U.S. warship and such surveys continued, but eight years later another naval survey vessel, the *Impeccable,* was deliberately harassed by several (unarmed) Chinese vessels while conducting surveys in the South China Sea. The *Impeccable* continued to conduct its surveys (escorted by a U.S. destroyer), but such harassment by Chinese ships has continued.[4]

As China's military capabilities improve, Beijing could become increasingly assertive in its responses to U.S. intelligence collection within its EEZ, knowing that the United States could no longer be confident of easily defeating China in a military conflict off of China's coast. For its part, the United States, accustomed to being able to enforce its position on freedom of navigation in international waters (as, for example, it did in the Gulf of Sidra incidents with Libya in 1981 and 1989), would probably not readily acquiesce to China's position. The result could be increased tensions between the United States and China and more frequent incidents or even deadly clashes. For the rest of the region, the result would be greater uncertainty about what the prevailing norms are for activities in other country's EEZs, and concern about China's willingness to use force to resolve international disputes.

Regardless of China's specific behavior in coming years, the 2020s are likely to be a time of power transition in East Asia, from a region in which the United States has controlled the seas and air above them and has had the capability to defend its allies against virtually any form of aggression, to one where China has the capability to, at a minimum, contest control of the seas and airspace and where an attempt to oppose a Chinese use of force will be dangerous and costly for any country, including the United States, that chooses to do so. Power transitions have historically been times of instability and conflict. Navigating the coming power transition in East Asia will require great skill and not a little luck on the part of both U.S. and Chinese leaders.

IMPLICATIONS FOR THE UNITED STATES

The findings of the preceding chapters of this book suggest several major implications for the United States. First, to maintain its edge over China in an era of constrained defense budgets, the U.S. military will need to make hard choices about what current capabilities should be preserved, what new capabilities should be acquired, and what capabilities should be divested. Most fundamentally, this implies the criticality of the U.S. military maintaining or improving its capabilities in the dimensions where the U.S. advantage over

China is greatest: organizational structure, logistics, and organizational culture. Given resource limitations, it also implies focusing on specific areas of warfare. Future conflict with China is not the only contingency the U.S. military should prepare for, but it is the contingency that entails the greatest risk of catastrophic defeat. Accordingly, the emphasis of U.S. capability development efforts should be on those capabilities that would be vital in the event of conflict with China. Based on the two scenarios analyzed in this book, these include air-to-air combat; active and passive defenses against surface-to-surface missiles (ballistic and cruise), both for fixed facilities such as air bases and for naval vessels; the ability, conversely, to attack ships and fixed facilities defended by highly capable surface-to-air missiles; aerial refueling capabilities; and the ability to detect and track the movements of Chinese ships and aircraft in the face of Chinese efforts to destroy or disrupt U.S. reconnaissance satellites and aircraft.

In the case of combat aircraft, another key finding is that quality is more important than quantity. In 2020, the U.S. Air Force will still have more than twelve hundred fighter aircraft and the U.S. Navy and Marine Corps will have another twelve hundred. Because of the limited usable basing available, however, a total of only six hundred U.S. fighter aircraft were able to participate in the Taiwan scenario analyzed in the previous chapter. Even if the U.S. military wishes to maintain enough fighter aircraft to simultaneously fight two major wars, unless the United States increases the number of usable (i.e., defendable) land bases and aircraft carriers in the western Pacific region, it is not clear what contingency would require more than a fraction of the other 880 U.S. Air Force fighters and 920 U.S. Navy and Marine Corps fighters that will be in the U.S. inventory in 2020 but would not be able to participate in a Taiwan contingency due to basing limitations.[5] Because of the limitations on the numbers of aircraft that can be operated from bases and aircraft carriers in the western Pacific, moreover, the combat capability of those limited numbers of aircraft is more important than the overall size of the U.S. inventory. Given that the funds available for defense spending are finite, therefore, the United States should eliminate less-capable fighter aircraft from its inventory and use the savings to further upgrade the capabilities of those that remain.

The same cannot be said of U.S. Navy warships, however. In particular, aircraft carriers *are* the bases from which naval aircraft operate. Everything else being equal, the more aircraft carriers available to participate in a conflict, the more air power the United States will be able to bring to bear. The key word here, however, is "available." In the Taiwan scenario analyzed in the previous chapter, for example, the United States has a total inventory of eleven aircraft carriers but only five are able to participate in the conflict because two are assumed to be undergoing long-term maintenance at the time of the conflict and the other four are based on the east coast of the United States where they are unable to reach the western Pacific in time to contribute to the operation. In the South China Sea scenario the limitation is even more severe, as only those ships based in the western Pacific or which happen to be in the region at the time the crisis begins are able to participate. Thus, in a conflict with China, the key issue with regard to naval capability (including naval aviation) will be how many ships are in or near the Pacific, particularly the western Pacific, at the time the conflict begins. Ships based in the Atlantic, although closer to potential hot spots in the Mediterranean and Persian Gulf than ships based on the West Coast of the United States, will be less likely to be able to contribute to scenarios involving China.

As this book has argued throughout, however, combat capability is not simply a function of the numbers and capabilities of major weapons platforms. In particular, in addition to organizational structure, doctrine, quality of personnel, quality of training, and organizational culture, there are a number of other types of systems that are key to being able to employ the capabilities of major weapons platforms. One of these is aerial refueling aircraft. In both scenarios analyzed, virtually all U.S. fighter aircraft were dependent on aerial refueling aircraft to engage in combat. Another important type of system is surveillance and reconnaissance systems, including satellites, unmanned aerial vehicles, and others. A third is the munitions carried by the major weapons platforms, such as air-to-air, surface-to-air, air-to-surface, and surface-to-surface missiles.

Over the longer term, maintaining its qualitative edge will require that the United States remain ahead of weaponry developments in China. Key factors in both of the scenarios examined, for example, were the limited range of China's antiship ballistic missiles, the small numbers of Chinese ballistic missiles capable of reaching Guam, China's lack of aerial refueling aircraft, and China's limited antisubmarine warfare capabilities. These allowed U.S. aircraft carriers, Guam-based aircraft, and submarines to conduct combat air patrols and attack ships while remaining relatively safe from counterattack. If China acquires longer-range antiship ballistic missiles, significant numbers of aerial refueling aircraft and conventional intermediate-range ballistic missiles, and significantly improved antisubmarine warfare capabilities, however, these limitations will no longer exist and the U.S. military will need to find new means of contesting air superiority over Taiwan and of sinking Chinese ships.

A second major implication of the analysis in this book is the importance of the capabilities of U.S. allies in any conflict with China. In the Taiwan scenario, the military capabilities of both Taiwan and Japan were key to the outcome. In the case of Taiwan, it contributed approximately 20 percent of the total air combat power defending the island during the first days of combat. This contribution, however, was dependent on Taiwan's air force being able to repair the runways at its air bases within a few hours of their being attacked by China's ballistic missiles. If a single ballistic missile attack were instead sufficient to put a runway out of operation for several days, then Taiwan's air force would essentially be out of the war after the first few hours of combat. Conversely, if Taiwan were able to restore its runways to operation within only an hour or so of their being damaged by ballistic missiles, then Taiwan's contribution to the air war would be significantly increased. Of course, the capabilities of Taiwan's fighter aircraft – and the pilots who were flying them and the commanders who were orchestrating them – would be critical as well. Regardless of how many were able to participate, mediocre aircraft flown by poorly led, incapable pilots would not be nearly as effective as high-quality aircraft flown by ably led, highly capable pilots. There are many other improvements that Taiwan could make to its defense that would greatly increase the difficulty for China of successfully invading and conquering the island.[6]

Japan also made important contributions in the Taiwan scenario. Of particular importance was the role played by Japan's Air Self-Defense Force, which not only deterred China from using manned aircraft to attack U.S. bases in Japan, but also reduced the effectiveness of Chinese cruise missile attacks on the air bases from which U.S. aircraft were operating. Along with the hardened shelters at the JASDF bases at Komatsu and Chitose (in addition to those at the joint U.S.-Japanese base at Misawa), this enabled U.S. combat aircraft operating from Japan to participate in the battle for air superiority over Taiwan. If more Japanese air bases, particularly those in southern Japan, possessed significant numbers of hardened shelters, along with rapid runway repair capabilities and the ability to service F-35s, which the Japanese Air Self-Defense Force itself will acquire beginning in 2016,[7] U.S. combat aircraft operating from Japan would be able to contribute even more effectively to the battle for air superiority.

A third major implication of the findings of this book, however, is that, although continuing to make efforts to preserve and prolong their military advantage over China is important, the United States and its allies in the region also need to accept adjust to the fact of China's growing military power. Even if they do not grow as rapidly in coming years as they have over the previous two decades, China's economy and military power are likely to continue to grow more rapidly than those of nations with mature economies such as the United States and Japan. This means that China will have an increasing say on developments in the region that affect its security. Even though Beijing's positions on issues may not be in the interests of other countries in the region or morally justifiable, to assume that the U.S. position will always prevail in every dispute is likely to result in increased frictions, tensions, and potentially even conflict with China. In some cases the United States will want to accept those costs and risks, but in others the United States will need to assess whether it is worth the costs and risks to stand its ground on an issue of minor importance to America but of vital importance to China. Determining which issue falls into which category will be a key challenge for the United States in coming years and one in which not just policy makers but the American public needs to be involved.[8]

IMPLICATIONS FOR CHINA

The nature of the growth of China's military capabilities has implications for China as well. China's growing military power will give Beijing the potential to alter some of the prevailing norms in the region. These include who controls the islands and reefs in the East China Sea and South China Sea and could expand to other areas, such as whether it is acceptable for one country to perform intelligence collection or military exercises within the EEZ of another country. China's leaders should consider carefully, however, whether changes to these norms are truly in China's long-term interest.

Another development that may already have occurred in response to China's growing military power is that Taiwan's leadership and people have apparently concluded that Taiwan is not capable of defending itself without the intervention of the United States. As a result, Taiwan's spending on defense fell from more than 3 percent of GDP in the 1990s to about 2 percent of GDP in 2011, even while China's defense spending more than tripled over the same period.[9] In other words, since the twenty-first century began, Taiwan has ceased spending enough on defense to defeat a Chinese attack and is now simply spending enough to hold out until the United States can come to its rescue.

As China's military capabilities further increase, to the point at which it could potentially invade and conquer Taiwan even in the face of U.S. intervention, its relationship with Taiwan is likely to change. Although actually attacking Taiwan would be extremely risky and costly for China, Taiwan's leaders will know that China's leaders could have little choice in the face of popular pressure under certain circumstances. This recognition is likely to make Taiwan's leaders more circumspect in their dealings with the mainland and in taking actions that could be interpreted as attempts to solidify or formalize Taiwan's de facto independence. China's growing military leverage over Taiwan could also cause Beijing to begin to exert pressure on Taiwan to enter into formal reunification negotiations.

China's leaders must be cautious, however, in how they make use of China's growing military power. First, they should recognize that China's military capabilities may not be as great as they appear. Modern doctrine, advanced weaponry, and well-educated personnel are important, but without an appropriate organizational structure and culture for implementing that doctrine and for taking advantage of the capabilities of the PLA's advanced weaponry and well-educated personnel, and without the logistical capabilities to sustain that weaponry and personnel, China's actual military power will likely be significantly less than the numbers and quality of its equipment and personnel would suggest. Lacking recognition of the PLA's continuing weaknesses, China's leaders could embark on a military operation that becomes a humiliating defeat or an excessively costly victory, as occurred with China's invasion of Vietnam in 1979 or the United States' invasion of Iraq in 2003.

China's leaders should also be aware that the actual or even threatened use of its military capabilities could provoke a response from the United States and countries in the region that would actually weaken China's influence. So far, there has not been a large-scale movement in Asia to counterbalance against China's growing power.[10] That could change, however, if Beijing began to use the threat of force more overtly and frequently, much less if it actually carried out those threats. Under such circumstances, the United States and countries in East Asia could begin to significantly increase their defense capabilities and move to strengthen the alliances between the United States and countries in the region, and countries in the region could begin to cooperate more closely with each other in security matters.[11] The net result could be that the United States and countries of East Asia increase their combined military capabilities by an amount greater than the improvement in China's military capabilities. In short, East Asia could begin to look like Europe did during the Cold War, an outcome that would make the entire region, including China (and the United States), worse off than before.

IMPLICATIONS FOR THE STUDY OF MILITARY POWER

The model of military power used in this study is more comprehensive than those used in the past and has a persuasive theoretical basis, but it has not been empirically validated. Although the importance of doctrine, organizational structure, weaponry, training, logistics, and organizational culture to the outcomes of military conflicts seems beyond question, it may be that some of these dimensions are significantly more important than others, which can therefore be discounted. Conversely, there may be important dimensions of military capability that were omitted from the model.

Even if the dimensions of military capability used in this study are both necessary and sufficient to describe the overall power of a military organization, moreover, the specific measures used in this study to assess capability in each of these dimensions, although also having a prima facie plausibility, have not been demonstrated to be the only or best criteria for assessing capability in those dimensions. To validate (or replace) the criteria used in this study, more in-depth studies would be needed of what specific characteristics of doctrine, organizational structure, weaponry, training, logistics, and organizational culture are associated with military success and failure.

There is also the question of how the different dimensions of military capability combine to produce overall military effectiveness. The model used in this study postulates that there are seven distinct dimensions of military capability and that a given military organization can fall anywhere along a continuum of capability in each of those seven dimensions. The most important measure of the outcome a military conflict, however, is largely unidimensional and binary: Either you win or you lose. Chapter Nine illustrated one method of assessing the likely outcome of a given military conflict that attempts to integrate the different dimensions of military capability – scenario analysis – but scenario analysis is a labor- and data-intensive process and even so requires broad guesses as to the operational effects of many of the dimensions. For example, in Chapter 9, a reasonably well-trained pilot operating within a centralized organization that discouraged individual initiative was considered to be 80 percent as effective as a superbly trained pilot operating within a more decentralized organization that encouraged individual initiative. Is 80 percent an accurate estimate of the effect of these differences? Can these differences even be translated into a single, fixed percentage that applies to all types of air-to-air combat? In-depth analysis of historical cases, therefore, is needed to identify, not just the relative importance of each dimension of military capability, but also how they interact with the other dimensions of military capability.

Despite these challenges, developing a valid model of military capability is an important task for both theoretical and practical reasons. At the theoretical level, as Biddle (2004) has pointed out, military power is central to many theories of international relations. If military power cannot be accurately assessed, then theories of international relations that depend on it cannot be accurately employed or tested.[12] Progress in the development of theories of international relations, therefore, requires an accurate model of what military capability actually is, as opposed to being an amorphous concept that is invoked but never defined, or which is represented only by indirect proxies, such as GDP or annual defense expenditures.

At the practical level, policy makers and researchers also need an accurate way of assessing the military capabilities of different nations, as important foreign policy choices, military deployments, and budget decisions depend on such assessments. During the Cold War, assessments of the military balance between North Atlantic Treaty Organization (NATO) and the Warsaw Pact, focused as they were on material measures such as numbers of tanks and soldiers, probably vastly overestimated the conventional military capabilities of the Warsaw Pact. This material bias carried over to estimates of the difficulty of expelling the Iraqi military from Kuwait in 1991. Estimates of the ease with which the U.S.-led coalition would defeat Iraq in 2003, on the other hand, informed as they were by the experience in 1991, were more accurate with respect to the conventional dimension of the conflict, but completely overlooked the difficulty the U.S. military would encounter in defeating an Iraqi insurgency.

Particularly given the challenge that will be posed by China's growing military capabilities in the future, it is important for U.S. leaders and policy researchers to accurately assess those capabilities. Assessments focused purely on material dimensions will likely lead to incorrect conclusions about how to counter China's capabilities that are also overly focused on material solutions. On the other hand, assessments that dismiss the Chinese military as culturally incapable of ever becoming an effective fighting force may lead to equally erroneous conclusions, as they neglect not only the possibility of cultural change within an organization, but also the degree to which appropriate adjustments in doctrine and organizational structure can compensate for weaknesses in organizational culture. The performance of the Soviet Army during World War II is instructive in this regard.[13]

There is no question that the capabilities of China's military are improving, but this improvement is more rapid in some dimensions than in others. Accurate assessments of these improvements and appropriate responses to them, by both American and Chinese leaders and researchers, require a multidimensional understanding of what military power is. This study has offered a prototype tool for measuring military power. Additional work is needed to validate and refine the tool, but it clearly provides one possible starting point for a more comprehensive, and, therefore, more useful, means for assessing military capability.

Notes

1 Introduction

1 For example, see Nathan and Ross, 1998, p. 146; Frankenstein, 1999, p. 199. Godwin, 1996b, p. 55, n. 5, attributes the term "junkyard army" to Alfred D. Wilhelm, then of the Atlantic Council. The originator of the term "world's largest military museum" is unclear.

2 "China Defense Budget to Increase 12.2 pct in 2014," 2014. Figures cited are in current dollars, but even after accounting for inflation China's defense budget nearly quintupled in real terms over this period. See National Bureau of Statistics of China, 2007; National Bureau of Statistics of China National Data website; Li, 2014. Officially announced defense budgets in China are believed to understate China's true defense spending by as much as a third. See, inter alia, Crane et al., 2005, pp. 91–134. Assuming the *proportion* by which the officially announced budgets understate China's actual defense spending has remained approximately constant over time, however; the growth rate in China's true defense spending should be about the same as the growth rate in the disclosed portion of its defense budget.

3 E.g., see Taiwan Affairs Office and the Information Office of the State Council, 2000.

4 96th Congress, 1979.

5 Goldstein, 2013, pp. 49–50.

6 Geller and Singer, 1998, pp. 72–75.

7 Studies that fall into this category include Shambaugh, 2002a; Council on Foreign Relations, 2003; Cordesman and Kleiber, 2007; Fisher, 2008; and Office of the Secretary of Defense, 2013.

8 Blasko, 2006, and Blasko, 2012, provide meticulously detailed descriptions of organization, personnel, deployment, doctrine, equipment, and training of the PLA Army. Studies of China's navy and related issues include Erickson et al., 2007; ONI, 2007; Howarth, 2008; O'Rourke, 2008; Holmes and Yoshihara, 2008; Erickson, Goldstein, and Lord, 2009; ONI, 2009; Cole, 2010; and Erickson and Goldstein, 2011. Reports on China's air force include NASIC, 2007; NASIC, 2010; and Allen, 2011b. Studies of China's defense industries include Medeiros et al., 2005, and Cheung, 2008.

Histories of the PLA include Ryan, Finkelstein, and McDevitt, 2003, and Burkitt, Scobell, and Wortzel, 2003. Studies of civil-military relations in China include Scobell and Wortzel, 2004; Li, 2006; and Finkelstein and Gunness, 2007. Studies of the PLA's combat doctrine include Mulvenon and Finkelstein, 2005; Cliff et al., 2007; and Cliff et al., 2011.

9 These include Shlapak, Orletsky, and Wilson, 2000; Tsang, 2006; and Shlapak et al., 2009. In addition, Bush and O'Hanlon, 2007, contains an appendix providing an analysis of China's capabilities to invade Taiwan.

10 The seminal work in the genre, and maybe the best known, is Bernstein and Munro, 1998. This book has been followed by a number of others, including Timperlake and Triplett, 1999; Gertz, 2000; Mosher, 2002; Menges, 2005; Carpenter, 2006; and Navarro, 2008.

11 For a typical example of how military power is represented in the media, see the graphic entitled "Defending China" in Page, 2013.

12 A description of how armored division equivalents were computed can be found in Congressional Budget Office, 1988, pp. 13–16. For examples of its use, see Posen, 1984–1985; Friedberg, 1987–1988; Millett, Murray, and Watman, 1986; Holmes, 1988; Cohen, 1988; Mearsheimer, Posen, and Cohen, 1989. Computer simulations used by the U.S. Department of Defense and its contractors were similarly based on the weapon systems the two sides possessed.

13 O'Hanlon, 2009, p. 75, cites analyses by Posen and Epstein that respectively estimated as many as eleven thousand or sixteen thousand coalition casualties. Other prewar casualty estimates apparently were as high as thirty thousand casualties, but it is not clear whether these estimates were based on analysis of the respective military forces or were simply guesses or worst-case planning factors. See Biddle, 1996, p. 142; O'Hanlon, 2009, p. 75.

14 O'Hanlon, 2009, p. 76, states that total coalition casualties (killed and wounded) were about fifteen hundred. A total of 147 U.S. military personnel died in combat during the 1991 Gulf War.

15 For examples of published works espousing this view, see Biddle, 1996, p. 139, fn. 1.

16 See Biddle (1996); Biddle, Hinkle, and Fisherkeller (1999); and Biddle (2004). Another popular explanation for the outcome of the Gulf War was that the Iraqi forces failed to fight and simply surrendered en masse. This explanation, too, is insufficient. Although large numbers of Iraqi forces surrendered without firing a shot, other forces fought determinedly but nonetheless were easily defeated in one-sided battles. See Biddle, 1996, pp. 149–152.

17 See Latimer, 2000; Kitchen, 2009, pp. 37–38.

18 See Fitzsimmons, 2013a, pp. 47–108, 167–230; Fitzsimmons, 2013b.

19 On the Battle of 73 Easting, see Biddle, 1996, pp. 146–147. On Lanchester's Laws, see O'Hanlon, 2009, pp. 67–70. Since Lanchester's equations are expressed in terms of continuous variables but losses are binary numbers, the result of no M1s lost was assumed to be equivalent to an expected loss of 0.49 or less according to Lanchester's equations. If the combat value of a T-72 is "1" and the combat value of an M1 is X, where X is a multiple of 1, then the value of X for which expected losses for the Iraqis

are 37 and expected losses for the United States are less than 0.5 is given by the equation $(9X)^2 / (37)^2 = 37/0.49$. Solving this equation for X gives $X = 35.7$.

20 See Biddle, 2004, pp. 150–180.

21 Biddle, 2004, pp. 191–196.

22 Biddle, 2004, p. 2.

23 For example, on the importance of culture, see Murray, 1999; on personnel quality, see Kavanagh, 2005 and Wardynski, Lyle, and Colarusso, 2009. In specific reference to the PLA, Blasko, 2012, p. 173, states, "The capabilities of modern systems vary according to . . . the training, logistics support, doctrine, and morale of the troops employing the weapons," but he does not further elaborate.

24 DOD *Dictionary of Military and Associated Terms*, 2013, p. A-49.

25 DOD *Dictionary of Military and Associated Terms*, 2013.

26 See Bianco, 1971, pp. 167–198; Blasko, 2006, pp. 2–4; Li, 2007, pp. 45–78.

27 Blasko, 2006, p. 4; Li, 2007, pp. 113–146; Cheung, 2008, pp. 23–25.

28 Blasko, 2006, p. 4; Cheung, 2008, pp. 23–25.

29 Blasko, 2006, pp. 2–4.

30 IISS, 1978, p. 56; National Bureau of Statistics of China, 2003, pp. 55, 284. The definitive work on the Sino-Vietnamese War from a Chinese perspective is O'Dowd, 2007.

31 Calculated based on National Bureau of Statistics of China, 2003, pp. 55, 58, 284.

32 The definitive account of the PLA's involvement in business activities is Mulvenon, 2001.

33 National Bureau of Statistics of China, 2007; Xinhua, 2013; National Bureau of Statistics of China National Data website; "China to Centralize Military Command to Improve Operations," 2014. These rates of increase are in real terms, after accounting for inflation. The average nominal rate of increase was nearly 15 percent.

34 For a detailed discussion, see Cliff et al., 2007.

35 For more on the CMC, see Li, 2002a; Shambaugh, 2002a, pp. 113–124; Shambaugh, 2002b.

36 Hu, Wang, and Zhang, 2007, pp. 22, 75–76, 78–82, 255–256, 281–283, 309–310.

37 Hu, Wang, Zhang, 2007, pp. 92–93, 255, 283, 309–310.

38 Note that this book focuses on the PLA's warfighting capabilities, not its capabilities to perform missions other than major combat operations, such as peacekeeping, disaster relief, suppression of domestic uprisings, and other actions it could be called upon to perform.

2 Doctrine

1 Griffith, 1990, pp. 21–22.

2 The *Department of Defense Dictionary of Military and Associated Terms* (2010), for example, states that doctrine "is authoritative but requires judgment in application."

3 Even within the U.S. military, there are differences between the services, with the U.S. Army having the reputation of being the most strict about adhering to doctrine and the U.S. Air Force having the reputation of being the least strict.

4 Johnson, Grissom, and Oliker, 2008, pp. 24–41.

5 Ibid.

6 Qiao and Wang, 1999.

7 For more on these magazines, see Wang, 2011, p. 158.

8 The collective term for these documents, that is, the Chinese term that corresponds to the English term "doctrine," is 作战条令. E.g., see Ren, 1999; *PLA Daily* Reporter, 1999; "Military Men Are Born to Win Victories," 2008; Yang, 2008; Yang, 2009.

9 China had no capability or expectations to conduct operations outside of its borders during these years. Any adversary, therefore, would have been an invader of China.

10 See Li, 1996, p. 443; Godwin, 1996a, pp. 466–467; Shambaugh, 2002a, pp. 62–64; Ng 2005, pp. 38–61; Fravel, 2005, pp. 88–89; Cliff et al., 2007, pp. 18–19. Before the 1960s, the PLA did not have its own doctrinal publications, relying instead on translated Soviet manuals. See "Military Men Are Born to Win Victories," 2008.

11 According to Yang, 2009, p. 113, the writing of the "second generation" of combat regulations occurred over a period from 1970 to about 1979. According to a textbook issued by the Academy of Military Sciences, the second generation "combined arms combat principles" (合成军队战斗概则), which represented the overarching document for this set of doctrinal publications, was issued in 1975. See Wang and Fang, 1999, p. 134.

12 Li, 1996, p. 446; Godwin, 1996a, pp. 464–465; Shambaugh, 2002a, pp. 63–64. The reasons for this assessment are somewhat unclear. Then-leader of China, Deng Xiaoping, attributed it to the strategic stalemate between the United States and Soviet Union. See ibid. It is also possible, however, that it was also a result of the normalization of relations with the United States in 1979 causing China's leaders to no longer be concerned about conflict with the United States (if they still were before 1979) while simultaneously reassuring them against the threat of Soviet invasion.

13 Li, 1996, pp. 444–456; Godwin, 1996a, pp. 466–472; Shambaugh, 2002a, pp. 64–69; Ng, 2005, pp. 61–104; Cliff et al., 2007, pp. 19–20; Yang, 2009, p. 114. A third generation of official combined arms combat principles was issued in 1987. See Wang and Fang, 1999, p. 134.

14 Finkelstein, 2007, p. 95. Although U.S. military doctrine periodically undergoes major revisions, there do not appear to be official overarching descriptors attached to different generations of doctrine. The doctrine known as AirLand Battle in the 1980s and 1990s, for example, applied only to the U.S. Army. There does not appear to have been an official descriptor for U.S. military doctrine as a whole during that period. Similarly, although the most recent edition of the U.S. Army's doctrine on operations, Field Manual 3–0, describes itself as "a revolutionary departure from past doctrine" it does not give a specific name to the new doctrinal conception it represents. See "Foreword" in Headquarters, Department of the Army, 2008.

15 Wang and Fang, 1999, pp. 124–138; Ren, 1999; Ng, 2005, pp. 106–122. According to Wang and Fang (1999, p. 126) and Yang (2008), the 1999 doctrinal publications

were the first to include campaign guidance documents (战役纲要). Previous generations of doctrine were limited to the "combat" (战斗), i.e., operational-tactical, level. Encyclopedia of China's Air Force Editorial Committee (2005, pp. 328–330) describes revisions to combat regulations for each of the PLA Air Force's major branches and specialties as well as for "composite force" (i.e., air force–wide) combat, all of which were issued in 1999. Previous versions are noted as having been issued between 1990 and 1995, but, based on the description in Ren (1999), those earlier versions were presumably based on the doctrinal concepts (particularly the 1987 combined arms combat principles) developed in the mid-1980s.

16 Wang and Fang, 1999, pp. 124–131; Encyclopedia of China's Air Force Editorial Committee, 2005, p. 328.

17 Wang and Fang, 1999, pp. 124, 129; Encyclopedia of China's Air Force Editorial Committee, 2005, p. 328. Specific descriptions of the types of campaigns described in the PLA Army, PLA Navy, or Second Artillery campaign guidances were not found. However, a classified textbook on Second Artillery Campaigns authored by the Second Artillery, which states that it is based on the joint campaign guidance and the campaign guidance for the Second Artillery, contains descriptions of nuclear counterattack campaigns (核反击战役) and conventional missile strike campaigns (常规导弹突击战役). See People's Liberation Army Second Artillery Force, 2004, pp. 297–337, 404.

18 Wang and Fang (1999, pp. 127, 135), after the headings for the sections titled "main contents" in its chapters on the joint campaign guidance and combined arms combat principles issued in January 1999, has the notation "omitted" (略). Textbooks on strategy, doctrine, and tactics include, inter alia, Wang and Zhang (2000), He (2001), Bi (2002), Lu (2004). Reference books include *Encyclopedia of China's Navy* (1999) and Encyclopedia of Air Force Editorial Committee (2005).

19 Wang and Fang, 1999, pp. 129–130; Fravel, 2005, p. 95; Ng, 2005, p. 122; Blasko, 2006, p. 104; Cliff et al., 2007, pp. 42–44.

20 Fravel, 2005, pp. 94–95, Ng, 2005, p. 122; Cliff et al., 2007, pp. 28–34.

21 Godwin 2001, p. 111; U.S. Secretary of Defense, 2001; Godwin, 2003, p. 278; Fravel, 2005, pp. 92, 93–94; Ng, 2005, pp. 119, 122; Blasko, 2006, pp. 100, 102; Cliff et al., 2007, pp. 28–34

22 Ibid.

23 Godwin, 2001, pp. 111–112, 113; U.S. Secretary of Defense, 2001; Godwin, 2003, pp. 278, 279; Ng, 2005, pp. 111–114; Cliff et al., 2007, pp. 38–41, 51–79.

24 Godwin, 2001, pp. 112, 113; U.S. Secretary of Defense, 2001; Godwin, 2003, pp. 278–280; Fravel, 2005, p. 94; Ng, 2005, pp. 117, 118, 122; Blasko, 2006, pp. 100–102; Cliff et al., 2007, pp. 28, 34–38.

25 Fravel, 2005, p. 95; Ng, 2005, pp. 117, 122; Blasko, 2006, pp. 102–103. Whether this belief is actually correct will be discussed in Chapter Three.

26 Cliff, 1996; Information Office of the State Council of the People's Republic of China, 2000; Stokes, 2005.

27 Dumbaugh, 2008, p. 2, n. 8. For more detail on possible conflict scenarios, see Johnson et al., 2009, pp. 37–39.

28 Wang and Fang, 1999, pp. 128–130.

29 Doctrinal guidance for a particular type of campaign, of course, does not indicate whether war plans for specific individual campaigns belonging to that type (e.g., an invasion of Taiwan, one particular possible "island offensive campaign") have been developed. It is unlikely that war plans would be written for a type of campaign for which there was no doctrinal guidance, however, and, even if a war plan for a given conflict had not been written in advance of the conflict, the existence of doctrinal guidance for the appropriate *type* of campaign would greatly facilitate the effective prosecution of the conflict.

30 Wang and Fang, 1999, p. 124. The 1999 air force campaign guidance did, however, include an air offensive campaign and publications of China's military described a Second Artillery "conventional missile strike campaign." See Wang and Zhang, 2000; People's Liberation Army Second Artillery Force, pp. 317–337. Thus, a coercive air and missile bombardment campaign against Taiwan could probably have been assembled from existing doctrinal elements if the Chinese leadership had so directed. However, such a campaign did not exist as a joint campaign type that had been subjected to the rigorous development and review process that the other joint campaign types had been.

31 Wang and Zhang, 2000, pp. 320–337. The 2006 edition of *Campaign Studies* does include "offensive campaigns against coral islands and reefs" (对珊瑚岛礁进攻战役) as a navy campaign. See Zhang, Yu, and Zhou, 2006, pp. 535–538. Note that the joint campaigns listed in Wang and Zhang (2000) closely, but not exactly, match those said to be included in the 1999 joint campaign guidance. Whereas the joint campaign guidance, for example, is said to include "island blockade" (岛屿封锁) and "island offensive" (岛屿进攻) campaigns, Wang and Zhang (2000, pp. 407–440) describes simply "blockade" (封锁) and "landing" (登陆) campaigns. An island blockade is clearly one type of blockade, but it is not the only type – blockades can also be imposed against continents – and an island offensive would normally entail an amphibious landing but would also include a ground offensive after the amphibious landing. In addition, Wang and Zhang (2000, pp. 474–484) includes a sixth type of joint campaign, an airborne campaign (空降战役), that was not among those said to have been included in the 1999 joint campaign guidance (it was also not included in the air force campaign guidance). Thus, although the campaigns included in Wang and Zhang, 2000, appear to be similar to those included in the official campaign guidance (the descriptors for the types of air force campaigns described in Wang and Zhang, 2000, for example, exactly match those said to be included in the 1999 air force campaign guidance), Wang and Zhang, 2000, clearly cannot be considered to be identical to or equivalent to the official campaign guidance.

32 Wang and Zhang (2000) describe possible army campaigns as including "mobile warfare campaigns" (机动战战役), "positional offense campaigns" (阵地进攻战役),

and "positional defense campaigns" (阵地防御战役). To be effective, however, especially in the face of South Korean and possibly U.S. air power, army operations in a war over Korea would have needed to be integrated with PLA Air Force and Second Artillery operations as part of a broader joint campaign.

33 Yang, 2009, p. 115.

34 Godwin, 2001, pp. 108–114; Finkelstein, 2001, pp. 125, 128.

35 See Luttwak, 2002, pp. 113–117. According to Luttwak (2002, p. 115), "the starting point of [a doctrine based on indirection and maneuver] is the avoidance of the enemy's strengths, followed by the application of some particular superiority against presumed enemy weaknesses, be they physical, psychological, technical, or organizational." These are precisely the terms used to describe the new doctrine promulgated by the PLA in 1999.

36 Wang and Fang, 1999, pp. 129, 130. See Cliff et al., 2007, pp. 23–50, for a detailed analysis of the aspects of China's doctrine that were designed for countering an adversary with superior military technology.

37 On the PLA Navy's operational doctrine, see Cole, 2001, pp. 139–144. On Second Artillery doctrine, see Medeiros, 2007, pp. 146–158, 165–169. Office of Naval Intelligence, 2007, has an eight-page chapter on doctrine, but this chapter discusses only how PLA doctrine is developed and implemented, not the actual content of that doctrine. Office of Naval Intelligence, 2009, has no discussion of doctrine at all.

38 Cliff et al., 2011, pp. 84–178.

39 Cliff et al., 2011, pp. 179–180, 182–184.

40 China's 2002 national defense white paper, issued in December 2002, still uses the term "local wars under modern, especially high-tech conditions" ("National Defense Policy," Information Office of the State Council of the People's Republic of China, 2002). The preface to an official book on Second Artillery Campaigns, dated July 1, 2003, uses the term "informationized local wars" (People's Liberation Army Second Artillery Force, 2004). China's 2004 and subsequent national defense white papers all use the phrase 信息化条件下局部战争 ("local wars under informationization requirements"). See Information Office of the State Council of the People's Republic of China, 2004.

41 Mulvenon, 2009. Note that Mulvenon and many others mistranslate "historical" (历史) in the phrase "historical missions for the new stage in the new century" as "historic," which would have been represented by a different Chinese term (历史性).

42 "National Defense Policy," Information Office of the State Council of the People's Republic of China, 2006a.

43 Cliff et al., 2011, pp. 179–186; Blasko, 2007, p. 318.

44 Yang, 2009, pp. 113, 114.

45 Articles implying the writing of the regulations was complete and that they would soon be issued include Xu et al., 2008; "Military Men Are Born to Win Victories," 2008; Bao, 2008; "New Year, New Measures, New Climate," 2009; Wang, 2009;

Liu et al., 2009; and Zhao and Zhang, 2009. The article implying that the regulations had been issued is Yang, 2009.

46 Yang, 2009, p. 115. This source also states that for the first time doctrine for the People's Armed Police was created. One example of the new type of campaign guidance that was added may be guidance for PLA political work during wartime 《中国人民解放军战时政治工作纲要》. See Bao, 2008.

47 According to Yang, 2009, p. 117, textbooks are revised at the same time as the doctrine is.

48 Zhang, Yu, and Zhou, 2006; Wang and Zhang, 2000. In addition, an airborne campaign, listed as a joint campaign in Wang and Zhang, 2000, is described as an air force campaign in Zhang, Yu, and Zhou, 2006. As noted above, however, an airborne campaign was not included in either the 1999 joint campaign guidance (or the 1999 air force campaign guidance), so it is not clear whether the inclusion of an airborne campaign as an air force campaign in Zhang, Yu, and Zhou, 2006, reflects its inclusion in the new air force campaign guidance.

49 See Chapter Six for more detail.

50 The disputed Senkaku Islands of the East China Sea are not coral islands, so it is not clear how relevant the "offensive campaign against coral islands and reefs" type would be to a conflict over territorial claims in the East China Sea.

51 Wang and Fang, 1999, pp. 129, 130.

52 Yang, 2009, pp. 112–113.

53 Wang and Liu, 2012; PLA General Staff Department, 2013.

54 Information Office, 2006a.

3 Organizational Structure

1 Jones, 2010, pp. 94–95, 98.

2 Jones, 2010, pp. 92–98, 120–129.

3 Jones, 2010, pp. 103–106, 131–132.

4 Jones, 2010, pp. 99–103.

5 Jones, 2010, pp. 106–108, 133.

6 Jones, 2010, pp. 109–115.

7 The purpose of this study is to assess the combat effectiveness of the Chinese military. As such, its interest in organization is limited to how organization directly affects a military's combat effectiveness during wartime. A military's organization, however, also *indirectly* affects its combat effectiveness through the organization's effects on the other dimensions of military capability – doctrine, personnel quality, training, and so forth. Since these other dimensions are primarily shaped during peacetime, the indirect effects of a military's organization on the military's overall capability, therefore, are a function of the organization's *peacetime* environment. The seminal study on this topic is Millett, Murray, and Watman, 1996.

8 This typology draws on Luttwak, 2001, pp. 113–117; and Liddell Hart, 2008, esp. pp. 121–124. Luttwak (2001) describes the first doctrinal type as one of "attrition,"

rather than "direct engagement." I prefer the term "direct engagement" as "attrition" implies a gradual wearing down over time whereas proponents of direct engagement would typically prefer to achieve their goals through a single decisive battle. Wars of attrition are often the result when militaries with doctrines of direct engagement are unable to achieve the decisive battle they seek. Liddell Hart (2008) refers to "direct approach" and "indirect approach."

9 On the U.S. Army during World War II, see Johnson, Grissom, and Oliker, 2008, pp. 24–41. On the German Army during the early years of World War II, see Deighton, 1979. Although Soviet operations during World War II largely consisted of direct engagements, from 1943 on the Soviet army began combining frontal assaults with "indirect" breakthrough and exploitation operations designed to isolate German units so that they could easily be defeated through encirclement and deprivation of supplies. See Griffith, 1990, pp. 130–134. For a detailed description of one such operation, the 1944 "Battle for White Russia," which resulted in the destruction of German Army Group Center, see Dunn, 2008.

10 Although the German army employed a doctrine of maneuver and indirection during the period of World War II when it was on the offensive, once Germany was on the defensive, Hitler continually refused to allow the army to yield ground. This resulted in more static defensive operations by the German army than its commanders would have preferred.

11 Griffith, 1990, p. 131.

12 Griffith, 1990, p. 132.

13 Luttwak, 2001, p. 115.

14 It could be argued that, to implement its doctrine, the PLA need not have an organic structure at all levels. If the principals of avoiding direct engagement with an adversary's combat forces and instead focusing the PLA best forces on attacks against key points apply only to broad domains of warfare (e.g., avoiding air-to-air combat), and not at lower operational and tactical levels, then only the top-most commanders would need to be given latitude to exercise initiative and flexibility and to coordinate directly with each other rather than up and down the chain of command. This is correct. Indeed, this was largely the approach adopted by the Soviet army during World War II, where, even within the tank, mechanized, and horse cavalry corps, which were given the best officers, only the higher ranking officers were expected to improvise and take initiative. This came at a price, however. At the tactical level Soviet units were considered only one-third as effective as their German counterparts. Thus, although the Soviet army was able to match and eventually surpass the German army in its skills at the operational level and above, overall victory was possible only because of the Soviet army's massive material superiority. See Griffith, 1990, pp. 131–132. The premise of China's doctrine since 1999, however, has been that China will *not* have material superiority over its most challenging opponent (the United States). Unless the PLA has extraordinary faith in the brilliance of its top commanders compared to their U.S. counterparts, therefore, for the principles of indirection and maneuver to enable it

to defeat a materially superior adversary, they would need to permeate all the way down to the tactical level. If they do not, then a mechanistic organizational structure would be the appropriate organizational structure for its doctrine, but that doctrine would have little hope of enabling it to defeat a materially superior adversary. As Fitzsimmons, 2013b, p. 3, states, "a materially inferior military force must be highly flexible and adaptable if it is to perform the range of military tasks required to defeat materially superior opponents."

15 See Blasko, 2006, pp. 36–42; Blasko, 2012, pp. 43–50; Cole, 2001, pp. 79–81; Cole, 2010, pp. 70–72.

16 Liu, 2003, pp. 66, 82.

17 Liu, 2003, p. 83; Blasko, 2006, pp. 36–44.

18 IISS, 2001, pp. 20, 188; "Operational Unit Diagrams"; "Army Command Structure." Both the PLA Army and the U.S. Army were relatively flat compared with business organizations: A corporation with nine organizational layers would typically have only about nine thousand employees. See Jones, 2010, p. 122.

19 Cole, 2002, pp. 481–488; Liu, 2003, p. 83. Cole, 2000, and Cole, 2002, make no mention of the base commander being in the chain of command. However, Office of Naval Intelligence, 2007, p. 7, states that this was the case and Cole, 2010, p. 67, in stating that the bases *lost* their responsibility for operational units in 2003, implies that they had such responsibility before 2003.

20 Numbered fleets are an organizational unit below the level of the two major fleets (Pacific and Atlantic) in the U.S. Navy. Which numbered fleet a ship belongs to depends on its geographic location. For example, in a conflict covering the entire Pacific theater, above the commander of a destroyer would have been a squadron commander, a battle group commander, either the Seventh Fleet commander (if the battle group was in the Western Pacific) or the Third Fleet commander (if the battle group was in the Eastern Pacific), and the overall maritime force commander for the Pacific theater. In a conflict limited to the Western Pacific, however, the Seventh Fleet commander might have been made overall maritime force com-mander for the theater and reported directly to the overall joint force commander for the conflict. The commanders of large ships, such as aircraft carriers and cruisers, would report directly to the commander of their battle group, rather than to a squadron commander. Personal communication from retired U.S. Navy captain.

21 None of the fleet commanders in the U.S. Navy in 2000 were female. See Botelho, 2014.

22 None of the fleet commanders or deputy fleet commanders in the PLA Navy in 2000 were female, so it is unlikely that the overall commander of PLA Navy forces in a military region in 2000 would have been a "her." See *Directory of PRC Military Personalities*, 2003.

23 IISS, 2001, pp. 20–21, 189–190. Note that China's military regions include only land areas, not sea areas. Thus, which ships would have been attached to which military regions is not clear. The North Sea Fleet was headquartered in the Jinan Military Region, the East Sea Fleet was headquartered in the Nanjing Military Region, and

the South Sea Fleet was headquartered in the Guangzhou Military Region. However, some North Sea Fleet units were based in the Beijing and Shenyang Military Regions. Whether these units would have assigned to the joint force commanders for the Beijing and Shenyang Military Regions, or to the joint force commander for the Jinan Military Region (assuming all three military regions were involved in the conflict) is unclear.

24 Allen, 2002b, pp. 384–391; Liu, 2003, p. 83. For nonaviation units they would have been platoon leader, company commander, battalion commander, regiment or brigade commander, and air corps, base, or command post commander. See Allen, 2002b, pp. 384–391. Note that the Chinese terms that Allen translates as "squadron" and "group" (中队 and 大队), I translate as "element" and "flight" for consistency with Western usage.

25 Private communication with former U.S. Air Force officer; "Air Expeditionary Force, Air and Space Expeditionary Task Force (ASETF)."

26 The PLA Air Force controlled a total of about four thousand aircraft. See IISS, 2001, pp. 190–191. Most of these were assigned to the seven MRAF's, but some were directly controlled by PLA Air Force headquarters. In a conflict, it is likely that additional aircraft would have been deployed to the involved military region(s), but many would undoubtedly have been retained in their home military regions.

27 The U.S. Air Force operated more than four thousand combat aircraft in 2001. See IISS, 2001, pp. 24–25. Contingency planning at the time allowed for up to half of these aircraft to be assigned to a single "major theater war." In addition, the overall commander of U.S. air forces in the conflict would have had control over significant numbers of surveillance and reconnaissance, aerial refueling, and transport aircraft. The overall commander of U.S. air forces during Operation Iraqi Freedom had control of more than eighteen hundred aircraft in March–April 2003, although more than half of the aircraft belonged to the U.S. Navy, U.S. Marine Corps, Great Britain, Australia, or Canada. See Moseley, 2003, p. 6.

28 IISS, 2001, p. 188; Gill, Mulvenon, Stokes, 2002, pp. 526–528; Hu, Wang, Zhang, 2007, p. 310; Stokes, 2012, p. 136. Note that here the term "base" (基地) refers to an organizational unit, not necessarily a single facility – most bases probably had multiple missile launch facilities associated with them. In addition to the six missile bases, moreover, the Second Artillery also had "assembly and testing bases" (装检基地), presumably a reference to units responsible for storing and mating nuclear warheads onto missiles. See Hu, Wang, and Zhang, 2007, p. 315. The number of these is unclear, but one assembly and testing base for each missile base may be a reasonable assumption (remembering that these "bases" are organizational units, and that the number of actual facilities for storing and mating warheads might have been greater).

29 Whether the joint force commander for a military region would have had command authority over the conventional ballistic missiles in that region is unclear. Figures 6-2 and 6-3 in Liu, 2003, pp. 82–83, although notional, do not show any surface-to-surface missile forces under the joint campaign command post for a

military region. Thus, it is possible that all Second Artillery missiles, including conventional ballistic missiles, would have been under the control of the "supreme headquarters" (统帅部) of the PLA. Since all three conventional ballistic missile brigades in 2000 belonged to a single missile base (Base 52), however, it seems likely that in this case the three conventional ballistic missile brigade commanders would have reported to a single officer (possibly the Base 52 commander) who had operational responsibility for all conventional ballistic missiles involved in the conflict. If this is correct, then there would still have been only two layers of officers between the commander of an individual missile launcher and the overall commander of the Second Artillery Force forces in the conflict: the battalion commander and the brigade commander.

30 Blasko, 2001, p. 312, citing Swaine, 1992, pp. 122–124. This statement refers to a peacetime situation, however, and might not have held in wartime.

31 Shambaugh, 2002a, p. 108.

32 Lewis and Xue, 2006, p. 146.

33 Interview with American specialist on PLA Air Force, September 2011.

34 Specifically, it employs a "multidivisional matrix structure," with the PLA Army, PLA Navy, PLA Air Force, and Second Artillery Force representing the "divisions." See Jones, 2010, pp. 170–171.

35 See Jones, 2010, pp. 169–170.

36 Blasko, Klapakis, and Corbett, 1996, p. 493; Dreyer, 1996, p. 334; Henley, 2000, p. 68; Blasko, 2006, p. 53; Hague, 2008, pp. 268–269; Cole, 2010, p. 118. Interview with American specialist on PLA Air Force, September 2011; interview with American specialist on PLA Army, October 2011.

37 Interview with American specialist on PLA Air Force, September 2011.

38 Johnson et al., 2009, pp. 44–49. Interview with American specialist on PLA Army, October 2011; interview with former U.S. Army battalion commander, September, 2011; Lewis and Xue, 2006, p. 145.

39 Lewis and Xue, 2006, pp. 115, 121.

40 Allen, 2002b, pp. 382–384; Cole, 2002, pp. 482–486; Finkelstein, 2002, pp. 126–127; Gill, Mulvenon, Stokes, 2002, pp. 520–526. Allen, 2011b, pp. 12–13.

41 Hu, Wang, Zhang, 2007, pp. 92–94, 297–298; *Directory of PRC Military Personalities*, 2003, pp. 87, 98, 113, 131, 141, 155, 170; Blasko, 2012, p. 35. The 2000 edition of *Directory of PRC Military Personalities* was not available for this study. Organizational changes between 2000 and 2003 are assumed to have been minor. Note that the forces of the North Sea Fleet were based in the Shenyang Military Region, Beijing Military Region, and Jinan Military Region.

42 IISS, 2001, p. 188; OSD, 2011, p. 4; IISS, 2011, pp. 230–231. Information Office, 2013, states that the PLA Army's "mobile operational units" in 2012 had a total of 850,000 personnel. This presumably excludes static and nonoperational units such as headquarters staffs above the corps level and nonmobile garrison units.

43 Blasko, 2012, pp. 43–51.

44 "Operational Unit Diagrams"; "Army Command Structure."

45 ONI, 2009; Cole, 2010, p. 67; IISS, 2011, p. 232.

46 Between 2000 and 2010 the U.S. Navy changed the term it used for its basic organizational unit, an aircraft carrier and associated escorts, from "aircraft carrier battle group" (CVBG) to "carrier strike group" (CSG).

47 None of the fleet commanders in the U.S. Navy in 2010 were female. See Botelho, 2014.

48 If a fleet commander had instead reported to an overall commander for U.S. naval forces in the theater, then that overall commander would have had up to three layers of officers between him and an individual ship captain. In this case, however, the overall commander might have had command over one hundred or more ships, thus justifying the additional command layer.

49 NASIC, 2011, pp. 21, 23; Allen, 2011b, pp. 10–11; Information Office, 2013. The PLA Air Force still had thirteen "command posts," but they no longer exerted independent command authority over divisions and brigades in their provinces. Instead, they reportedly simply acted "on behalf of" the MRAF commander. See NASIC, 2011, p. 23.

50 Private communications with a former U.S. Air Force officer and with an air force researcher at the RAND Corporation.

51 The total number of aircraft operated by the PLA Air Force had fallen from about four thousand in 2000 to approximately twenty-five hundred in 2010. The total number of aircraft in the U.S. Air Force had fallen from about seventy-two hundred in 2000 to about forty-four hundred in 2010. See IISS, 2001, pp. 25, 190; IISS, 2011, pp. 64–65, 234.

52 IISS, 2001, p. 188.

53 Office of the Secretary of Defense, 2011, p. 78; Stokes, 2012, pp. 136, 143, 145. Not all of these missiles were necessarily controlled by the Second Artillery, but the majority likely were. How the GLCMs were organized is not clear. If they were organized in a way similar to the SRBMs, then at most two brigades would have been needed to control the between forty and fifty-five GCLM launchers estimated to be in service at the time.

54 Interview with American specialist on PLA Air Force, September 2011.

55 Interviews with former U.S. Army officers, September 2011.

56 Cooper, 2011, p. 8.

57 Personal communication from Chinese military officer, October 2011.

58 Interview with American specialist on PLA Air Force, September 2011; interview with American specialist on PLA Army, October 2011; Allen, 2011b, pp. 31–32.

59 Interview with American specialist on PLA Air Force, September 2011; interview with American specialist on PLA Army, October 2011; personal communication from American specialist on PLA Air Force, October 2011.

60 Blasko, 2006, p. 27; Allen, 2011b, pp. 12–16; personal communication from American specialist on PLA Air Force, October 2011.

61 Allen, 2011b, pp. 12–16; personal communication from American specialist on PLA Air Force, October 2011.

62 Fabey, 2014, p. 38.

63 Personal communication from Chinese military officer, October 2011.

64 E.g., see "PLA to Carry Out Structural and Organizational Reform," 2013; Zhao, 2014. In a puzzling response to Zhao, 2014, and others, the Ministry of National Defense described the claim that "the Chinese military has verified that it will establish a joint operational command in due course" as "baseless," but then went on to say "we will ... in due time ... establish the joint operational command system." See "MND Clarifies Rumors About 'Joint Operational Command,'" 2014.

65 There are indications of a possible intent to increase the size of the other services relative to the PLA Army, but, as of 2014, the extent of adjustment planned was unclear. See "Advance Military Work By Revolving Closely around the Ability to Fight and Win Battles," 2013.

66 See "Advance Military Work By Revolving Closely around the Ability to Fight and Win Battles," 2013.

4 Weaponry

1 Office of the Under Secretary of Defense (Comptroller)/Chief Financial Officer, p. 10.

2 E.g., Biddle, 2004, which is a major critique of the emphasis of material factors in determining combat outcomes, nonetheless acknowledges that military technology does have an effect, although it sees it as a "second-order effect" relative to how forces are employed (p. 160). This perspective is consistent with that of the present study, which regards quality of weaponry as just one of seven important dimensions of military capability.

3 See Epstein, 1987, p. 69; O'Neill, 1996.

4 O'Neill, 1996, describes how the author calculated that the WEI of his all-terrain bicycle was double that of the best armored personnel carrier for which a WEI had been reported.

5 This chapter relies primarily on the International Institute of Strategic Studies's annual publication *The Military Balance* (IISS, 2001, 2002, 2003, 2004, 2005, 2006, 2007, 2008, 2009, 2010, 2011) for estimates of the numbers of each type of system in service for a given year. The numbers provided in *The Military Balance* are not always consistent from year to year, but are assumed to be roughly accurate in aggregate. In some cases other sources, such as the U.S. Department of Defense's annual report on the Chinese military (OSD, 2009, 2010, 2011) or the *Jane's* series of publications have been used to correct or adjust the estimates in *The Military Balance*. The *Jane's* series of publications has been used as the primary source of information about the capabilities of individual weapon systems.

6 IISS, 2001, pp. 20, 188; IISS, 2002, p. 145 (the data in IISS, 2002, are in some instances more detailed than those in IISS, 2001, and I assume that they are still roughly accurate for China in 2000); Brune, Lange, and Oertel, 2010, p. 12.

7 Ibid. The PLA Army operated an estimated twelve hundred self-propelled cannons and fourteen thousand towed artillery pieces in 2000. The U.S. Army operated twenty-five hundred self-propelled cannons and fifteen hundred towed artillery pieces.

8 IISS, 2001, pp. 20, 188; IISS, 2002, p. 145; "NORINCO Type WZ501 Infantry Fighting Vehicle," 2010.

9 IISS, 2001, pp. 20, 188; IISS, 2002, p. 145.

10 Ibid.

11 IISS, 2001, pp. 21, 189.

12 IISS, 2001, pp. 21, 189; "CSS-N-1 'Scrubbrush' (SY-1/HY-1/FL-1), 2011; "CSS-N-2 'Safflower' CSSC-2 'Silkworm'; CSS-N-3/CSSC-3 'Seersucker' (HY-2/FL-3A)," 2011; "CSS-N-4 `Sardine' (YJ-8/C-801); CSS-N-6 (YJ-83/C-802/Noor); YJ-62/C-602; YJ-82; CY-1," 2011; "Standard Missile 1/2/3/5/6 (RIM-66/67/156/161/165/174)," 2011; "RIM-7 SeaSparrow/RIM-162 Evolved SeaSparrow; Mk 57 NSSMS, IPDMS; AN/SWY-1(V) SDSMS," 2011. I consider the one-hundred-mile range SM-2 missiles mounted on U.S. Ticonderoga–class cruisers and Arleigh Burke–class destroyers to be long-range surface-to-air missiles. I consider surface-to-air missiles of ranges between ten and fifty miles, including the 15.5-mile range Uragan (SA-N-7) systems on the two Sovremenny-class destroyers in the PLA Navy and the 25-mile range SM-1 systems on the thirty-five Oliver Hazard Perry–class frigates in the U.S. Navy at the time, to be "medium-range." Five Chinese destroyers and eleven frigates were fitted with short-range surface-to-air missiles including the eight-mile range HQ-7 (based on the French Crotale system) or the six-mile HQ-61. The twenty-two Spruance class destroyers in the U.S. Navy were equipped with the ten-mile range Sea Sparrow short-range surface-to-air missile. Eleven destroyers and approximately thirty frigates in the Chinese Navy had no surface-to-air missiles.

13 IISS, 2001, pp. 21, 189; "Kilo Class (Project 877EKM/636)," 2011; "Song Class (Type 039/039G)," 2011; "Han Class (Type 091/091G)," 2011; "Romeo Class (Project 633)," 2011; "Ming Class (Type 035)," 2011; Office of Naval Intelligence, 2009, p. 22; Cole, 2010, p. 97.

14 IISS, 2001, pp. 19, 21–23, 190.

15 IISS, 2001, pp. 19, 25, 190.

16 IISS, 2001, pp. 20, 188, 191; IISS, 2002, pp. 145–146. The twenty-five millimeter chain gun on the sixty-eight hundred Bradley fighting vehicles and Linebacker air defense vehicles in the U.S. Army could be used against low-altitude airborne targets such as helicopters.

17 IISS, 2001, p. 188; "DF-11 (CSS-7/M-11)," 2011; "DF-15 (CSS-6/M-9)," 2011; "MGM-140/-164/-168 ATACMS (M39)," 2011. The ATACMS Block 1A had a warhead weighing 350 pounds as compared to the eighteen hundred pound warhead on the DF-11 and the eleven hundred to 1,650 pound warhead on the DF-15. Approximately 250 Block 1A missiles had been delivered by 2000, in addition to 1,650 one-hundred-mile-range Block 1 missiles with twelve hundred pound warheads. Thus, at ranges of one hundred miles or less, U.S. SRBMs were capable of delivering four

times as much high explosive as China's. At ranges between one hundred and 185 miles, however, China's ballistic missiles were capable of delivering at least five and a half times as much high-explosive as were U.S. missiles, albeit less accurately, and the U.S. had no ballistic missiles with ranges greater than 185 miles, whereas China had more than 160 DF-15s.

18 The F-117 stealth fighter had a unrefueled combat radius of about seven hundred miles and the B-2 stealth bomber had an unrefueled combat radius of twenty-six hundred miles to thirty-eight hundred miles, depending on the flight profile and payload. See Laur and Llanso, 1995, p. 82; "Northrop Grumman (Northrop) B-2A Spirit," 2010.

19 IISS, 2001, pp. 19, 188; Office of the Secretary of Defense, 2001, pp. 14–16. The number of shorter range missiles was probably between sixty and 130. IISS, 2001, p. 188, indicates that China had fifty DF-21 and sixty to eighty DF-3A medium- and intermediate-range missiles, but Office of the Secretary of Defense, 2001, states that China had "over 100 nuclear warheads," implying that, after deducting the twenty DF-5s and twenty DF-4s, the total number of DF-21 and DF-3A missiles was "over" sixty.

20 "ZiYuan-2/JianBing-3 series," 2010; "Feng Huo (Zhongxing 2X/ShenTong series)," 2010.

21 IISS, 2001, p. 19; "NOSS (Naval Ocean Surveillance System)," 2010.

22 Office of the Secretary of Defense, 2000; Office of the Secretary of Defense, 2002.

23 Insufficient information was available to assess changes in the quality of equipment of individual soldiers over the period under study. However, evidence suggests that the quality of this equipment still lagged considerably behind that of the United States in 2010. Lightweight Kevlar helmets, for example, which were introduced into the U.S. military in the 1980s, were still not in widespread usage in the PLA in 2010. (Prior to 1979, the PLA did not wear helmets at all. Horrific rates of head and neck injuries during China's border war with Vietnam in that year resulted in the PLA's first steel helmets being rushed into service.) Similarly, as late as 2014 Chinese soldiers were generally not issued body armor, whereas the use of body armor was ubiquitous in the U.S. military. An entire infantry company, moreover, reportedly possessed only two radio sets, used by the commander and political commander to communicate with higher echelons. Communication between the company commander and his platoon leaders (as well as between platoon leaders and their squad leaders) was apparently conducted by yelling or, presumably, the time-honored device of runners. Similarly, although units in 2010 supposedly spent a quarter of their training time in night training (see Chapter Six), an entire company in 2014 was said to possess only one night vision device. See "How Much Does PLA Soldier's Individual Equipment Cost?" 2014.

24 IISS, 2001, p. 20; IISS, 2011, pp. 58, 231.

25 A "gun" is a cannon that fires directly at its target. A "howitzer" is a cannon that fires its shell in a high trajectory so that it falls onto its target from a steep angle. A "gun-howitzer" is a cannon designed to be capable of employing either type of trajectory.

26 IISS, 2011, pp. 58, 231; "PLZ-07 122 mm Self-Propelled Howitzer," 2011; "NOR-INCO 155 mm Self-Propelled Gun Howitzer PLZ-05," 2011.

27 IISS, 2001, p. 188; IISS, 2011, pp. 57, 58, 230, 231; "ZBD-04 Infantry Fighting Vehicle," 2011; "Chinese Amphibious Assault Vehicle ZBD2000 (ZBD-05)," 2010; "NORINCO Airborne Assault Vehicle (AAV) ZLC2000 (ZBD-03)," 2011. I consider the "Type-92," which IISS 2011 lists as "an armored infantry fighting vehicle," to be an armored personnel carrier, as the basic WZ551, to which "Type-92" appears to refer (see IISS, 2001, p. 188), appears to be armed with only a 0.50 caliber machine gun. I assume that "Type-92A" referred to in IISS, 2011, p. 231, is the infantry fighting vehicle version of the WZ551, which is armed with a turret-mounted twenty-five millimeter cannon. See "NORINCO WZ551 Armoured Personnel Carrier," 2010.

28 IISS, 2011, pp. 58, 231; "CHAIG WZ-10," 2011. The Z-9W and Z-9WA versions of the Z-9 are armed (see "HAI (Eurocopter) Z-9 Haitun," 2011) as are the U.S. AH-6 and OH-58D.

29 IISS, 2011, pp. 57, 58, 230, 231. Although IISS 2011 lists them as multirole helicopters, I consider the PLA Army's Mi-17, SA-316, and Z-9/Z-9B helicopters to be transport helicopters. The only areas in which numbers had increased significantly over 2000 were self-propelled cannons, which had increased by more than 40 percent over 2000, and transport helicopters, which had quadrupled.

30 "Luyang I (Type 052B) class," 2011; "SA-N-7 'Gadfly' (3K90 M-22 Uragan/Shtil)/SA-N-7B 'Grizzly' (9K37 Ezh/Shtil-1)/SA-N-7C 'Gollum' (9M317/Shtil-2)," 2011; "Luyang II (Type 052C) class," 2011; "HHQ-9," 2011; "CSS-N-4 'Sardine' (YJ-8/C-801), 2011; "CSS-N-6 (YJ-83/C-802/Noor)," 2011; "YJ-62/C-602," 2011; "YJ-82," 2011; "CY-1," 2011; "RGM-84/UGM-84 Harpoon (GWS 60)," 2011. Analysis of the (limited) historical data available on the use of antiship cruise missiles suggests that the damage caused by an antiship cruise missile impact is best approximated as a function of its kinetic energy (one-half of the product of its mass and the square of its speed). See Hughes, 2000, p. 159. Since the YJ-62 flies at approximately the same speed as the YJ-83 and Harpoon but weighs 50 percent more than they do, on average a YJ-62 impact should cause 50 percent more damage than a YJ-83 or Harpoon impact. See "CSS-N-6 (YJ-83/C-802/Noor)," 2011; "YJ-62/C-602," 2011; "RGM-84/UGM-84 Harpoon (GWS 60)," 2011.

31 "Luzhou class (Type 051C)," 2011; "SA-N-6 'Grumble' (V601 Fort/Rif)/SA-N-20 'Gargoyle' (Fort-M/Rif-M)," 2011.

32 "Jiangkai I (Type 054) Class," 2011; Cole, 2010, p. 94; "Jiangwei II (Type 053H3) Class," 2011; "Jiangkai II (Type 054A) Class," 2011; "HHQ-16," 2011; IISS, 2011, p. 232; ONI, 2009, p. 18.

33 IISS, 2011, pp. 58–59, 232; "Arleigh Burke (Flight IIA) Class," 2011. The eighty-one Ticonderoga-class cruisers and Arleigh Burke–class destroyers the U.S. Navy operated in 2010 were all armed with the one-hundred-mile-range SM-2ER surface-to-air missile. The SM-1 surface-to-air missiles and Harpoon antiship cruise missiles on the twenty Perry-class frigates remaining in the U.S. Navy's inventory in 2010, however, had all been removed after 2000, turning these ships into antisubmarine

warfare-only platforms. See "Oliver Hazard Perry Class," 2011. Presumably the assumption was that, when there was threat of attack by enemy aircraft or surface ships, the frigates would operate together with cruisers or destroyers, which would provide protection for them from attack by enemy aircraft or surface ships.

34 Cole, 2010, p. 102; IISS, 2011, pp. 58–59, 232. As noted above, the antiship cruise missiles had been removed from the twenty Perry-class frigates in the U.S. Navy inventory. In addition, the antiship cruise missiles for the two littoral combat ships that had been commissioned by 2010 had not yet been acquired.

35 Cole, 2010, pp. 86–95, 97–104; IISS, 2011, p. 232.

36 Cole, 2010, pp. 99–104; IISS, 2011, p. 232.

37 ONI, 2009, pp. 18, 20; IISS, 2011, p. 232; "Houbei (Type 022) Class," 2011.

38 "Kilo Class (Project 877EKM/636)," 2011.

39 "Yuan Class (Type 041)," 2011; Office of Naval Intelligence, 2009, pp. 22–23; OSD, 2011, p. 4.

40 "Shang Class (Type 093)," 2011; Office of Naval Intelligence, 2009; "Han Class (Type 091/091G)," 2011.

41 IISS, 2011, pp. 231–232; "Song Class (Type 039/039G)," 2011.

42 IISS, 2011, pp. 58, 231–232. U.S. submarines in 2010 were no longer equipped with antiship cruise missiles – they relied entirely on their stealth and torpedoes to attack surface ships. See "Los Angeles class," 2011.

43 IISS, 2011, p. 232; "HAIC Q-5," 2011; "SAC Y-8 (Special Mission Versions)," 2011. The number of fighter aircraft operated by the PLA Navy in 2010 is unclear. IISS reported 250 J-6s (MiG-19s), forty J-7s (MiG-21s), and forty-two J-8s (Chinese-designed twin-engine fighters based on the MiG-21) in 2000. The number of reported PLA Navy J-8s rose to 320 in 2005, then fell again to forty-eight in 2008, and remained at that level through 2010. Meanwhile, the number of reported J-7s fell to twenty-six in 2002, then rose back up to thirty-six in 2008 and remained at that level through 2010. Finally, the number of reported J-6s fell to zero in 2008 and remained at that level through 2010. The result of these fluctuations was that the total number of PLA Navy fighters reported by IISS rose from 332 in 2000 to nearly six hundred in 2005 then fell to just more than one hundred in 2010. See IISS, 2001, p. 190; IISS, 2002, p. 147; IISS, 2003, p. 154; IISS, 2004, p. 172; IIISS, 2005, p. 273; IISS, 2006, p. 267; IISS, 2007, p. 349; IISS, 2008, p. 379; IISS, 2009, p. 385; IISS, 2010, p. 402; IISS, 2011, p. 233. This degree of variably calls into question the reliability of the estimates of Chinese naval aviation for any given year.

44 IISS, 2011, pp. 56, 58, 60.

45 "CAC J-10 Meng Long," 2011; IISS, 2011, p. 234; "SAC (Sukhoi Su-27) J-11," 2011; "SD-10, SD-10A (PL-12)," 2011; "LT-2 Laser Guided Bomb (LS-500J)," 2011; "Fei Teng Guided Bombs (FT-1, FT-2, FT-3, FT-5, FT-6)," 2011; "KD-63 (YJ-63), K/AKD-63," 2011; "KD-88 (K/AKD-88)," 2011; "YJ-91, KR-1 (Kh-31P)," 2011.

46 IISS, 2011, pp. 64–65, 234.

47 "KS-1/KS-1A (HQ-12)," 2011; "Hongqi-2," 2011; "HQ-9/FT-2000," 2011; "S-300P," 2011.

48 OSD, 2009, p. 66; IISS, 2011, pp. 58, 231, 234.

49 Publicly available information does not indicate what proportion of the more than one thousand SRBMs China possessed in 2010 were the more-accurate versions.

50 IISS, 2011, p. 230; OSD, 2011, p. 78; "DF-11 (CSS-7/M-11)," 2011; "DF-15 (CSS-6/M-9)," 2011; "DF-21 (CSS-5)," 2011; Kato, 2011. For more on the potential effects of Chinese ballistic missile attack on Taiwanese and U.S. forces, see Cliff et al., 2007, pp. 81–83 and Shlapak et al., 2009, pp. 31–51. Although there are Patriot missile batteries with antiballistic missile capabilities on both Taiwan and Okinawa, these batteries would be overwhelmed by the number of ballistic missiles that China could launch at a single time.

51 OSD, 2010, p. 66; OSD, 2011, pp. 4, 34–35, 78; IISS, 2011, pp. 56, 230; "XIA class (Type 092)," 2011.

52 "ZiYuan-2/JianBing-3 Series," 2010; "Feng Huo (Zhongxing 2X/ShenTong Series)," 2010; Union of Concerned Scientists Satellite Database, 2011; "Yaogan Series," 2010; "NOSS (Naval Ocean Surveillance System)," 2010; "Tianhui Series," 2010; "Shijian Series," 2011; "Misty," 2010; "Improved Crystal," 2010; "TacSat Series," 2010; "WorldView Series," 2011; "GeoEye Series," 2010; OSD, 2011, p. 35; "Lacrosse/Onyx Series," 2011; "Defense Support Program (DSP)," 2010; "Chinastar (Zhongwei)," 2010; "China Telecommunications Broadcast Satellite Co (ChinaSat)," 2010; "Space Based Infrared System (SBIRS)," 2011; "STSS (Space Tracking and Surveillance System)," 2011; "Beidou/Compass Series," 2011; "Chinasat/Zhongxing/STTW series," 2011. In addition to electro-optical reconnaissance satellites, China has also used film-based photo-reconnaissance satellites that return their film to earth for developing after being in orbit for three or four weeks. In 2000, no such satellites had been launched for four years, but an additional five missions were conducted from 2003 to 2005. See "Fanhui Shi Weixing 3 (FSW-3)/JianBing-4 Series," 2010. Given the time between launch and recovery, such satellites obviously cannot be used for battlefield intelligence collection once a conflict has started. The Tianhui satellite launched in 2010 had a reported resolution of about sixteen feet. The Ziyuan 2 satellites, one of which was operational in 2000 and two of which were operational in 2010, had an estimated resolution of about ten feet. The four optical reconnaissance satellites of the Yaogan series operational in 2010 were estimated to have a resolution of about two and a half feet, and the three synthetic aperture radar satellites in the Yaogan series operational in 2010 were estimated to have a resolution of fifteen to sixty feet. Synthetic aperture radar satellites have the advantage of being able to collect images through clouds and while the satellite is on the night side of the earth. Yaogan 6, a presumed SAR satellite, apparently failed to operate correctly. See Hagt and Durnin, 2011, p. 737. The Shijian 6 series of satellites appear to be electronic intelligence satellites. The Shijian 11 series appear to be early warning satellites. The three military telecommunication satellites in operation in 2010 were Zhongxing 20, Zhongxing 20A, and Zhongxing 22A. Zhongxing 20, launched in 2003, was probably nearing the end of its operational life, estimated at eight years, hence the launching of Zhongxing 20A, its apparent replacement.

The civilian telecommunications satellites operational in 2010 that were controlled by state-owned corporations included Chinasat 5A, Chinasat 6B, Chinasat 9, probably Chinasat 5B (although it was apparently no longer operational by September 2011), and possibly Chinasat 5C (a "backup" for Chinasat 5B that was launched in September 2010, although it was apparently also not operational by September 2011).

53 "Chinese Anti-Satellite Test Sets Off Washington's Alarms," 2007; Morring, 2007, p. 20; Mathews, 2008; "Shijian series," 2011; Perrett, 2011, p. 32.

54 Office of the Secretary of Defense, 2011, p. 37; Wortzel, 2014, p. 19.

55 Krekel, Adams, and Bakos, 2012, pp. 27–36; Xu, 2013, p. 64.

56 For a discussion of these issues, see, for example, Crane et al., 2005, pp. 91–134.

57 This assumes that the PLA regards the funds as having been expended at the time the equipment is ordered, as the U.S. military does, rather than when it is delivered. Some weapon systems, notably ships, take much longer than a year from the time they are ordered to when they enter service.

58 Information Office of the State Council of the People's Republic of China, 2000a; National Bureau of Statistics of China, 2010; Information Office of the State Council of the People's Republic of China, 2011.

59 "Annual Data"; "China 2015 Defense Budget to Grow 10.1 Pct, Lowest in 5 Years," 2015; Li, 2015, p. 2.

60 It is possible that the growth rate of defense spending in the second half of the period 2009–2019 will be greater than the growth rate during the first half of the period. If the growth rate in overall defense spending increases to 7.5 percent per year in the period 2014–2019 and procurement spending increases at the same rate over this period, then total procurement expenditures over the period 2009–2019 will be only 3.4 percent greater than if procurement spending grows at 5.5 percent during this period. Thus, the projections that follow are not highly sensitive to assumptions about the growth in the PLA's procurement spending in the period 2014–2019.

61 Assuming a 5.5 percent annual growth rate in procurement spending in the period 2009–2019, this ratio is 2.17.

62 IISS, 2002, p. 145; IISS, 2011, p. 231; IISS, 2014, p. 44. Since there is no program to develop a new main battle tank for the U.S. military that is likely to result in a fielded system by 2020, the number of main battle tanks in the U.S. military in 2020 is assumed to be unchanged from 2014.

63 IISS, 2001, p. 188; IISS, 2011, p. 231.

64 IISS, 2014, pp. 44, 48, 232. Since there is no program to develop a new artillery weapon for the U.S. military that is likely to result in a fielded system by 2020, the number of artillery pieces in the U.S. military in 2020 is assumed to be unchanged from 2014.

65 IISS, 2010, p. 402; IISS, 2011, pp. 231, 233; IISS, 2014, p. 44. Since there is no program to develop a new infantry fighting vehicle for the U.S. military that is likely to result in a fielded system by 2020, the number of infantry fighting vehicles in the U.S. military in 2020 is assumed to be unchanged from 2014.

66 IISS, 2001, p. 188; IISS, 2002, p. 147; IISS, 2011, p. 231; IISS, 2014, pp. 44, 48. Since there is no program to develop a new armored personnel carrier for the U.S. military that is likely to result in a fielded system by 2020, the number of armored personnel carriers in the U.S. military in 2020 is assumed to be unchanged from 2014.

67 IISS, 2001, p. 189; IISS, 2002, p. 146; IISS, 2011, p. 231; IISS, 2014, pp. 44, 49. The number of each major category of helicopter in the U.S. military in 2020 is assumed to be unchanged from 2014.

68 IISS, 2001, p. 189; IISS, 2002, p. 146; IISS, 2011, p. 231; IISS, 2014, pp. 44, 49. The number of each major category of helicopter in the U.S. military in 2020 is assumed to be unchanged from 2014.

69 IISS, 2001, p. 188; IISS, 2002, p. 145; IISS, 2011, pp. 58, 231.

70 These would include four Sovremenny-class, two Luzhou-class, two Luyang I–class, and eighteen Luyang II– and Luyang III–class ships. Older destroyer designs are assumed to have been retired by 2020.

71 Three Jiangwei II–class frigates were built between 2000 and 2010. If procurement of these ships increased at an average annual rate of 5.5 percent between 2010 and 2020, another seven would be constructed. No additional Jiangwei II–class ships entered service after 2010, however, with production shifting to the newer Jiangkai I and Jiangkai II designs. The number of Jiangkai II–class ships estimated to enter service between 2010 and 2020, therefore, was increased by four, taking the place of the seven additional less-sophisticated (and, presumably, less-expensive) Jiangwei II–class ships. The ten Jiangwei II–class ships in the fleet in 2010, however, were assumed to remain in service through 2020. See IISS, 2001, p. 189; IISS, 2011, p. 232.

72 Department of Defense, 2014, p. 40.

73 IISS, 2011, p. 232; "Houbei (Type 022) class," 2013; Jiangdao (Type 056) class, 2013.

74 The size of China's attack submarine force grew from fifty-four boats in 2010 to fifty-six in 2013. See Office of the Secretary of Defense, 2011, p. 74; Office of the Secretary of Defense, 2014, p. 77.

75 "China's Russian Kilo Buy May Put Song Submarine Future in Doubt," 2002.

76 IISS, 2001, p. 189; ONI, 2009, p. 21; IISS, 2011, pp. 58, 231–232; Office of the Under Secretary of Defense (Comptroller)/CFO, 2011, p. 6-6; Department of Defense, 2014, p. 40.

77 IISS, 2001, p. 190; IISS, 2011, pp. 60–61, 233; "SAC 'J-15'," 2011; Department of Defense, 2014, p. 40; Department of the Navy, 2014a.

78 IISS, 2001, p. 190; IISS, 2011, p. 233; Department of Defense, p. 40.

79 "Kuznetsov (Orel) Class (Project 1143.5/6)," 2011; Department of Defense, 2014, p. 40; Staff Reporters, 2014b; OSD, 2011, pp. 3, 46.

80 Fulghum et al., 2011; "First Flight for Second Chinese Stealth Aircraft," 2012; IISS, 2001, p. 190; IISS, 2011, p. 234; OSD, 2011, p. 32; Department of Defense, 2014, p. 40; Department of the Air Force, 2014a. The older-generation J-8 remained in production during the 2000s. Published estimates of how many were in service fluctuated from year to year, however, and information on how many older models were phased out in favor of newer types in a given year is not available. As a result, it

is not possible to estimate how many J-8s were produced between 2000 and 2010. Assuming the J-8 was no longer in production after 2010, the resources that were used for its production between 2000 and 2010 could be applied to production of the J-10 and J-11 during the period 2010 and 2020. Given the lack of information about how many J-8s were actually produced, however, this potential contribution has been ignored.

81 IISS, 2001, p. 190; IISS, 2011, p. 234.

82 "XAC H-6."

83 IISS, 2011, p. 234; Department of Defense, 2014, p. 40.

84 "S-300P," 2011; OSD, 2009, p. 66; IISS, 2001, pp. 188, 191; IISS, 2011, pp. 58, 231, 234. The U.S. military currently has no plans to acquire additional land-based surface-to-air missile launchers or dedicated antiaircraft guns.

85 IISS, 2001, p. 188; OSD, 2011, p. 78; OSD, 2009, p. 66; "DF-21 (CSS-5)," 2011; "DF-11 (CSS-7/M-11)," 2011; "DF-15 (CSS-6/M-9)," 2011. Statement that cost of a missile is roughly proportional to its range is based on independent analysis by the author. It is possible, moreover, that the PLA could acquire even longer-range conventional ballistic missiles by 2020. The 2013 edition of the U.S. Department of Defense's annual report to Congress on the Chinese military states that China is developing intermediate-range conventional ballistic missiles with ranges between 1,860 miles and 3,110 miles, which could reach targets as far away from China as Guam. See OSD, 2013, pp. 5, 42.

86 OSD, 2011, p. 78; "C-602 (HN-1/-2/-3/YJ-62/X-600/DH-10/CJ-10/HN-2000)," 2011.

87 IISS, 2001, p. 188; IISS, 2011, p. 230. China is also said to be developing a new road-mobile ICBM that might be capable of carrying multiple independently targetable reentry vehicles (MIRVs). See OSD, 2011, p. 3.

88 IISS, 2011, p. 230. These projections of China's future nuclear forces assume that China already possesses or will produce the fissile material needed for their warheads.

89 U.S. numbers are based on Department of Defense, 2014, p. 41.

90 "ZiYuan-2/JianBing-3 Series," 2010; "Feng Huo (Zhongxing 2X/ShenTong Series)," 2010; Union of Concerned Scientists Satellite Database, 2011; "Yaogan Series," 2010; "Tianhui Series," 2010; "Shijian Series," 2011; "Misty," 2010; "Improved Crystal," 2010; "TacSat Series," 2010; "WorldView Series," 2011; "GeoEye Series," 2010; "Lacrosse/Onyx Series," 2011; "Defense Support Program (DSP)," 2010; "Chinastar (Zhongwei)," 2010; "Space Based Infrared System (SBIRS)," 2011; "STSS (Space Tracking and Surveillance System)," 2011; "Beidou/Compass Series," 2011; "Chinasat/Zhongxing/STTW Series," 2011.

91 Weeden, 2014; Gruss, 2014.

92 OSD, 2011, p. 37. The power requirements for lasers and microwaves capable of destroying satellites in medium earth orbit (about fifteen thousand miles above the earth's surface) and geostationary orbit (22,236 miles above the earth's surface), where most navigation, early warning, and communications satellites reside, are much higher than those for destroying satellites in low earth orbit (about three

hundred miles above the earth's surface), as the energy absorbed by the satellite diminishes according to the square of the distance from the laser or microwave source.

5 Personnel

1 This incident is described in Wardynski, Lyle, and Colarusso, 2009, pp. 25–26. No specific date is given for the experiment.

2 How well the personnel actually *perform* depends on the degree to which they are employed in positions that match their capabilities and the degree to which the incentive structure within which they operate motivates them to use those capabilities.

3 Scribner, Smith, Baldwin, and Phillips, 1986; Teachout and Pellum, 1991; Winkler, Fernandez, and Polich, 1992; Orvis, Childress, and Polich, 1992; all as cited in Kavanagh, 2005, pp. 27–32.

4 Albrecht, 1979; Horowitz and Sherman, 1980; Moore, 1981; Marcus, 1982; Hammon and Horowitz, 1990; Beland and Quester, 1991; Hammon and Horowitz, 1992; Doyle, 1998; all as cited in Kavanagh, 2005, pp. 5–13, 16–23.

5 Griffith, 1990, pp. 52–94. Quote is from p. 56.

6 Griffith, 1990, pp. 131–132.

7 Albrecht, 1979; Horowitz and Sherman, 1980; Moore, 1981; Armor et al., 1982; Marcus, 1982; Scribner, Smith, Baldwin, and Phillips, 1986; Hammon and Horowitz, 1990; Beland and Quester, 1991; Teachout and Pellum, 1991; Buddin et al., 1992; Hammon and Horowitz, 1992; Orvis, Childress, and Polich, 1992; Winkler, Fernandez, and Polich, 1992; Doyle, 1998; Gerlach, 2009; Rodriguez, 2009. Assessments of personnel quality in the U.S. military also often use speed of promotion as an indicator of individual capability. E.g., see Buddin et al., 1992; Quester and Lee, 2001; Lewis, 2004. However, promotion speed is a useful indicator only of the relative quality of individuals within an organization, not for assessing changes over time in an organization or for comparing one organization to another.

8 Cole, 2010. p. 120.

9 E.g., see Miller, 2006, p. 22; Gunness, 2007, p. 189; Corbett, O'Dowd, Chen, 2008, pp. 141, 156.

10 Li, 2003, p. 82.

11 Li, 2003, p. 82; Bickford, 2007, p. 175.

12 Blasko, 2006, p. 63. This began to change in the 2003, when (small numbers of) recent division, brigade, and regiment commanders were added to the teaching staff of the PLA's National Defense University. See ibid.

13 Dreyer, 1996, p. 320; Bickford, 2007, p. 177; Corbett, O'Dowd, Chen, 2008, p. 142; NASIC, 2010, p. 33.

14 National Bureau of Statistics of China, 2010, Table 3–7.

15 Cole, 2001, p. 116; Blasko, 2006, p. 49; ONI, 2007, p. 73; NASIC, 2010, p. 36.

16 ONI, 2007, p. 73; NASIC, 2010, p. 36; Allen, 2011b, p. 26; McCauley, 2011, p. 16.

17 IISS, 2001, pp. 188–190, estimates the size of the PLA Army as approximately 1,600,000 and the size of the PLA Navy, Air Force, and Second Artillery as 250,000, 420,000, and "100,000+," for a total of 770,000+. IISS estimates should be regarded as approximate, however, because as recently as 2013 IISS was estimating the size of the PLA Navy and Air Force as 255,000 and 300,000–330,000, respectively, but the PRC's 2012 defense white paper, issued in April 2013, revealed their sizes to be 235,000 and 398,000.

18 The overall size of the PLA was 2.5 million in 2000. However, this number includes an unknown number of (uniformed but rankless) civilian officials (文职干部 – see Blasko, 2006, p. 20). Officers and civilian officials are often collectively referred to as "cadres" (干部 – e.g., see Information Office, 2002a, "Cadre Training"). NASIC, 2010, p. 35, states that 1.6 million of the 2.3 million personnel in the PLA in 2008 were enlisted, implying that the remaining seven hundred thousand were cadres. Information Office, 2006b, 〈四、人民解放军〉, states that the number of cadres was reduced by 170,000 when the PLA as a whole was reduced from 2.5 million to 2.3 million between 2003 and 2005. This implies that there were approximately 870,000 cadres and 1,630,000 enlisted personnel in 2000, before the reductions. If a third of the noncivilian PLA personnel were officers, four-ninths were conscripts, and two-ninths were NCOs in 2000, this would imply that there were approximately 1.1 million conscripts, 550,000 NCOs, and 800,000 officers. These estimates are highly approximate, however, and should not be regarded as authoritative.

19 Dreyer, 1996, p. 323.

20 ONI, 2007, pp. 75, 77; Blasko, 2008, p. 105; Cole, 2010, p. 120.

21 Blasko, 2006, p. 50.

22 Blasko, 2006, p. 52.

23 Corbett, O'Dowd, and Chen, 2008, p. 144.

24 According to Corbett, O'Dowd, and Chen, 2008, p. 144, "most" PLA officers had at least a three-year technical degree in 1998. Li Zhiguo, 2003, p. 82, states that approximately 65 percent of officers had three-year technical degrees or four-year bachelor's degrees. Information Office, 2002a, "Cadre Training," however, states that 80 percent of *cadres* possessed college degrees. Since, as noted earlier, the term "cadre" encompasses both military officers and civilian officials in the PLA, it is possible that the percentage of military officers with college degrees was less than 80 percent, although the 65 percent figure that Li cites a year later would only be mathematically possible if fewer than 60 percent of PLA cadres were officers. A more likely explanation is that Li's figure was out of date. If we assume that the percentage of PLA officers with college degrees grew steadily from 10 percent in 1980 to 80 percent in 2002, then approximately 74 percent of officers would have had college degrees in 2000.

25 Bickford, 2007, p. 182, cites Information Office, 2002a, "Cadre Training," in saying 80 percent of officers had college degrees in 2002. He then goes on to say that 72 percent of officers held degrees from "*dazhuan*" (three-year technical colleges)

in 2002, implying that 90 percent (72%/80% = 0.90) of college degrees were from three-year technical colleges. As noted above, however, Information Office, 2002a, "Cadre Training," actually states that 80 percent of *cadres* held college degrees, not officers, so it is not clear if Bickford's 72 percent figure also refers to all cadres or only to officers.

26 Mulvenon, 1997, p. 13; Bickford, 2007, p. 174.

27 According to Bickford, 2007, p. 176, forty-six thousand graduates of civilian colleges joined the PLA between 1992 and 1999. Bickford, 2007, does not indicate the number recruited in 2000 or before 1992, but Blasko, 2006, p. 58, states that ten thousand graduates of civilian colleges and universities were being accepted into the PLA each year in the early 2000s. If we therefore assume that ten thousand civilian college graduates joined the PLA in 2000 but that the number who joined before 1992 was negligible, then the total number of civilian college graduates in the PLA in 2000 would have been about fifty-six thousand, roughly 7 percent of the eight hundred thousand or so officers in the PLA in 2000. Providing a smaller estimate, Corbett, O'Dowd, and Chen, 2008, p. 143, state that only 36,600 graduates of civilian colleges, less than 5 percent of the PLA officer corps, joined the PLA between the date of the Fourteenth CPC National Congress (1992) and 2000. Why the Bickford and Corbett, O'Dowd, and Chen figures are inconsistent is not clear.

28 Conversely, the average graduate of a civilian university in China in 2000 was probably more capable than his counterpart in the United States, as China's civilian colleges in the 1990s were highly selective. Of the 17.3 million students who graduated from high school in 1996, for example, only 5.6 percent enrolled in college. Thus, college graduates in China in 2000 represented a highly elite portion of the population. See National Bureau of Statistics of China, 1997, Table 18-1.

29 Office of the Under Secretary of Defense, Personnel and Readiness, undated, Tables D-11 and D-17.

30 Figures do not add to 100 percent because of rounding.

31 Officers constituted 14.9 percent of U.S. active duty military personnel in 2000, and 97.3 percent of officers had at least a college degree. One percent of enlisted personnel did not have a high school diploma or GED. Among enlisted personnel in the U.S. Army, Navy, and Marine Corps, 6.8 percent had at least a two-year college degree. Statistics on the number of enlisted personnel in the U.S. Air Force holding two-year college degrees were not available, but if the percentage were comparable to that of the other services, then approximately 6 percent of U.S. military personnel (6.8 percent of enlisted personnel and 2.7 percent of officers) probably held two year-college degrees. The percentage of enlisted personnel in the U.S. military in 2000 with four-year college degrees is assumed to be negligible. See Office of the Under Secretary of Defense, Personnel and Readiness, undated, Tables D-11 and D-17; Office of the Assistant Secretary of Defense (Force Management Policy), 2001, Tables 3.7, 4.13, and B-23.

32 According to Bickford, 2007, p. 175, the PLA awarded 22,500 advanced degrees between 1992 and 2003. Assuming the number of PLA members holding advanced degrees awarded before 1992 was negligible, and that the number of degrees awarded each year between 1992 and 2003 was roughly constant, then about sixteen thousand members of the PLA, 0.6 percent of the entire PLA, would have held advanced degrees in 2000. Alternatively, Information Office, 2002a, "Cadre Training," states that the PLA had thirty thousand cadres with master's or doctor's degrees, 1.2 percent of the entire PLA. It is possible, however, that a disproportionate number of these were held by cadres who were civilian officials.

33 ONI, 2007, p. 73; NASIC, 2010, p. 36; Allen, 2011b, p. 26; McCauley, 2011, p. 16.

34 Office of the Under Secretary of Defense, Personnel and Readiness, Table D-12.

35 E.g., see Blasko, 2006, pp. 56–57.

36 Office of the Assistant Secretary of Defense (Force Management Policy), 2001, Tables B-46, B-48, D-16, D-26.

37 Blasko, 2008, pp. 103–104; NASIC, 2010, pp. 38–39; ONI, 2007, p. 75.

38 Blasko, 2006, p. 50; ONI, 2007, p. 77; Blasko, 2008, p. 126; NASIC, 2010, p. 37. According to some reports, however, bribes, rather than innate ability, were the distinguishing criteria for those selected for military service, with payments as high as 50,000 to 100,000 yuan (about $8,000 to $16,000) being required to be selected. See Staff Reporters, 2014a; Shi, 2014.

39 Blasko, 2008, pp. 105, 109; Wang Yifeng, 2010; NASIC, 2010, p. 39; Fang, 2010; Allen, 2011b, p. 27; Wang, 2015, p. 9.

40 Blasko, 2008, pp. 126–127; Fang, 2010; Li, 2011; Gan and Wang, 2010; Xiang, Bei, and Deng, 2011.

41 Wang, 2015, p. 9.

42 Blasko, 2006, p. 52; ONI, 2007, p. 77; Blasko, 2008, pp. 110–111; NASIC, 2010, p. 44. It is not clear how many civilian college graduates became NCOs each year. In 2003 the number was 630 and in 2004 it was more than one thousand, but data for subsequent years were not available. One article (Wang Yifeng, 2010) states that in 2008, thirty-nine thousand civilian college graduates joined the PLA, but it is not clear if this number includes college graduates who were accepted for officer training and/or college graduates who became ordinary conscripts.

43 ONI, 2007, p. 82; Gunness and Vellucci, 2008, p. 211.

44 NASIC, 2010, p. 35; McCauley, 2011, p. 16.

45 Blasko, 2006, p. 54; Blasko, 2008, pp. 100, 116; Information Office, 2006b, 〈四、人民解放军〉; McCauley, 2011, pp. 16, 17. Note that Information Office, 2006a, "Completing the Reduction of 200,000 Troops," mistranslates 干部 (cadre) as "officer." (It later mistranslates 文职干部 – civilian officials – as "NCOs.")

46 ONI, 2007, p. 84; Blasko, 2008, p. 115.

47 Blasko, 2008, p. 115.

48 According to NASIC, 2010, p. 35, 1.6 million of the 2.3 million people in the PLA in 2008 were enlisted, meaning that the remaining seven hundred thousand were "cadres" – officers or civilian officials. Assuming that at least fifteen thousand of

these were civilian officials, then officers would represent less than 30 percent of military personnel.

49 Wang, 2010. In 2013, the vice-president of the PLA Air Force Command Academy was quoted as saying "At present you can hardly find an officer who does not hold a bachelor's degree or higher." See Choi, 2013.

50 Blasko, 2006, p. 58.

51 Blasko, 2006, p. 58; Bickford, 2007, p. 178.

52 Blasko, 2006, p. 58; Gunness, 2007, p. 194.

53 According to Blasko, 2006, p. 58, eight thousand National Defense Students enrolled in college in 2004. According to Corbett, O'Dowd, and Chen, 2008, p. 143, eleven thousand enrolled in 2006. Assuming that 90 percent of these students graduated four years later (in 2008 and 2010), and estimating the number of National Defense Students who graduated in 2004, 2005, 2006, and 2009 based on the assumption that the number of graduating students grew linearly from 2004 to 2010, then a total of 41,950 would have graduated from 2003 to 2010. Allen, 2011a, p. 11, states that, as of September 2011, thirteen thousand PLA Air Force National Defense Students had graduated, a number that seems to be broadly consistent with this estimate. (Assuming that the number of National Defense Students continued to grow at a linear rate in 2011, by September 2011, 53,200 would have graduated. The thirteen thousand who joined the PLA Air Force would represent about 24 percent of these. If the number of National Defense Students who entered the PLA Air Force constituted the same proportion as PLA Air Force personnel constituted of the PLA as a whole – about 17 percent – then it is possible that as many as seventy-five thousand National Defense Students had entered the PLA by September 2011.

54 NASIC, 2010, p. 33; Allen, 2011a, p. 11. The "less than 25 percent" estimate assumes that at most thirty-five thousand of the thirty-five to fifty thousand civilian college graduates who became officers before 2001 remained in the force in 2010, and that roughly 110,000 graduates of civilian colleges became officers between 2001 and 2010. The 110,000 estimate, in turn derives from the estimate above that forty-two thousand National Defense Students were commissioned by 2010, and a report from 2002, before National Defense Students began entering the force, that "more than 10,000 graduates" of civilian colleges joined the PLA each year. See Blasko, 2006, p. 58. If we assume, based on this report, that an average of eleven thousand ordinary civilian college graduates became officers in the PLA in 2001 and 2002, and that this number decreased each year thereafter as the number of National Defense Student graduates increased, so that an average total of eleven thousand graduates of civilian colleges became officers each year throughout the decade, then 110,000 would have become officers from 2001 to 2010. If there were seven hundred thousand officers in the PLA in 2010, 145,000 (35,000 + 110,000) graduates of civilian colleges would have represented at most about 21 percent of the officer corps, potentially more if the size of the officer corps was significantly less (i.e., if the proportion of civilian cadres within the seven hundred thousand figure was large).

55 Blasko, 2006, p. 63; Gunness, 2007, p. 193; Wang, 2010.

56 Blasko, 2006, pp. 47, 55; ONI, 2007, p. 61; NASIC, 2010, pp. 29, 31.

57 Bickford, 2007, p. 177; Gunness, 2007, pp. 191, 195; NASIC, 2007, pp. 30, 33; Allen, 2011b, p. 23.

58 Blakso, 2006, p. 55.

59 Bickford, 2007, p. 181; Corbett, O'Dowd, Chen, 2008, pp. 161–162.

60 The annual attrition rate that would result in only half of NCOs remaining in service beyond four terms (fourteen years) is 4.83 percent (because $(1-0.0483)^{14} = 0.5$). Since the new NCO program had only been in place since 1999, and no NCO had served more than thirteen years as an NCO before 1999, I assume that the structure of NCO ranks in 2010 was the same as what it would eventually reach in the steady state with a 4.83 percent annual attrition rate, except that I assume that there were no NCOs that had served more than twenty-four years in 2010. This results in 28 percent of NCOs being senior NCOs. Of course, many junior and midgrade NCOs probably also had three-year technical degrees in 2010, especially since the PLA was now recruiting civilian college graduates to become NCOs. Conversely, since the requirement that all senior NCOs have three-year degrees was only imposed in 2008, it seems unlikely that all senior NCOs did in fact hold such degrees in 2010. I assumed that the number of junior and midgrade NCOs holding three-year technical degrees was at least as great as the number of senior NCOs who did not hold such degrees. Hence the estimate that at least 28 percent of NCOs had degrees from technical colleges in 2010.

61 As noted above, according to Bickford, 2007, p. 175, the PLA awarded 22,500 advanced degrees between 1992 and 2003, and, beginning in 2003, eighteen hundred students a year were enrolled in three-year advanced study programs at civilian universities. Assuming that essentially all of them received advanced degrees three years later, by 2010 about 10,800 would have received degrees. Meanwhile, assuming that, from 2003 to 2010, PLA institutions continued to award advanced degrees at the rate they had between 1992 and 2003, and that virtually all advanced degree holders remained on active duty in the PLA, then about 47,600 officers would have held advanced degrees in 2010. This does not include civilians who received advanced degrees and then were recruited into the PLA. As noted above, in footnote 48, by 2008 there were at most seven hundred thousand officers in the PLA.

62 NASIC, 2010, p. 35; McCauley, 2011, p. 16.

63 Office of the Under Secretary of Defense, Personnel and Readiness, undated, Tables B-18, B-26, D-11. Figures on the proportion of U.S. enlisted personnel who held two-year college degrees in 2010 were not available, but the proportion was assumed to be roughly the same as it was in 2000 (6.8 percent). Information on degree status for 9.5 percent of U.S. officers was not available; the degree status distribution for this population was assumed to be roughly the same as for the 90.5 percent for whom it was available.

64 Wardynski, Lyle, and Colarusso, 2009, p. 6, notes that this proportion is a Congressional mandate for the U.S. Army. Similar proportions were assumed to apply to the

U.S. Navy, Marine Corps, and Air Force. Unlike China, there is no evidence that suggests that, in the U.S. military, graduates of military academies are less capable than graduates of civilian universities.

65　More than 20 percent of high school graduates enrolled in full-time colleges in China in 2006, as compared to 5.6 percent in 1996. See National Bureau of Statistics of China, 2007, Table 21–2, and National Bureau of Statistics of China, 1997, Table 18–1. On improvements in quality of instruction at PLA academies, see Bickford, 2007, p. 175.

66　Office of the Under Secretary of Defense, Personnel and Readiness, undated, Table D-12.

67　Office of the Under Secretary of Defense, Personnel and Readiness, undated, Tables D-11, D-12, D-17, D-18.

68　Perhaps more importantly, the *quality* of experience in the PLA military was markedly different from that in the U.S. military, as much of the U.S. military in 2010 had significant amounts of recent combat experience in Iraq and Afghanistan. This issue will be addressed in the next chapter.

69　NASIC, 2010, p. 35; Cole, 2010, p. 124. The date by which this goal is to be achieved is not specified. More recently there have been indications that the number of officers will be cut even more significantly than these numbers. See "PLA to Carry Out Structural and Organizational Reform," 2014.

70　National Bureau of Statistics of China, 2010, Table 20–2.

71　Blasko, 2012, p. 61.

72　Junior and midlevel NCOs are assumed to only have high school diplomas.

73　This assumes that none of the officers who received advanced degrees between 1992 and 2010 will have retired by 2020. Although this is unlikely to be true, it also seems likely that the rate at which officers receive advanced degrees will increase between 2010 and 2020 as compared to the 2003–2010 period.

6　Training

1　As one example, Biddle, Hinkle, and Fisherkeller, 1999, pp. 20–22, describes how, in the Battle of La Haye du Puits, three American divisions attacked elements of the German LXXXIV Corps in Normandy in July 1944. The opposing forces, terrain, and objectives were similar for all three American divisions. The best-trained of the three divisions, the Eighty-Second Airborne, achieved the fastest rate of advance and the fewest casualties per square mile of ground captured. The worst-trained division, the Ninetieth Infantry, had the slowest rate of advance and suffered the most casualties per square mile of ground captured, even though it was significantly better equipped than the Eighty-Second Airborne.

2　"Joint Training Policy and Guidance for the Armed Forces of the United States," 2012, p. C-4; "The Joint Training System: A Guide for Senior Leaders," 2012, p. A-3; Headquarters, Department of the Army, 2011, p. 2-2; *The U.S. Army Training Concept*, 2011, p. 13.

3 Headquarters, Department of the Army, 2011, p. 2-5.
4 "Joint Training Policy and Guidance for the Armed Forces of the United States," 2012, pp. C-3–C-4; "The Joint Training System: A Guide for Senior Leaders," 2012, p. A-3.
5 "Joint Training Policy and Guidance for the Armed Forces of the United States," 2012, p. C-4; "The Joint Training System: A Guide for Senior Leaders," 2012, p. A-3; Headquarters, Department of the Army, 2011, p. 2–2; *Leadership and Force Development*, 2011, pp. 44–45.
6 Headquarters, Department of the Army, 2011, p. 2–4; *The U.S. Army Training Concept*, 2011, p. 13; *Leadership and Force Development*, 2011, pp. 43–44.
7 "Joint Training Policy and Guidance for the Armed Forces of the United States," 2012, pp. C-4–C-5; "The Joint Training System: A Guide for Senior Leaders," 2012, p. A-3; Headquarters, Department of the Army, 2011, pp. 2-3–2-5; *The U.S. Army Training Concept*, 2011, p. 13; *Leadership and Force Development*, 2011, p. 45.
8 "Joint Training Policy and Guidance for the Armed Forces of the United States," 2012, pp. C-4–C-5; Headquarters, Department of the Army, 2011, p. 2-2; *The U.S. Army Training Concept*, 2011, p. 13; *Leadership and Force Development*, 2011, pp. 43, 45; Moore et al., 1995, pp. 15–16.
9 Dong and Su, 2001; Combined Arms Tactics Training Bureau, 2001b; Su, Li, and Liao, 2002; Wang, Sun, and Tang, 2002; Sun and Su, 2003; Blasko, 2006, pp. 119–120, 145; ONI, 2007, pp. 28, 91–92. Note that the U.S. Chairman of the Joint Chiefs of Staff also issues annual training guidance. See, e.g., "Joint Training Policy and Guidance for the Armed Forces of the United States," 2012, pp. C-1–C-2.
10 Blasko, Klapakis, and Corbett, 1996, p. 490; "Fundamental Basis for [PLA] Operational Training in the New Period," 1999; *PLA Daily Reporter*, 1999; Gu and Su, 2001; Combined Arms Tactics Training Bureau, 2001a; Fan, 2002; Yang and Su, 2002; Commentator, 2002; Xiao, Hu, and Liu, 2008. Shambaugh, 2002a, p. 97, states that the training guidelines were "revised and reissued in January 1999," but this appears to be a reference to the GSD's annual assignment of training work, as a search of *PLA Daily* found no reference to the issuance of new training guidelines between December 1995 and June 2001.
11 Blasko, 2006, pp. 37–44.
12 E.g., Office of the Secretary of Defense, 2002, p. 26, notes that "[PLA Navy] training and exercise activity in 2001 was limited, with the Navy reportedly participating in only a handful of exercises. Moreover, the normal end-of-year multifleet exercise apparently was cancelled" and "[PLA Air Force] and [PLA Navy] fighter pilot tactical training continues, albeit slowly."
13 Yang, Yang, and Su, 2002.
14 Sun and Su, 2003.
15 Blasko, Klapakis, and Corbett, 1996, p. 495; Cole, 2001, pp. 133–136; Blasko, 2006, pp. 163–164. During basic training political training represented 40 percent of training time (Blasko, 2008, p. 107). In the mid-1980s, 30 percent of a soldier's time was said to be devoted to nonmilitary activities (Cole, 2001, p. 247, n. 101).

16 Henley, 2000, pp. 61–62; Blasko, 2006, p. 38; Puska, 2010, p. 555. The authoritative study of the PLA's involvement in commercial activities is Mulvenon, 2001.

17 Ren, 1999; "Fundamental Basis for [PLA] Operational Training in the New Period," 1999; Ma, 1999; *PLA Daily Reporter*, 1999. The quotes are from "Fundamental Basis for [PLA] Operational Training in the New Period," 1999 and Ma, 1999.

18 Su, Li, and Liao, 2002; Wang, Sun, and Tang, 2002; Yang and Su, 2002; Wu, 2002; Sun and Su, 2003; correspondence with researcher, Chinese Academy of Military Science. Note that different Western sources translate the name of the *Military Training and Evaluation Guidelines* differently. For example, Blasko (2006) uses the translation "Military Training and Evaluation *Program*" and ONI (2007) uses "*Outline* of Military Training and Evaluation." Consultation with a native speaker of Chinese, however, confirms that "guidelines" is the most accurate translation of the Chinese term 大纲.

19 Blasko, Klapakis, and Corbett, 1996, pp. 493, 516–517, 523; Dreyer, 1996, p. 322; Cole, 2001, pp. 124–129; Shambaugh, 2002a, pp. 95–96; Blasko, 2006, pp. 51, 146; "Joint Field Training by the Three Services like a Raging Wildfire," 2009; "Frequently Asked Questions." Quote is from Cole, 2001, p. 125.

20 Blasko, Klapakis, and Corbett, 1996, pp. 517–519; Cole, 2001, p. 129; Gu and Su, 2001; Yang and Su, 2002; Shambaugh, 2002a, pp. 95–96; Puska, 2002, pp. 229–231; Sun and Su, 2003; Blasko, 2006, pp. 146–150.

21 Blasko, Klapakis, and Corbett, 1996, pp. 488–499; Gu and Su, 2001; Dong and Su, 2001; Combined Arms Tactics Training Bureau, 2001a; Cole, 2001, pp. 124–133; Office of the Secretary of Defense, 2002, p. 27; Shambaugh, 2002a, pp. 94–105; Puska, 2002, pp. 239–240, 243; Su, Li, and Liao, 2002; Wang, 2002; Xia, 2002; Commentator, 2002; Sun and Su, 2003. Quote is from Cole, 2001, pp. 124–125.

22 Cheung, 1999, p. 239; Puska, 2002, pp. 232–238; Blasko, 2006, pp. 147, 160, 164–167; ONI, 2007, p. 44.

23 Blasko, Klapakis, and Corbett, 1996, pp. 492–493; Dong and Su, 2001; Su, Li, and Liao, 2002; Wang, Sun, and Tang, 2002; Li, 2002b; Wu, 2002; Shambaugh, 2002a, pp. 96, 97.

24 "International Security Cooperation," Information Office, 2000a; Blasko, 2012, p. 5.

25 "Building a New System for Training under Informationization Conditions," 2008.

26 Xiao, Hu, and Liu, 2008; Mulvenon, 2009.

27 Xiao, Hu, and Liu, 2008; Liu, 2008; Liu and Wu, 2008; "Building a New System for Training under Informationization Conditions," 2008; Liu and Wu, 2010b; Yan and Liu, 2011a; Liu and Hu, 2011b.

28 Liu, 2008; Liu and Wu, 2008; "Building a New System for Training under Informationization Conditions," 2008; Xiao, Hu, and Liu, 2008.

29 Cole, 2010, p. 138; Gu and Liu, 2011 refers to the responsibility of "Party Committee leaders" (i.e., unit commanders and political commissars) for organizing and leading training.

30 Wang, 2009.

31 Yang, Yang, and Su, 2002; ONI, 2007, pp. 87–101; "Building a New System for Training under Informationization Conditions," 2008; ONI, 2009, pp. 34–41; Zhang, 2010; Cole, 2010, pp. 131–137; Guo, 2011.

32 Cole, 2010, p. 141; Blasko, 2012, pp. 35, 45, 201–203.

33 Liu, 2008; Wang, 2009; Dong, 2009.

34 Gu and Liu, 2011; Cai and Zheng, 2013.

35 Liu, 2008; Liu and Wu, 2008; "Building a New System for Training under Informationization Conditions," 2008; Xiao, Hu, and Liu, 2008; Huang, 2010; Blasko 2012, 190–194. Quotes are from Huang, 2010.

36 "Building a New System for Training under Informationization Conditions," 2008; Wu and Liu, 2009; Yu and Liu, 2009; Huang, 2010.

37 Liu, 2008; Yu and Liu, 2009; Liu and Hu, 2011a.

38 NASIC, 2007, pp. 33–35; ONI, 2007, pp. 87–101; Liu, 2008; ONI, 2009, pp. 34–41; "Joint Field Training by the Three Services like a Raging Wildfire," 2009; Liu and Wu, 2010b; Cole, 2010, pp. 130–137; NASIC, 2010, pp. 61–66; Allen, 2011b, pp. 33–40; Blasko, 2012, pp. 175–179, 183–200; Fuell, 2014, p. 9. Quotes are from Fuell, 2014, p. 9.

39 NASIC, 2007, pp. 33–35; ONI, 2007, pp. 87–101; Liu and Wu, 2008; "Building a New System for Training under Informationization Conditions," 2008; Xiao, Hu, and Liu, 2008; ONI, 2009, pp. 34–41; Cole, 2010, pp. 131–137; Liu and Wu, 2010a; Zhou, Jiang, and Fang, 2010; Wang, 2010; Wu and Cai, 2010; Huang, 2010; Gu and Liu, 2011; Blasko, 2012, pp. 176–182, 197–200, 203–206; Fuell, 2014, p. 9.

40 Dong and Su, 2001; Su, Li, and Liao, 2002; Wang, Sun, and Tang, 2002; Li, 2002b; Wu, 2002; Liu and Wu, 2008; "Building a New System for Training under Informationization Conditions," 2008; Blasko, 2012, p. 177.

41 Dong, 2009; Zhang, 2010; Gu and Liu, 2011; Yan and Liu, 2011b.

42 "Deployment of the Armed Forces," Information Office, 2011.

43 Zhang, 2010; Liu and Wu, 2010b; Allen, 2011b, pp. 38–39; Yan and Liu 2011a; Liu and Cai, 2011; Liu and Hu, 2011b; Gu and Liu, 2011; Liu and Hu, 2011a; Blasko, 2012, p. 210.

44 Zhang, 2010; Liu and Wu, 2010a; Huang, 2010; Liu and Wu, 2010b; Wu and Cai, 2010; Gu and Liu, 2011; Liu and Hu, 2011a; Yan and Liu, 2011b.

7 Logistics

1 This categorization is largely based on, but not identical to, *Joint Logistics*, 2008, pp. I-9 – II-15.

2 *Joint Logistics*, 2008, pp. II-11–II-12 includes *combat* engineering (constructing or destroying barriers and obstacles, laying or removing mines, etc.) as a logistic function but in this study combat engineering is regarded as a type of combat operation and is included by implication in the analysis in the other chapters of this book (e.g., on weaponry or training).

3 Dumond et al., 2001, p. iii.

4 Cheung, 1999, p. 233.

5 Allen, 2011b, p. 41; Blasko, 2012, p. 149.

6 Cheung, 1999, pp. 228, 230–235, 239–241; Henley, 2000, pp. 55–67, 62–64, 71, 73; Shambaugh, 2002a, p. 139; Blasko, 2006, pp. 44, 118–119, 165; Puska, 2010, pp. 554, 570. Quotes are from Cheung, 1999, p. 234 and Henley, 2000, p. 55.

7 Cheung, 1999, p. 235; Allen, 2002, pp. 263, 279; Shambaugh, 2002a, p. 139; Blasko, 2006, pp. 29, 44, 118.

8 Cheung, 1999, pp. 234–235; Blasko, 2006, p. 165.

9 If the conflict had been protracted, the ability of PLA and civilian defense industry factories to replenish those stocks as they were depleted would have become important, but I not have attempted to assess that capability for this study.

10 Henley, 2000, p. 60; Blasko, 2006, p. 165.

11 Cheung, 1999, pp. 228, 230, 234; Henley, 2000, pp. 55, 62–64, 71, 73; Allen, 2002, pp. 278–279; Blasko, 2006, pp. 44, 118; Button et al., 2007, p. 80.

12 One analyst, for example, estimated that the PLA Air Force would have had difficulty supplying the thirty to fifty million gallons of aviation fuel required by a relatively small-scale war. Allen, 2002, pp. 278–279.

13 Private communication with expert on PLA Army.

14 Chinese divisions consist of three infantry or armored regiments, an artillery regiment, an air defense regiment, and other support units. In the U.S. Army, an Infantry Brigade Combat Team (IBCT) has about thirty-six hundred soldiers and six hundred vehicles, and requires about three hundred tons of supplies a day in heavy combat operations. A Chinese infantry regiment is smaller than an IBCT, with about twenty-eight hundred soldiers (the number of vehicles in a Chinese infantry regiment is unclear). If we assume that the supply requirements of the Chinese infantry regiment are proportionately smaller, then it would consume two to two hundred and fifty tons of supplies a day. In the U.S. Army, a Heavy Brigade Combat Team (HBCT) has about thirty-eight hundred soldiers and eighteen hundred vehicles, including about two hundred armored vehicles, and requires six hundred tons of supplies a day in heavy combat operations. A Chinese armored regiment has about a third as many soldiers (twelve hundred) and half as many armored vehicles (one hundred or more) as an HBCT, implying a daily supply requirement of about 250 tons in heavy combat. If we assume that the supply requirements of the artillery regiment (eleven hundred soldiers) and air defense regiment (one thousand soldiers) are similar to those of the armored regiment, and that the remainder of the division (thirteen hundred to thirty-three hundred soldiers) requires another hundred to two hundred tons of supplies a day, then a Chinese infantry or armored division would consume about thirteen hundred to fourteen hundred tons of supplies a day in heavy combat. See Blasko, 2006, pp. 39–42; Button et al., 2007, pp. 75–86; O'Hanlon, 2009, pp. 144–147.

15 Cheung, 1999, p. 237; 2001, 2006, 2007; National Bureau of Statistics of China, 2001; U.S. Census Bureau, 2002; U.S. Census Bureau, 2003; U.S. Census Bureau, 2004–2005; National Bureau of Statistics of China, 2006; National Bureau of

Statistics of China, 2007. Before 2007, Chinese statistics on highway mileage did not include "village roads." Since U.S. highway mileage statistics include all public road and street mileage in the fifty states and District of Columbia, total Chinese highway mileage in 2000 was estimated by multiplying the reported highway mileage for 2000 by the ratio of the total highway mileage reported for 2005 in National Bureau of Statistics, 2007 (which included village roads) to that reported in National Bureau of Statistics, 2006 (which did not include village roads). Despite China's lack of petroleum pipelines, the PLA expected pipelines to be the primary means for transporting fuel supplies. See Blasko, 2006, p. 118.

16 As one example, in 2001 the author traveled by car from Lhasa to Katmandu along the China-Nepal "Friendship Highway," the main artery connecting China with South Asia. At the time, although in the process of being upgraded and expanded, much of this "highway" was an unpaved two-lane dirt road.

17 Cole, 2001, pp. 103–104; IISS, 2001, pp. 21, 22, 25, 190.

18 National Bureau of Statistics of China, 2001; Bureau of Transportation Statistics, 2012.

19 U.S. Census Bureau, 2001. Panama and Liberia had the world's largest merchant fleets according to ship registrations, but most of the ships registered in those countries were owned by foreign entities. The Chinese flag not generally being regarded as a "flag of convenience," the vast majority of the ships registered in China were probably owned by Chinese companies.

20 IISS, 2001, pp. 190; Cole, 2001, p. 80; "Yuliang (Type 079) Class," 2013; "Yukan (Type 072) Class," 2013; "Yuhai (Type 074) (Wuhu-A) Class," 2013; "Yudao Class (Type 073)," 2013; "Yuting I (Type 072 II) Class," 2013; "US 1–511 (shan) Class," 2005; "Ilyushin Il-76," 2012; "SAC Y-8," 2013; "Xian (Antonov) Y-7," 2012; Button et al., 2007, pp. 75–86; Denmark, 2012, p. 302. A 2001 study by a Chinese military analyst of the logistics challenges associated with amphibious operations against Taiwan concluded that the Chinese logistics system was not capable of providing the necessary supplies. The author of that study recommended that supplies during the initial phase of battle be provided by helicopters, with mobilization of civilian ships occurring once China had seized Taiwan and the Strait. See Puska, 2010, p. 577.

21 Cheung, 1999, pp. 228, 230, 234, 239; Henley, 2000, pp. 55, 62–64, 71, 73; Allen, 2002, pp. 283–284; Blasko, 2006, pp. 44, 118–119; ONI, 2007, p. 44

22 Allen, 2002, pp. 280, 285. U.S. aircraft participating in Operation Desert Storm in 1991 flew an average of two thousand sorties a day. Even during the relatively small-scale contingency with Serbia over Kosovo in 1999, participating U.S. aircraft flew an average of five hundred sorties a day.

23 Henley, 2000, pp. 63–64; Allen, 2002, pp. 273–275.

24 Cheung, 1999, pp. 228, 230, 234; Henley, 2000, pp. 55, 62–64, 71, 73; Blasko, 2006, pp. 44, 118–119.

25 IISS, 2001, pp. 190; "Yantai (Type 073) Class," 2013; "Danlin Class," 2013; "Hongqi Class," 2013; "Dayun (Type 904) Class Supply Ships," 2013; "Dandao Class," 2013;

Button et al., 2007, pp. 75–86. The precise transport capacity of the PLA Navy's cargo ships is not clear, but the PLAN's landing ships were collectively estimated to be capable of carrying about twenty thousand tons of cargo. Assuming the cargo capacity to displacement ratio for the seventy-five thousand tons of cargo ships was roughly similar to that for the 110,000 tons of landing ships, this implies that the cargo ships would have been able to carry twelve thousand to fifteen thousand tons of cargo. In the U.S. Army, an IBCT, which has about thirty-six hundred soldiers, weighs about twenty-four hundred tons including all of its equipment. Since a Chinese infantry regiment has fewer soldiers (about twenty-eight hundred), I assume it weighs a proportionately smaller amount: about nineteen hundred tons. An HBCT, which has more than two hundred armored vehicles, weighs about twenty thousand tons including all of its equipment. Since the weight of an armored unit appears to be primarily a function of the number of vehicles it has (e.g., an HBCT has 6 percent more soldiers than an IBCT but weighs eight times as much), I assume that a Chinese armored regiment, which has about half as many armored vehicles as an HBCT, weighs about half as much as an HBCT: about ten thousand tons. I assume that the artillery and air defense regiments of the Chinese division weigh about five thousand tons each (i.e., less than an armored regiment but more than an infantry regiment), and that the remainder of the division (thirteen hundred to three thousand soldiers) weighs another thousand to two thousand tons. For a light infantry division comprising three infantry regiments, this gives a total weight of about seventeen thousand tons. For an understrength armored division comprising two armored regiments instead of the usual three, it gives a total weight of about thirty-two thousand tons. See Blasko, 2006, pp. 39–42; Button et al., 2007, pp. 75–86.

26 IISS, 2001, pp. 190, 210; Cole, 2001, pp. 80, 84, 103; Allen, 2002, p. 277; "US 1–511 (shan) Class," 2005; Button et al., 2007, pp. 75–86; "Yuliang ('Type 079) Class," 2013; "Yukan ('Type 072) Class," 2013; "Yuhai ('Type 074) (Wuhu-A) Class," 2013; "Yudao Class ('Type 073)," 2013; "Yuting I ('Type 072 II) Class," 2013 . Using the assumptions above, a partly mechanized division comprising two light infantry regiments and one armored regiment would weigh about twenty-five thousand tons, greater than the estimated twenty thousand ton total lift capacity of the Chinese amphibious fleet in 2000. If the division's artillery regiment were left behind (on the assumption that, at least initially, naval gunfire, surface-to-surface missiles, and aircraft would substitute for artillery support), the remainder of this composite division would weigh about twenty thousand tons.

27 Henley, 2000, p. 73.

28 Cheung, 1999, pp. 228, 230, 234; Henley, 2000, pp. 55, 62–64, 71, 73; Blasko, 2006, pp. 44, 118–119, 166; "Qiongsha Class," 2013.

29 Puska, 2010, p. 590.

30 Puska, 2010, pp. 570, 574–576; Cole, 2010, p. 67; Denmark, 2012, p. 297; Blasko, 2012, pp. 38–39.

31 Blasko, 2012, pp. 35, 213, 222.

32 Cole, 2010, pp. 67, 68, 72, 93, 202.

33 ONI, 2007, p. 44; Blasko, 2012, pp. 166, 169; Cole, 2010, pp. 132, 134, 190.

34 Puska, 2010, p. 596.

35 Puska, 2010, pp. 590–594.

36 Puska, 2010, pp. 577, 579, 580, 593.

37 Puska, 2010, pp. 577, 593; Cole, 2010, p. 132; IISS, 2011, pp. 231–232; Blasko, 2012, pp. 34–35, 173.

38 Puska, 2010, p. 569. See also Garnaut, 2012.

39 Hille, 2012; Staff Reporters, 2014a.

40 Denmark, 2012, pp. 304–305, 307–309; Blasko, 2012, p. 215.

41 Cole, 2010, pp. 132, 157, 184, 202; Denmark, 2012, pp. 309–310.

42 Denmark, 2012, pp. 297, 298, 301–302.

43 Puska, 2010, pp. 570, 576–577, 592, 596; Blasko, 2012, pp. 52, 134.

44 Puska, 2010, pp. 575, 583–584; Blasko, 2012, pp. 34, 40, 52, 85, 89–102.

45 Blasko, 2012, pp. 48–50, 112, 149, 169.

46 Private communication with expert on PLA Army.

47 Puska, 2010, p. 583; Blasko, 2012, pp. 34, 134; National Bureau of Statistics of China, 2011; U.S. Census Bureau, 2011; Bureau of Transportation Statistics, 2012.

48 ONI, 2007, p. 44; Cole, 2010, pp. 68, 72, 93, 202; Puska, 2010, pp. 591–592; IISS, 2011, pp. 59–60, 232–233; Military Sealift Command; Denmark, 2012, pp. 310, 311.

49 National Bureau of Statistics of China, 2011; Maritime Administration, 2011; Bureau of Transportation Statistics, 2012; IISS, 2011, p. 233; "Yantai (Type 073) Class," 2013; "Danlin Class," 2013; "Hongqi Class," 2013; "Dayun (Type 904) Class Supply Ships," 2013; "Dandao Class," 2013. An additional twelve hundred large merchant ships were registered in Hong Kong in 2010. How many were owned by Chinese corporations, however, is unclear. (All or virtually all merchant ships registered in mainland China are presumed to have been owned by Chinese corporations.)

50 IISS, 2011, pp. 233, 234; "Yunshu (Yudeng III) Class," 2013; "Yuting II (Type 072 III) Class," 2013; "Yuzhao (Type 071) Class," 2013; "Yudeng (Type 073) Class," 2013; "Yubei (Type 074A) Class," 2013; "Yuliang (Type 079) Class," 2013; "Yukan (Type 072) Class," 2013; "Yuhai (Type 074) (Wuhu-A) Class," 2013; "Yuting I (Type 072 II) Class," 2013; "Ilyushin Il-76," 2012; "SAC Y-8," 2013; "Xian (Antonov) Y-7," 2012.

51 ONI, 2007, pp. 44, 50; Cole, 2010, p. 68; Allen, 2011b, p. 42; Blasko, 2012, pp. 134, 149, 169, 203–204.

52 Allen, 2011b, p. 42; Blasko, 2012, pp. 40, 50, 52, 85, 89–102, 112, 134, 149.

53 ONI, 2007, p. 50; Cole, 2010, p. 202; Allen, 2011b, p. 42; Denmark, 2012, pp. 310–311.

54 Button et al., 2007, p. 80; Puska, 2010, p. 583; Blasko, 2012, pp. 49, 149; Denmark, 2012, p. 304.

55 As in 2000, a Chinese infantry regiment is assumed to weigh about nineteen hundred tons, an infantry division to weigh about seventeen thousand tons, and a full armored division to weigh about forty-two thousand tons.

56 Blasko, 2012, pp. 112, 134; Denmark, 2012, pp. 304, 311–312.

57 National Bureau of Statistics of China, 2011.

58 IISS, 2011, p. 272; Denmark, 2012, p. 303. As in 2000, a Chinese infantry division is assumed to weigh about seventeen thousand tons and an armored regiment to weigh about ten thousand tons.

59 Allen, 2011b, p. 42; Blasko, 2012, pp. 112, 215; ONI, 2007, p. 50; Denmark, 2012, p. 303.

60 Puska, 2010, p. 575; Blasko, 2012, pp. 48, 52, 89–102, 112, 169; "Anwei (Type 920) Class," 2013; "Ankang Class," 2013.

61 Puska, 2010, pp. 591–592, 594; Denmark, 2012, pp. 300, 309.

62 "Yubei (Type 074A) Class," 2013; "Yuting II (Type 072 III) Class," 2013; "Yunshu (Yudeng III) Class," 2013.

63 For a description of Velocity Management, see Dumond et al., 2001.

64 "Yantai (Type 073) Class," 2013; "Dayun (Type 904) Class Supply Ships," 2013; "SAC Y-9," 2013; "XAC Y-20," 2013; Sweetman and Perrett, 2013, p. 26.

65 Cole, 2010, p. 198; "Fuchi (Type 903) Class," 2013.

66 Blasko, 2012, pp. 50, 96–99. Each maneuver regiment of the two mechanized infantry divisions is assumed to weigh about five thousand tons (intermediate between the nineteen hundred tons estimated above for a light infantry regiment and the ten thousand tons estimated for an armored regiment). The division is assumed to also have one artillery and one air defense regiment, each weighing five thousand tons as well, and various other elements weighing another two thousand tons. The armored brigade is assume to weigh fifteen thousand tons (intermediate between the ten thousand tons estimated for a Chinese armored regiment and the twenty thousand tons of a U.S. HBCT, which has roughly twice as many soldiers (thirty-nine hundred) as Blasko estimates for a Chinese armored brigade (two thousand).

8 Organizational Culture

1 On the relationship between organizational culture and performance in general, see Kotter and Heskett, 1992; Denison, 1997; Cameron and Quinn, 2011. For an argument about the relationship between military culture and military effectiveness, see Murray, 1999.

2 Schein, 2010, pp. 23–33; 73–156; Jones, 2010, pp. 179–182; Cameron and Quinn, 2011, pp. 18–21.

3 Kotter and Heskett, 1992, pp. 28–43; Schein, 2010, p. 14; Jones, 2010, p. 180.

4 See Cameron and Quinn, 2011; Denison, 1997.

5 Denison, 1997, pp. 4–16; Denison, Haaland, and Goelzer, 2004, pp. 99–100; Cameron and Quinn, 2011, pp. 41–56. Denison's methodology has subsequently subdivided each of the four clusters into three subclusters. E.g., see Denison, Haaland, and Goelzer, 2004. See also "Denison Model," Denison Consulting website (as of June 21, 2013: www.denisonconsulting.com/model).

6 Denison, 1997, pp. 6–8; Denison, Haaland, and Goelzer, 2004, p. 100; Cameron and Quinn, 2011, pp. 46–48.

7 Denison, 1997, pp. 8–11; Denison, Haaland, and Goelzer, 2004, p. 100; Cameron and Quinn, 2011, pp. 41–43.

8 Denison, 1997, pp. 13–14; Denison, Haaland, and Goelzer, 2004, p. 100; Cameron and Quinn, 2011, pp. 43–46.

9 Denison, 1997, pp. 11–13; Denison, Haaland, and Goelzer, 2004, p. 100; Cameron and Quinn, 2011, pp. 49–51.

10 Denison, Haaland, and Goelzer, 2004, p. 103; Cameron and Quinn, 2011, pp. 27–28.

11 See Mattox, 2013.

12 Headquarters, Department of the Army, 2005, pp. iv, 1-14–1-16, 1-18; "Department of the Navy Core Values Charter"; "The United States Navy"; "The Navy Ethos"; "United States Air Force Core Values"; "The Airman's Creed." The foreign militaries whose values were examined are the Canadian, British, Australian, New Zealand, and Israeli militaries. See Barrett, 2012, pp. 18–22.

13 Headquarters, Department of the Army, 2005, pp. iv, 1-15; "Department of the Navy Core Values Charter"; "The United States Navy"; "United States Air Force Core Values"; Barrett, 2012, pp. 18–22.

14 Headquarters, Department of the Army, 2005, p. 1-16; "Department of the Navy Core Values Charter"; "The United States Navy"; "The Navy Ethos"; "United States Air Force Core Values"; Barrett, 2012, pp. 18–22.

15 Fitzsimmons, 2013a, pp. 20–21, identifies group loyalty as one of the cultural norms associated with military effectiveness.

16 Headquarters, Department of the Army, 2005, pp. iv, 1-11, 1-16; "Department of the Navy Core Values Charter"; "The United States Navy"; "United States Air Force Core Values"; "The Airman's Creed."

17 Barrett, pp. 18–22.

18 Headquarters, Department of the Army, 2005, p. iv; "The Airman's Creed."

19 Headquarters, Department of the Army, 2005, pp. iv, 1-16.

20 "The Navy Ethos"; "The Airman's Creed."

21 Barrett, 2012, p. 21.

22 Headquarters, Department of the Army, 2005, p. iv; "The Navy Ethos."

23 "United States Air Force Core Values."

24 Headquarters, Department of the Army, 2005, pp. iv, 1-16; "Department of the Navy Core Values Charter"; "The United States Navy"; "United States Air Force Core Values"; "The Airman's Creed"; Barrett, 2012, pp. 18–21.

25 Headquarters, Department of the Army, 2005, pp. iv, 1-16, 1-18; "Department of the Navy Core Values Charter"; "The United States Navy"; "The Airman's Creed"; Barrett, 2012, p. 21.

26 Headquarters, Department of the Army, 2005, p. 1-16.

27 Headquarters, Department of the Army, 2005, p. iv; "The Profession of Arms," 2010.

28 "Department of the Navy Core Values Charter"; "The United States Navy."

29 Barrett, 2012, pp. 18–22.

30 Fitzsimmons, 2013a, pp. 20–21, identifies "technical expertise" as one of the cultural norms associated with military effectiveness.

31 Mattox, 2013, p. 61.
32 Headquarters, Department of the Army, 2005, pp. 1-15–1-16; "Department of the Navy Core Values Charter"; "The United States Navy"; "The Navy Ethos"; "United States Air Force Core Values"; Barrett, 2012, pp. 18, 19, 21.
33 Headquarters, Department of the Army, 2005, pp. 1-12, 1-14.
34 "The Profession of Arms," 2010, pp. 4, 5.
35 "Department of the Navy Core Values Charter"; "The United States Navy"; "United States Air Force Core Values."
36 Moten, 2010, p. 22.
37 Pierce, 2010, pp. xiv–xv.
38 "The Profession of Arms," 2010, p. 5.
39 "United States Air Force Core Values."
40 "The Navy Ethos"; "Department of the Navy Core Values Charter"; "The United States Navy."
41 Barrett, 2012, pp. 18–22.
42 Headquarters, Department of the Army, 2005, p. 1-16; "Department of the Navy Core Values Charter"; "The United States Navy"; "United States Air Force Core Values."
43 "Department of the Navy Core Values Charter"; "The United States Navy"; "United States Air Force Core Values."
44 "The Profession of Arms," 2010, p. 4.
45 Headquarters, Department of the Army, 2008, p. A-2.
46 "Department of the Navy Core Values Charter"; "The United States Navy."
47 Moten, 2010, p. 22; Barrett, 2012, pp. 18, 38, 39.
48 It could be argued that obedience is implied by the values of moral integrity and/or discipline, as these require following laws and regulations, and military regulations invariably require obedience to (lawful) orders. However, the value of obedience would seem to be broader than merely obeying statements that are clearly orders. A military in which members did not feel compelled to obey instructions or requests from their superiors that were not actual "orders" would be very different from most militaries. Note also that in Western militaries "obedience" includes not just obedience to higher-ranking officers but obedience to civilian authority as well. See Headquarters, Department of the Army, 2005, p. 1-14; Snider, Oh, and Toner, 2009, p. 12; "The Profession of Arms," 2010, p. 5; Moten, 2010, pp. vi, 19, 20, 22; Barrett, 2012, pp. 22, 40. For the PLA it includes obedience to the CPC.
49 Headquarters, Department of the Army, 2005, p. 1-12.
50 Pierce, 2010, pp. iv, v, xiv, 37, 66; Barrett, 2012, p. 39; Fitzsimmons, 2013b, pp. 20–21.
51 Headquarters, Department of the Army, 2005, p. 1-14; "The Profession of Arms," 2010, p. 4; Pierce, 2010, pp. iv, v, xiv, 13, 16, 36, 37, 62, 64, 66–67; Barrett, 2012, pp. 16, 38; Fitzsimmons, 2013b, p. 20; Murray, undated, p. 141.
52 Biddle, 2004, pp. 82–83, 94–99, 106–107; "Department of the Navy Core Values Charter"; "The United States Navy"; Pierce, 2010, pp. iv, v, xiv, 12, 16, 17, 36, 37, 62, 64, 66; Barrett, 2012, p. 16; Fitzsimmons, 2013b, p. 20.

53 Deighton, 1979; Keegan, 1988, pp. 9–95; Dunn, 2008, p. 6; Pierce, 2010, pp. iv, xiv, 13, 16, 62, 64, 66.

54 "The Navy Ethos."

55 See Miller, 2011, p. 44.

56 It should also be noted that organizational cultures are not monolithic. Each suborganization within a larger organization has its own subculture, and these can vary significantly from each other. See Schein, 2010, pp. 55–71. Given the small number of survey respondents and their heavily constrained scope of contact with the PLA, characterizing different subcultures within the PLA was obviously not feasible in this study. Thus, although the questionnaire responses may accurately represent PLA culture "on average," they are probably less accurate as characterizations of any given suborganization within the PLA.

57 Two people who had not had significant direct contact with the PLA since 1995 were excluded.

58 One response was excluded because the average year of contact was 2005 – precisely between 2000 and 2010. This response, however, was generally consistent with the other nine: For only one of the twenty-two values assessed (*expertise*) would including this response in either of the two groups have changed the median response for that group by a full category (from "somewhat less" to "about the same" if it had been included in the group for which the average year of contact was closer to 2010).

59 Although the questionnaire responses are ordinal data (that is, a response of "2" simply means greater than "1" but less than "3," not "precisely midway between '1' and '3'"), it is possible that the median response (i.e., the value for which half of the responses are higher and half are lower) will fall between two of the defined categories. If, for example, of the four sets of questionnaire responses associated with 2000, two indicated that PLA culture supported a given value "somewhat less" than U.S. military culture (coded as "2") and two indicated that PLA culture supported that value "about the same" as U.S. military culture (coded as "3"), then the median response would be between "somewhat less" and "about the same." Medians that fall between two categories are indicated by the use of "½."

60 *Responsibility*, for which the median response was between "much less" ("1") and "somewhat less" ("2") in 2000, but was "about the same" ("3") in 2010, and *self-sacrifice*, for which the median response was between "somewhat less" ("2") and "about the same" ("3") in 2000, but was "somewhat more" ("4") in 2010.

61 Several questionnaire responders (three out of the total of ten responders) took the initiative to note that the term "patriotism" means something different to Chinese than it does to Americans. One asserted that the American concept simply does not exist in China, and another stated that what Chinese conceive of as "patriotism," Americans would regard as more akin to "nationalism." The difference, according to this responder, is that "patriotism" focuses on the virtues of one's own country whereas "nationalism" reflects a desire to see one's own country's interests advanced at the expense of those of other countries.

62 The value *patriotism* does not clearly fit into any of the Cameron and Quinn or Denison value clusters. It appears to be similar to values such as teamwork and loyalty, but in the context of organizational culture these generally refer to teamwork within and loyalty to the organization, not to the larger nation-state in which the organization is embedded.

63 Deighton, 1979; Keegan, 1988, pp. 9–95; Biddle, 2004, pp. 82–83, 94–99, 106–107; Headquarters, Department of the Army, 2005, pp. 1-12, 1-14; Dunn, 2008, p. 6; "The Profession of Arms," 2010, p. 4; "Department of the Navy Core Values Charter"; "The United States Navy"; Pierce, 2010, pp. iv, v, xiv, 12, 13, 16, 17, 36, 37, 62, 64, 66–67; Barrett, 2012, pp. 16, 38, 39; Murray, undated, p. 141 .

64 Pierce, 2010, pp. 86–87.

65 Even the generally top-down Soviet military in World War II was able to implement blitzkrieg principles and achieved its greatest successes, such as the destruction of Germany's Army Group Center in June–July 1944, when its commanders were allowed to exercise initiative and take risks. See Griffith, 1990, pp. 131–134; Dunn, 2008, p. 6. Consistent with this, Blasko, Klapakis, and Corbett (1996, pp. 493–494) states that "In a local war fought under high technology conditions it is likely that small units (companies, battalions, or regiments) will be required to operate more independently than the PLA has been accustomed to operating in the past. ... Such an environment will require a level of initiative, exchange of information and confidence in subordinates not yet common in Chinese society."

66 The greater number of relative strengths and weaknesses in 2010 as compared to 2000 is a result of small changes in the medians between 2000 and 2010. In 2000, five medians were "3" or greater and four were between "2" and "3." In 2010, all five of the medians that had been "3" or greater in 2000 remained "3" or greater, but three of the four medians that had been between "2" and "3" in 2000 had also become "3" or greater (in addition, one median that had been between "2" and "3" in 2000 fell to "2" in 2010, and one median that had been between "1" and "2" rose to "3" in 2010). Similarly, in 2000, five medians were between "1" and "2" or worse, and eight were "2." In 2010, all five medians that had been between "1" and "2" or worse in 2010 were still between "1" and "2" or worse, but four medians that had been "2" in 2000 had fallen to between "1" and "2" or worse.

67 As stated above, *patriotism* does not clearly fit into any of the four value clusters described by Cameron and Quinn and Denison, nor does *courage*.

68 In addition to providing ratings of the degree to which PLA culture supported the twenty-two identified values, survey respondents were asked to provide "any additional thoughts or observations about PLA culture" they might have.

69 Pierce, 2010, pp. 86–87.

70 It is not a coincidence that the PLA's doctrine is inconsistent with both its organizational culture and its organizational structure, as organizational structure is an important source of organizational culture. See Jones, 2010, pp. 196–197.

71 Schein, 2010, pp. 273–296.

72 See Garnaut, 2012, p. 16; Perlez, 2012b; Chan, 2015.

73 See Lee and Guvin, 2013, pp. 11–12; Graaf, 2007, pp. 53–54. Perhaps surprisingly to Westerners, corruption is not necessarily associated with a low importance assigned to moral integrity. In many societies, including China's, corruption is in fact a response to moral imperatives, specifically the responsibility of a person to aid family members and friends when possible. See Graaf, 2007, pp. 53–55, and Madsen, 1984. Adherence to laws and regulations was intended to be captured by the value of "discipline" in the survey used for this chapter, but, interestingly, this was an area in which the PLA was rated relatively highly (see Tables 8.1 and 8.2). It is possible, however, that the survey respondents were primarily thinking of different aspects of discipline, such as adherence to specific orders and instructions.

9 Scenario Analysis

1 It should be understood that scenarios are not predictions of future conflicts. Scenario analysis seeks to describe hypothetical conflicts that approximate important character-istics of potential future conflicts. Most potential future conflicts never occur, however, and, when they do occur, they never exactly match the characteristics described in any scenario analysis. The purpose of scenario analysis is to identify hypothetical conflicts such that, when an actual conflict or crisis does occur, it will at least share some similarities with one of the scenarios that were analyzed, so that insights derived from the scenario analyses will be applicable to the actual conflict. The scenarios described in this chapter were chosen because they appear, at present, to be among the *more* likely conflict scenarios involving China, but the choice of them should not be considered to be the reflection of a belief that either of them is *likely* to occur.

2 Analysis of the effects of alternative estimates of the performance of individual weapon systems that was conducted but is not described here supports this assertion, as the overall outcomes of the scenarios were not highly sensitive to assumptions about the performance of any one type of weapon.

3 See Cliff et al., 2007, pp. 29–34, for arguments as to why the Chinese leadership might wish to launch a preemptive surprise attack.

4 Tokyo could also, of course, choose to not allow U.S. forces to operate out of Japanese territory in this conflict. This scenario, however, assumes that Japan allows them to operate out of concern that refusing to do so would weaken U.S. security guarantees to Japan at a time when China has clearly become aggressive and belligerent.

5 A historical example involving China of such mutual restraint occurred during the 1958 Kinmen Crisis, when Beijing did not allow its aircraft to bomb the Nationalist-held island of Kinmen as long as Nationalist aircraft did not bomb the Chinese mainland. See Morgan et al., 2008, p. 188.

6 Another possible participant in the conflict would be South Korea. This scenario, however, assumes that Seoul opposes U.S. military aircraft participating in the conflict from bases in Korean territory and that the United States accepts this restriction. According to a former South Korean official, when the United States

inquired in 2003 about the possibility of using forces in South Korea in the event of a Taiwan contingency, Seoul refused to grant permission. See Lee, 2014.

7 China's leadership would undoubtedly hope that the attacks in preparation for an invasion would be sufficient to convince Taiwan to capitulate. If those attacks were not sufficient, however, then the only way to compel Taiwan to accept unification would be to invade and occupy the island.

8 Staff Writer with CNA, 2014, p. 3.

9 As of 2012, Taiwan's army was estimated to have two hundred thousand personnel and five armored, one armored infantry, two special operations, three aviation, and twenty-eight light infantry brigades. See IISS, 2013, p. 335.

10 Cole, 2013; author's personal observations based on his interactions with Taiwan's military.

11 "Lockheed Martin (General Dynamics) F-16 Fighting Falcon," 2012; "AIDC F-CK-1 Ching Kuo," 2012; Kan, 2013, pp. 9–10, 16–17; "Boeing AH-64 Apache," 2013.

12 Cole, 2006, pp. 76–78; Ministry of National Defense, 2011, p. 116; Cole, 2013; Wang, 2013; Staff Writer with CNA, 2014, p. 3; Pan, 2014, p. 3.

13 In 2001, the average conscript in Taiwan's military was twenty-two years old and the average NCO was 24.7 years old. See Cole, 2006, p. 77. Since the average conscript in 2001 would have been halfway through a two-year term, if we assume that NCOs had on average joined the military at the same age as the average conscript, this would imply that the average NCO had 3.7 years of experience in 2001. If Taiwan has successfully implemented an all-volunteer military by 2020, then presumably the proportion of new recruits will go down and the average tenure of NCOs will go up, but it seems unlikely that the average enlisted person in Taiwan's military will have seven years of experience, as will be the case in both the PLA and U.S. military in 2020. All enlisted personnel in Taiwan's military in 2020 are assumed to have at least a high school education but, similar to the U.S. military, only a small percentage are assumed to have higher levels of education, whereas about a fifth of enlisted personnel in the PLA will hold three-year degrees.

14 In the case of U.S. Marine Corps aviation, the F-35B is supposed to replace both the AV-8 and the F/A-18. Most AV-8s are planned to remain in service through 2027, however. See Carey, 2013. Through 2020, therefore, the F-35B is assumed to only have replaced F/A-18s.

15 Department of the Navy, 2014a, 2014b, 2014c; Department of the Air Force, 2014a; Department of Defense, 2014a. Ships were not assumed to be available in 2020 unless their planned year of commissioning was 2019 or earlier. Planned years of commissioning are listed in Department of the Navy, 2014d.

16 The budget documents issued in March 2014 do not allow for the possible effects of "budget sequestration" mandated by the U.S. Congress's Budget Control Act of 2011. Budget sequestration was imposed in Fiscal Year 2013 (FY2013), reducing the Department of Defense budget by $50 billion. The Bipartisan Budget Act of 2013 suspended sequestration for FY2014 and FY2015, but sequestration could be reimposed after FY2015. The 2020 U.S. force structure projected here assumes that

U.S. Congress acts to remove the sequestration limits or at least continues to suspend them through FY2019. In addition to the possible effects of sequestration, however, if past performance is any guide, the budget documents issued in April 2013 are probably too optimistic in terms of the costs to implement the planned defense program. In 2012, for example, the Congressional Budget Office estimated that the U.S. Defense Department's plan for the FY2013 to FY2017 period would cost 5 percent more to execute than the amount that the Defense Department had actually budgeted. See Congressional Budget Office, 2012, pp. 25–37. The budget for the 2015 to 2019 fiscal years issued in March 2014 is likely too small by a similar amount. The overall effect on the total U.S. inventory in 2020, however, is assumed to be minor. Finally, some acquisition programs that were ongoing in March 2014 will undoubtedly subsequently be canceled. However, since it is impossible to predict which ones will be canceled, all programs underway in 2014 are assumed to continue at least through 2019.

17 The Department of Defense's 2014 Quadrennial Defense Review report states that the U.S. Navy will operate twenty-one Ticonderoga-class cruisers in FY2019, but ten or eleven of the ships will be laid-up for a long-term modernization program and will not have crews. Thus, these ships are assumed to not be available for combat. See Department of Defense, 2014b, p. 40.

18 The Department of Defense's 2014 Quadrennial Defense Review report indicates an intention to reduce the number of fighter aircraft in the U.S. Air Force to 971. See Department of Defense, 2014b, p. 40. This number, however, refers to the "Primary Aircraft Inventory (PAI)" – the number of aircraft funded for full-time operations in a given year. The Air Force typically maintains a greater number of fighters in operational condition but employs them at only about 80 percent of what would be considered a full-time usage rate. Thus, the actual number of operational fighter aircraft, referred to as the "Total Aircraft Inventory (TAI)" is generally about 25 percent greater than the PAI. This table, therefore, shows a total of 1,210 fighter aircraft (F-22s, F-35As, F-15s, and F-16s).

19 The Department of Defense's 2014 Quadrennial Defense Review report indicates that the U.S. Air Force will be employing ninety-six bombers in FY2019: 44 B-52s, 36 B-1s, and 16 B-2s. See Department of Defense, 2014b, p. 40. The 2010 Quadrennial Defense Review report, however, also stated that the Air Force would only operate ninety-six bombers. See Department of Defense, 2010, p. 47. In fact, as of 2014, total U.S. Air Force inventory comprised 144 bombers. See IISS, 2014, pp. 51–52. This again reflects the difference between PAI and TAI numbers. Since the number of PAI bombers in the 2014 Quadrennial Defense Review report is unchanged from that in the 2010 report, the total number of bombers actually in the U.S. Air Force inventory in 2020 is assumed to be unchanged from 2014.

20 Department of Defense, 2014b, p. 40, indicates that the U.S. Air Force will operate 54 KC-10s, 54 K-46s, and 335 KC-135s in FY2019. By June 2020, however, an additional ten K-46s are scheduled to be completed. Since the total number of K-46s and KC-135s in FY2019 (389) will be essentially unchanged from 2014

(291, see IISS, 2014, pp. 51-52), ten KC-135s are assumed to be taken out of service during that period, leaving the combined total number of KC-46s and KC-135s in service unchanged.

21 The Department of Defense's 2014 Quadrennial Defense Review report indicates that the U.S. Air Force will be employing 231 MQ-9 and 32 RQ-4 unmanned reconnaissance aircraft in FY2019. See Department of Defense 2014b, p. 40. However, as of 2014 both aircraft were still in production and by the beginning of FY2019 the Air Force is scheduled to have accepted delivery of 273 MQ-9s and forty-five RQ-4s. By June 2020 the Air Force is scheduled to have accepted delivery of 323 MQ-9s and forty-five RQ-4s.

22 The Department of Defense's 2014 Quadrennial Defense Review report indicates that the U.S. Air Force will be employing twenty-seven command and control aircraft in FY2019: eighteen E-3s, six E-8s, and three E-4 Advanced Airborne Command Posts. See Department of Defense, 2014b, p. 40. The 2010 Quadrennial Defense Review report, however, also stated that the Air Force would operate twenty-seven command and control aircraft. See Department of Defense, 2010, p. 47. In fact, as of 2014, total U.S. Air Force inventory comprised thirty-two E-3s and seventeen E-8s (along with four E-4s). See IISS, 2014, pp. 51–52. This again apparently reflects the difference between PAI and TAI numbers. Since the number of PAI command and control aircraft in the 2014 Quadrennial Defense Review report is unchanged from that in the 2010 report, the total number of E-3s and E-8s in the U.S. Air Force inventory in 2020 is assumed to be unchanged from 2014.

23 Specific optical/infrared, synthetic aperture radar, and maritime surveillance satellite programs are not in the public record, but this scenario assumes that in 2020 the United States operates roughly the same number of such satellites as were in operation in 2013.

24 "Destroyers – DDG," undated; "Zumwalt (DDG 1000) Class," 2013. An additional difference in capabilities between the Zumwalt-class and the Arleigh Burke–class and Ticonderoga-class ships will be the Zumwalt-class ships' capability to bombard land targets more than seventy miles away using its two 155 millimeter guns, but this capability does not appear to be relevant to a Chinese invasion of Taiwan.

25 "Littoral Combat Ship Class – LCS," undated; "Independence Class Littoral Combat Ship Flight 0," 2013; "Freedom Class Littoral Combat Ship Flight 0," 2013; "Oliver Hazard Perry Class," 2011; Department of the Navy, 2014d. The antisurface warfare capabilities of these ships will be extremely limited, consisting of ship-launched thirty-three-pound Griffin missiles, helicopter-launched Hellfire missiles, thirty millimeter cannons, and machine guns. See "Independence Class Littoral Combat Ship Flight 0," 2013; "Freedom Class Littoral Combat Ship Flight 0," 2013; "Griffin," 2013. These weapons will be of utility primarily against light boats and fast attack craft, not major warships.

26 Department of the Air Force, 2014a, pp. 8–21.

27 "P-8A Multi-mission Maritime Aircraft (MMA)," undated; Sweetman, 2013; Department of the Navy, 2014a. Estimated delivery dates for the P-8 were not available, but

102 will have been ordered through the end of FY2018. Assuming the average time between when they are ordered and when they are delivered is the same for the P-8 as it is for other aircraft, most of these aircraft should have been delivered by mid-2020.

28 Butler and Sweetman, 2013, pp. 20–23.

29 "Terminal High-Altitude Area Defence," 2013; Department of Defense, 2014a, pp. 3–5.

30 "Standard Missile," undated; "RIM-66/-67/-156 Standard SM-1/-2, RIM-161 Standard SM-3, and RIM-174 Standard SM-6," 2013; Department of the Navy, 2014b, pp. 35–37.

31 "AGM-158 JASSM," 2012; Sweetman, 2013; Department of the Air Force, 2014b, pp. 12, 20, 30, 37. Delivery dates were not available but all JASSM-ERs ordered through the end of FY2019 (i.e., by September 30, 2019) are assumed to have been delivered by mid-2020.

32 See Chapter Five.

33 See Chapter Six.

34 See Chapter Seven.

35 For example, from the port of Xiamen to central Taiwan (e.g., the area around Taichung) is approximately 175 miles. At an average speed of fifteen knots (the top speed of most of China's amphibious landing ships is seventeen to eighteen knots), this would take ten hours to travel. Forces departing from Xiamen, however, would be potentially subject to attack by Taiwan's forces on the island of Jinmen, which is positioned between Xiamen and the open ocean. From the next-nearest major port, and the nearest actual PLA Navy base, Shantou, to central Taiwan is approximately 250 miles. This would take approximately fifteen hours to travel at fifteen knots.

36 Specifically, there are at least sixteen PLA Air Force bases in the Nanjing and Guangzhou MRs that are within five hundred miles of Taiwan. See "China>Air Force," 2013. (Distances are to the point 24.00 degrees north, 121.00 degrees east, approximately in the center of Taiwan, and were estimated using the website www. indo.com/distance/. "China > Air Force," 2013, does not include all military air bases in China as, for example, neither it nor "China > Navy," 2013, lists the obviously military air base at Zhangzhou near Xiamen, but is assumed to include most of them.) Assuming that all the JH-7, Su-27/Su-30/J-11, and J-10 aircraft currently stationed at these bases remain at their current locations, but that in the years or months leading up to 2020 each regiment of J-7, J-8, Q-5, JZ-8 (a reconnaissance version of the J-8), and JJ-7 (a trainer version of the J-7) aircraft currently stationed at these bases is replaced by a regiment of twenty-four J-10s, and that a regiment of twenty-four J-10s is stationed at each PLA Air Force base in the Nanjing or Guangzhou MRs that is within five hundred miles of Taiwan but that at present does not appear to have aircraft permanently stationed there, then there would be sufficient capacity at these bases to support all three hundred J-10s postulated to be available for this conflict. According to "CAC J-10 Meng Long," 2013, the J-10 has

an estimated combat radius of only 345 miles, but this is presumably using internal fuel only, as the F-16, an aircraft of comparable size and performance, has a combat radius of 845 miles when carrying one thousand gallons of external fuel. See "Lockheed Martin F-16 Fighting Falcon," 2012. The J-10 has an estimated maximum internal fuel storage capacity of about thirteen hundred gallons. Assuming that a combat radius of 345 miles reflects 60 percent of the fuel being consumed in transit, with another 30 percent of the fuel available for combat maneuvers and a 10 percent safety reserve, and that, because of the increased drag caused by external fuel tanks, each gallon of external fuel is only half as efficient as a gallon of internal fuel, then to increase the J-10's combat radius by 155 miles (i.e., total transit distance by 310 miles), would require about five hundred gallons of external fuel, which would weigh about thirty-three hundred pounds – well within the J-10's maximum payload of 14,500 pounds (some of this payload capacity would be devoted to the weapons the J-10 carried, but, since the J-10 would be performing purely air-to-air combat initially, these weapons would weigh much less than the remaining 11,200 pounds of payload capacity). The external fuel tanks would be emptied and jettisoned before the aircraft reached the area of combat, to avoid compromising the aircraft's performance during combat.

There are an additional seventeen PLA Air Force bases in the Nanjing and Guangzhou MRs that are more than five hundred miles but less than 750 miles from Taiwan. Assuming that all the H-6, Su-30, KJ-2000 aircraft currently stationed at these bases remain at their current locations but that, in the years or months leading up to the conflict, each regiment of J-7, J-8, or JJ-7 currently stationed at these bases is replaced by a regiment of twenty-four Su-27s, Su-30s, J-11s, or J-20s, and that a regiment of twenty-four Su-27s, Su-30s, J-11s, or J-20s is stationed at each of these bases that at present does not appear to have aircraft permanently stationed there, then there would be sufficient capacity at these bases to support all 325 Su-27s, Su-30s, J-11s, and J-20s postulated to be available for this conflict. The Su-27, Su-30, and, presumably, the J-11 that is based on them, all have combat radii of more than nine hundred miles. See "Sukhoi Su-27," 2013 and "Sukhoi Su-30M," 2013. The J-20 is assessed to be an even longer-range aircraft with a combat radius of at least eleven hundred miles. See Kopp, 2011. Thus, all of these aircraft would easily be able to engage in air-to-air combat over Taiwan from these bases without needing to be refueled en route.

37 Since so little information about China's counterspace systems is publicly available, Chapter Four did not provide estimates of the numbers of ground-launched anti-satellite missiles, co-orbital satellite interceptors, ground-based antisatellite lasers, and high-power microwave beams China might have in 2020. The numbers of each of these types of systems shown in Table 9.2, therefore, are arbitrary.

38 A similar proportion of PLA Navy ships would presumably also be unavailable at any given time. However, this scenario assumes that the 20 percent undergoing long-term overhaul are included within the one-third of all PLA Navy ships that are withheld from the Taiwan operation.

39 The Japanese Ground Self-Defense Forces also operate Patriot batteries at various locations in Japan, including near the joint U.S.-Japanese air base at Misawa and at the JASDF bases of Naha on Okinawa and Chitose on Hokkaido. Each Japanese battery consists of five launchers with a total inventory of about eight missiles per launcher. See "Japan > Air Force," 2013; "MIM-104 Patriot," 2013.

40 This would represent a very large-scale commitment of U.S. naval forces and would severely reduce the number of ships available for normal peacetime operations in other parts of this world. The assumption of this scenario, however, is that, with China mobilizing an even greater proportion of its own naval and air forces, the United States is preparing for a full-scale, albeit geographically confined, war with China.

41 Amphibious assault carriers would normally carry six F-35Bs, along with about twenty helicopters used primarily for transporting and supporting the marines carried onboard the ship. In this scenario, the amphibious assault carriers are assumed to be used primarily as small aircraft carriers, and therefore to have removed some of the helicopters to provide room for additional F-35s, and to have a minimal onboard marine contingent.

42 Okinawa is just more than four hundred miles from China, and some versions of the DF-15, have ranges of five hundred miles or more, as does the reported DF-16 SRBM, which might enter service by 2020. See "DF-15 (CSS-6/M-9)," 2012, and "DF-16," 2012. Distances estimated using Google Earth.

43 "Kadena Air Base," undated.

44 "Marine Aircraft Group 36," undated. Currently two squadrons of V-22 tiltroter aircraft are based at Futenma.

45 The U.S. Air Force air base at Kunsan in South Korea is closer to the Taiwan Strait than Iwakuni but, as stated in note 6, the South Korean government is assumed to not grant permission for U.S. forces based in South Korea to participate in this conflict.

46 "DF-21 (CSS-5)," 2013.

47 Based on Google Earth images dated April 2012, Iwakuni appeared to have at least eight potential aircraft parking areas that could be approximated by rectangles of dimensions 2,000 feet by 300 feet, 700 feet by 750 feet, 650 feet by 350 feet, 750 feet by 1,450 feet, 400 feet by 350 feet, 750 feet by 200 feet, 1,200 feet by 150 feet and 400 feet by 400 feet. Also, construction was underway on what might have been an additional parking area of about 1,800 feet by 750 feet. In addition, aircraft could potentially be dispersed along the two 9,200 taxiways parallel to the main runway, along a 4,100-foot segment of what appeared to be an abandoned runway, and along a 5,300-foot segment of a taxiway parallel to that runway. Stillion and Orletsky, 1999, pp. 11–15, postulates that a missile could carry one-pound submunitions, each with a lethal radius of approximately twenty feet, whose total weight would equal about 75 percent of the weight of a unitary warhead carried by the same missile. The DF-21 has an estimated payload of six hundred kilograms (see "DF-21 (CSS-5)," 2013). If we assume, therefore, that it carries $600 \times 0.75 \times 2 = 900$ half-kilogram

(since China uses the metric system) submunitions, and that these submunitions are released in a uniform pattern with each submunition five meters from the six nearest other submunitions, then they will cover a roughly circular area about 293 meters (960 feet) in diameter. Virtually all aircraft in such an area would be within the lethal radius of at least one submunition (even allowing for some irregularity in the distribution because of wind and imperfections in the release mechanism, as well as the likelihood that some submunitions would fail to detonate), and therefore highly likely to be damaged or destroyed. A total of approximately forty-five such DF-21 missiles would be sufficient to cover all possible parking areas at Iwakuni (indeed, the entire base could be covered by about seventy missiles, regardless of how large the actual parking areas within it were). Assuming, as per Stillion and Orletsky, 1999, a warhead reliability rate of 85 percent, then more than 80 percent of the aircraft parked at Iwakuni would be unusable or destroyed after such an attack.

48 As of 2014, there was one squadron of twelve Marine Corps F/A-18s permanently stationed at Iwakuni and usually a second squadron deployed there on a temporary basis. In 2017, however, a squadron of sixteen F-35B short takeoff/vertical landing aircraft will be deployed to Iwakuni. See Butler, 2013a, p. 43. This scenario assumes that the F/A-18s currently stationed at Iwakuni will be withdrawn at the time the F-35Bs are deployed, and that, at the time of the conflict, the F-35Bs stationed at Iwakuni have all been embarked onboard U.S. amphibious assault carriers.

49 Based on Google Earth. This requires that the DF-21s be based in northeastern Jilin province and overfly North Korea. Under international law, this would be a violation of North Korea's neutrality in the conflict. The scenario being examined here assumes (1) that Beijing would be willing to accept any resulting political repercussions and (2) that this violation of North Korea's neutrality would not cause Pyongyang to join in the conflict on the side of the United States, Japan, and Taiwan.

50 Based on Google Earth.

51 See Shlapak et al., 2009, pp. 45–46.

52 Based on analysis using Google Earth. At points during the Vietnam War, more than 120 B-52 heavy bombers were based at Andersen. E.g., see Tilford, 1991, pp. 255, 262.

53 Based on Google Earth. Distances are great circle route distances. Actual flying distances would be somewhat greater unless Indonesia granted overflight rights, which would make it a combatant in this conflict under international law and seems unlikely in this scenario.

54 These aircraft would generally not fly to the Taiwan Strait, of course, but rather to patrol or refueling stations well away from China's coast.

55 An alternative approach would be to conduct a blockade of Taiwan and attempt to force the island into submission by cutting off its access to imported food, energy, and so forth. Although a successful blockade could indeed eventually force Taiwan to surrender, historically blockades have taken a very long time – years, typically – to succeed. See Glosny, 2004. Assessing whether China would be capable of

successfully blockading Taiwan would represent analysis of a different scenario, but in any case the assumption of the present scenario is that the Chinese leadership, even if they believed a blockade to be feasible, are unwilling to wait the time needed for one to succeed.

56 Zhang, Yu, and Zhou, 2006, pp. 316–330.

57 Zhang, Yu, and Zhou, 2006, pp. 316–330.

58 Zhang, Yu, and Zhou, 2006, pp. 322–323.

59 Zhang, Yu, and Zhou, 2006, pp. 323–330.

60 See Cliff et al., 2011, pp. 165–178. Since heavy combat forces are not parachute-deployable, the purpose of the airborne assault would be to aid the amphibiously landed forces in breaking out of their beachheads, interdicting Taiwanese counter-attacks against the beachheads, or seizing a port or airfield through which add-itional combat forces could be brought to Taiwan.

61 *Campaign Studies* describes the targets that would be attacked, but not the order in which they would be attacked or with what assets. A RAND study on Chinese air force operations (Cliff et al., 2011) describes the likely sequence of operations and targets for the PLA Air Force in an air superiority campaign, but has no information on how these would be coordinated with the actions of assets con-trolled by other services, such as the ballistic missiles and GLCMs operated by the Second Artillery Force.

62 Given the threat posed by U.S. nuclear attack submarines and other dangers, this scenario assumes that the PLA Navy would, at least initially, keep its own carriers close to China's coast and on the periphery of the conflict where they would force the U.S. to devote assets to tracking their location and hedging against an incursion by them while limiting their vulnerability to U.S. attack.

63 E.g., see Libicki, 2011, p. 3.

64 On the use of cyber warfare in recent conflicts, see Healey, 2013, esp. pp. 164–231.

65 Satellites, because they travel in repeating and, therefore, highly predictable orbits, are relatively easy to intercept under normal circumstances. However, China would not be able to attack all U.S. satellites simultaneously with ground-launched antisatellite missiles since not all U.S. satellites would be passing over Chinese territory at the same time. Once U.S. satellite operators realized that their satellites were under attack, they would likely begin regularly slightly changing their orbits before they passed over Chinese territory. These slight changes would likely be sufficient to cause an antisatellite missile to be unable to intercept the satellite if launched based on the last-known orbital parameters. After each orbital maneuver, it would take some time (at least several orbital passes) for Chinese satellite-tracking radars and telescopes to reacquire a satellite and determine its new orbital param-eters, at which point the satellite might change its orbit again. (Each orbital change would consume some of the satellite's onboard fuel, which is needed to periodically reboost the satellite in response to the friction caused by the residual amount of atmosphere at the altitude at which imagery satellites orbit. Thus, the numerous orbital changes involved in preventing the satellite from being intercepted would

significantly shorten the operational lifetime of the satellite. The satellites are assumed to have enough onboard fuel, however, to remain in orbit for the duration of the conflict.) The net effect of these actions and counteractions is represented in simplified form in this scenario by saying that half of the antisatellite missile attacks miss and that it takes the PLA several days to expend all of its antisatellite missiles. The precise number of satellites destroyed does not have a significant effect on the overall outcome of this scenario.

66 This scenario assumes that China in 2020 does not possess high-altitude antisatellite missiles or "co-orbital" antisatellite weapons capable of intercepting and disrupting or destroying other satellites in higher orbits, although, as of 2014, there was evidence that China was attempting to develop such a capability. See Smith, 2013; Weeden, 2014.

67 See "Global Positioning System (GPS)/Navstar Constellation," 2012.

68 As of 2013, 40 percent of U.S. satellite-relayed military communications were relayed by commercial satellites and this proportion was projected to increase to 68 percent in the future. See Butler, 2013b, p. 56.

69 These satellites, of course, would generally be available to China as well. China could also attempt to deny U.S. access to these satellites by, before the conflict, signing leases on their transponders so that there would be no additional transponders available for the United States to use.

70 "Taiwan Deploys Advanced Early Warning Radar," 2013.

71 "AN/FPS-115 'Pave Paws' Radar," 2005.

72 The newest versions of the DF-15 (DF-15B) are estimated to have a "circular error probable" (CEP – the radius of a circle centered on the target within which the warhead would have a 50 percent probability of landing) of about sixteen feet, meaning that they will strike within sixteen feet of their aim points 50 percent of the time. See "DF-15 (CSS-6/M-9)," 2012. If the aim point was the exact center of the radar, the missile would have to miss by more than three times this distance to miss the radar entirely. This of course assumes that the DF-15B is as accurate as estimated *and* that the location of the radar in three-dimensional space relative to the launch point of the missile is known with precision.

73 If each missile had an 80 percent probability of striking the radar, two missiles would have a 96 percent chance that at least one of them would strike the radar $(1 - (0.2)^2 = 0.96)$ and three missiles would have a more than 99 percent chance of hitting it $(1 - (0.2)^3 = 0.992)$.

74 "MIM-104 Patriot," 2013.

75 If the Taiwanese military frequently relocated its Patriots in the days leading up to the attack, their positions might not be known at the time of the ballistic missile attacks, in which case they might survive the initial attacks. However, since the Patriot cannot fire while being relocated and some time is required to deploy it again once it reaches a new firing location, it would also not be capable to intercepting missiles or aircraft initially.

76 "PAC-3," 2013; "Terminal High-Altitude Area Defence," 2013.

77 Each THAAD battery has six launchers, each with eight ready rounds. Since missile defense firing doctrine generally allocates two interceptors to each incoming missile, this implies a maximum of twenty-four intercepts. It is conceivable that, faced with a large volley of ballistic missiles, the THAAD operators could opt to use only one interceptor per incoming missile, accepting a lower probability of success with each intercept. It seems unlikely, however, that THAAD could conduct forty-eight intercepts in the approximately two minutes in which the missiles would be within its engagement envelope. Thus, THAAD is assumed to be capable of intercepting no more than twenty-four missiles from a single volley. Even twenty-four successful intercepts is probably highly optimistic for THAAD. However, since THAAD has no combat record to suggest its actual effectiveness, PLA planners would need to allow for the possibility that THAAD performed as well as theoretically possible.

78 The best approach would be to first launch a salvo of forty-five missiles at the THAAD battery. If 20 percent of the missiles failed or went off course, there would still be thirty-six missiles headed at the THAAD battery, of which at most thirty-two could be intercepted by THAAD and the four Patriot batteries, ensuring that at least four would get through and put the THAAD system out of action with a high degree of confidence. At this point a second salvo of twenty missiles could be launched, five at each of the four Patriot batteries. Again assuming that 20 percent of these missiles failed or went off course, there would still be an average of four headed at each Patriot battery. It is possible that one or two Patriots might survive such an attack, but the effect of the remaining Patriots on subsequent salvos of missiles launched at the base would be minor.

79 "Japan > AIR FORCE," 2013.

80 If 20 percent of the missiles failed or went off course, there would still be thirty-two missiles headed at the THAAD battery, of which at most thirty could be intercepted by THAAD and the three Patriot batteries, ensuring that at least two would get through and put the THAAD system out of action with a high degree of confidence.

81 Each squadron is assumed to consist of twenty F-2s (see note 89, below), of which sixteen (80 percent) are available for combat each day (a typical "readiness rate" for military aircraft). The endurance of the F-2 is not publicly available, but the F-16, on which the F-2 is based, has a range of two thousand miles, about 60 percent of 3,450 mile range of the F-15, which has a published endurance of five hours and fifteen minutes. See "F-16 Fighting Falcon" 2012; "F-15 Eagle," 2012; "Boeing (McDonnell Douglas) F-15 Eagle," 2013. Assuming the optimum cruising speeds are about the same for the two aircraft, this would imply that the F-2 has an unrefueled endurance of about three hours. Since Misawa is 160 miles from Matsushima, the aircraft would spend approximately fifteen minutes in transit each way. If they stayed on patrol until they had only an hour and fifteen minutes of fuel left (i.e., until they could use an hour's worth of fuel in combat and still have enough to fly home), then each aircraft would spend an hour and a half on patrol each flight. Since each flight would last only two hours, each aircraft is assumed to

be able to perform four such flights each day (i.e., to spend a total of eight hours flying each day, a good but not spectacular sortie rate).

82 "Mitsubishi F-2," 2012.

83 Personal communication from John Stillion, Center for Strategic and Budgetary Assessments.

84 Cruise missiles have smaller radar cross-sections than aircraft and fly closer to the ground, making them harder to detect and track. On the other hand they represent no threat to intercepting aircraft and thus the intercepting aircraft can engage it from the optimal relative position for a missile launch without putting itself at risk. In addition, cruise missiles do not maneuver or employ other countermeasures in an attempt to evade an incoming air-to-air missile. Since the net effect of these differences is unclear, the AAM-4 and AIM-120 are assumed to have approximately the same probability of successful intercept against cruise missiles as the AIM-120 has demonstrated against manned aircraft.

85 "Japan > Air Force," 2013; "MIM-104 Patriot," 2013.

86 The Patriot does not have a significant combat record against aircraft or cruise missiles (the only aircraft known to have been shot down by a Patriot being a British Tornado GR4 and a U.S. Navy F/A-18C in "friendly fire" incidents in Iraq in 2003 and no engagements against cruise missiles are known to have occurred) and a 60 percent success rate would be far greater than surface-to-air missiles have historically demonstrated. However, the AIM-120 air-to-air missile has also performed far better than older generations of radar-guided air-to-air missiles such as the AIM-7 Sparrow, which had a success rate of 8 percent during the Vietnam War (personal communication from John Stillion, Center for Strategic and Budgetary Assessments). Thus, it is not unreasonable to assume that the Patriot, being similarly modern, would perform roughly as well as the AIM-120.

87 If 55 of 240 CJ-10s were shot down, then the probability of any given missile not being shot down would be 185/240 = 0.77. Assuming that each missile that was not shot down had a 70 percent probability of hitting and rendering a shelter unusable, then the probability that a given missile would hit and destroy a shelter would be 0.77 × 0.7 = 0.54. The probability that at least one of the four missiles fired at each shelter would destroy it would be 1 minus the probability that none of four missiles fired at the shelter hit it (i.e., there are two possibilities – either none of the missiles hits the shelter and renders it unusable or at least one does): $1 - (1 - 0.54)^4 = 0.955$. Thus, on average, 60 × 0.955 = 57 shelters would be rendered unusable.

88 In this scenario, seventy-two F-35As are based at Misawa. Because of the long transit times between Misawa and Taiwan (a minimum of about two and half hours each way, not including diversions to refuel), the most efficient way to use these aircraft would be for them to remain aloft for the maximum amount of time normally allowed for U.S. Air Force fighter pilots in a single flight – twelve hours – periodically refueling them with tanker aircraft. Assuming that each aircraft is able to conduct one twelve-hour flight per day, and that 80 percent of them are able to fly on any given day, then on average twenty-nine of them would be in the air at any

one time, with the remaining forty-three on the ground. This means that each shelter would have a 43/60 = 0.72 probability of holding an aircraft. Assuming that a shelter being rendered unusable would also render any aircraft inside unusable, if fifty-seven shelters were destroyed, on average 0.72 × 57 = 41 aircraft would be destroyed with them.

89 Japan has an estimated two hundred operational F-15Js divided among ten squadrons, suggesting that each squadron has about twenty aircraft. See "Japan > Air Force," 2013. If 20 percent of a squadron's aircraft were unavailable on any given day because of maintenance problems, then the two squadrons would have an average of about thirty-two aircraft available for combat each day. If we assume that F-15Js have the same endurance as F-15C/Ds (five and a quarter hours), that, as with Japan's F-2s, the aircraft land when they have only an hour of fuel remaining, and that each aircraft is able to make two such flights per day, and that transit time to and from Komatsu would occupy fifteen minutes of each flight (Gifu is only seventy-five miles from Komatsu), then there would be an average of 32 × 4 × 2/ 24 = 10.7 of them in the air at any one time.

90 Japan's F-15Js were originally equipped to carry four AIM-7 Sparrow radar-guided air-to-air missiles, and U.S. F-15s now carry eight AIM-120s. The AAM-4 is intermediate in weight between the AIM-7 Sparrow and AIM-120, so each F-15J is assumed to be able to carry six AAM-4s. See "Boeing (Mitsubishi) F-15J Eagle," 2013; "Boeing (McDonnell Douglas) F-15 Eagle," 2013; "AIM-7 Sparrow," 2013; "AIM-120 AMRAAM (Advanced Medium Range Air-to-Air Missile)," 2013; "Type 99 (AAM-4)," 2013.

91 The probability of a given missile not being shot down would be 16/56 = 0.29. Assuming that each missile that was not shot down had a 70 percent probability of hitting and rendering a shelter unusable, then the probability that a given missile would hit and destroy a shelter would be 0.29 × 0.7 = 0.20. The probability that at least one of the four missiles fired at each shelter would destroy it would be 1 − (1 − 0.2)^4 = 0.59. Thus, on average, 14 × 0.59 = 8.3 shelters would be rendered unusable. Assuming 80 percent readiness and that, as at Misawa, each F-35 performs a single twelve-hour flight per day (Komatsu is somewhat closer to Taiwan than Misawa, but transit time would still be at least two hours each way), then on average ten aircraft would be in the air at any one time, with the remaining fourteen on the ground.

92 If, on a typical day, 20 percent of the aircraft were unable to conduct flight operations because of maintenance problems, that would leave ninety-six F-22s and eighty KC-135s able to fly that day. It would take the F-22s about four hours to fly from Guam to Taiwan, including "stops" for refueling from tanker aircraft, and four hours to fly back. If the F-22s spent four hours flying combat air patrols after arriving over Taiwan, the total time in the air would be twelve hours, the maximum normally allowed for U.S. Air Force fighter pilots on a single flight. After returning to Guam, each F-22 is assumed to require about twelve hours on the ground for maintenance and refueling before being able to take off again. The KC-135s, as large aircraft with more than one pilot, would be allowed to stay in the air

for a longer period, but it is assumed that after each flight they would need to spend a proportionately longer period on the ground for maintenance, with the result that, on average, they also would spend about half of their time in the air and half of their time on the ground. Thus, in any twenty-four-hour period, ninety-six of the F-22s and eighty of the KC-135s would spend about twelve hours in the air and twelve hours on the ground, and the remaining twenty-four F-22s and twenty KC-135s that were unable to conduct flight operations that day would spend the entire twenty-four hours on the ground. This would result in an average of seventy-two F-22s and sixty KC-135s being on the ground at any one time.

93 Based on Google Earth and assuming the warhead on the intermediate-range missile is approximately the same size as that on the medium-range DF-21.

94 Reloading and repositioning the PLA's conventional ballistic missile launchers is assumed to take approximately eight hours.

95 As noted earlier, F-15C/Ds have an endurance of five and a quarter hours. If each combat air patrol lasted four and a quarter hours (i.e., the aircraft landed when they had one hour of fuel remaining) and each operationally available aircraft conducted two such patrols each day, then each operationally available aircraft would spend about 35 percent of a day in the air. If 80 percent of the fifty-four F-15s at Kadena were available on a given day, then on average $54 \times 0.80 \times 0.35 = 15.1$ would be in the air at a time.

96 "Japan > Air Force," 2013; Ministry of Defense, Part II, Chapter 5, Section 1.

97 If we assume, as before, that each operationally available F-15J at Naha conducts two combat air patrols each day, that 80 percent of them are available on any given day, and that the aircraft land when they have only an hour of fuel remaining, then there would be an average of $32 \times 4.25 \times 2/24 = 11.3$ of them in the air at any one time. Since Naha is only thirteen miles from Kadena, the aircraft can begin protecting Kadena virtually as soon as they are airborne.

98 If forty of sixty CJ-10s were shot down, then the probability of any given missile being shot down would be $40/60 = 0.67$. Assuming that each missile that was not shot down had a 70 percent probability of hitting and destroying its target, then the probability that a given missile would hit and destroy a shelter would be $(1 - 0.67) \times 0.70 = 0.23$. The probability that at least one of the four missiles fired at each shelter would destroy it would be $1 - (1 - 0.23)^4 = 0.65$. Thus, on average, $15 \times 0.65 = 9.8$ shelters would be destroyed. The Patriots at Kadena are assumed to have been put out of action by ballistic missile attacks and, because cruise missiles fly close to the ground, the Japanese Patriots at Naha are assumed to be unable to engage them.

99 Assuming an 80 percent readiness rate, thirty-two F-15Js would be available for combat on any given day. If, as before, each flight lasts four and a quarter hours, then each F-15J would be conducting combat air patrols for three and a half hours per flight, as it would take twenty to twenty-five minutes each way to fly the 230 miles from Akita to the area around Chitose. Thus, at any given time there would be $32 \times 3.5 \times 2/24 = 9.3$ F-15Js conducting combat air patrols.

100 The nine F-15Js would shoot down an average of $9 \times 6 \times 0.6 = 32.4$ CJ-10s. The three JASDF Patriot batteries would have a total of sixty missiles available to fire. Assuming a 60 percent intercept rate, they would shoot down another thirty-six CJ-10s. The probability of a given CJ-10 reaching its target, therefore, would be $(112 - 32.4 - 36)/112 = 0.39$ and, assuming that 70 percent of CJ-10s that reached their targets destroyed them, the probability of a given shelter being destroyed would be $1 - (1 - 0.39 \times 0.7)^4 = 0.72$. Since the transit times from Chitose to Taiwan would be more than three hours, each F-35A at Chitose is assumed to conduct one twelve-hour flight per day. Assuming an 80 percent readiness rate for the forty-eight F-35As based at Chitose in this scenario, this would mean that nineteen of them would be in the air at any given time, leaving twenty-nine on the ground – more than the number of shelters at Chitose.

101 Shlapak et al., 2009, p. 62.

102 The PLA could also attempt to damage the runways at the air bases in Japan being used by U.S. aircraft but, given the PLA's more-limited inventory of medium-range ballistic missiles, these would be more effectively used to attack unprotected aircraft at those air bases.

103 See "DF-15 (CSS-6/M-9)," 2012.

104 According to Shlapak et al., 2009, Figure 3.4 (p. 41), three missiles with a CEP of eighty-two feet (twenty-five meters) would have a roughly 90 percent probability of successfully damaging a given section of runway, four such missiles would have a roughly 95 percent probability, and five such missiles would have a roughly 99 percent probability. For runways of nine thousand feet or less, damaging the runway at its approximate midpoint would be sufficient to prevent it from being usable until the runway was repaired, as fighter jets need at least five thousand feet of usable runway to take off and land. Runways longer than nine thousand feet would need to be targeted in two places to ensure that no undamaged segment of five thousand or more feet remained after the attack. Taiwan's three air bases with a single runway of nine thousand feet or less, therefore, could each be put out of action with 90 percent confidence by three missiles, but its six air bases with either a single runway longer than nine thousand feet or two runways of less than nine thousand feet would each require eight missiles to be put out of action with 90 percent confidence. This is because for a runway to be damaged in two places, or for two runways to both be damaged, with at least 90 percent confidence, requires that each aim point have a 95 percent probability of being damaged ($0.95 \times 0.95 = 0.90$). For Taiwan's one air base with two runways longer than nine thousand feet (Tainan), approximately twenty missiles would be required ($0.99^4 = 0.96$). See Shlapak et al., 2009, pp. 41–42. Thus, a total of seventy-seven missiles would be required to put Taiwan's ten air bases out of action with a probability of at least 90 percent each. On average, therefore, such an attack would leave Taiwan with only one of its ten air bases still operational. (Specifically,

there would be a 35 percent probability that none of Taiwan's air bases would still be operational, a 39 percent probability that only one would still be operational, and a 26 percent probability that two or more would still be operational.)

105 If we assume an 80 percent readiness rate for Taiwan's 280 fighters and that each flies two two-hour combat air patrols per day (F-16s have a maximum in-air endurance of about three hours – F-CK-1s, which are also single-engine fighters but weigh about 73 percent as much as an F-16, carry about 65 percent as much fuel internally, and are therefore assumed to also have a maximum in-air endurance of about three hours), then an average of thirty-seven would be in the air at the time of the missile attack, of which about four would be from the one air base still operational after the ballistic missile attack. The average air base would have twenty-eight fighters, so the thirty-three fighters from the nine nonoperational air bases would be added to those based at the one still-operational base, for a total of about sixty-one. (Given Taiwan's small geographic size, all fighters are assumed to be in range of the one still-operational base and able to land there after the ballistic missile attack. This is probably optimistic for Taiwan given the chaos and confusion that would undoubtedly follow the ballistic missile attack and some aircraft would probably run out of fuel or have to land on highways or civilian airfields where they would be out of action until they could refuel and return to one of Taiwan's air force bases. However, the overall outcome of this scenario is not highly sensitive to this assumption.)

106 It would take approximately one day for the equipment and ground crews needed to fuel, arm, and maintain the F-35s to be flown in and begin operating.

107 The F-22s, with their ability to cruise at Mach 1.2, would be able to make the transit in somewhat less time than the F-35s, although they would still have to slow down twice each way to refuel. The overall effect of the greater transit speed of the F-22s on the number of aircraft the U.S. would be able to maintain over Taiwan, however, would be minor.

108 After its initial attacks, the PLA would no longer have the capability to attack Guam with land-based missiles, as its conventionally armed intermediate-range ballistic missiles would all be expended and its ground-launched land-attack cruise missiles would not have the range to reach Guam. The PLA could, however, attempt to attack Guam with land-attack cruise missiles launched by H-6 bombers. Such an operation would be quite risky for the bombers. If they attempted to pass between Taiwan and the main islands of Japan, they would risk being intercepted by U.S. fighters operating over Taiwan or transiting between Taiwan and Japan. Alternatively, they could attempt to pass through the Strait of Luzon south of Taiwan, but they would have to pass within about 160 miles of Taiwan (the Balintang Channel appears to have a half-mile wide corridor of international airspace – passage farther south would entail violating Philippine airspace) and thus could be intercepted by U.S. fighters operating over Taiwan. China would also have to divert fighters from the battle for air

superiority over Taiwan to escort the bombers, otherwise the bombers would be highly vulnerable to interception.

109 Since the roughly four-hundred-mile transit from Kadena to Taiwan and back would require an additional hour of flying time each way, total flying time would be six hours per flight. Since this exceeds the maximum duration of the F-15, the F-15s would need to be refueled at some point during their patrols.

110 The transit time to and from Komatsu would be about three hours. If each F-35 based at Komatsu spent four hours patrolling over Taiwan, total flight time would be about ten hours, as compared to twelve hours for aircraft flying from Guam. Each F-35 based at Komatsu is therefore assumed to be able to fly once every twenty hours. Transit times from Misawa and Chitose would be closer to four hours, therefore each F-35 operating from these bases is assumed to fly once every twenty-four hours.

111 The F/A-18E/F has an endurance of two hours and fifteen minutes when flying combat air patrols (see "Boeing F/A-18 Super Hornet," 2014). Assuming an 80 percent readiness rate and that each aircraft flies two self-protection combat air patrols a day, a total of twenty-seven aircraft would be needed to keep an average of four aircraft in the air at all times ($27 \times 0.8 \times 2.25 \times 2 / 24 = 4$). This would leave forty-eight F-35Cs, forty-five F-35Bs, and one hundred F/A-18E/Fs available for flying combat air patrols over Taiwan.

112 Assuming a readiness rate of 80 percent and that each aircraft is able to make one nine-hour flight (five hours in transit to and from the carrier and four hours on station over Taiwan) per day. This represents a lower operational rate than U.S. Air Force aircraft are assumed to be able to sustain from land bases (nine out of twenty-four hours instead of twelve out of twenty-four hours), but U.S. aircraft carriers generally operate on a "twelve hours on, twelve hours off" system. That is, the carrier conducts high-intensity air operations for about twelve hours, then ceases for the next twelve hours so that the flight deck crews can rest. (If multiple carriers are present, their schedules are staggered so that at any one time about half of the carriers are conducting flight operations.) Thus, in any twenty-four-hour period, an aircraft would only be able to perform one nine-hour flight.

113 These numbers assume that sufficient aerial refueling aircraft are available to support these fighters (and the E-2, E-3, F/A-18G, and RC-135 aircraft also needed to support them). Confirming whether the remaining ninety-five KC-135, thirty-six KC-10, and forty-five KC-46 aircraft available to the United States in this scenario (in addition to the one hundred KC-135s operating from Guam, which are assumed to be needed to support the F-22s and F-35As based there) would be able to support these operations when flying out of locations such as Australia goes beyond the scope of this analysis but would be an important check on the validity of its findings.

114 Not including its forty-four carrier-based J-15s.

115 The PLA Navy has another 160 JH-7s available to it, but these are assumed to be configured for naval strike missions, not ground attack.

116 In this scenario, U.S. fighter aircraft also conduct at most two flights a day, but each such flight is allowed to last up to six hours. The PLA's flights to Taiwan from various bases in mainland China, however, would only take two or three hours per flight.

117 See Cliff et al., 2011, pp. 85–115, for a description of how the PLA would conduct an offensive air campaign.

118 E.g., by U.S. E-3 or Taiwanese E-2 aircraft operating east of Taiwan.

119 Given that subsequent raids would be arriving every four hours, Taiwan would not be able to send this many fighters to meet every raid, since that would imply six flights per day for each operational aircraft. As will be seen, however, by the time of the next raid, the aircraft sent to meet it will likely be coming from a different air base.

120 The PLA's JH-7s are assumed to be focused on their ground attack missions and to have negligible air-to-air combat capability.

121 This may not seem enough of an advantage for these aircraft, which are far more expensive than their predecessors. Historically, however, qualitative advantages of even this magnitude in fighter aircraft have rarely been observed. At the end of World War II, for example, the German Luftwaffe formed an elite unit of highly experienced pilots and Me-262 jet fighters, the most advanced fighter aircraft of the time, called Jagdverband 44. Based on its combat record, each aircraft in this unit had an effective combat power equivalent to 3.01 allied fighters. Personal communication from John Stillion, Center for Strategic and Budgetary Assessments.

122 China is assumed to devote all of its J-20s to offensive operations. Thus, China's 120 fighters would consist of an average of ten J-20s and 110 J-10s, J-11s, Su-27s, and Su-30s. Since Taiwan has 210 F-16s and seventy F-CK-1s initially, thirty-six of its forty-eight fighters are assumed to be F-16s and twelve are assumed to be F-CK-1s.

123 If we consider China's total air-to-air combat power to be "100," then a 50 percent advantage for United States and Taiwan would mean that their combined air-to-air combat power was about "150." If an air-to-air combat power of 150 caused losses of "5" to a force with an air-to-air combat power of 100, then an air-to-air combat power of 100 should cause losses of $100/150 \times 5 = 3.3$ to an air-to-air combat power of 150. Losses of 3.3 out of 150 are $3.3/150 = 2.2\%$.

124 This may be optimistic for Taiwan, given that the Chinese fighters would outnumber the U.S. and Taiwanese fighters.

125 Such as the YJ-91. See "YJ-91 (KR-1/Kh-31P/AS-17 'Krypton')," 2012.

126 If we assume that each JH-7 carries two KD-88 air-to-surface missiles, that it fires them both at a single shelter, and that each missile has a 70 percent probability of destroying its target, then the probability of a targeted shelter being destroyed is $1 - (1 - 0.7)^2 = 0.91$. Thus, fourteen JH-7s would be expected to destroy $14 \times 0.91 = 12.7$ shelters. Since sixty aircraft would be using Taiwan's one operational air base, that would mean that 220 aircraft were spread among the other nine bases, or an average of about twenty-four aircraft per base. If each base other than Chia Shan or Taitung, where aircraft are stored in mountainside tunnels that are virtually

invulnerable to attack by conventional weapons, has fifty shelters on average, then approximately 48 percent of the shelters at bases where aircraft are unable to fly due to runway damage will contain aircraft. Assuming the JH-7s concentrate their attacks on such air bases, then 13 x 0.48 = 6.2 of the destroyed shelters will contain aircraft.

127 Since seventy of the PLA's 220 SRBM launchers are deployed to Zhejiang province and dedicated to attacking Okinawa in this scenario, only 150 would be available for attacking Taiwan. To fire a salvo of seventy-five missiles every four hours thus assumes that each missile launcher can be reloaded and repositioned for firing at least once every eight hours.

128 Taiwan begins the conflict with 280 fighters. The first air raid results in the loss of one of Taiwan's fighters in air-to-air combat and six are destroyed on the ground, leaving 273, or an average of about twenty-seven at each of Taiwan's ten airfields.

129 If the twenty-five F-15s that survived the initial ballistic missile attack on Kadena had a readiness rate of 80 percent, then an average of ten would be in the air at any given time (each of the twenty operational aircraft flies two six-hour sorties a day, meaning that they spend half of their time in the air). This would leave fifteen F-15s on the ground, five of them in shelters and ten parked in the open. Of the ten parked in the open, approximately 80 percent (eight) would be destroyed by the second ballistic missile attack. If the probability of each of the five still-usable shelters being destroyed is, as before, 0.65, then an average of three shelters, each with an F-15 inside, would be destroyed. The fourteen surviving F-15s would be able to keep an average of $14 \times 0.80 \times 4 \times 2/24 = 3.7$ aircraft in the air over Taiwan at a time.

130 Of the thirty-one F-35s at Misawa, an average of twelve would be in the air at any one time, leaving nineteen on the ground, with three in the three surviving shelters and the remaining sixteen parked in the open. Of the seventy missiles launched at Misawa, 20 percent (fourteen) are assumed to fail or fly off course, and the three JASDF Patriot batteries at Misawa are each assumed to intercept one of the remaining 56 missiles. Thus, each of the sixteen F-35s parked in the open would have a $53/70 = 0.76$ probability of being hit by a submunition.

131 Of the twenty-eight F-35s at Chitose, an average of eleven would be in the air any one time, leaving seventeen on the ground, with eight in the eight still-usable shelters and the remaining nine parked in the open. Of the sixty-five missiles launched at Chitose, 20 percent (thirteen) are assumed to fail or fly off course, and the three JASDF Patriot batteries at Chitose are each assumed to intercept one of the remaining fifty-two missiles. Thus, each of nine F-35s aircraft parked in the open would have a $49/65 = 0.75$ probability of being hit by a submunition, meaning that, on average, seven would be damaged or destroyed. Each individual CJ-10 would, as before, have a 0.39 probability of destroying a shelter, meaning that each of eight surviving shelters would have a 0.73 probability of being destroyed resulting in an average of six shelters (each with an F-35 inside) being destroyed. If the PLA

had intelligence about which shelters were still usable after the first attack (e.g., from satellites or human agents near Chitose), fewer CJ-10s could be used.

132 Of the nineteen surviving F-35s at Misawa, an average of eight would be in the air at any one time, leaving eleven on the ground, with three in the three still-usable shelters and the remaining eight parked in the open. Of the seventy missiles launched at Misawa, 20 percent (fourteen) are assumed to fail or fly off course, and the three JASDF Patriot batteries at Misawa are each assumed to intercept one of the remaining fifty-six missiles. Thus, each of the eight F-35s parked in the open would have a $53/70 = 0.76$ probability of being hit by a submunition.

133 "C-602 (HN-1/-2/-3/YJ-62/X-600/DH-10/CJ-10/HN-2000)," 2012.

134 Two CJ-10s are launched at each aim point at Chitose. As before, the F-15Js and Patriots defending Chitose respectively intercept thirty-two and thirty-six CJ-10s. Thus, given an 80 percent reliability rate, a given missile would have a probability of $(1 - 68/260) \times 0.8 = 0.59$ of hitting its aim point. The probability of at least one of the two missiles hitting its aim point would be $1 - (1 - 0.59)^2 = 0.83$. Assuming an 80 percent readiness rate, six of the fifteen F-35s still operating at Chitose would be in the air at any one time, leaving nine on the ground. Of these, two would be parked inside the two remaining usable shelters, leaving seven parked in the open. Those parked in the open would each have a 0.83 probability of being destroyed by a missile, meaning that, on average, $7 \times 0.83 = 5.8$ would be destroyed.

135 Based on Google Earth, approximately fifty-five CJ-10s would be required to cover all of the parking areas at Komatsu (including those at the small commercial airport that shares a runway with the JASDF base, which would probably have to suspend operations during the conflict). If two CJ-10s were launched at each aim point in the parking areas in Komatsu and two more were launched at each of the fourteen shelters at Komatsu (assuming the PLA did not have accurate information on which of the fourteen had already been destroyed), then a total of 138 missiles would be needed. Of these, forty would be intercepted by the F-15Js patrolling near Komatsu, meaning that a given missile would have a probability of $(1 - 40/138) \times 0.8 = 0.57$ of reaching its aim point. The probability of at least one of the two missiles hitting its aim point would be $1 - (1 - 0.57)^2 = 0.81$. Assuming an 80 percent readiness rate, five of the twelve F-35s still operating at Komatsu would be in the air at any given time, on average, meaning that seven would be on the ground. Of these, two would be parked inside the two remaining usable shelters, leaving five parked in the open. Those parked in the open would each have a 0.81 probability of being destroyed by a missile meaning that, on average, $5 \times 0.81 = 4.0$ would be destroyed. The two shelters with aircraft parked inside would each have a 0.81 probability of being hit by a missile which would have a 0.7 probability of destroying it, meaning that, on average, $2 \times 0.81 \times 0.7 = 1.1$ additional aircraft would be destroyed inside of a shelter.

136 With the exception of the U.S. Marine Corps F-35Bs operating from the amphibious assault carriers, which would not be replaced, as the only other short

takeoff/vertical landing aircraft available, the A/V-8, has very limited air-to-air combat capabilities.

137 As noted at the beginning of this section, the PLA is assumed to devote a third of its fighters to defensive combat air patrols over mainland China. If the PLA maintained this ratio throughout the conflict, then, as fighters flying offensive missions were shot down or otherwise destroyed, some of them would be replaced by fighters that had previously been flying defense combat air patrols. Specifically, every time three fighters flying offensive missions were shot down, they would be replaced by one fighter that had been flying defensive combat air patrols. Thus, the loss of every three offensive fighters would reduce the number of fighters flying offensive missions by only two. Nonetheless, this drawdown rate would be significantly faster than that of the U.S., which in most cases would be replacing a lost aircraft by one either equally capable or at least two-thirds as capable.

138 Two additional factors would contribute to this result. First, whereas most U.S. aircraft would participate in only one combat per day (the exceptions being those flying from Kadena and Komatsu), each PLA aircraft would participate in two. Thus, each aircraft lost by the PLA would have twice the impact as an equivalent aircraft lost by the United States. Second, as noted at the beginning of this section, the PLA's weakness in repair and maintenance would result in fewer and fewer aircraft being available each day, apart from combat losses. Note that this result assumes that the United States has sufficient air-to-air missiles available to continue to fight effectively over many days.

139 For a discussion of the challenges the U.S. military encountered in attempting to carry out such an operation against Serbian forces in 1999, see Hosmer, 2001, pp. 82–85.

140 While in port, the amphibious ships would be particularly vulnerable to attack, as they would be stationary and easily attacked by precision-guided weapons such as JASSM. For this reason, the amphibious ships might be loaded with troops, equipment, and supplies before the initiation of hostilities, and patrol up and down along China's coast under cover of China's navy and aircraft. If so, this would be further reason for a fairly rapid invasion of Taiwan, as the forces could not easily be sustained at sea indefinitely.

141 From a point fifty thousand feet above sea level, a straight line to the earth's horizon touches down 275 miles away. Radar waves are refracted by the earth's atmosphere, however, with the effect that the radar horizon is somewhat farther away, as if the radius of the earth were about a third greater than it actually is. As a result, the radar horizon from fifty thousand feet is about 315 miles away.

142 Butler and Sweetman, 2013, pp. 20–23.

143 Submarines patrolling north and south of the Taiwan Strait might also detect the approach of the invasion fleet, although they would have to trail an antenna on the ocean's surface to communicate their discovery, risking revealing themselves.

144 Half of the thirteen Los Angeles–class, ten Virginia-class, and two Seawolf-class submarines are assumed to succeed in intercepting Chinese landing convoys

headed toward Taiwan. PLA Navy antisubmarine forces (ships and helicopters) escorting each convoy are assumed to sink or drive away half of the approximately six Los Angeles–class submarines that succeed in intercepting convoys and 20 percent of the much-stealthier five Virginia and one Sea Wolf–class submarine that succeed in intercepting convoys. Each submarine is assumed to launch two torpedoes at each landing ship (submarine sonar operators would be able to identify the amphibious landing ships by the sounds of their propellers) and to use 80 percent of the torpedoes it carries (twenty-six in the case of Los Angeles–class submarines, thirty-eight for the Virginia class, and fifty for the Seawolf class). Modern torpedoes are extremely lethal and generally a single hit would be sufficient to sink or disable a ship the size of landing ship. (During World II, an average of 1.3–1.4 torpedoes were required to put a fifteen-thousand-ton ship out of action; see Hughes, 2000, p. 157. Modern torpedoes, however, are designed to explode deep below the keel of the target ship, creating a water jet that often causes the target ship to split in half and sink after a single hit.) If we assume that each torpedo has a 0.70 probability of hitting and sinking or disabling a landing ship, then each pair of such torpedoes would have a 0.91 probability of putting its target out of action. Thus, the three Los Angeles–class submarines that succeeded in intercepting convoys and avoiding being sunk or driven off would be able to sink or disable $3 \times 20/2 \times 0.91 = 27.3$ landing ships; the four Virginia-class submarines would be able to sink or disable $4 \times 30/2 \times 0.91 = 54.6$ landing ships; and the one Seawolf-class submarine be able to sink or disable $1 \times 40/2 \times 0.91 = 18.2$ landing ships. Collectively these would total one hundred of the 180 landing ships.

145 In 2020 this will primarily be the Joint Standoff Weapon (JSOW), a guided glide bomb that has a range of up to 80 miles and of which the U.S. Navy will possess more than five thousand in 2020. See "AGM-154 JSOW (Joint Standoff Weapon) and JSOW-ER," 2013 and Department of the Navy, 2014b. By 2020, however, the U.S. Navy and U.S. Air Force may have begun to field a longer-range antiship missile based on the AGM-158B JASSM-ER, which has a range of approximately six hundred miles. See "LRASM Missiles: Reaching for a Long-Range Punch," 2014 and "AGM-158A JASSM (Joint Air-to-Surface Standoff Missile), AGM-158B JASSM-ER and LRASM," 2014. This system would potentially enable U.S. forces to attack Chinese ships from locations outside of the range of Chinese fighters and ship-based surface-to-air missiles.

146 Taiwan's naval forces are assumed to be patrolling east of Taiwan and, when the approach of the Chinese invasion fleet was detected, to attempt to close with and interdict it. It is not clear that this effort would be effective, however. For Taiwan's navy to stay out of range of the PLA's land-based naval strike aircraft, its ships would need to stay about nine hundred miles away from the Taiwan Strait. At that distance it would take more than a day for them to steam to within range of the Taiwan Strait, at which point the invasion force would probably already have landed. While en route, moreover, Taiwan's ships would be subject to attack by the PLA Navy's aircraft, submarines, and surface ships, reducing the number of

Taiwanese ships that would actually arrive within range of the Taiwan Strait. If Taiwan chose to keep its ships closer to the Strait, on the other hand, then the PLA would have several days to find and attack them with its aircraft, submarines, and surface ships, with the result that there would probably be very few Taiwanese ships left by the time the invasion fleet began steaming toward Taiwan.

147 "Hsiung Feng 1/2/3 (Male Bee)," 2013, states that some Hsiung Feng 2 missiles are being used for coastal defense and that a mobile launch vehicle has been developed for them, but information on how many such vehicles and missiles are in service is not available.

148 While unloading troops and equipment on Taiwan's beaches, moreover, the landing ships, now stationary targets, would be vulnerable to attacks by precision-guided weapons such as JASSMs carried by B-1s. As noted in Chapter Seven, the PLA would also be able to transport a regiment of paratroopers each day. Unless they landed in a strategic but lightly defended location, however, the main utility of these forces would be to delay any Taiwanese attempts to counterattack the beachhead.

149 The thirteen U.S. attack submarines that did not succeed in intercepting the first wave of landing ships would presumably be available to intercept the second wave (those that did succeed are assumed to have been sunk or expended their torpedoes). If again half of them succeeded in intercepting amphibious ships, they would be able to sink another forty to fifty ships.

150 Assuming that at twenty to twenty five ships were sunk in transit by the three of the six U.S. attack submarines that did not succeed in intercepting any landing ships during the first two trips.

151 E.g., see Banyan, 2014.

152 See Burgess, 2012.

153 "Grounded Ship Is Philippines' Last Line of Defence," 2013; Agence France-Presse, 2013; Calunsod, 2013; Fonbuena, 2013; Banyan, 2014.

154 At an average transit speed of fifteen knots. The most-distant Philippine-held feature, Commodore Reef, is approximately 780 miles from the nearest Chinese naval base (at Sanya, on Hainan Island).

155 "KAI T-50 Golden Eagle," 2012.

156 It is unclear whether, assuming it acquired two additional aircraft carriers by 2020, the PLA would assign all three of them to a single fleet or distribute them between the three fleets. This scenario assumes that at least one carrier is based in the South Sea Fleet but that, even if more than one is based there, the PLA leadership does not commit more than one to the operation on the assumption that the increased tempo of carrier takeoff and landing practice (which would be required in preparation for a military operation) on more than one carrier would be observed by U.S. intelligence and reveal the existence of preparations for a major military operation.

157 See "China > Navy," 2014. In 2020, the South Sea Fleet is assumed to control six Luyang III–class destroyers, four Luyang II–class destroyers, fourteen Jiangkai II–class frigates, two Jiangwei-class frigates, ten Jiangdao-class corvettes, four Type 093A/095–class nuclear attack submarines, two Shang-class nuclear attack

submarines, four Kilo-class conventionally powered attack submarines, four Yuan-class conventionally powered attack submarines, four Song-class conventionally powered attack submarines, and twenty-two Houbei-class fast attack missile craft.

158 "Yudeng (Type 073III) Class," 2013; "Yuhai (Type 074) (Wuhu-A) Class," 2013; "Yuliang (Type 079) Class," 2013; "Yunshu (Type 073IV) Class," 2013; "Yuting I (Type 072 II) Class," 2013; "Yuting II (Type 072 III) Class," 2013; "Yuzhao (Type 071) Class," 2013.

159 Distance calculated using Google Earth. The Philippine-occupied feature closest to the Chinese landmass is Northeast Cay. Locations of Philippine-occupied islands based on "Spratly Islands," undated.

160 This assumes that no new bases in the region are constructed between 2013 and 2020 and that (1) each regiment of J-7, JJ-7, or J-8 fighters currently based within one thousand miles of the most-distant Philippine-occupied feature, Commodore Reef, is replaced by a regiment of Su-27/Su-30/J-11s or JH-7s; (2) a regiment of Su-27/Su-30/J-11s or JH-7s is stationed at each of the two other PLA Air Force bases within one thousand miles of Commodore Reef (Suixi and Shantou Northeast); (3) the regiment of H-6D naval bombers and regiment of H-6U aerial refueling aircraft currently based at Lingshui and the regiment of JH-7 naval fighter-bombers currently based at Ledong continue to be based there; and (4) a regiment of J-20s is stationed at Nanning Wuxu, approximately 1,080 miles from Commodore Reef. Although there are two other PLA Air Force bases that would be within J-20 range of at least some of the Philippine-held features of the South China Sea, it seems unlikely that the PLA would base more than a third or so of the approximately sixty J-20s it is projected to have in 2020 within a single military region. Chinese air base locations are based on Google Earth and "China > Navy," 2013, and "China>Air Force," 2013.

161 "CNO's Navigation Plan, 2014–2018"; Pellerin, 2014.

162 See "The Carrier Strike Group" for the composition of a typical aircraft carrier strike group.

163 "Kadena Air Base," undated.

164 "Mission," undated.

165 Butler, 2013a, p. 43.

166 Holt, 2013. In the past, B-1 and B-2 bombers have also been deployed to Guam. However, Holt, 2013, implies that only B-52s would be deployed to Guam in the future.

167 "35th Fighter Wing Mission," 2009.

168 "Mission," undated.

169 Zhang, Yu, and Zhou, 2006, pp. 535–538.

170 Since the landing force does not set sail until after the initial clash, it would not reach the Philippine-occupied features until the expiration of the forty-eight hour period in any case.

171 Each of the thirteen Song-class and Yuan-class submarines can attack any ship that passes across a fifty-mile segment – twenty-five miles on either side of the submarine – of the two-thousand-mile arc.

172 Note that if the ships had begun heading directly toward the South China Sea when China's ships left port but before the Chinese ships attacked the Philippine ships, once the conflict began, U.S. military leaders would likely direct the U.S. ships to steam out of range of China's antiship ballistic missiles and JH-7 naval strike aircraft before the U.S. president announced the intention to defend the Philippines with military force.

173 Assuming a steaming speed of twenty knots. An alternative approach would be to begin sailing directly toward the South China Sea as soon as the Chinese fleet was detected leaving port. This would enable the carrier group to arrive in the seas to the east of the northern Philippine island of Luzon, seven hundred to eight hundred miles from the Philippine-held features of the South China Sea, in about three days. This approach, however, would require that the ships sail within range of China's northerly antiship ballistic missile brigade and land-based naval strike aircraft. Detailed analysis of the effects of Chinese ballistic missile, aircraft, and submarine attacks, not reproduced here, suggests that such an approach would likely result in both the fleet carrier based at Yokosuka and the amphibious assault carrier based at Sasebo being put out of action before they reached their destination.

174 The redeployments of the F-35As, P-8s, aerial refueling aircraft, and other support-ing aircraft would require considerable airlift to relocate the personnel, equip-ment, and ordnance needed to fuel, arm, and maintain the aircraft. The transport aircraft needed to relocate these personnel, equipment, and ordnance are assumed to be available.

175 Alternatively, the carrier aircraft could land in the Philippines to refuel. That, however, would potentially put them at risk for attack by the intermediate-range ballistic missiles China possesses in this scenario.

176 Submarine-launched antiship cruise missiles are launched from torpedo tubes. The Song-class, Yuan-class, and Kilo-class all have six torpedo tubes, so each would be able to launch six missiles at a time. The Type 093A– and Type 095–class are assumed to have the same number of torpedo tubes as their predeces-sor, the Shang (Type 093)–class, which has six torpedo tubes as well. See "Song class (Type 039/039G)," 2011; "Yuan class (Type 041)," 2011; "Kilo class (Project 877EKM/636)," 2011; "Shang class (Type 093)," 2011. The launch of the first salvo of missiles would disclose the submarines' positions, particularly that of the Song-class/Yuan-class and Shang-class/Type 093A/Type 095 submarines, which would be less than twenty-five miles away from the carrier group. Disclosing their positions would make these submarines subject to attack by American P-8s and ship-based antisubmarine warfare helicopters. The submar-ines are therefore assumed to be unable to launch a second salvo of antiship cruise missiles.

177 The F/A-18E/F has an endurance of two hours and fifteen minutes when flying combat air patrols. See "Boeing F/A-18 Super Hornet," 2014. If each F/A-18 flies two combat air patrols a day then, assuming an 80 percent readiness rate for the 42 F/A-18s on the carrier, an average of $42 \times 0.8 \times 2.25 \times 2 / 24 = 6.3$ will be in the air at any one

time. Since the F-35C has a combat radius of 690 miles, as opposed to 915 miles for the F/A-18E/F, it is assumed to have an endurance of one hour and thirty minutes when flying a combat air patrol 175 miles from the carrier (the two hours and fifteen minutes endurance for the F/A-18E/F is also based on it being 175 miles from the carrier). See "Lockheed Martin F-35 Lightning II," 2013; "Boeing F/A-18 Super Hornet," 2013. If each F-35C flies two combat air patrols per day, then, assuming an 80 percent readiness rate for the 12 F-35Cs on the carrier, an average of $12 \times 0.8 \times 1.5 \times 2 / 24 = 1.2$ will be in the air at any one time.

178 F/A-18E/Fs are capable of carrying eleven different weapons at a time. A more-typical maritime air superiority load-out, however, is two AIM-9 "Sidewinder" short-range air-to-air missiles and four AMRAAMs. The initial design of the F-35 will only be capable of carrying two AMRAAMs. Thus, between them the six F/A-18s and one F-35 would be carrying about 26 AMRAAMS. See "Boeing F/A-18 Super Hornet," 2013; "Lockheed Martin F-35 Lightning II," 2013.

179 The probability of each missile successfully locking onto a ship is assumed to be 0.8. The AMRAAMs are assumed to have a 0.6 probability of shooting down each of the fourteen YJ-82s that lock onto a ship, but only half that probability (i.e., 0.3) of shooting down each of the five supersonic 3M-54E1s.

180 The carrier group's long-range surface-to-air missiles and short-range air defenses are also assumed to have a combined probability of 0.6 or 0.3 of intercepting the incoming YJ-82s and 3M-54E1s.

181 According to Schulte, 1994, p. 24, on average the equivalent of approximately two Exocet missiles are required to put a ship the size of an Arleigh Burke–class destroyer (more than eight thousand tons) out of action. The YJ-82 has a weight of eighteen hundred pounds and a speed of Mach 0.9, as compared as compared to 1,440 pounds and Mach 0.93 for an Exocet, and thus is roughly equivalent to an Exocet. See "Destroyers – DDG"; "CSS-N-4 'Sardine' (YJ-8/C-801)," 2011; "YJ-82," 2011.

182 The 3M-54 has a weight of 4,230 pounds and a terminal speed of Mach 2.9. If the striking power of a missile is, as Schulte finds, primarily a function of its kinetic energy ($\frac{1}{2}$ mass $\times$ velocity^2), then the 3M-54 would have twenty-nine times the striking power of an Exocet (see Schulte, 1994, pp. 22–30). If, instead, as seems more plausible, the *momentum* of a missile (mass $\times$ velocity) is a better measure of the striking power of an antiship cruise missile, then the 3M-54 would still have nine times the striking power of an Exocet. The largest ship for which Schulte estimates the number of antiship cruise missiles needed to put it out of action is fifteen thousand tons, with Schulte estimating that approximately two Exocet-equivalent missiles would be sufficient, on average. See Schulte, 1994, p. 24. Therefore, although Schulte does not extrapolate his data to a ship the size of a Nimitz-class carrier (97,000 tons), given that the number of missiles needed to put a ship out of action is less than proportional to the size of the ship, it seems likely that a single 3M-54E1 would be sufficient to put even a Nimitz-class aircraft carrier out of action. See "SS-N-27A 'Sizzler' (3M54)," 2012; "Aircraft Carriers – CVN."

183 The probability of the carrier not being hit by either 3M-54E1 would be $0.8 \times 0.8 = 0.64$. The probability that it would be hit by at least one of these missiles, therefore, would be $1 - 0.64 = 0.36$. This assumes the missiles have an equal probability of striking any of the ships in the formation. Although it is possible that the missile would seek the largest ship in the formation (as indicated by the strength of its radar reflection), there would also be significant efforts to jam or spoof the missile's seeker, which would likely make it difficult for the missile to determine which ship was the largest.

184 If the 3M-54E1s struck two of the cruiser and destroyers escorting the carrier, however, then the carrier would be left with a single escort ship.

185 The F/A-18C/D can carry four JSOWs. The F/A-18E/F has a payload approximately twenty-two hundred pounds greater than that of the F/A-18C/D and has two additional locations for carrying external stores. Since a JSOW weighs approximately eleven hundred pounds, the F/A-18E/F should be able to carry two additional JSOWs. See "AGM-154 JSOW (Joint Standoff Weapon) and JSOW-ER," 2013; "Boeing (McDonnell Douglas) F/A-18 Hornet," 2014; "Boeing F/A-18 Super Hornet," 2013.

186 Assuming an operational readiness rate of 80 percent for both sides, nineteen F-22s would be matched against eighteen J-15s. As earlier in this chapter, each fifth-generation F-22 is assumed to be the equivalent of three fourth-generation aircraft such as the J-15.

187 The F/A-18s are assumed to remain outside of the range of the Chinese air defense destroyers escorting the carrier. If the thirty-four operationally available F/A-18s launch all of their JSOWs and each JSOW has a 0.8 probability of hitting one of the ships, then a total of 163 JSOWs will hit ships. If the JSOWs are targeted randomly, then the probability of a given ship not being hit by one will be $(33/34)^{163} = 0.0077$. The JSOW is about 74 percent of the weight of an Exocet but flies 5 percent faster and thus has roughly 80 percent of the destructive power of an Exocet. See "AGM-154 JSOW (Joint Standoff Weapon) and JSOW-ER," 2013. Since most of China's landing ships are less than two thousand tons, a single JSOW hit should be sufficient to put the ship out of action. See Hughes, 2000, p. 160. Even if the ship were not put out of action, however, the casualties to the troops and equipment carried onboard would likely be such that they were no longer combat-effective. The probability that none of the ships would be able to land a combat-effective force, therefore, would be $(1 - 0.0077)^{34} = 0.77$.

188 Assuming 80 percent of the Chinese fighters within range of the landing areas are operational at any given time.

189 Again, assuming sufficient aerial refueling aircraft were available.

190 There would be a combined probability of nearly 50 percent that one of the two carriers would be put out of action.

191 The twenty-five F/A-18s would launch 150 JSOWs. If the JSOWs were targeted randomly against the landing ships and each JSOW had a 0.8 probability of hitting a landing ship and rendering the unit it was carrying combat ineffective, then the

probability that a given ship would not be hit by a JSOW would be $(33/34)^{120}$ = 0.0278. On average, therefore, $34 \times 0.0278 = 0.94$ ships would not be hit by JSOWs.

192　The potential actions of the Los Angeles–class submarine operating in the South China Sea have not been considered so far. Given the dispersion of the landing groups, it would not be possible for the submarine to position itself such that it could attack all of them. It could, however, put itself in position to attack the Chinese LPD group, if the LPD group attempted to conduct landings on one or more of the islands that the initial landing attempt had failed to seize.

193　Of course, the prolonged buildup of tensions would potentially also allow China to attempt to position ships and submarines so that they could launch a large-scale attack on the carrier group(s) at the outset of hostilities. If such an attack succeeded in putting all U.S. carriers in the area out of action, then the landings would likely succeed. Given that U.S. nuclear attack submarines would also be patrolling in the area, however, a significant number of Chinese surface ships might be sunk in the process.

194　See "LRASM," 2013.

195　The LRASM was originally not planned to enter service until 2023. However, recently there have been indications that the system will enter production in 2017, meaning that some (roughly 70) might be available by 2020. See Warwick, 2013; "LRASM Missiles: Reaching for a Long-Range Punch," 2014; Lescher, 2014.

10　Conclusion

1　A partial exception to this generalization might be North Korea, whose leadership has cultivated an image of irrationality that has forced other countries in the region to respond to threats of actions despite the fact that such actions would likely be suicidal for the ruling regime in Pyongyang.

2　"Japan Protests as Record Number of Chinese Ships Converge near Senkakus," 2013.

3　Whitlock, 2014.

4　Pedrozo, 2009, pp. 101–102; Gertz, 2013.

5　Not all of these aircraft would actually be available to participate in combat. Some would be needed, even during a wartime, for training, testing, and as replacements for aircraft lost during the conflict. The U.S. Air Force, for example, plans to have a total of only 971 "combat-coded" fighter aircraft in 2020. See Department of Defense, 2014b, p. 40. However, that would still leave 650 fighters available for other conflicts while a war with China was going on. Although circumstances can change, as of this time it is difficult to imagine what adversary in 2020 would require twice as many fighters to defeat as China.

6　For examples, see Murray, 2008.

7　Butler, 2011.

8　In the author's view, issues such as the defense of Taiwan and of democratic U.S. allies Japan and the Philippines are examples of issues on which the United States will want to stand its ground, but others may differ.

9 Council for Economic Planning and Development, 2012, pp. 51, 183. Because Taiwan's economy has continued to grow since the 1990s, the absolute level of defense spending in Taiwan in 2011 was about the same as in the late 1990s.

10 See Medeiros et al., 2008; Fei, 2011.

11 Some of these responses are beginning to occur. See Medeiros et al., 2008, pp. 49–55; Fei, 2011, pp. 89–97, 116–120; Calunsod, 2013; Mogato and Torode, 2014.

12 Biddle, 2004, pp. 191–192. As Biddle (2004, pp. 192–193) also points out, and this study has reiterated, the concept of a single measure of military capability of a nation that applies in all situations is itself problematic, as the military capability a nation is able to bring to bear will depend on the specific nature and location of the conflict.

13 See Griffith, 1990, pp. 131–135.

Works Cited

"35th Fighter Wing Mission," Misawa Air Base website, October 7, 2009. As of September 23, 2013: www.misawa.af.mil/library/factsheets/factsheet.asp?id=14099

96th Congress. "Taiwan Relations Act," Public Law 96–8, 1979. As of March 23, 2012: www.ait.org.tw/en/taiwan-relations-act.html

"Advance Military Work by Revolving Closely around the Ability to Fight and Win Battles," *Qiushi Online*, February 1, 2013.

Agence France Press, "Philippines: Chinese Military in South China Sea Threatens Peace," June 30, 2013. As of September 18, 2013: www.defensenews.com/article/20130630/DEFREG03/306300006/Philippines-Chinese-Military-South-China-Sea-Threatens-Peace

"AGM-86 Air-Launched Cruise Missile (ALCM) and CALCM," *Jane's Air-Launched Weapons*, February 25, 2013.

"AGM-154 JSOW (Joint Standoff Weapon) and JSOW-ER," *Jane's Air-Launched Weapons*, April 29, 2013.

"AGM-158 JASSM," *Jane's Strategic Weapon Systems*, December 20, 2012.

"AGM-158A JASSM (Joint Air-to-Surface Standoff Missile), AGM-158B JASSM-ER and LRASM," *Jane's Air-Launched Weapons*, May 7, 2013.

"AIDC F-CK-1 Ching Kuo," *Jane's Aircraft Upgrades*, October 24, 2012.

"AIM-7 Sparrow," *Jane's Air-Launched Weapons*, July 15, 2013.

"AIM-120 AMRAAM (Advanced Medium Range Air-to-Air Missile)," *Jane's Air-Launched Weapons*, July 18, 2013.

"Air Expeditionary Force, Air and Space Expeditionary Task Force (ASETF)," Federation of American Scientists website. As of August 11, 2014: http://fas.org/man/dod-101/usaf/unit/aef.htm

"Aircraft Carriers – CVN," United States Navy Fact File, America's Navy website. As of September 20, 2013: www.navy.mil/navydata/fact_display.asp?cid=4200&tid=200&ct=4

Albrecht, Mark. *Labor Substitution in the Military Environment: Implications for Enlisted Force Management.* Santa Monica, CA: RAND Corporation, 1979.

Allen, Kenneth W. "Chinese Air Force Officer Recruitment, Education, and Training," *China Brief*, Volume XI, Issue 22, November 30, 2011a, pp. 9–13.

"Logistics Support for PLA Air Force Campaigns," in Scobell and Wortzel, eds., *China's Growing Military Power*, 2002, pp. 251–306.

The Ten Pillars of the People's Liberation Army Air Force: An Assessment. Washington, DC: Jamestown Foundation, 2011b.

"Amphibious Assault Ships – LHA/LHD/LHA(R)," United States Navy Fact File, America's Navy website. As of July 1, 2013: www.navy.mil/navydata/fact_display. asp?cid=4200&tid=400&ct=4

"Amphibious Transport Dock – LPD," United States Navy Fact File, America's Navy website. As of September 20, 2013: www.navy.mil/navydata/fact_display.asp? cid=4200&tid=600&ct=4

"AN/FPS-115 'Pave Paws' Radar," *Jane's C4ISR & Mission Systems: Land*, June 22, 2005.

"Ankang Class," *Jane's Fighting Ships*, February 15, 2013.

"Annual Data" (年度数据), National Bureau of Statistics of China website. As of August 21, 2014: http://data.stats.gov.cn/workspace/index;jsessionid=C643 B274223070AD9E0090A34DE3B4A3?m=hgnd

"Anwei (Type 920) Class," *Jane's Fighting Ships*, February 15, 2013.

"Arleigh Burke (Flight IIA) Class," *Jane's Fighting Ships*, August 9, 2011.

Armor, David J., Richard L. Fernandez, Kathy Bers, Donna S. Schwarzback, S. Craig Moore, and Leola Cutler. *Recruit Aptitudes and Army Job Performance: Setting Enlistment Standards for Infantrymen.* Santa Monica, CA: RAND Corporation, 1982.

"Army Command Structure," U.S. Army website. As of February 27, 2014: www.army. mil/info/organization/unitsandcommands/commandstructure/

"Attack Submarines – SSN," United States Navy Fact File, America's Navy website. As of September 20, 2013: www.navy.mil/navydata/fact_display.asp?cid=4100&tid= 100&ct=4

Banyan. "The Pressure on the Sierra Madre," *The Economist*, March 22, 2014, p. 46.

Bao Guojun (包国俊). 〈军事科学与时俱进繁荣发展〉 ("Military Science Develops Flourishingly with the Times"), 《解放军报》 [*PLA Daily*], November 26, 2008, p. 3.

Barrett, Lieutenant Colonel Clark C. "Finding The 'Right Way': Toward an Army Institutional Ethic." Carlisle Paper. Carlisle, PA: Strategic Studies Institute, U.S. Army War College, 2012. As of June 22, 2013: www.strategicstudiesinstitute.army. mil/pubs/display.cfm?pubID=1129

"Beidou/Compass Series," *Jane's Space Systems and Industry*, August 31, 2011.

Beland, Russell, and Aline Quester. "The Effects of Manning and Crew Stability on the Material Condition of Ships," *Interfaces*, Vol. 21, No. 4, July–August 1991, pp. 111–120.

Bernstein, Richard, and Ross H. Munro. *The Coming Conflict with China.* New York: Vintage Books, 1998.

Bi Xinglin (薛兴林), ed. 《战役理论学习指南》 [*Campaign Theory Study Guide*]. Beijing: National Defense University Press, 2002.

Bianco, Lucien. *Origins of the Chinese Revolution, 1915–1949.* Stanford, CA: Stanford University Press, 1971.

Bickford, Thomas J. "Searching for a Twenty-first Century Officer Corps," in Finkelstein and Gunness, eds., *Civil-Military Relations in Today's China*, 2007, pp. 171–186.

Biddle, Stephen. *Military Power: Explaining Victory and Defeat in Modern Battle.* Princeton: Princeton University Press, 2004.

"Victory Misunderstood: What the Gulf War Tells Us about the Future of Conflict," *International Security*, Vol. 21, No. 2 (Fall 1996), pp. 139–179.

Biddle, Stephen, Wade P. Hinkle, and Michael Fisherkeller. "Skill and Technology in Modern Warfare," *Joint Forces Quarterly*, Summer 1999, pp. 18–27.

Blasko, Dennis J. *The Chinese Army Today: Tradition and Transformation for the 21st Century*. London and New York: Routledge, 2006.

The Chinese Army Today: Tradition and Transformation for the 21st Century (Second Edition). London and New York, Routledge, 2012.

"PLA Ground Force Modernization and Mission Diversification: Underway in All Military Regions," in Kamphausen and Scobell, eds., *Right-Sizing the People's Liberation Army*, 2007, pp. 281–373.

"PLA Conscript and Noncommissioned Officer Individual Training," in Kamphausen, Scobell, and Tanner, eds., *The "People" in the PLA*, 2008, pp. 99–137.

Blasko, Dennis J., Philip T. Klapakis, and John F. Corbett. "Training Tomorrow's PLA: A Mixed Bag of Tricks," *China Quarterly*, No. 196 (June 1996), pp. 488–524.

"Boeing AH-64 Apache," *Jane's All the World's Aircraft*, February 7, 2013.

"Boeing F/A-18 Super Hornet," *Jane's All the World's Aircraft*, February 7, 2013.

"Boeing (McDonnell Douglas) F-15 Eagle," *Jane's Aircraft Upgrades*, June 27, 2013.

"Boeing (McDonnell Douglas) F/A-18 Hornet," *Jane's Aircraft Upgrades*, March 24, 2014.

"Boeing (Mitsubishi) F-15J Eagle," *Jane's Aircraft Upgrades*, May 1, 2013.

Botelho, Greg. "Tighe Becomes First Woman to Command a Numbered U.S. Navy Fleet," CNN U.S., April 3, 2014. As of August 12, 2014: www.cnn.com/2014/04/03/us/navy-female-commander/

Brune, Sophie-Charlotte, Sascha Lange, and Janka Oertel. *Military Trends in China: Modernising and Internationalising the People's Liberation Army*. Berlin: Stiftung Wissenschaft und Politik, German Institute for International and Security Affairs, February 2010.

Buddin, Richard, Daniel Levy, Janet Hanley, and Donald Waldman. *Promotion Tempo and Enlisted Retention*. Santa Monica, CA: RAND Corporation, 1992.

"Building a New System for Training under Informationization Conditions,"《解放军报》[*PLA Daily*], August 1, 2008.

Bureau of Transportation Statistics, Research and Innovative Technology Administration, U.S. Department of Commerce. "National Transportation Statistics," 2012. As of March 25, 2013: www.rita.dot.gov/bts/sites/rita.dot.gov.bts/files/publications/national_transportation_statistics/index.html

Burgess, Joe. "Territorial Claims in South China Sea," *New York Times*, May 31, 2012. As of September 18, 2013: www.nytimes.com/interactive/2012/05/31/world/asia/Territorial-Claims-in-South-China-Sea.html?_r=0

Burkitt, Laurie, Andrew Scobell, and Larry Wortzel, eds. *The Lessons of History: The Chinese People's Liberation Army at 75*. Carlisle, PA: U.S. Army War College, 2003.

Bush, Richard, and Michael O'Hanlon. *A War like No Other: The Truth about China's Challenge to America*. Hoboken, NJ: John Wiley and Sons, 2007.

Butler, Amy. "Delay Tactics," *Aviation Week and Space Technology*, July 15, 2013a, pp. 42–43.

"Japan Selects F-35," Aviation Week website, December 20, 2011. As of October 3, 2013: www.aviationweek.com/Blogs.aspx?plckBlogId=Blog:27cc4a53-dcc8-42d0-bd3a-01329aef79a7&plckPostId=Blog%3A27cc4a53-dcc8-42d0-bd3a-01329aef79a7Post%3Ac711918b-7a3b-45f5-9486-d4047341b1f1

"Spotty Comms," *Aviation Week and Space Technology*, March 18, 2013b, pp. 56–57.

Butler, Amy, and Bill Sweetman. "Return of the Penetrator," *Aviation Week and Space Technology*, December 9, 2013, pp. 20–23.

Button, Robert W., John Gordon IV, Jessie Riposo, Irv Blickstein, and Peter A. Wilson. *Warfighting and Logistic Support of Joint Forces from the Joint Sea Base*. Santa Monica, CA: RAND Corporation, 2007.

"C-602 (HN-1/-2/-3/YJ-62/X-600/DH-10/CJ-10/HN-2000)," *Jane's Strategic Weapon Systems*, October 24, 2012.

"CAC J-10 Meng Long," *Jane's All the World's Aircraft*, July 3, 2013.

Cai Yingting (蔡英挺) and Zheng Weiping (郑卫平). 〈始终牢记强军之要 加紧推进军事斗争准备〉("Always Bear in Mind the Key to a Strong Military, Push Harder Preparations for Military Struggle"), 《求是理论网》[Seeking Truth Theory Online], March 1, 2013.

Calunsod, Ronron. "Philippines Upgrades Military to End China 'Bullying' in S. China Sea," Kyodo, July 3, 2013.

Cameron, Kim S., and Robert E. Quinn. *Diagnosing and Changing Organizational Culture: Based on the Competing Values Framework* (Third Edition). San Francisco: Jossey-Bass, 2011.

Cary, Bill. "AV-8B Harrier II Retirement Is Stretched to 2030," AIN Online, June 7, 2013. As of August 28, 2014: www.ainonline.com/aviation-news/ain-defense-perspective/2013-06-07/av-8b-harrier-ii-retirement-stretched-2030

Carpenter, Ted Galen. *America's Coming War with China: A Collision Course over Taiwan*. New York: Palgrave Macmillan, 2006.

"CHAIG WZ-10," *Jane's All the World's Aircraft*, June 9, 2011.

Chan, Minnie. "Hu Jintao's Weak Grip on China's Army Inspired President Xi Jinping's Military Shake-Up: Sources," *South China Morning Post*, March 11, 2015.

Chen Shoumin (陈守民) and Wu Tianmin (武天敏). 〈迈开联合训练新步伐－总参探索实践我军信息化条件下联合训练综述〉("Taking New Strides toward Joint Training – Summary of GSD Exploration of and Experimentation with [PLA] Training Under Conditions of Informationization"), 《解放军报》[PLA Daily], January 19, 2009.

Cheng, Dean. Abstract of "Evolving PLA Concepts of Jointness: 'Unified Joint Operations' and 'Coordinated Joint Operations'" (full article is not publicly available). As of July 1, 2011: www.cna.org/sites/default/files/2.pdf

Cheung, Tai Ming. *Fortifying China: The Struggle to Build a Modern Defense Economy*. Ithaca, NY: Cornell University Press, 2008.

"Reforming the Dragon's Tail: Chinese Military Logistics in the Era of High-Technology Warfare and Market Economics," in Lilley and Shambaugh, eds., *China's Military Faces the Future*, 1999, pp. 228–246.

"China > Air Force," *Jane's Sentinel Security Assessment: China and Northeast Asia*, March 1, 2013.

"China > Navy," *Jane's Sentinel Security Assessment: China and Northeast Asia*, September 24, 2014.

"China 2015 Defense Budget to Grow 10.1 pct, Lowest in 5 Years," *China Military Online*, March 5, 2015. As of April 7, 2015: http://eng.chinamil.com.cn/news-channels/2015-03/05/content_6381499.htm

"China Defense Budget to Increase 12.2 pct in 2014," website of the Ministry of National Defense, People's Republic of China, March 5, 2014. As of August 21, 2014: http://eng.mod.gov.cn/DefenseNews/2014–03/05/content_4494705.htm

"China Telecommunications Broadcast Satellite Co (ChinaSat)," *Jane's Space Systems and Industry*, November 29, 2010.

"China to Centralize Military Command to Improve Operations," Reuters, January 3, 2014. As of January 6, 2014: www.reuters.com/article/2014/01/03/us-china-military-idUSBREA0200Y20140103

"China's Russian Kilo Buy May Put Song Submarine Future in Doubt," *Jane's Defence Weekly*, June 6, 2002.

"Chinasat/Zhongxing/STTW series," *Jane's Space Systems and Industry*, July 27, 2011.

"Chinastar (Zhongwei)," *Jane's Space Systems and Industry*, May 5, 2010.

"Chinese Amphibious Assault Vehicle ZBD2000 (ZBD-05)," *Jane's Armour and Artillery*, October 12, 2010.

"Chinese Anti-satellite Test Sets Off Washington's Alarms," *Aerospace Daily and Defense Report*, January 19, 2007, p. 2.

Choi Chi-yuk. "Progress Slow in Developing Fighter Jets, Major General Zhu Heping Says," *South China Morning Post*, April 6, 2013.

Cliff, Roger. "China's Peaceful Unification Strategy," *American Asian Review*, Vol. XIII, No. 4, Winter 1996.

Cliff, Roger, Mark Burles, Michael S. Chase, Derek Eaton, and Kevin L. Pollpeter. *Entering the Dragon's Lair: Chinese Antiaccess Strategies and Their Implications for the United States*. Santa Monica, CA: RAND Corporation, 2007.

Cliff, Roger, John Fei, Jeff Hagen, Elizabeth Hague, Eric Heginbotham, and John Stillion. *Shaking the Heavens and Splitting the Earth: Chinese Air Force Employment Concepts in the 21st Century*. Santa Monica, CA: RAND Corporation, 2011.

Cliff, Roger, and Toy Reid. "Roiling the Waters in the Taiwan Strait," *International Herald Tribune*, March 21, 2006.

"CNO's Navigation Plan, 2014–2018," undated. As of September 20, 2013: www.navy.mil/cno/index.asp

Cohen, Eliot A. "Toward Better Net Assessment: Rethinking the European Conventional Balance," *International Security*, Vol. 13, No. 1, Summer 1988, pp. 50–89.

Cole, Bernard D. *The Great Wall at Sea: China's Navy Enters the Twenty-first Century*. Annapolis, MD: Naval Institute Press, 2001.

——— "The Organization of the People's Liberation Army Navy (PLAN)," in Mulvenon and Yang, eds., *The People's Liberation Army as Organization*, 2002, pp. 458–509.

——— *Taiwan's Security: History and Prospects*. London and New York: Routledge, 2006.

——— *The Great Wall at Sea: China's Navy in the Twenty-first Century*. Annapolis, MD: Naval Institute Press, 2010.

Cole, J. Michael. "Taiwan's "All-Volunteer" Military: Vision or Nightmare?," *The Diplomat*, July 9, 2013.

Combined Arms Tactics Training Bureau, Military Training Department, GSD (总参军训部合同战术训练局). 〈构建训战一致的新模式〉("Construct a New Model of Uniformity Between Training and Warfare"),《解放军报》[*PLA Daily*], August 14, 2001a.

("Integrating Unity and Diversity – Implementing the New Guidance Method"). 《解放军报》[*PLA Daily*], August 28, 2001b.

Commentator (评论员). 〈立足全局规;范我军训练实践〉("Standardize [the PLA's] Training Practices Based on the Overall Situation"),《解放军报》[*PLA Daily*], March 22, 2002.

Congressional Budget Office. *Long-Term Implications of the 2013 Future Years Defense Program*. July 2012.

U.S. Ground Forces and the Conventional Balance in Europe. (Washington, DC: U.S. Government Printing Office, 1988). As of August 4, 2014: https://www.cbo.gov/sites/default/files/cbofiles/ftpdocs/55xx/doc5540/doc01b-entire.pdf

Cooper, Cortez A. "Joint Anti-Access Operations: China's 'System-of-Systems' Approach." Testimony presented before the U.S.-China Economic and Security Review Commission, January 27, 2011.

Corbett, John F., Jr., Edward C. O'Dowd, and David Chen. "Building the Fighting Strength: PLA Officer Accession, Education, Training, and Utilization," in Kamphausen, Scobell, and Tanner, eds., *The "People" in the PLA*, 2008, pp. 139–189.

Cordesman, Anthony H., and Martin Kleiber. *Chinese Military Modernization: Force Development and Strategic Capabilities*. Washington, DC: CSIS Press, 2007.

Council for Economic Planning and Development. *Taiwan Statistical Data Book 2012*. Taipei, Taiwan, 2012.

Council on Foreign Relations. *Chinese Military Power*. New York: Council on Foreign Relations, 2003.

Cordesman, Anthony, and Martin Kleiber. *Chinese Military Modernization: Force Development and Strategic Capabilities*. Washington, DC: Center for Strategic and International Studies, 2007.

Crane, Keith, Roger Cliff, Evan Medeiros, James Mulvenon, and William Overholt. *Modernizing China's Military: Opportunities and Constraints*. Santa Monica, CA: RAND Corporation, 2005.

"Cruisers – CG," United States Navy Fact File, America's Navy website. As of September 20, 2013: www.navy.mil/navydata/fact_display.asp?cid=4200&tid=800&ct=4

"CSS-N-1 'Scrubbrush' (SY-1/HY-1/FL-1); CSS-N-2 'Safflower' CSSC-2 'Silkworm'; CSS-N-3/CSSC-3 'Seersucker' (HY-2/FL-3A)," *Jane's Naval Weapon Systems*, July 4, 2011.

"CSS-N-4 'Sardine' (YJ-8/C-801)," *Jane's Naval Weapon Systems*, July 4, 2011.

"CSS-N-6 (YJ-83/C-802/Noor)," *Jane's Naval Weapon Systems*, July 4, 2011.

"CY-1," *Jane's Naval Weapon Systems*, July 4, 2011.

"Dandao Class," *Jane's Fighting Ships*, February 15, 2013.

"Danlin Class," *Jane's Fighting Ships*, February 15, 2013.

"Dayun (Type 904) Class Supply Ships," *Jane's Fighting Ships*, February 11, 2013.

"Defense Support Program (DSP)," *Jane's Space Systems and Industry*, December 3, 2010.

Deighton, Len. *Blitzkrieg: From the Rise of Hitler to the Fall of Dunkirk*. New York: Knopf, 1979.

Denison, Daniel R. *Corporate Culture and Organizational Effectiveness.* www.deni
sonculture.com, 1997.

Denison, Daniel R., Stephanie Haaland, and Paulo Goelzer. "Corporate Culture and
Organizational Effectiveness: Is Asia Different from the Rest of the World?"
Organizational Dynamics, Vol. 33, No. 1, pp. 98–109, 2004.

Denmark, Abraham M. "PLA Logistics 2004–11: Lessons Learned in the Field,"
in Kamphausen, Lai, and Tanner, eds., *Learning by Doing*, 2012, pp. 297–335.

Department of Defense, "Department of Defense Fiscal Year (FY) 2015 President's
Budget Submission, Missile Defense Agency Defense Wide Justification Book
Volume 2b of 2: Procurement, Defense-Wide," March 2014a. As of August 27,
2014: http://comptroller.defense.gov/Portals/45/Documents/defbudget/fy2015/bud
get_justification/pdfs/02_Procurement/2_PROCUREMENT_MasterJustification
Book_Missile_Defense_Agency_PB_2015_Vol_2.pdf

Department of Defense. *Quadrennial Defense Review 2014.* Washington, DC,
March 2014b. As of August 27, 2014: www.defense.gov/pubs/2014_Quadrennial_
Defense_Review.pdf

Department of Defense. *Quadrennial Defense Review Report.* Washington DC,
February 2010. As of August 28, 2014: www.defense.gov/qdr/images/QDR_as_of_
12Feb10_1000.pdf

Department of Defense Dictionary of Military and Related Terms, Joint Publication
1–02, November 8, 2010 (as amended through 15 May 2011). As of July 1, 2011:
www.dtic.mil/doctrine/new_pubs/jp1_02.pdf

Department of the Air Force. "Department of Defense Fiscal Year (FY) 2015 President's Budget Submission, Air Force Justification Book Volume 1 of 2: Aircraft
Procurement, Air Force," March 2014a. As of September 16, 2014: www.saffm.hq.
af.mil/shared/media/document/AFD-140310-041.pdf

Department of the Air Force. "Department of Defense Fiscal Year (FY) 2014 President's Budget Submission, Air Force Justification Book Volume 1: Missile Procurement, Air Force," March 2014b. As of September 12, 2014: www.saffm.hq.af.
mil/shared/media/document/AFD-140310-044.pdf

Department of the Navy. "Department of Defense Fiscal Year (FY) 2015 President's
Budget Submission, Navy Justification Book, Volume 1 of 4: Aircraft Procurement, Navy, Budget Activity 01–04," March 2014a. As of August 29, 2014: www.
finance.hq.navy.mil/FMB/15pres/APN_BA1–4_BOOK.pdf

Department of the Navy. "Department of Defense Fiscal Year (FY) 2015 President's
Budget Submission, Navy Justification Book, Volume 1: Weapons Procurement,
Navy," March 2014b. As of September 12, 2014: www.finance.hq.navy.mil/fmb/
15pres/WPN_BOOK.PDF

Department of the Navy. "Fiscal Year (FY) 2015 Budget Estimates, Justification of
Estimates: Shipbuilding and Conversion, Navy," March 2014c. As of August 29,
2014: www.finance.hq.navy.mil/FMB/15pres/SCN_BOOK.pdf

"Department of the Navy Core Values Charter." Department of the Navy Legal
Community Public Website. As of June 22, 2013: http://ethics.navy.mil/content/
corevaluescharter.aspx

"Destroyers – DDG." United States Navy Fact File, America's Navy website, undated.
As of June 27, 2013: www.navy.mil/navydata/fact_display.asp?cid=4200&tid=900
&ct=4

"DF-11 (CSS-7/M-11)," *Jane's Strategic Weapon Systems*, June 21, 2011.

"DF-25," *Jane's Strategic Weapon Systems*, June 21, 2011.

"DF-15 (CSS-6/M-9)," *Jane's Strategic Weapon Systems*, August 12, 2012.

"DF-16," *Jane's Strategic Weapon Systems*, September 5, 2012.

"DF-21 (CSS-5)," *Jane's Strategic Weapon Systems*, June 12, 2013.

Dictionary Editing Office, Language Research Institute, Chinese Academy of Social Sciences (中国社会科学院语言研究所词典编辑室). 《现代汉语词典》 (*Modern Chinese Dictionary*). Beijing: Commercial Printing House, 2002.

Directory of PRC Military Personalities. 2003. No publication information provided.

Directory of PRC Military Personalities. 2010. No publication information provided.

"Dock Landing Ship – LSD," United States Navy Fact File, America's Navy website. As of September 20, 2013: www.navy.mil/navydata/fact_display.asp?cid=4200&tid=1000&ct=4

DOD Dictionary of Military and Associated Terms, Joint Publication 1–02, November 8, 2010, as amended through October 15, 2013. As of January 3, 2014: www.dtic.mil/doctrine/dod_dictionary/acronym/d/18303.html

Dong Guishan (董贵山). 〈在化解难题中推进联合训练〉 ("Push Forward Joint Training While Solving Difficult Problems"), 《解放军报》 [*PLA Daily*], November 26, 2009, p. 10.

Dong Wenjiu (董文久) and Su Ruozhou (苏若舟).〈新的军事训练与考核大纲颁发〉 ("New Military Training and Evaluation Guidelines Issued"), 《解放军报》 [*PLA Daily*], August 10, 2001.

Doyle, Mary Anne. *Youth vs. Experience in the Enlisted Air Force: Productivity Estimates and Policy Analysis*. Santa Monica, CA: RAND Corporation, 1998.

Dreyer, June Teufel. "The New Officer Corps: Implications for the Future," *China Quarterly*, Vol. 146, June 1996, pp. 315–335.

Dumbaugh, Kerry. "Tibet: Problems, Prospects, and U.S. Policy." Congressional Research Service, July 30, 2008.

Dumond, John, Marygail K. Brauner, Rick Eden, John Folkeson, Kenneth Girardini, Donna Keyser, Eric Peltz, Ellen M. Pint, and Mark Y.D. Wang. *Velocity Management: The Business Paradigm That Has Transformed U.S. Army Logistics*. Santa Monica, CA: RAND Corporation, 2001.

Dunn, Walter S., Jr. *Soviet Blitzkrieg: The Battle for White Russia, 1944*. Mechanicsburg, PA: Stackpole Books, 2008.

Encyclopedia of China's Air Force Editorial Committee. *Encyclopedia of China's Air Force*. Beijing: Aviation Industry Press, 2005.

Encyclopedia of China's Navy 《中国海军百科全书》. Beijing: Haichao Press, 1999.

Epstein, Joshua M. *Strategy and Force Planning: The Case of the Persian Gulf*. Washington, DC: Brookings Institution, 1987.

Erickson, Andrew S., and Lyle J. Goldstein, eds. *Chinese Aerospace Power: Evolving Maritime Roles*. Annapolis, MD: Naval Institute Press, 2011.

Erickson, Andrew S., Lyle J. Goldstein, and Carnes Lord, eds. *China Goes to Sea: Maritime Transformation in Comparative Historical Perspective*. Annapolis, MD: Naval Institute Press, 2009.

Erickson, Andrew S., Lyle J. Goldstein, William Murray, and Andrew Wilson, eds. *China's Future Nuclear Submarine Force*. Annapolis, MD: Naval Institute Press, 2007.

"F-15 Eagle," Official Web Site of the U.S. Air Force, May 21, 2012. As of July 30, 2013: www.af.mil/information/factsheets/factsheet.asp?id=101

"F-16 Fighting Falcon," Official Web Site of the U.S. Air Force, May 21, 2012. As of July 30, 2013: www.af.mil/information/factsheets/factsheet.asp?id=103

Fabey, Michael. "China Unfurls," *Aviation Week & Space Technology*, July 28, 2014, pp. 37–38.

Fan Changlong (范长龙). 〈贯彻大纲"知"纲为要〉("In Implementing the Guidelines, 'Knowing' the Guidelines is Necessary"),《解放军报》[*PLA Daily*], January 9, 2002.

Fang Wei (房炜). 〈大学生士兵职业生涯规;划教育探析〉("Examination of Career Planning Education for College Student Soldiers")《安徽警官职业学院学报》(*Journal of Anhui Vocational College of Police Officers*), No. 6, 2010, pp. 67–71.

"Fanhui Shi Weixing 3 (FSW-3)/JianBing-4 Series," *Jane's Space Systems and Industry*, June 17, 2010.

"FDNF Ships," Commander Fleet Activities Sasebo website. As of September 20, 2013: www.cnic.navy.mil/regions/cnrj/installations/cfa_sasebo/about/fdnf_ships.html

Fei, John F. "Beyond Rivalry and Camaraderie: Explaining Varying Asian Responses to China." PhD Dissertation, Pardee RAND Graduate School, 2011.

"Fei Teng Guided Bombs (FT-1, FT-2, FT-3, FT-5, FT-6)," *Jane's Air-Launched Weapons*, January 25, 2011.

"Feng Huo (Zhongxing 2X/ShenTong Series)," *Jane's Space Systems and Industry*, May 5, 2010.

Finkelstein, David M. "China's National Military Strategy: An Overview of the "Military Strategic Guidelines." Kamphausen and Scobell, eds., *Right-Sizing the People's Liberation Army*, 2007, pp. 69–140.

"Commentary on Doctrine." Mulvenon and Yang, eds., *Seeking Truth from Facts*, 2001, pp. 119–130.

Finkelstein, David M., and Kristen Gunness, eds. *Civil Military Relations in Today's China: Swimming in a New Sea*. Armonk, NY: M. E. Sharpe, 2007.

"First Flight for Second Chinese Stealth Aircraft," *Aviation Week and Space Technology*, November 5, 2012.

Fisher, Richard. *China's Military Modernization: Building for Regional and Global Reach*. Santa Barbara, CA: Praeger, 2008.

Fitzsimmons, Scott. *Mercenaries in Asymmetric Conflicts*. Cambridge: Cambridge University Press, 2013a.

"When Few Stood Against Many: Explaining Executive Outcomes' Victory in the Sierra Leonean Civil War," *Defence Studies*, Vol. 13, Issue 2, 2013b, pp. 245–269.

Flanagan, Stephen J. and Michael E. Marti, eds. *The People's Liberation Army and China in Transition*. Washington, DC: National Defense University Press, 2003.

"Fleet Information," Commander, Navy Region Hawaii website. As of October 3, 2014: www.cnic.navy.mil/regions/cnrh/about/fleet_information.html

Fonbuena, Carmela, "Up to 5 Chinese Ships Circling Panatag, Ayungin," Rappler. com, August 28, 2013. As of September 18, 2013: www.rappler.com/nation/37520-chinese-ships-panatag-ayungin

Frankenstein, John. "China's Defense Industries: A New Course?" Mulvenon and Yang, eds., *The People's Liberation Army in the Information Age*, 1999, pp. 187–216.

Fravel, M. Taylor. "The Evolution of China's Military Strategy: Comparing the 1987 and 1999 Editions of *Zhanluexue*." Mulvenon and Finkelstein, eds., *China's Revolution in Doctrinal Affairs*, 2005, pp. 79–99.

"Freedom Class Littoral Combat Ship Flight o," *Jane's Fighting Ships*, April 10, 2013.

"Frequently Asked Questions," U.S. Navy website. As of March 2, 2015: https://www.navy.com/faq.html

Friedberg, Aaron L. "The Assessment of Military Power: A Review Essay," *International Security*, Vol. 12, No. 3, Winter 1987–1988, pp. 190–202.

"Fuchi (Type 903) Class," *Jane's Fighting Ships*, February 14, 2013.

Fuell, Lee. "Broad Trends in Chinese Air Force and Missile Modernization." Presentation to the U.S.-China Economic and Security Review Commission, January 30, 2014.

Fulghum, David A., Bill Sweetman, Bradley Perrett, and Robert Wall. "China's Stealth Aircraft Program Will Face Advanced Defenses," *Aviation Week and Space Technology*, January 17, 2011, p. 20.

"Fundamental Basis for [PLA] Operational Training in the New Period"〈新时期我军作战训练的基本依据〉,《解放军报》[*PLA Daily*], January 25, 1999.

Gan Peirong (甘培荣) and Wang Desong (王德松).《抓好大学生士兵入伍训练教育管理》("Take Charge of Induction Training, Education, and Management for College Student Soldiers")《政工学刊》(*Journal of Political Work*), No. 9, 2010, pp. 36–37.

Garnaut, John. "The Rot Inside," *The Age*, April 14, 2012, p. 16.

Geller, Daniel S., and J. David Singer. *Nations at War: A Scientific Study of International Conflict*. Cambridge: Cambridge University Press, 1998.

"GeoEye Series," *Jane's Space Systems and Industry*, May 5, 2010.

Gerlach, James M. *A Comprehensive Officer Sabbatical Program: Rethinking the Military Officer Career Path*. Carlisle Barracks, PA: U.S. Army War College, 2009.

Gertz, Bill. "China Begins to Build Its Own Aircraft Carrier," *Washington Times*, August 1, 2011a. As of December 14, 2011: www.washingtontimes.com/news/2011/aug/1/china-begins-to-build-its-own-aircraft-carrier/?page=all

"Inside the Ring," *Washington Times*, March 10, 2011b.

"Inside the Ring: New Naval Harassment in Asia," *Washington Times*, July 17, 2013.

The China Threat: How the People's Republic Targets America. Washington, DC: Regnery, 2000.

"Global Positioning System (GPS)/Navstar Constellation," *Jane's Space Systems and Industry*, October 22, 2012.

Glosny, Michael A. "Strangulation from the Sea? A PRC Submarine Blockade of Taiwan," *International Security*, Vol. 28, No. 4, Spring 2004, pp. 125–160.

Godwin, Paul H. B "From Continent to Periphery: PLA Doctrine, Strategy and Capabilities towards 2000." *China Quarterly*, No. 146 (June 1996a), pp. 464–487.

"'PLA Incorporated': Estimating China's Military Expenditure." Segal and Yang, eds., *Chinese Economic Reform*, 1996b, pp. 55–77.

"Compensating for Deficiencies: Doctrinal Evolution in the Chinese People's Liberation Army: 1978–1999." Mulvenon and Yang, eds., *Seeking Truth from Facts*, 2001, pp. 87–118.

"PLA Doctrine and Strategy: Mutual Apprehension in Sino-American Military Planning." Flanagan and Marti, eds., *The People's Liberation Army and China in Transition*, 2003, pp. 261–284.

Goldstein, Avery. "First Things First: The Pressing Danger of Crisis Instability in U.S.-China Relations," *International Security*, Vol. 37, No. 4, Spring 2013, pp. 49–89.

Gons, Eric Stephen. "Access Challenges and Implications for Airpower in the Western Pacific." PhD Dissertation, Pardee RAND Graduate School, 2011.

Graaf, Gjalt de. "Causes of Corruption: Towards a Contextual Theory of Corruption," *Public Administration Quarterly*, Spring 2007, pp. 39-86.

"Griffin," *Jane's Weapons: Naval*, January 4, 2013.

Griffith, Paddy. *Forward into Battle: Fighting Tactics from Waterloo to the Near Future* (Revised Edition). New York: Ballantine Books, 1990.

"Grounded Ship Is Philippines' Last Line of Defence," AFP, May 23, 2013.

Gruss, Mike. "U.S. State Department: China Tested Anti-satellite Weapon," *Space News*, July 28, 2014.

Gu Boliang (顾伯良) and Su Ruozhou (苏若舟). 〈新年度训练教学有新目标〉 ("Training and Teaching in the New Year Have New Targets"),《解放军报》 [*PLA Daily*], February 2, 2001.

Gu Qingren (谷庆仁) and Liu Feng'an (刘逢安). 〈全军开展贯彻军事训练与考核大纲专项执法监察〉 ("Entire PLA Initiates Legal Inspection of Implementation of Special Topics of Military Training and Evaluation Guidelines"),《解放军报》 [*PLA Daily*], May 13, 2011.

Gunness, Kristen A. "Educating the Officer Corps: The Chinese People's Liberation Army and Its Interactions with Civilian Academic Institutions," in Finkelstein and Gunness, eds., *Civil Military Relations in Today's China*, 2007, pp. 187–201.

Gunness, Kristen A. and Fred Vellucci. "Reforming the Officer Corps: Keeping the College Grads In, the Peasants Out, and the Incompetent Down," in Kamphausen, Scobell, and Tanner, eds., *The "People" in the PLA*, 2008, pp. 191–231.

Guo Jianyue (郭建跃). 〈机关基础训练，一个都不能少〉 ("Training in Staff Headquarters, Everyone Is Required"),《解放军报》 [*PLA Daily*], May 9, 2011.

"HAI (Eurocopter) Z-9 Haitun," *Jane's All the World's Aircraft*, June 9, 2011.

Hagt, Eric, and Matthew Durnin. "Space, China's Tactical Frontier," *Journal of Strategic Studies*, Vol. 34, No. 5, October 2011, pp. 733–761.

"HAIC Q-5," *Jane's Aircraft Upgrades*, February 9, 2011.

Hammon, Colin, and Stanley Horowitz. *Relating Flying Hours to Aircrew Performance: Evidence for Attack and Transport Missions*. Washington, DC: Institute for Defense Analyses, IDA Paper P-2609, June 1992.

Flying Hours and Crew Performance. Washington, DC: Institute for Defense Analyses, IDA Paper P-2379, March 1990.

"Han Class (Type 091/091G)," *Jane's Fighting Ships*, February 11, 2011.

Harrison, Todd. *Analysis of the FY 2012 Defense Budget*. Washington, DC: Center for Strategic and Budgetary Assessments, 2011. As of March 27, 2012: www.csbaonline. org/publications/2011/07/analysis-of-the-fy2012-defense-budget/

He Diqing (何涤清).《战役学教程》 [*Textbook on Campaign Studies*]. Beijing: Military Science Press, 2001.

Headquarters, Department of the Army. *The Army*. Field Manual No. 1. Washington, DC, June 14, 2005.

Headquarters, Department of the Army. *Operations*. Field Manual No. 3–0. Washington, DC, February 2008. As of July 1, 2011: www.fas.org/irp/doddir/army/fm3–0.pdf (document is marked as approved for unlimited public distribution but could not be found on any publicly accessible U.S. government website)

Headquarters, Department of the Army. *Training Units and Developing Leaders for Full Spectrum Operations.* Field Manual No. 7-0. Washington, DC, February 2011.

Healey, Jason, ed. *A Fierce Domain: Conflict in Cyberspace, 1986 to 2012.* Cyber Conflict Studies Association in Partnership with the Atlantic Council, 2013.

Henley, Lonnie. "PLA Logistics and Doctrine Reform, 1999–2009," in Puska, ed., *People's Liberation Army after Next,* 2000, pp. 55–77.

"HHQ-16," *Jane's Naval Weapon Systems,* November 12, 2010.

"HHQ-7/FM-80/FM-90N," *Jane's Naval Weapon Systems,* January 17, 2011.

"HHQ-9," *Jane's Naval Weapon Systems,* May 12, 2011.

Hille, Kathrin. "Chinese General Faces Corruption Probe," *Financial Times,* February 1, 2012.

Holmes, James R. "Integrated Chinese Saturation Attacks: Mahan's Logic, Mao's Grammar," in Erickson and Goldstein, eds., *Chinese Aerospace Power,* 2011, pp. 407–422.

Holmes, James R., and Toshi Yoshihara. *Chinese Naval Strategy in the 21st Century: The Turn to Mahan.* London and New York: Routledge, 2008.

Holmes, Kim R. "Measuring the Conventional Balance in Europe," *International Security,* Vol. 12, No. 4, Spring 1988, pp. 166–173.

Holt, Staff Sgt. Katherine. "Barksdale AFB: B-52's Deploying to Guam, Part of Routine Rotation of Continuous Bomber Presence on Guam," Pacific News Center website, August 28, 2013. As of September 23, 2013: www.pacificnewscenter.com/index.php?option=com_content&view=article&id=37232:barksdale-afb-b-52s-deploying-to-guam-part-of-routine-rotation-of-continuous-bomber-presence-on-guam&catid=45:guam-news&Itemid=156

"Hongqi-2," *Jane's Land-Based Air Defence,* August 25, 2011.

"Hongqi Class," *Jane's Fighting Ships,* February 15, 2013.

Horowitz, Stanley, and Allan Sherman. "A Direct Measure of the Relationship Between Human Capital and Productivity," *Journal of Human Resources,* Vol. 15, No. 1, Winter 1980, pp. 67–76.

Hosmer, Stephen T. *Why Milosevic Decided to Settle When He Did.* Santa Monica, CA: RAND Corporation, 2001.

"Houbei (Type 022) Class," *Jane's Fighting Ships,* December 9, 2013.

"How Much Does PLA Soldier's Individual Equipment Cost?" China Military Online, December 5, 2014. As of April 7, 2015: http://english.chinamil.com.cn/news-channels/2014-12/05/content_6257426.htm

Howarth, Peter. *China's Rising Sea Power: The PLA Navy's Submarine Challenge.* London and New York: Routledge, 2008.

"HQ-9/FT-2000," *Jane's Land-Based Air Defence,* October 11, 2011.

"Hsiung Feng 1/2/3 (Male Bee) [sic]," *Jane's Strategic Weapon Systems,* October 19, 2012.

Hu Guangzheng (胡光正), Wang Jingchao (王京朝), and Zhang Qindong (张秦洞). 《军制》 [*Military Organization*]. Military Encyclopedia of China (Second Edition). Beijing: Encyclopedia of China Publishing House, 2007.

Huang Qunming (黄群明). 〈浅说执行多样化军事任务准备〉 ("Overview of Implementing Preparation for Diversified Military Tasks"), 《解放军报》 [*PLA Daily*], March 4, 2010.

Hughes, Capt. Wayne P., Jr. *Fleet Tactics and Coastal Combat* (Second Edition). Annapolis, MD: Naval Institute Press, 2000.

IISS. See International Institute for Strategic Studies.

"Ilyushin Il-76," *Jane's All the World's Aircraft*, October 17, 2012.

"Improved Crystal," *Jane's Space Systems and Industry*, September 2, 2011.

"Independence Class Littoral Combat Ship Flight 0," *Jane's Fighting Ships*, April 10, 2013.

Information Office of the State Council of the People's Republic of China. *China's National Defense in 2000*. Beijing: 2000a.

Information Office of the State Council of the People's Republic of China. *China's National Defense in 2002*. Beijing: 2002a. As of July 6, 2011: www.china.org.cn/e-white/20021209/index.htm

Information Office of the State Council of the People's Republic of China (中华人民共和国 国务院新闻办公室).《2002年中国的国防》[*China's National Defense in 2002*]. Beijing: 2002b. As of February 28, 2012: www.mod.gov.cn/affair/2011–01/06/content_4249946_5.htm

《2004年中国的国防》[*China's National Defense in 2004*]. Beijing: 2004. As of July 22, 2011: www.china.com.cn/ch-book/20041227/index.htm

China's National Defense in 2006. Beijing: 2006a. As of July 6, 2011: www.china.org.cn/english/features/book/194421.htm

《2006年中国的国防》[*China's National Defense in 2006*]. Beijing, 2006b. As of March 1, 2012: www.mod.gov.cn/affair/2011–01/06/content_4249948.htm

China's National Defense in 2008. Beijing: 2009. As of July 6, 2011: www.china.org.cn/government/whitepaper/node_7060059.htm

China's National Defense in 2010. Beijing: 2011. As of July 6, 2011: www.china.org.cn/government/whitepaper/node_7114675.htm

The Diversified Employment of China's Armed Forces. Beijing, April 2013. As of February 28, 2014: http://eng.mod.gov.cn/Database/WhitePapers/index.htm

《一个中国的原则与台湾问题》[*The One China Principle and the Taiwan Issue*]. Beijing: February 2000b. As of July 2, 2011: www.china.com.cn/ch-book/taiwan/itaiwan.htm.

International Institute for Strategic Studies (IISS). *The Military Balance 1978/1979*. London: Routledge, 1978.

The Military Balance 1986/1987. London: Routledge, 1986.

The Military Balance 2001/2002. London: Routledge, 2001.

The Military Balance 2002/2003. London: Routledge, 2002.

The Military Balance 2003/2004. London: Routledge, 2003.

The Military Balance 2004/2005. London: Routledge, 2004.

The Military Balance 2005/2006. London: Routledge, 2005.

The Military Balance 2006. London: Routledge, 2006.

The Military Balance 2007. London: Routledge, 2007.

The Military Balance 2008. London: Routledge, 2008.

The Military Balance 2009. London: Routledge, 2009.

The Military Balance 2010. London: Routledge, 2010.

The Military Balance 2011. London: Routledge, 2011.

The Military Balance 2013. London: Routledge, 2013.

The Military Balance 2014. London: Routleadge, 2014.

"Japan Protests as Record Number of Chinese Ships Converge near Senkakus," Kyodo, April 23, 2013.

"Japan > Air Force," *Jane's Sentinel Security Assessment: China and Northeast Asia*, March 1, 2013.

"Jiangdao (Type 056) Class," Jane's Fighting Ships, December 31, 2013.

"Jiangkai I (Type 054) Class, *Jane's Fighting Ships*, January 10, 2011.

"Jiangkai II (Type 054A) Class," *Jane's Fighting Ships*, February 11, 2011.

"Jiangwei II (Type 053H3) Class," *Jane's Fighting Ships*, February 11, 2011.

Johnson, David E., Adam Grissom, and Olga Oliker. *In the Middle of the Fight: An Assessment of Medium-Armored Forces in Past Military Operations*. Santa Monica, CA: RAND Corporation, 2008.

Johnson, David E., Jennifer D.P. Moroney, Roger Cliff, M. Wade Markel, Laurence Smallman, and Michael Spirtas. *Preparing and Training for the Full Spectrum of Military Challenges: Insights from the Experiences of China, France, the United Kingdom, India, and Israel*. Santa Monica, CA: RAND Corporation, 2009.

"Joint Field Training by the Three Services like a Raging Wildfire" 〈三军演兵场·联合训练如如火茶〉,《解放军报》[*PLA Daily*], March 18, 2009.

Joint Logistics. Joint Publication 4-0. July 18, 2008.

"Joint Training Policy and Guidance for the Armed Forces of the United States," Chairman of the Joint Chiefs of Staff Instruction 3500.01G, March 15, 2012.

"Kadena Air Base," The Official Web Site of Kadena Air Base, undated. As of July 10, 2013: www.kadena.af.mil/main/welcome.asp

"KAI T-50 Golden Eagle," *Jane's All the World's Aircraft*, October 22, 2012.

Kamphausen, Roy, and Andrew Scobell, eds. *Right-Sizing the People's Liberation Army: Exploring the Contours of China's Military*. Carlyle, PA: U.S. Army War College, 2007.

Kamphausen, Roy, David Lai, and Andrew Scobell, eds. *The PLA at Home and Abroad: Assessing the Operational Capabilities of China's Military*. Carlisle, PA: U.S. Army War College, 2010.

Kamphausen, Roy, Andrew Scobell, and Travis Tanner, eds. *The "People" in the PLA: Recruitment, Training, and Education in China's Military*. Carlisle, PA: U.S. Army War College, 2008.

Kan, Shirley A. "Taiwan: Major U.S. Arms Sales since 1990," Congressional Research Service, July 23, 2013.

Kato, Yoichi. "U.S. Commander Says China Aims to Be a 'Global Military' Power," Asahi.com, December 28, 2010. As of November 28, 2011: www.asahi.com/english/TKY201012270241.html

Kavanagh, Jennifer. *Determinants of Productivity for Military Personnel: A Review of Findings on the Contribution of Experience, Training, and Aptitude to Military Performance*. Santa Monica, CA: RAND Corporation, 2005.

"KD-63 (YJ-63), K/AKD-63," *Jane's Air-Launched Weapons*, March 28, 2011.

"KD-88 (K/AKD-88)," *Jane's Air-Launched Weapons*, January 20, 2011.

Keegan, John. *The Price of Admiralty: The Evolution of Naval Warfare*. New York: Viking, 1988.

"Kilo Class (Project 877EKM/636)," *Jane's Fighting Ships*, January 10, 2011.

Kitchen, Martin. *Rommel's Desert War*. Cambridge: Cambridge University Press, 2009.

Kopp, Carlo. "An Initial Assessment of China's J-20 Stealth Fighter," *China Brief*, Vol. 11, Issue 8, May 6, 2011.

Kotter, John P., and James L. Heskett. *Corporate Culture and Performance*. New York: Free Press, 1992.

Krekel, Bryan, Patton Adams, and George Bakos. "Occupying the Information High Ground: Chinese Capabilities for Computer Network Operations and Cyber Espionage," 2012. As of March 12, 2014: http://origin.www.uscc.gov/sites/default/files/Research/USCC_Report_Chinese_Capabilities_for_Computer_Network_Operations_and_Cyber_%20Espionage.pdf

"KS-1/KS-1A (HQ-12)," *Jane's Land-Based Air Defence*, November 18, 2011.

"Kuznetsov (Orel) Class (Project 1143.5/6)," *Jane's Fighting Ships*, March 10, 2011.

"Lacrosse/Onyx Series," *Jane's Space Systems and Industry*, August 31, 2011.

Latimer, Jon. *Operation Compass 1940: Wavell's Whirlwind Offensive*. Oxford: Osprey Publishing, 2000.

Laur, Colonel Timothy M., and Steven L. Llanso. *Encyclopedia of Modern U.S. Military Weapons*. New York: Berkeley Books, 1995.

Leadership and Force Development, Air Force Doctrine Document 1–1, Washington, DC, November 8, 2011.

Lee, Wang-Sheng and Cahit Guven. "Engaging in Corruption: The Influence of Cultural Values and Contagion Effects at the Micro Level," Discussion Paper No. 7685, Institute for the Study of Labor, October 2013.

Lee Yong-in. "New Book Reveals US Abandoned Military Plans," *The Hankyoreh*, May 15, 2014.

Lehman, John, and Harvey Sicherman, eds. *America the Vulnerable: Our Military Problems and How to Fix Them*. Philadelphia, PA: Foreign Policy Research Institute, undated. As of March 24, 2014: www.fpri.org/docs/BookAmericatheVulnerable.pdf

Lescher, Rear Admiral William K., Department of the Navy, "FY 2015 President's Budget," March 4, 2014. As of October 5, 2014: http://web.archive.org/web/20140305002625/www.finance.hq.navy.mil/FMB/15pres/DON_PB15_Press_Brief.pdf

Lewis, Mark R. "Army Transformation and the Junior Officer Exodus." *Armed Forces and Society*, Vol. 31, No. 1, 2004, pp. 63–93.

Li Keqiang. "Report on the Work of the Government," March 5, 2014. As of August 21, 2014: http://online.wsj.com/public/resources/documents/2014GovtWorkReport_Eng.pdf

"Report on the Work of the Government," March 5, 2015. As of April 7, 2014: http://download.xinhuanet.com/2015lhwaiwen/zfgzbg/2015zfgzbgEng.pdf

Li, Nan, ed. *Chinese Civil-Military Relations: The Transformation of the People's Liberation Army*. Oxford and New York: Taylor & Francis, 2006.

"The PLA's Evolving Warfighting Doctrine, Strategy and Tactics, 1985–95: A Chinese Perspective." *China Quarterly*, No. 146 (June 1996), pp. 443–463.

"The Central Military Commission and Military Policy in China," in Mulvenon and Yang, eds., *The People's Liberation Army as Organization*, 2002a, pp. 45–94.

Li Shunhua (李顺华). 〈严训还需细考〉 ("To Train Rigorously Must Also Evaluate in Detail"),《解放军报》[*PLA Daily*], July 2, 2002b.

Li, Xiaobing. *A History of the Modern Chinese Army*. Lexington, KY: University Press of Kentucky, 2007.

Li Yong (李勇). 〈新形势下大学生士兵管理教育问题探讨〉 ("Investigation of Problems in the Management and Education of College Student Soldiers in the New Environment").《柴达木开发研究》(*Qaidam Development Studies*), No. 2, 2011, pp. 42–44.

Li Zhiguo (李治国). 〈军官继续教育与新型军事人才培养〉 ("Continuing Officer Education and Development of the New Type of Military Talent")《继续教育》 (*Continuing Education*), Supplemental Issue, 2003, p. 82.

Libicki, Martin C. "Chinese Use of Cyberwar as an Anti-Access Strategy: Two Scenarios." Testimony presented before the U.S. China Economic and Security Review Commission, January 27, 2011.

Liddell Hart, B. H. *Strategy*. BN Publishing, 2008.

Lilley, James R., and David Shambaugh, eds. *China's Military Faces the Future*. Armonk, NY: M. E. Sharpe, 1999.

"Littoral Combat Ship Class – LCS," United States Navy Fact File, America's Navy website, undated. As of June 27, 2013: www.navy.mil/navydata/fact_display.asp?cid=4200&tid=1650&ct=4

Liu Feng'an (刘逢安). 〈深化训练内容改革积极推进训练转变《军事训练与考核大纲》编修工作扎实推进〉 ("Deepen Training Content Reform, Advance Transformation of Training: 'Military Training and Evaluation Guidelines' Revision Work Steadily Advancing"),《解放军报》[*PLA Daily*], April 17, 2008.

Liu Feng'an (刘逢安) and Cai Pengcheng (蔡鹏程). 〈在深化改革中加快转变战斗力生成模式〉 ("While Deepening Reform, Develop Model for Accelerating Transformation of Combat Power"),《解放军报》[*PLA Daily*], January 14, 2011.

Liu Feng'an (刘逢安) and Hu Junhua (胡君华). 〈描绘"十二五"时期军事训练科学发展蓝图〉 ("Drawing the Blueprint for the Scientific Development of Military Training during the Twelfth Five Year Plan Period"),《解放军报》[*PLA Daily*], September 23, 2011a.

〈提高基于信息系统体系作战能力〉 ("Raise Ability to Conduct Operations Based on Information Systems"),《解放军报》[*PLA Daily*], March 29, 2011b.

Liu Feng'an (刘逢安) and Wu Tianmin (武天敏). 〈新一代《军事训练与考核大纲》颁发〉 ("New Generation of 'Military Training and Evaluation Guidelines' Issued"),《解放军报》[*PLA Daily*], July 25, 2008.

〈深化训练模式，方法和管理改革〉 ("Deepen Reform of Training Models, Methods, and Management")《解放军报》[*PLA Daily*], January 8, 2010a.

(武天敏). 〈训练转变：在风雨中奋力前行〉 ("Transforming Training: Pushing Forward in the Wind and Rain"),《解放军报》[*PLA Daily*], November 2, 2010b.

Liu Xiaohua (刘孝华), Wu Dilun (吴弟伦), Liu Feng'an (刘逢安), and Wu Tianmin (武天敏). 〈具有战略意义的深刻变革—我军军事训练从机械化向信息化条件下转变综述〉 ("A Deep Transformation of Strategic Significance: A Summary of the Transformation of PLA Military Training from Mechanization to Informationization Conditions"),《解放军报》[*PLA Daily*], September 2, 2009.

Liu Wei (刘伟), Wang Zhongyuan (王忠远), and Wang Lingjiang (王令江).《战区联合战役指挥概论》[*An Introduction to Joint Theater Command*]. Beijing: National Defense University Press, 2003.

"Lockheed Martin F-16 Fighting Falcon," *Jane's All the World's Aircraft*, August 3, 2012.

"Lockheed Martin (General Dynamics) F-16 Fighting Falcon," *Jane's Aircraft Upgrades*, August 29, 2012.

"Lockheed Martin F-35 Lightning II," *Jane's All the World's Aircraft*, February 7, 2013.

"Los Angeles Class," *Jane's Fighting Ships*, April 10, 2013.

"LRASM Missiles: Reaching for a Long-Range Punch," Defense Industry Daily, July 2, 2014. As of October 2, 2014: www.defenseindustrydaily.com/lrasm-missiles-reaching-for-a-long-reach-punch-06752/

"LT-2 Laser Guided Bomb (LS-500J)," *Jane's Air-Launched Weapons*, January 26, 2011.

Lu Lihua (芦利华).《军队指挥理论学习指南》[*Military Command Theory Study Guide*]. Beijing: National Defense University Press, 2004.

Luttwak, Edward N. *Strategy: The Logic of War and Peace* (Revised Edition). Cambridge, MA: Belknap Press, 2002.

"Luyang I (Type 052B) Class," *Jane's Fighting Ships*, January 10, 2011.

"Luyang II (Type 052C) Class," *Jane's Fighting Ships*, February 11, 2011.

"Luzhou Class (Type 051C)," *Jane's Fighting Ships*, August 9, 2011.

Ma Xiaochun (马晓春).〈认真学习贯彻新一代作战条令〉("Carefully Study and Implement New Generation of Warfighting Doctrine"),《解放军报》[*PLA Daily*], February 5, 1999.

Madsen, Richard. *Morality and Power in a Chinese Village*. Berkeley, CA: University of California Press, 1984.

Marcus, A. J. *Personnel Substitution and Navy Aviation Readiness*. Alexandria, VA: Center for Naval Analyses, 1982.

"Marine Aircraft Group 36," Official Website of the United States Marine Corps, undated. As of July 10, 2013: www.1stmaw.marines.mil/SubordinateUnits/MarineAircraftGroup36/About

Maritime Administration, U.S. Department of Commerce. "Top 25 Flag of Registry," updated December 15, 2011. As of March 25, 2013: www.marad.dot.gov/library_landing_page/data_and_statistics/Data_and_Statistics.htm

Mathews, Jim. "U.S. Navy Intercepts Crippled Satellite with Modified SM-3 Missile," Aviation Week Intelligence Network, February 20, 2008.

Mattox, John Mark. "Values Statements and the Profession of Arms: A Reevaluation," *Joint Forces Quarterly*, Issue 66, 1st quarter 2013, pp. 59–63.

Mayer, Daryl. "KC-46 Progressing on Track," Air Force Material Command website, April 9, 2013. As of July 10, 2013: www.afmc.af.mil/news/story.asp?id=123343686

McCauley, Kevin. "Non-Commissioned Officers and the Creation of a Volunteer Force," *China Brief*, Vol. XI, Issue 18, September 30, 2011, pp. 14–19.

Mearsheimer, John J., Barry R. Posen, and Eliot A. Cohen. "Reassessing Net Assessment," *International Security*, Vol. 13, No. 4, Spring 1989, pp. 128–179.

Medeiros, Evan S. "'Minding the Gap': Assessing the Trajectory of the PLA's Second Artillery," in Kamphausen and Scobell, eds., *Right-Sizing the People's Liberation Army*, 2007, pp. 143–189.

Medeiros, Evan S., Roger Cliff, Keith Crane, and James C. Mulvenon. *A New Direction for China's Defense Industry*. Santa Monica, CA: RAND Corporation, 2005.

Medeiros, Evan S., Keith Crane, Eric Heginbotham, Norman D. Levin, Julia F. Lowell, Angel Rabasa, and Somi Seong. *Pacific Currents: The Responses of U.S. Allies and Security Partners in East Asia to China's Rise*. Santa Monica, CA: RAND Corporation, 2008.

Menges, Constantine C. *China: The Gathering Threat*. Nashville, TN: Thomas Nelson, 2005.

"MGM-140/-164/-168 ATACMS (M39)," *Jane's Strategic Weapon Systems*, October 27, 2011.

"Military Men Are Born to Win Victories: The Military's Fifth Generation of Doctrine Awaiting Approval" 〈军人生来为战胜：我军第五代作战条令正在报批〉,《人民网》(People's Net), March 23, 2008. As of November 5, 2012: http://military.people.cn/GB/8221/7032631.html

Military Sealift Command. "Combat Logistics Force," undated. As of March 25, 2013: www.msc.navy.mil/PM1/

Miller, Frank. "Changing the Landscape of Civil-Military Relations in China: The PLA Responds to Recruiting and Retention Challenges," in Scobell and Wortzel, eds., *Shaping China's Security Environment*, 2006, pp. 15–34.

"Negotiating with the Chinese," *International Affairs: The Professional Journal of the Foreign Area Officer Association*, Vol. 14, No. 3, August 2011, pp. 41–45.

Millett, Allan R., Williamson Murray, and Kenneth H. Watman. "The Effectiveness of Military Organizations," *International Security*, Vol. 11, No. 1, Summer 1986, pp. 37–71.

"MIM-104 Patriot," *Jane's Land Warfare Platforms: Artillery and Air Defense*, April 10, 2013.

"Ming Class (Type 035)," *Jane's Fighting Ships*, February 11, 2011.

Ministry of Defense, "Defense of Japan 2014." As of September 19, 2014: www.mod.go.jp/e/publ/w_paper/2014.html

Ministry of National Defense, "National Defense Report" Editing Committee. *National Defense Report, The Republic of China*, 2011. Taipei, Taiwan: Ministry of National Defense, 2011.

"Mission," Commander, Patrol and Reconnaissance Force Seventh Fleet website, undated. As of September 23, 2013: www.cprf7f5f.navy.mil/72mission.html

"Misty," *Jane's Space Systems and Industry*, July 8, 2010.

"Mitsubishi F-2," *Jane's All the World's Aircraft*, October 22, 2012.

"MND Clarifies Rumors About 'Joint Operational Command,'" Ministry of National Defense, People's Republic of China website, January 6, 2014. As of February 25, 2014: http://eng.mod.gov.cn/DefenseNews/2014–01/06/content_4482143.htm

Mogato, Manuel, and Greg Torode. "Philippine, Vietnamese Navies to Unite against China over Beers and Volleyball," Reuters, April 10, 2014.

Moore, S. Craig. *Demand and Supply Integration for Air Force Enlisted Work Force Planning: A Briefing*. Santa Monica, CA: RAND Corporation, August 1981.

Moore, S. Craig, Lawrence M. Hasner, Bernard D. Rostker, Suzanne M. Holroyd, and Judith C. Fernandez. *A Framework for Characterization of Military Unit Training Status*, Santa Monica, CA: RAND Corporation, 1995.

Morgan, Forrest E., Karl P. Mueller, Evan S. Medeiros, Kevin L. Pollpeter, and Roger Cliff. *Dangerous Thresholds: Managing Escalation in the 21st Century*. Santa Monica, CA: RAND Corporation, 2008.

Morring, Frank, Jr. "China Asat Test Called Worst Single Debris Event Ever," *Aviation Week and Space Technology*, February 12, 2007, p. 20.

Mosher, Stephen. *Hegemon: China's Plan to Dominate Asia and the World*. New York: Encounter Books, 2002.

Moseley, Lt Gen T. Michael. "Operation IRAQI FREEDOM – By the Numbers." Assessment and Analysis Division, USCENTAF, April 30, 2003. As of August 11, 2014: www.afhso.af.mil/shared/media/document/AFD-130613-025.pdf

Moten, Matthew. "The Army Officers' Professional Ethic – Past, Present, and Future." Volume 2, Professional Military Ethics Monograph Series. Carlisle, PA: Strategic Studies Institute, U.S. Army War College, February 2010.

"Multirole ASM (KD-88)," *Jane's Strategic Weapon Systems*, December 20, 2012

Mulvenon, James. "Chairman Hu and the PLA's 'New Historic Missions.'" *China Leadership Monitor*, No. 27, Winter 2009.

    Professionalization of the Senior Chinese Officer Corps: Trends and Implications. Santa Monica, CA: RAND Corporation, 1997.

    Soldiers of Fortune: The Rise and Fall of the Chinese Military-Business Complex, 1978–1998. New York: M. E. Sharpe, 2001.

Mulvenon, James, and David Finkelstein, eds. *China's Revolution in Doctrinal Affairs: Emerging Trends in the Operational Art of the Chinese People's Liberation Army.* Alexandria, VA: CNA, 2005 (document is undated but CNA website gives publication date as November 2005). As of July 1, 2011: www.cna.org/sites/default/files/DoctrineBook.pdf

Mulvenon, James C., and Andrew N. D. Yang, eds. *Seeking Truth from Facts: A Retrospective on Chinese Military Studies in the Post-Mao Era.* Santa Monica CA: RAND Corporation, 2001.

    The People's Liberation Army as Organization: Reference Volume 1.0. Santa Monica, CA: RAND Corporation, 2002.

Mulvenon, James C., and Richard H. Yang, eds. *The People's Liberation Army in the Information Age.* Santa Monica CA: RAND Corporation, 1999.

Murray, William S. "Revisiting Taiwan's Defense Strategy," *Naval War College Review*, Vol. 61, No. 3, Summer 2008, pp. 13–38.

Murray, Williamson. "Does Military Culture Matter?" in Lehman and Sicherman, eds., *America the Vulnerable*, undated but reprint of 1999 article in *Orbis*, pp. 134–151.

Nathan, Andrew J., and Robert S. Ross. *The Great Wall and the Empty Fortress: China's Search for Security.* New York: W. W. Norton and Company, 1998.

National Air and Space Intelligence Center (NASIC). *China: Connecting the Dots: "Strategic Challenges Posed by a Re-Emergent Power.* Wright-Patterson Air Force Base, Ohio, 2007.

    People's Liberation Army Air Force 2010. Wright-Patterson Air Force Base, Ohio, 2010.

National Bureau of Statistics of China. *China Statistical Yearbook 1997.* Beijing: China Statistics Press, 1997. As of February 27, 2012: www.stats.gov.cn/ndsj/information/nj97/ml97.htm

    China Statistical Yearbook 2001. Beijing: China Statistics Press, 2001. As of March 25, 2013: www.stats.gov.cn/english/statisticaldata/yearlydata/YB2001e/ml/indexE.htm

    China Statistical Yearbook 2003. Beijing: China Statistics Press, 2003.

    China Statistical Yearbook 2006. Beijing: China Statistics Press, 2007. As of March 25, 2013: www.stats.gov.cn/tjsj/ndsj/2006/indexch.htm

    China Statistical Yearbook 2007. Beijing: China Statistics Press, 2007. As of March 7, 2012: www.stats.gov.cn/tjsj/ndsj/2007/indexch.htm

    China Statistical Yearbook 2010. Beijing: China Statistics Press, 2010. As of December 9, 2011: www.stats.gov.cn/tjsj/ndsj/2010/indexch.htm

China Statistical Yearbook 2011. Beijing: China Statistics Press, 2010. As of March 25, 2013: www.stats.gov.cn/tjsj/ndsj/2011/indexch.htm

National Bureau of Statistics of China National Data website. As of January 6, 2014: http://data.stats.gov.cn/workspace/index?m=hgnd

The National Military Strategy of the United States of America 2011: Redefining America's Military Leadership, 2011. As of July 1, 2011: www.jcs.mil//content/files/2011–02/020811084800_2011_NMS_-_08_FEB_2011.pdf

Navarro, Peter. *The Coming China Wars: Where They Will Be Fought and How They Can Be Won.* Upper Saddle River, NJ: FT Press, 2008.

"Navy Organization," U.S. Navy website. As of February 27, 2014: www.navy.mil/navydata/organization/org-top.asp

"New Year, New Measures, New Climate: A Scan of the Results Brought by Rectification to a Portion of the First Group of PLA Units to Participate in Study and Practice Activities" 〈新年新举措新气象—全军首批参加学习实践活动部分单位整改落实成果扫描〉,《解放军报》[*PLA Daily*], February 1, 2009, p. 6.

"NOSS (Naval Ocean Surveillance System)." *Jane's Space Systems and Industry,* August 30, 2010.

Ng, Ka Po. *Interpreting China's Military Power: Doctrine Makes Readiness.* London: Routledge, 2005.

"NORINCO 155 mm Self-Propelled Gun Howitzer PLZ-05," *Jane's Armour and Artillery,* February 21, 2011.

"NORINCO Airborne Assault Vehicle (AAV) ZLC2000 (ZBD-03)," *Jane's Armour and Artillery,* October 12, 2011.

"NORINCO Type WZ501 Infantry Fighting Vehicle," *Jane's Armour and Artillery,* November 18, 2010.

"NORINCO WZ551 Armoured Personnel Carrier," *Jane's Armour and Artillery,* November 23, 2010.

"Northrop Grumman (Northrop) B-2A Spirit," *Jane's Aircraft Upgrades,* December 3, 2010.

O'Dowd, Edward C. *Chinese Military Strategy in the Third Indochina War: The Last Maoist War.* London: Routledge, 2007.

Office of Naval Intelligence (ONI). *China's Navy 2007.* Washington, DC, 2007.

The People's Liberation Army Navy: A Modern Navy with Chinese Characteristics. Washington, DC, 2009.

Office of the Assistant Secretary of Defense (Force Management Policy). *Population Representation in the Military Services: Fiscal Year 2000.* November 2001. As of August 15, 2014: http://prhome.defense.gov/RFM/MPP/AP/POPREP/

Annual Report to Congress: Military Power of the People's Republic of China, 2000.

Annual Report to Congress: Military Power of the People's Republic of China, 2002.

Office of the Secretary of Defense. *Annual Report to Congress: Military and Security Developments Involving the People's Republic of China,* 2010.

Annual Report to Congress: Military and Security Developments Involving the People's Republic of China, 2011.

Annual Report to Congress: Military and Security Developments Involving the People's Republic of China, 2013.

Annual Report to Congress: Military and Security Developments Involving the People's Republic of China, 2014.

Annual Report to Congress: Military Power of the People's Republic of China, 2009.

Proliferation: Threat and Response, 2001. As of November 16, 2011: www.fas.org/irp/threat/prolif00.pdf

Office of the Under Secretary of Defense (Comptroller)/Chief Financial Officer. "Fiscal Year 2014 Budget Request and FY 2013 Update," April 2013. As of March 3, 2014: http://comptroller.defense.gov/Portals/45/Documents/defbudget/fy2014/FY2014_Budget_Request.pdf

Program Acquisition Costs by Weapon System, February 2011. As of December 14, 2011: http://comptroller.defense.gov/defbudget/fy2012/FY2012_Weapons.pdf

Office of the Under Secretary of Defense, Personnel and Readiness. *Population Representation in the Military Services: Fiscal Year 2010.* Undated. As of August 15, 2014: http://prhome.defense.gov/RFM/MPP/AP/POPREP/

Population Representation in the Military Services: Fiscal Year 2011. Undated. As of August 15, 2014: http://prhome.defense.gov/RFM/MPP/AP/POPREP/

O'Hanlon, Michael E. *The Science of War.* Princeton: Princeton University Press, 2009.

"Ohio Class," *Jane's Fighting Ships,* April 9, 2013.

"Oliver Hazard Perry Class," *Jane's Fighting Ships,* March 24, 2011.

O'Neill, Barry. "How to Measure the Military Worth of a Weapon, at Least in Theory," April 1991, rev. March 1996. As of March 3, 2014: www.sscnet.ucla.edu/polisci/faculty/boneill/index_files/weapnew.htm

ONI. See Office of Naval Intelligence.

"Operational Unit Diagrams," U.S. Army website. As of February 27, 2014: www.army.mil/info/organization/unitsandcommands/oud/

O'Rourke, Ronald. *China Naval Modernization: Implications for U.S. Navy Capabilities.* Hauppauge, NY: Nova Science Publishers, 2008.

Orvis, Bruce, Michael Childress, and J. Michael Polich. *Effect of Personnel Quality on the Performance of Patriot Air Defense System Operators.* Santa Monica, CA: RAND Corporation, 1992.

"P-8A Multi-mission Maritime Aircraft (MMA)," United States Navy Fact File, America's Navy website, undated. As of June 28, 2013: www.navy.mil/navydata/fact_display.asp?cid=1100&tid=1300&ct=1

"PAC-3," *Jane's Strategic Weapon Systems,* April 10, 2013.

Page, Jeremy. "For Xi, a 'China Dream' of Military Power," *Wall Street Journal,* March 13, 2013. As of October 13, 2014: http://online.wsj.com/news/articles/SB10001424127887324128504578348774040546346

Pan, Jason. "Military Intake on Track: Ministry," *Taipei Times,* November 19, 2014, p. 3.

Pedrozo, Captain Raul. "Close Encounters at Sea: The USNS Impeccable Incident," *Naval War College Review,* Vol. 62, No. 3, Summer 2009, pp. 101–111.

Pellerin, Cheryl. "Hagel: U.S. to Send 2 More Aegis Ships to Japan," American Forces Press Service, April 6, 2014. As of October 3, 2014: www.defense.gov/news/news article.aspx?id=121992

People's Liberation Army Second Artillery Force (中国人民解放军第二炮兵).《第二炮兵战役学》[Study of Second Artillery Campaigns]. Beijing: Liberation Army Press, 2004.

Perlez, Jane. "Continuing Buildup, China Boosts Military Spending More than 11 Percent," *New York Times,* March 4, 2012a.

"Corruption in Military Poses a Test for China," *New York Times*, November 15, 2012b.

Perrett, Bradley. "China's First Space Docking Follows Precise Launch," *Aviation Week and Space Technology*, November 7, 2011, p. 32.

Pierce, James G. "Is the Organizational Culture of the U.S. Army Congruent with the Professional Development of Its Senior Level Officer Corps?" The Letort Papers. Carlisle, PA: Strategic Studies Institute, U.S. Army War College, September 2010.

PLA Daily Reporter. 〈认真贯彻作战条令不断提高"打赢"能力〉 ("Faithfully Implement Warfighting Regulations, Continuously Raise "Fight and Win" Capability"), 《解放军报》 [*PLA Daily*], February 25, 1999.

PLA General Staff Department (解放军总参谋部). 〈紧紧围绕能打仗 打胜仗推进军事工作〉 ("Advance Military Work By Revolving Closely Around the Ability to Fight and Win Battles"),《求是》 [*Qiushi*], February 1, 2013. As of June 23, 2013: www.qstheory.cn/zxdk/2013/201303/201301/t20130129_209019.htm

"PLA to Carry Out Structural and Organizational Reform," Ministry of National Defense, People's Republic of China website, November 28, 2013. As of February 25, 2014: http://eng.mod.gov.cn/DefenseNews/2013–11/29/content_4477126.htm

"PLZ-07 122 mm Self-Propelled Howitzer," *Jane's Armour and Artillery*, February 21, 2011.

Posen, Barry R. "Measuring the European Conventional Balance: Coping with Complexity in Threat Assessment," *International Security*, Vol. 9, No. 3, Winter 1984–1985, pp. 47–88.

Puska, Susan M, ed. *People's Liberation Army After Next*. Carlisle, PA: U.S. Army War College, 2000.

"Rough but Ready Force Projection: An Assessment of Recent PLA Training," in Andrew Scobell and Larry M. Wortzel, eds., *China's Growing Military Power*, 2002, pp. 223–250.

"Taming the Hydra: Trends in China's Military Logistics since 2000," in Kamphausen, Lai, and Scobell, eds., *The PLA at Home and Abroad*, 2010, pp. 553–612.

Qiao Liang (乔良), and Wang Xiangsui (王湘穗).《超限战 : 全球化时代战争与战法》 (*Unrestricted Warfare: War and Warfighting Methods in an Age of Globablization*). Beijing: Liberation Army Arts and Literature Press, 1999.

"Qiongsha Class," *Jane's Fighting Ships*, February 14, 2013.

Quester, Aline O., and Gary Lee. *Senior Enlisted Personnel: Do We Need Another Grade?* Alexandria, VA: CNA, 2001.

Ren Xiangdong (任向东). 〈中国陆海空三军实施新一代作战条令〉 ["China's Army, Navy, and Air Force Implement A New Generation of Warfighting Regulations"].《了望》 [*Outlook*], July 23, 1999.

"RGM-84/UGM-84 Harpoon (GWS 60)," *Jane's Naval Weapon Systems*, August 19, 2011.

"RIM-7 SeaSparrow/RIM-162 Evolved SeaSparrow; Mk 57 NSSMS, IPDMS; AN/SWY-1(V) SDSMS," *Jane's Naval Weapon Systems*, March 14, 2011.

"RIM-66/-67/-156 Standard SM-1/-2, RIM-161 Standard SM-3, and RIM-174 Standard SM-6," *Jane's Strategic Weapon Systems*, June 11, 2013.

Rodriguez, Jacob. "Predicting the Military Career Success of United States Air Force Academy Cadets." *Armed Forces and Society*. Vol. 36, No. 1, 2009, pp. 65–85.

"Romeo Class (Project 633)," *Jane's Underwater Warfare Systems*, August 11, 2011.

Ryan, Mark, David Finkelstein, and Michael McDevitt, eds. *Chinese Warfighting: The PLA Experience since 1949*. Armonk, NY: M. E. Sharpe, 2003.

"S-300P," *Jane's Land-Based Air Defence*, March 30, 2011.

"SA-N-6 'Grumble' (V601 Fort/Rif)/SA-N-20 'Gargoyle' (Fort-M/Rif-M)," *Jane's Naval Weapon Systems*, November 11, 2010.

"SA-N-7 'Gadfly' (3K90 M-22 Uragan/Shtil)/SA-N-7B 'Grizzly' (9K37 Ezh/Shtil-1)/ SA-N-7C 'Gollum' (9M317/Shtil-2)," *Jane's Naval Weapon Systems*, March 30, 2011.

"SAC 'J-15'," *Jane's All the World's Aircraft*, June 9, 2011.

"SAC Y-8," *Jane's All the World's Aircraft*, February 11, 2013.

"SAC Y-8 (Special Mission versions)," *Jane's All the World's Aircraft*, October 17, 2011.

"SAC Y-9," *Jane's All the World's Aircraft*, January 2, 2013.

"SAC (Sukhoi Su-27) J-11," *Jane's All the World's Aircraft*, June 9, 2011.

Schein, Edgar H. *Organizational Culture and Leadership* (Fourth Edition). San Francisco: Jossey-Bass, 2010.

Schulte, John C. *An Analysis of the Historical Effectiveness of Antiship Cruise Missiles in Littoral Warfare*. Monterey, CA: Naval Postgraduate School, September 1994.

Scobell, Andrew, and Larry M. Wortzel, eds. *China's Growing Military Power: Perspectives on Security, Ballistic Missiles, and Conventional Capabilities*, Carlisle, PA: U.S. Army War College, 2002.

eds. *Civil-Military Change in China*. Carlisle, PA: U.S. Army War College, 2004.

eds. *Shaping China's Security Environment: The Role of the People's Liberation Army*. Carlisle, PA: U.S. Army War College, 2006.

Scribner, Barry, D. Alton Smith, Robert Baldwin, and Robert Phillips. "Are Smart Tankers Better? AFQT and Military Productivity," *Armed Forces and Society*, Winter 1986, pp. 193–206.

"SD-1/HQ-61 (CSA-N-2)," *Jane's Naval Weapon Systems*, March 22, 2011.

"SD-10, SD-10A (PL-12)," *Jane's Air-Launched Weapons*, January 20, 2011.

"Seawolf Class," *Jane's Fighting Ships*, April 10, 2013.

Secretary of State Rice, Secretary of Defense Rumsfeld, Minister of Foreign Affairs Aso, and Minister of State for Defense Nukaga, "United States–Japan Roadmap for Realignment Implementation," May 1, 2006. As of September 20, 2013: www.mofa.go.jp/region/n-america/us/security/scc/doc0605.html

Segal, Gerald, and Richard H. Yang. *Chinese Economic Reform: The Impact on Security*. London: Routledge, 1996.

Shambaugh, David. *Modernizing China's Military: Progress, Problems, and Prospects*. Berkeley: University of California Press, 2002a.

"The Pinnacle of the Pyramid: The Central Military Commission," in Mulvenon and Yang, eds., *The People's Liberation Army as Organization*, 2002b, pp. 95–121.

"Shang Class (Type 093)," *Jane's Fighting Ships*, February 11, 2011.

Shi, Ting. "In China, Joining the Army Will Cost You," *Bloomberg Businessweek*, July 17, 2014.

"Shijian Series," *Jane's Space Systems and Industry*, October 26, 2011.

Shlapak, David A., David T. Orletsky, Toy I. Reid, Murray Scot Tanner, and Barry Wilson. *A Question of Balance: Political Context and Military Aspects of the China-Taiwan Dispute*. Santa Monica, CA: RAND Corporation, 2009.

Shlapak, David A., David T. Orletsky, and Barry Wilson. *Dire Strait?: Military Aspects of the China-Taiwan Confrontation and Options for U.S. Policy*. Santa Monica, CA: RAND Corporation, 2000.

Smith, Marcia S. "Surprise Chinese Satellite Maneuvers Mystify Western Experts," SpacePolicyOnline.com, August 19, 2013. As of August 23, 2013: www.spacepoli cyonline.com/news/surprise-chinese-satelllite-maneuvers-mystify-western-experts

Snider, Don M., Paul Oh, and Kevin Toner. "The Army's Professional Military Ethic in an Era of Persistent Conflict." *Professional Military Ethics Monograph Series.* Carlisle, PA: Strategic Studies Institute, U.S. Army War College, October 2009.

"Song Class (Type 039/039G)," *Jane's Fighting Ships*, February 11, 2011.

"Space Based Infrared System (SBIRS)," *Jane's Space Systems and Industry*, June 23, 2011.

"Spratly Islands," Google Maps website, undated. As of September 25, 2013: https:// maps.google.com/maps/ms?ie=UTF8&hl=en&msa=0&msid=11204781077030786 7127.0004460b96d655257cc9c&ll=11.070603,115.708008&spn=9.563619,20.566406 &t=k&z=6

"SS-N-27A 'Sizzler' (3M54)," *Jane's Naval Weapons*, October 9, 2012.

Staff Reporters. "Ex-PLA Top General Xu Caihou Held in Cash for Rank Probe," *South China Morning Post*, March 19, 2014a.

Staff Reporters. "Work under Way on China's Second Aircraft Carrier at Dalian Yard," *South China Morning Post*, January 19, 2014b.

Staff Writer with CNA. "President Reiterates Plan to Reduce Size of Military Force," *Taipei Times*, February 14, 2014, p. 3.

"Standard Missile 1/2/3/5/6 (RIM-66/67/156/161/165/174)," *Jane's Naval Weapon Systems*, May 10, 2011.

"Standard Missile," United States Navy Fact File, America's Navy website, undated. As of June 28, 2013: www.navy.mil/navydata/fact_display.asp?cid=2200&tid=1200 &ct=2

Stillion, John, and David T. Orletsky. *Airbase Vulnerability to Conventional Cruise-Missile and Ballistic Missile Attacks: Technology, Scenarios, and U.S. Air Force Responses.* Santa Monica, CA: RAND Corporation, 1999.

Stokes, Mark A. "The Chinese Joint Aerospace Campaign: Strategy, Doctrine, and Force Modernization." Mulvenon and Finkelstein, eds., *China's Revolution in Doctrinal Affairs*, 2005, pp. 221–305.

   "The Second Artillery Force and the Future of Long-Range Precision Strike," in Tellis and Tanner, eds., *Strategic Asia 2012–13*, 2012, pp. 127–160.

"STSS (Space Tracking and Surveillance System)." *Jane's Space Systems and Industry*, July 4, 2011.

Su Kui (苏巍), Li Zhiqiang (李志强), and Liao Jianlin (寥健林).〈把针对性训练引向深入〉("Draw Directed Training Deeper").《解放军报》[*PLA Daily*], March 26, 2002.

"Sukhoi Su-27," *Jane's All the World's Aircraft*, February 1, 2013.

"Sukhoi Su-30M," *Jane's All the World's Aircraft*, February 1, 2013.

Sun Kaixiang (孙开香), and Su Ruozhou (苏若舟).〈总参部署新年度军事训练工作〉("GSD Issues New Year's Military Training Work"),《解放军报》[*PLA Daily*], January 17, 2003.

Sweetman, Bill. "Decision Time: Tactical Aircraft Transition Choices Loom for U.S. Navy," *Aviation Week and Space Technology*, June 24, 2013, pp. 45–46.

Sweetman, Bill, and Bradley Perrett. "Avic Y-20 Airlifter Awaits Better Engines," *Aviation Week and Space Technology*, February 4, 2012, p. 26.

"TacSat Series," *Jane's Space Systems and Industry*, August 16, 2010.

Taiwan Affairs Office and the Information Office of the State Council, People's Republic of China. *The One-China Principle and the Taiwan Issue*. February 2000. As of January 6, 2014: http://english.gov.cn/official/2005-07/27/content_17613.htm

"Taiwan Deploys Advanced Early Warning Radar," Channel NewsAsia, February 3, 2013. As of February 3, 2013: www.channelnewsasia.com/stories/afp_asiapacific/view/1251961/1/.html

"Taiwan > Army," *Jane's Sentinel Security Assessment: China and Northeast Asia*, June 13, 2012.

Teachout, Mark, and Martin Pellum. *Air Force Research to Link Standards for Enlistment to On-the-Job Performance*. Brooks Air Force Base, TX: Air Force Human Resources Laboratory, AFHRL-TR-90-90, February 1991.

Tellis, Ashley J., and Travis Tanner. *Strategic Asia 2012–13: China's Military Challenge*. Seattle and Washington, DC: National Bureau of Asian Research, 2012.

"Tenant Commands," Naval Base Guam website. As of September 20, 2013: www.cnic.navy.mil/regions/jrm/installations/navbase_guam/about/tenant_commands.html

"Terminal High-Altitude Area Defence," *Jane's Strategic Weapon Systems*, April 10, 2013.

"The Airman's Creed," the official website of the U.S. Air Force. As of June 22, 2013: www.af.mil/shared/media/document/afd-070418-013.pdf

"The Carrier Strike Group," America's Navy website. As of September 20, 2013: www.navy.mil/navydata/ships/carriers/powerhouse/cvbg.asp

"The Joint Training System: A Guide for Senior Leaders," Chairman of the Joint Chiefs of Staff Guide 3501, June 8, 2012.

"The Navy Ethos," America's Navy website. As of June 22, 2013: www.navy.mil/features/ethos/navy_ethos2.html

"The Profession of Arms: An Army White Paper," Center for the Army Profession and Ethic, Combined Arms Center, U.S. Army Training and Doctrine Command, December 8, 2010. As of June 22, 2013: http://cape.army.mil/doctrine.php

"The United States Navy," America's Navy website. As of June 22, 2013: www.navy.mil/navydata/nav_legacy.asp?id=193

The U.S. Army Training Concept, 2012–2020, TRADOC Pamphlet 525-8-3, Fort Monroe, VA, January 7, 2011.

"Tianhui Series," *Jane's Space Systems and Industry*, September 2, 2010.

Tilford, Earl H., Jr. *Setup: What the Air Force Did in Vietnam and Why*. Maxwell Air Force Base, AL: Air University Press, June 1991.

Timperlake, Edward, and William C. Triplett II. *Red Dragon Rising: Communist China's Military Threat to America*. Washington, DC: Regnery Publishing, 1999.

Tsang, Steve, ed. *If China Attacks Taiwan: Military Strategy, Politics, and Economics*. London and New York: Routledge, 2006.

"Type 99 (AAM-4)," *Jane's Air-Launched Weapons*, August 6, 2013.

"UGM-109 Tomahawk," *Jane's Naval Weapon Systems*, April 13, 2013.

Union of Concerned Scientists Satellite Database, September 1, 2011 version. As of November 29, 2011: www.ucsusa.org/nuclear_weapons_and_global_security/space_weapons/technical_issues/ucs-satellite-database.html

"United States Air Force Core Values," Peterson Air Force Base website. As of June 22, 2013: www.peterson.af.mil/shared/media/document/AFD-090212-058.pdf

U.S. Census Bureau, U.S. Department of Commerce. *Statistical Abstract of the United States, 2001*. As of March 25, 2013: www.census.gov/prod/www/statistical_abstract.html

Statistical Abstract of the United States, 2002. As of March 25, 2013: www.census.gov/prod/www/statistical_abstract.html

Statistical Abstract of the United States, 2003. As of March 25, 2013: www.census.gov/prod/www/statistical_abstract.html

Statistical Abstract of the United States, 2004–2005. As of March 25, 2013: www.census.gov/prod/www/statistical_abstract.html

Statistical Abstract of the United States, 2011. As of March 25, 2013: www.census.gov/compendia/statab/2011/2011edition.html

U.S. Department of Defense. *National Defense Strategy*. 2008. As of July 1, 2011: www.defense.gov/pubs/2008NationalDefenseStrategy.pdf

Program Acquisition Costs by Weapon System, 2002. As of July 6, 2011: http://comptroller.defense.gov/Docs/fy2003_weabook.pdf

Program Acquisition Costs by Weapon System, 2003. As of July 6, 2011: http://comptroller.defense.gov/Docs/fy2004_weabook.pdf

Program Acquisition Costs by Weapon System, 2004. As of July 6, 2011: http://comptroller.defense.gov/Docs/fy2005_weabook.pdf

Program Acquisition Costs by Weapon System, 2005. As of July 6, 2011: http://comptroller.defense.gov/Docs/fy2006_weabook.pdf

Program Acquisition Costs by Weapon System, 2006. As of July 6, 2011: http://comptroller.defense.gov/Docs/fy2007_weabook.pdf

Program Acquisition Costs by Weapon System, 2007. As of July 6, 2011: http://comptroller.defense.gov/Docs/fy2008_weabook.pdf

Program Acquisition Costs by Weapon System, 2009. As of July 6, 2011: http://comptroller.defense.gov/defbudget/fy2010/FY2010_Weapons.pdf

U.S. Department of Defense. *Quadrennial Defense Review Report*. February 2010. As of July 1, 2011: www.defense.gov/qdr/images/QDR_as_of_12Feb10_1000.pdf

U.S. Secretary of Defense. *Annual Report on the Military Power of the People's Republic of China*, 2001.

"US 1–511 (shan) Class," *Jane's Fighting Ships*, October 28, 2005.

"Virginia Class," *Jane's Fighting Ships*, April 9, 2013.

Wang An (王安), and Fang Ning (方宁).《军队条令条例教程》[*Textbook on Military Regulations and Ordinances*]. Beijing: Military Science Press, 1999.

Wang, Chris. "Date for All-Volunteer Military Delayed," *Taipei Times*, September 13, 2013, p. 1.

Wang Hongshan (王洪山), and Liu Shengdong (刘声东).〈习近平：富国和强军相统一 巩固国防和强大军队〉("Xi Jinping: Rich Nation and Strong Military Are Inseparable, Solidify National Defense and Strengthen the Military"),《求是》(*Qiushi*), December 12, 2012. As of June 23, 2013: www.qstheory.cn/yw/201212/t20121213_199792.htm

Wang Houqing (王厚卿), and Zhang Xingye (张兴业), eds.《战役学》[*Campaign Studies*]. Beijing: National Defense University Press, 2000.

Wang Jiping (王继平).〈把战训一致落到实处〉("Bring Uniformity between Training and Warfare into Reality"),《解放军报》[*PLA Daily*], May 28, 2002.

Wang Shengkui (王盛槐), Sun Xiaobo (孙晓波), and Tang Baodong (唐保东).〈按纲施训的四大关系〉("The Four Great Relationships of Training According to the Guidelines"),《解放军报》[*PLA Daily*], June 4, 2002.

Wang Shumei. "The PLA and Student Recruits: Reforming China's Conscription System." Institute for Security and Development Policy, January 2015.

Wang Xixin (王西欣). 〈打造与时代同步的核心军事能力〉("Build a Core Military Capability That Is in Step with the Times"),《解放军报》[*PLA Daily*], May 2, 2009.

Wang Yifeng (王逸峰). 〈关于调整我军军官学历于军衔对应关系思考〉("Thoughts on Adjusting the Correspondence between Officer Degree and Rank")《法制研究》[*Research on Rule of Law*] No. 2, 2010, pp. 60–64.

Wang, Zheng. "Understanding China's Military Strategy: The Challenge to Researchers." *Asia Policy*, No. 12 (July 2011), pp. 157–160.

Wardynski, Casey, David S. Lyle, and Michael J. Colarusso. *Towards a U.S. Army Officer Corps Strategy for Success: A Proposed Human Capital Model Focused upon Talent*. Carlyle, PA: Strategic Studies Institute, April 2009.

Warwick, Graham. "Sneak Attacker," *Aviation Week and Space Technology*, September 16, 2013, p. 42.

Weeden, Brian. "Through a Glass, Darkly: Chinese, American, and Russian Anti-Satellite Testing in Space," *Space Review*, March 17, 2014. As of October 9, 2014: www.thespacereview.com/article/2473/1

"What Changes Has the Promulgation and Implementation of the New Guidelines Brought to Military Training?" 〈新大纲颁布实行给军事训练带来哪些变化?〉. 《解放军报》[*PLA Daily*], March 18, 2009, p. 2.

Whitlock, Craig. "Pentagon: China Tried to Block U.S. Military Jet in Dangerous Mid-Air Intercept," *Washington Post*, August 22, 2014.

Winkler, John, Judith Fernandez, and J. Michael Polich. *Effect of Aptitude on the Performance of Army Communications Officers*. Santa Monica, CA: RAND Corporation, 1992.

"WorldView Series," *Jane's Space Systems and Industry*, January 26, 2011.

Wortzel, Larry M. *The Chinese People's Liberation Army and Information Warfare*. Carlisle Barracks, PA: United States Army War College Press, 2014.

Wu Dilun (吴弟伦) and Liu Feng'an (刘逢安). 〈总参部署全军新年度军事训练工作强调以提高核心军事能力为根本着力点〉("GSD Allocates Military Training Work for New Year, Emphasis on Raising Core Military Capabilities as Basic Point of Exertion"),《解放军报》[*PLA Daily*], January 7, 2009.

Wu Pinxiang (吴品祥). 〈把握按纲施训的着力点〉("Grasp the Exertion Point of Training According to Guidelines"),《解放军报》[*PLA Daily*], May 21, 2002.

Wu Tianmin (武天敏) and Cai Pengcheng (蔡鹏程). 〈野外驻训：我们"放虎归山"〉 ("Field Training: We 'Set the Tiger Loose in the Mountains'"),《解放军报》 [*PLA Daily*], October 14, 2010.

"XAC H-6," *Jane's All the World's Aircraft*, July 8, 2013.

"XAC JH-7," *Jane's All the World's Aircraft*, July 8, 2013.

"XAC Y-20," *Jane's All the World's Aircraft*, January 28, 2013.

"XIA Class (Type 092)," *Jane's Fighting Ships*, January 10, 2011.

Xia Guofu (夏国富). 〈以创新求落实〉("Seek Realization through Innovation"), 《解放军报》[*PLA Daily*], June 4, 2002.

"Xian (Antonov) Y-7," *Jane's Aircraft Upgrades*, August 13, 2012.

Xiang Fei (项菲), Bei Ying (北英), and Deng Minghui (邓明辉). 〈浅谈大学生士兵的教育管理〉. ("An Overview of Educational Administration for College Student Soldiers").《学理论》(*Theory Research*). No. 18, 2011, pp. 187–188.

Xiao Yunhong (肖运洪), Hu Junhua (胡君华), Liu Feng'an (刘逢安). 〈三次转变带来军事训练持续发展〉 ("Three Transformations Bring Continued Development of Military Training"), 《解放军报》[*PLA Daily*], October 13, 2008.

Xinhua. "China's Economy to Grow 7.5%," December 3, 2013. As of January 6, 2014: http://europe.chinadaily.com.cn/business/2013–12/03/content_17148523.htm

Xu Shengliang (徐生梁), Peng Fei (逢飞), Ding Haiming (丁海明), and Bao Guojun (包国俊). 〈情系中国军事"思想库"—党中央, 中央军委关心军事科学院建设和发展纪实〉 ("Inside China's Military 'Think Tank': A Chronicle of the Party Center and CMC's Concern for the Construction and Development of the Academy of Military Sciences"), 《解放军报》[*PLA Daily*], March 21, 2008.

Xu Xingguo (徐兴国). 《我军信息作战力量建设研究》[*Study of the Development of Our Military's Information Operations Power*]. Beijing: Academy of Military Science Press, 2013.

Yan Yong (闫勇), and Liu Feng'an (刘逢安). 〈四总部通报表彰全军军事训练以及师旅级单位全军爱军精武标兵〉 ("Announcement from Four General Departments Praises PLA's First Rank Division- and Brigade-Level Training Units and Model Soldiers"), 《解放军报》[*PLA Daily*], January 1, 2011a.

〈全军年度军事训练考核和等级评定工作展开〉 ("PLA-Wide Annual Military Training, Evaluation, and Grade Assessment Work Begins"), 《解放军报》[*PLA Daily*], November 19, 2011b.

Yang Guang (杨光), Yang Huicheng (杨会成), and Su Ruozhou (苏若舟). 〈认真贯彻军事训练条例努力开创依法治训新局面〉 ("Faithfully Implement Military Training Regulations, Diligently Initiate a New Aspect of Administering Training Based on Law"), 《解放军报》[*PLA Daily*], September 13, 2002.

Yang Huicheng (杨会成) and Su Ruozhou (苏若舟). 〈总参部署新年度军事训练和院校教育工作〉 ("GSD Allocates Military Training and Academic Educational Work for New Year"), 《解放军报》[*PLA Daily*], January 11, 2002.

Yang Zhiyuan (杨志远). 〈我军新一代作战条令出台的前前后后〉 ["The Period of the Appearance of Our Military's New Generation of Warfighting Regulations"]. 《解放军报》[*PLA Daily*], October 8, 2008, p. 27.

〈我军编修作战条令的创新发展及启示〉 ["Innovative Development in Revising the PLA's Operational Doctrine and Its Implications"], 《中国军事科学》[*China Military Science*], No. 6, 2009, pp. 113–118.

"Yantai (Type 073) Class," *Jane's Fighting Ships*, February 15, 2013.

"Yaogan Series," *Jane's Space Systems and Industry*, August 18, 2010.

"YJ-62/C-602," *Jane's Naval Weapon Systems*, July 4, 2011.

"YJ-82," *Jane's Naval Weapon Systems*, July 4, 2011.

"YJ-8K (C-801K), YJ-82K (C-802K), YJ-83K (C-802AK), YJ-83KH (CM-802AKG)," *Jane's Air-Launched Weapons*, August 21, 2013.

"YJ-91, KR-1 (Kh-31P)," *Jane's Air-Launched Weapons*, March 28, 2011.

"YJ-91 (KR-1/Kh-31P/AS-17 'Krypton')," *Jane's Strategic Weapon Systems*, December 5, 2012.

Yoshihara, Toshi, and James R. Holmes. *Red Star Over the Pacific: China's Rise and the Challenge to U.S. Maritime Strategy*. Annapolis, MD: Naval Institute Press, 2010.

Yu Ping (余平) and Liu Feng'an (刘逢安). 〈总参全面部署兵种军事业务工作强调把提高核心军事能力摆在突出位置〉 ("GSD Comprehensively Allocates

Military Work for Services and Branches, Emphasizes Putting Raising Core Military Capabilities in a Prominent Position"),《解放军报》[*PLA Daily*], January 20, 2009.

"Yuan Class (Type 041)," *Jane's Fighting Ships*, February 11, 2011.

"Yubei (Type 074A) Class," *Jane's Fighting Ships*, February 11, 2013.

"Yudao Class (Type 073)," *Jane's Fighting Ships*, February 13, 2013.

"Yudeng (Type 073III) Class," *Jane's Fighting Ships*, December 31, 2013.

"Yuhai (Type 074) (Wuhu-A) Class," *Jane's Fighting Ships*, December 9, 2013.

"Yukan (Type 072) Class," *Jane's Fighting Ships*, December 31, 2013.

"Yuliang (Type 079) Class," *Jane's Fighting Ships*, December 9, 2013.

"Yunshu (Type 073IV) Class," *Jane's Fighting Ships*, December 31, 2013.

"Yuting I (Type 072 II) Class," *Jane's Fighting Ships*, December 31, 2013.

"Yuting II (Type 072 III) Class," *Jane's Fighting Ships*, December 9, 2013.

"Yuzhao (Type 071) Class," *Jane's Fighting Ships*, December 31, 2013.

"ZBD-04 Infantry Fighting Vehicle," *Jane's Armour and Artillery*, October 12, 2011.

Zhang Yuliang (张玉良), Yu Shusheng (郁树胜), and Zhou Xiaopeng (周晓鹏), eds. 《战役学》[*Campaign Studies*]. Beijing: National Defense University Press, 2006.

Zhang Wei (张炜). 〈破解联训考评难〉("Unraveling Why Joint Evaluation Is Difficult"),《解放军报》[*PLA Daily*], January 3, 2010.

Zhao Guojie (赵国杰) and Zhang Qiang (张强). 〈重视战术思想研究〉("Emphasize the Study of Tactical Concepts"),《解放军报》[*PLA Daily*], September 17, 2009, p. 10.

Zhao Shengnan. "New Joint Command System 'On Way,'" *China Daily*, January 3, 2014. As of February 25, 2014: http://usa.chinadaily.com.cn/china/2014–01/03/content_17212780.htm

Zhou Bing (周兵), Jiang Yun (姜云), and Fang Yunfei (方云飞). 〈野外驻训：聚焦装备管理与技术保障〉("Field Training: Focus on Equipment Management and Technical Support"),《解放军报》[*PLA Daily*], August 26, 2010.

"ZiYuan-2/JianBing-3 Series," *Jane's Space Systems and Industry*, June 17, 2010.

"Zumwalt (DDG 1000) Class," *Jane's Fighting Ships*, April 10, 2013.

Index

CPSIA information can be obtained
at www.ICGtesting.com
Printed in the USA
LVOW03s0123290917

550422LV00011BA/136/P